Frames of Mind

Other Books by Howard Gardner

The Quest for Mind (1973; second edition, 1981)

The Arts and Human Development (1973)

The Shattered Mind (1975)

Developmental Psychology (1978; second edition, 1982)

Artful Scribbles: The Significance of Children's Drawings (1980)

Art, Mind, and Brain: A Cognitive Approach to Creativity (1982)

FRAMES
OF
MIND

The Theory of
Multiple Intelligences

HOWARD GARDNER

BasicBooks
A Division of HarperCollins*Publishers*

Library of Congress Cataloging in Publication Data

Gardner, Howard.
  Frames of mind.

  Includes bibliographical references and index.
  1. Intellect. I. Title.
BF431.G244 1983   153   83–70765
ISBN 0–465–02508–0 (cloth)
ISBN 0–465–02509–9 (paper)

Introduction to the Paperback Edition Copyright © 1985 by Howard Gardner
Copyright © 1983 by Howard Gardner
Printed in the United States of America
Designed by Vincent Torre
Cloth 85 86 87 88 HC 15 14 13 12 11 10 9 8
Paper 92 93 94 95 96 HC 20 19 18 17 16

For Ellen

CONTENTS

Contents

Part III

Implications and Applications

REINTRODUCING
FRAMES OF MIND

I have been gratified by the extended discussion of *Frames of Mind*, both by colleagues with a professional interest in issues of intelligence and by members of the general public who are concerned about psychology and education. Publication of a paperbound edition and new printings of the original hardbound edition give me an opportunity to clarify certain points and to mention some lines of work undertaken since the completion of the original manuscript early in 1983.

In writing *Frames of Mind*, I sought to undermine the common notion of intelligence as a general capacity or potential which every human being possesses to a greater or lesser extent. At the same time, I also questioned the assumption that intelligence, however defined, can be measured by standardized verbal instruments, such as short-answer, paper-and-pencil tests. At the time of writing, I had not fully appreciated the extent to which these conceptions of intelligence and intelligence testing are entrenched in our society. Perhaps this entrenchment helps to explain why many readers have not fully appreciated the nature of my challenge.

In an effort to help you enter this work, and to forestall these common misinterpretations, I would ask new readers to perform two thought experiments. First of all, try to forget that you have ever heard of the concept of intelligence as a single property of the human mind; or of that instrument called the intelligence test, which purports to measure intelligence once and for all. Second of all, cast your mind widely about the world and think of all the roles or "end states"—vocational and avocational—that have been prized by cultures during various eras. Consider, for example, hunters, fishermen, farmers, shamans, religious leaders, psychiatrists, military leaders, civil leaders, athletes, artists, musicians, poets, parents, and scientists. Honing in closer, then, consider the three end states with which I begin *Frames of Mind*—the Puluwat sailor, the Koranic student, and the Parisian composer at her microcomputer.

In my view, if we are to encompass adequately the realm of human cognition, it is necessary to include a far wider and more universal set of competences than has ordinarily been considered. And it is necessary to remain open to the possibility that many—if not most—of these competences do not lend themselves to measurement by standard verbal methods, which rely heavily on a blend of logical and linguistic abilities.

With such considerations in mind, I have formulated a definition of what I call an "intelligence." An intelligence is the ability to solve problems, or to create products, that are valued within one or more cultural settings. Note that nothing has been said here about the sources of these abilities, or about the proper means of "testing" these capacities. Building upon this definition, and drawing especially on biological and anthropological evidence, I then introduce eight distinct criteria for an intelligence and propose seven human competences that basically fulfill these criteria. The major portion of the book provides a detailed description of the evidence for, and the mode of operation of, each particular intelligence. There follows a critique of the theory in terms of those deficiencies that were most evident to me at the time of writing. I conclude with some considerations of how intelligences do—and can—develop within a culture and how they can be mobilized in various educational settings.

When one puts forth a new theory, it is sometimes helpful to indicate the perspectives to which it is most radically opposed. This tack seems especially important inasmuch as a number of critics have been unable—or unwilling—to abandon these traditional perspectives. I introduce two exhibits in this regard. The first comes from an advertisement for an intelligence test. This ad begins:

Need an individual test which quickly provides a stable and reliable estimate of intelligence in 4 or 5 minutes per form? Has three forms? Does not depend on verbal production or subjective scoring? Can be used with the severely physically handicapped (even paralyzed) if they can signal yes-no? Handles two year olds and superior adults within the same short series of items and the same format?

And it continues in this vein. While I shall avoid judging the value of this test, I can state unequivocally that the description implies a wonderland of testing which I find to be illusory. I might add that I am equally suspicious of claims to test intelligence (whatever it might be) by means of reaction-time measures or brain waves. These measures may well correlate with I.Q.'s—all the more reason, from my perspective, for calling I.Q.'s into question.

My second exhibit comes from a more venerable source—a well-known quotation from Samuel Johnson. The redoubtable doctor once defined "true genius" as "a mind of large general powers, accidentally determined to some particular direction." While I do not question that some individuals may have the potential to excel in more than one sphere, I strongly challenge the notion of large general powers. To my way of thinking, the mind has the potential to deal with several different kinds of *content*, but an individual's facility with one content has little predictive power about his or her facility with other kinds of content. In other words, genius (and, *a fortiori*, ordinary performance) is likely to be specific to particular contents: human beings have evolved to exhibit several intelligences and not to draw variously on one flexible intelligence.

Having set a context that I hope will allow readers to accept—at least provisionally—the perspective of *Frames of Mind*, I turn now to some frequent criticisms. *Frames* has been viewed as a useful study of human talents but not a valid examination of intelligence. As stated in the book itself, I place no particular premium on the word *intelligence*, but I do place great importance on the equivalence of various human faculties. If critics were willing to label language and logical thinking as talents as well, and to remove these from the pedestal they currently occupy, then I would be happy to speak of multiple talents. But I strongly resist any attempt to use a contrast between intelligence and talent as a veiled attempt to ignore or minimize the range of critical human abilities.

Lest you think that this is simply a pedantic quarrel about terminology, consider the current definition of gifted children. The vast majority of programs for gifted children have as their chief (if not sole) criterion for admission a score on intelligence tests in the superior range (usually above 130). A program that recognized the range of intelligences proposed here would select children in a radically different way.

An important claim of the theory—though one that remains to be adequately tested—is that each intelligence is relatively independent of the others, and that an individual's intellectual gifts in, say, music, cannot be inferred from his or her skills in mathematics, language, or interpersonal understanding. In an effort to rebut this contention, several critics have pointed out that there are generally positive correlations (a so-called positive manifold) among tests for different faculties (for example, space and language) and that, therefore, these abilities are not uncorrelated. I fear, however, that I cannot accept these correlations at face value. Nearly all current tests are so devised that they call principally upon linguistic and logical facility (as well as a certain speed, flexibility, and perhaps superficiality as well). Accordingly, individuals with these skills are likely to do well even in tests of musical or spatial abilities, while those who are not especially facile linguistically and logically are likely to be impaled on such standardized tests.

Tests of the various intelligences must each be posed by appropriate means. Thus, a measure for bodily intelligence should involve the use of the body in such activities as learning a game or a dance (and not a set of questions about such activity); an assessment of spatial ability should involve navigation about an unfamiliar environment (and not a series of geometric rotations requiring multiple-choice responses); an estimate of musical acuity should require mastery of a composition (either in performance or in analysis) and not a series of tonal discriminations. Only when such "intelligence-fair" instruments have been devised will it be possible to determine whether there are nontrivial correlations among the separate intelligences.

This comment on the limits of standardized testing raises a more general question about the relationship between the present theory and standard psychometric analysis. I recognize the great achievement involved in the development of a science of test construction and evaluation. I also acknowledge that standardized tests provide an adequate assessment of scholastic potential (though certainly no better an estimate than school grades). Where I part company from the mainstream of psychometric practice is in my insistence that an analysis of cognition must include all human problem-solving and product-fashioning skills and not just those that happen to lend themselves to testing via a standard format. Whatever their original purposes and strengths, standardized tests are now expected to assess all human capacities—a burden to which they are not equal. Rather than allowing the testing tail to wag the assessment dog, I call for the development of means of assessment that are fully adequate to the range of human skills which deserve to be probed.

A persistent confusion among readers, for which I must bear primary responsibility, is an equation of the possession of a particular intelligence and the attainment of a particular adult end state. In truth, nearly any adult end state of any consequence in any culture will involve a blend of intelligences; an intelligence in pure form can be observed only in a freak. Thus, a competent musical performer will certainly exhibit musical intelligence but must equally exhibit some bodily kinesthetic skills (so as to be able to achieve subtle effects at will); interpersonal intelligence (so as to be able to communicate effectively with an audience); logical mathematical skills (so that one can ultimately make a profit); and so on. It is for convenience that I have resorted to musicians as examples of musical intelligence; in the workaday world, only the blend of intelligences in an intact individual makes possible the solving of problems and the creation of products of significance. Nonetheless, despite the cooperation of intelligences in any complex human activity, I would insist that the isolation of a particular intelligence is the proper move en route to a more veridical view of the structure of human cognition.

After several decades in which intelligence testing continued apace, but theoretical work was virtually nonexistent, there has been an enormous revival of interest in the theoretical issues concerning intelligence(s). In addition to the individuals on whose works I comment in chapters 2, 11, and 12, I want to mention several other recent contributors: Jonathan Baron, whose definition stresses the point that intelligent individuals act rationally, evaluating all the available evidence even when it goes against their predilections;[1] John Horn, who has distinguished between more and less "fluid" forms of intelligence and has emphasized the hierarchical relations among different intellectual factors;[2] and Robert Sternberg, who has synthesized a vast amount of information about intelligence and has also put forth a triarchic theory of intellect, which encompasses internal manipulation of information, sensitivity to the external context, and the relationship between these two components of intellect.[3] Mihaly Csikszentmihalyi and Rick Robinson have drawn the important distinction between a universal biologically based notion (intelligence) and the more culturally derived notions of a domain and a field.[4] In recent essays, I have had the opportunity to respond specifically to frameworks proposed by Jerry Fodor[5] and Sternberg.[6] Such continuing interchanges should help to advance our still modest understanding of human intellective processes.

With my colleagues I have also had the opportunity to carry forward some of the work begun in *Frames of Mind*. Joseph Walters and I have studied crystallizing experiences.[7] In these fertile encounters with an object or a situation, one discovers that one possesses a hitherto unsuspected combination of intelligences, and proceeds to develop that strand of talent. Such encounters occur with ordinary individuals, as when a youngster

1. *Rationality and Intelligence* (New York: Cambridge University Press, in press).
2. "Trends in the Measurement of Intelligence," in R. J. Sternberg and D. K. Detterman, eds., *Human Intelligence: Perspectives on Its Theory and Measurement* (Norwood, N.J.: ABlex, 1979).
3. "Toward a Triarchic Theory of Human Intelligence," *Behavioral and Brain Sciences* 7(1984):269–87.
4. "Culture, Time, and the Development of Talent," in R. Sternberg and J. Davidson, eds., *Conceptions of Giftedness* (New York: Cambridge University Press, in press).
5. H. Gardner, "The Centrality of Modules. A Comment on J. A. Fodor, *The Modularity of Mind*," *Behavioral and Brain Sciences*, in press.
6. H. Gardner, "Assessing Intelligences: A Comment on 'Testing Intelligence without IQ Tests' by Robert Sternberg," *Phi Delta Kappan*, June 1984, pp. 699–700.
7. "Crystallizing Experiences," in R. Sternberg and J. Davidson, eds., *Conceptions of Giftedness* (New York: Cambridge University Press, in press).

discovers a special gift at chess or bowling, as well as with the gifted, as when young Einstein's receipt of a compass stimulated his thinking about physical forces. Joseph Walters, Mara Krechevsky, and I have also begun the difficult but intriguing task of tracing through the developmental trajectories of particular intelligences.[8] In our first study, we compared the principal stages of development in normal and gifted children in two intellectual domains: music (performance as well as composition) and logical-mathematical thought (science as well as mathematics). In the course of the latter study, we relied heavily on the reports by classroom teachers, who have been able to follow their former students for up to several decades. We found that these teachers possess a unique repository of knowledge about which factors tend to predict future involvement with a field, as well as those that prove indifferent predictors of the later course of development. Surprisingly, this source of information has gone virtually untapped by researchers in educational psychology.

Practical as well as theoretical issues are now being addressed. Working closely with my long-time colleague David Feldman, and with the support of a grant from the Spencer Foundation, my colleagues and I have been attempting to develop new means for assessing intellectual propensities (as we call them) in the pre-school years. Our working assumption is that it may prove possible to tap children's individual profiles of strengths and weaknesses by observing them at play (and at work) in an enriched environment—one that provides ample opportunity for exhibiting proclivities in various of the intelligences. Assuming that such an assessment is feasible, we plan to produce Propensities Reports. In these brief essays, we describe a child's particular profile of intellectual strengths and weaknesses and offer concrete suggestions about which activities at home, at school, and in the community might be appropriate for the child to engage in during this period of life.

Frames of Mind diverges from other approaches in the emphasis it places on the development and deployment of human competences. Whatever the ultimate fate of the theory as science, I hope that discussion and application of the theory will contribute to more effective educational practice. The most rewarding aspect of issuing the book has been the extent to which individuals "in the field" have sought to incorporate its various themes into their daily educational activities.

HOWARD GARDNER

Cambridge, Massachusetts, January 1985

8. "The Development of Two Intelligences: Reports from Teachers," Harvard Project Zero Working Paper, 1985.

PREFACE

As indicated in the following note about the Project on Human Potential, this book had an unusual genesis. It came to be written because of the foresight and generosity of a foundation that sought clarification of a concept in its charter—"human potential." The executive director of the foundation, Willem Welling, and the chairman of the board of directors, Oscar van Leer, conceived of a project to investigate human potential and asked several of us at the Graduate School of Education at Harvard to respond to their daunting challenge. The project drew together a group of colleagues from diverse backgrounds who have had the chance to collaborate over the past four years. The story of that collaboration will be related elsewhere, but it is germane to record that it has enabled me to range more broadly and to reflect more probingly about a gamut of issues than I could have done without the flexible support of the van Leer Foundation. My first and greatest debt is to Willem Welling, Oscar van Leer, and their associates at the Bernard van Leer Foundation.

I wish to thank my senior colleagues on the Project on Human Potential—Gerald Lesser, Robert LeVine, Israel Scheffler, and Merry White for their continuous and continuing stimulation, constructive criticism, and support. Our interactions have genuinely changed the way in which I think about many issues and have helped materially with the writing and rewriting of this book. From the first, I have been blessed with incredibly talented, insightful, and hard-working research assistants, and I want to thank them individually and mention their area of contribution to this study: Lisa Brooks (genetics), Linda Levine (psychology), Susan McConnell (neurobiology), Susan Pollak (history and philosophy), William Skryzniarz (international develop-

Preface

ment), and Claudia Strauss (anthropology). In a day when scholarship is little esteemed among talented young persons, they have shown exemplary independence and dedication: I am pleased that they are all pursuing careers in the world of scholarship. Other members of the Project to whom I am indebted in various ways include Leonie Gordon, Margaret Herzig, Francis Keppel, Harry Lasker, and Lois Taniuchi. For their generous administrative support, I wish to thank Deans Paul Ylvisaker and Blenda Wilson and, more recently, Deans Patricia Graham and Jerome Murphy.

While, in the first instance, this book is a report on human potentials as viewed from a psychobiological perspective, it also represents an effort to pull together findings from two lines of research which I have been pursuing over the past dozen years. One line is the development, in normal and gifted children, of symbol-using capacities, particularly in the arts—a line I have been carrying out at Harvard Project Zero. The other has been the breakdown of cognitive capacities in individuals suffering from brain damage, which I have been pursuing at the Boston Veterans Administration Medical Center and the Boston University School of Medicine. A conception of different intelligences—the "frames of mind" of my title—has emerged as the most appropriate and comprehensive way of conceptualizing the human cognitive capacities whose development and breakdown I have been studying. I am grateful to have the opportunity to present in this volume the theoretical framework that has emerged from these efforts at synthesis, and to offer some tentative suggestions about the educational implications of the framework. And I want to take this opportunity to thank the various agencies that have generously supported my research over ten years: The Veterans Administration, which granted me a sabbatical so that I could concentrate on this synthesis; the Department of Neurology of Boston University School of Medicine, the Medical Research Division of the Veterans Administration, and the National Institute of Neurological Diseases, Communication Disorders and Stroke, all of which have supported my work in neuropsychology; and, for their support of the work of my colleagues and me at Harvard Project Zero on normal and gifted children, the Spencer Foundation, the Carnegie Corporation, the Markle Foundation, the National Science Foundation, and the National Institute of Education. A large debt is owed to that innovative institution the MacArthur Foundation, which furnished me much needed security during a perilous period for researchers in the social sciences.

I want finally to express my appreciation to those individuals who have made particular contributions to this book. A number of my colleagues read the entire manuscript, or large sections of it, and offered extremely helpful comments. I wish to record my appreciation to Tom Carothers, Michael Cole, Yadin Dudai, David Feldman, Norman Geschwind, Linda Levine, David Olson, Susan McConnell, Sidney Strauss, William Wall, and Ellen Winner. Dolly Appel served as principal word processor and supervisor of the preparation of the physical manuscript and did so in a skillful, helpful, and cheerful manner which I greatly admired. Jasmine Hall generously offered to prepare the index. Linda Levine aided me with numerous aspects of the physical and conceptual manuscript and undertook with great ingenuity and energy the preparation of the extensive reference notes. I don't know what I would have done without her intelligences! And as with my two most recent books, my colleagues at Basic Books were an unfailing source of support: I especially thank my editor Jane Isay and her assistant Mary Kennedy, as well as Judith Greissman, Janet Halverson, Phoebe Hoss, Lois Shapiro, and Vincent Torre—and the proofreader, Pamela Dailey.

I wish to thank the following individuals and publishers for permitting me to reproduce copyrighted materials:

To Dr. Roger N. Shepard for permission to reproduce the spatial rotation figure from R. N. Shepard and J. Metzler, "Mental Rotation of Three-Dimensional Objects," *Science*, Vol. 171, pp. 701–703, Fig. 1, 19 February 1971.

To Academic Press for permission to reproduce a drawing by Nadia from L. Selfe, *Nadia: A Case of Extraordinary Drawing Ability in an Autistic Child*, 1977.

To the American Association for the Advancement of Science for permission to reproduce the spatial rotation figure from R. N. Shepard and J. Metzler, "Mental Rotation of Three-Dimensional Objects," *Science*, Vol. 171, pp. 701–703, Fig. 1, 19 February 1971.

To Harper & Row for permission to quote material from Kenneth Clark, *Another Part of the Wood: A Self-Portrait*, 1974.

To John Murray Publishers, Ltd. for permission to quote material from Kenneth Clark, *Another Part of the Wood: A Self-Portrait*, 1974.

To A. D. Peters & Company for permission to quote passages from Stephen Spender, *The Making of a Poem*, 1955.

Cambridge, Massachusetts
June 1983

NOTE ON THE PROJECT
ON HUMAN POTENTIAL

The Bernard van Leer Foundation of The Hague, Netherlands, is an international nonprofit institution dedicated to the cause of disadvantaged children and youth. It supports innovative projects that develop community approaches to early childhood education and child care, in order to help disadvantaged children to realize their potential.

In 1979, the foundation asked the Harvard Graduate School of Education to assess the state of scientific knowledge concerning human potential and its realization. Proceeding from this general directive, a group of scholars at Harvard has over the past several years been engaged in research exploring the nature and realization of human potential. Activities sponsored by the Project on Human Potential have included reviews of relevant literature in history, philosophy, and the natural and social sciences, a series of international workshops on conceptions of human development in diverse cultural traditions, and the commissioning of papers and books.

The principal investigators of the Project represent a variety of fields and interests. Gerald S. Lesser, who chaired the Project's steering committee, is an educator and developmental psychologist, a principal architect in the creation of educational television programs for children. Howard Gardner is a psychologist who has studied the development of symbolic skills in normal and gifted children, and the impairment of such skills in brain-damaged adults. Israel Scheffler is a philosopher who has worked in the areas of philosophy of education, philosophy of science, and philosophy of language. Robert LeVine, a social anthropologist, has worked in subsaharan Africa and Mexico, studying family life, child care, and psychological development. Merry White is a sociologist and Japan specialist who

Note on the Project on Human Potential

has studied education, formal organizations, and the roles of women in the Third World and Japan. This wide range of interests and disciplines enabled the Project to take a multifaceted approach to issues of human potential.

The first volume published under the aegis of the Project is Howard Gardner's *Frames of Mind*, a study of human intellectual potentials which draws not only on psychological research but also on the biological sciences and on findings about the development and use of knowledge in different cultures.

The second book of the Project to appear is Israel Scheffler's *Of Human Potential*, which treats philosophical aspects of the concept of potential. Sketching the background of the concept and placing it in the context of a general theory of human nature, this treatment then proposes three analytical reconstructions of the concept and offers systematic reflections on policy and the education of policy makers.

The third volume is *Human Conditions: The Cultural Basis of Educational Development*, by Robert A. LeVine and Merry I. White. Emphasizing the crucial role of cultural factors in the progress of human development, the book offers new models for development based on the social anthropology of the lifespan and the social history of family and school.

To provide background for the study of diversity in development, the Project established teams of consultants in Egypt, India, Japan, Mexico, the People's Republic of China, and West Africa. Selected papers presented by these consultants in Project workshops appear in *The Cultural Transition: Human Experience and Social Transformations in the Third World and Japan*, a fourth volume, edited by Merry I. White and Susan Pollak. Representatives of international development agencies were also engaged as consultants and correspondents over the five-year period of the Project. Through such international dialogue and research, the Project has sought to create a new multidisciplinary environment for understanding human potential.

Part I

Background

1

The Idea of
Multiple
Intelligences

A YOUNG GIRL spends an hour with an examiner. She is asked a number of questions that probe her store of information (Who discovered America? What does the stomach do?), her vocabulary (What does *nonsense* mean? What does *belfry* mean?), her arithmetic skills (At eight cents each, how much will three candy bars cost?), her ability to remember a series of numbers (5,1,7,4,2,3,8), her capacity to grasp the similarity between two elements (elbow and knee, mountain and lake). She may also be asked to carry out certain other tasks—for example, solving a maze or arranging a group of pictures in such a way that they relate a complete story. Some time afterward, the examiner scores the responses and comes up with a single number—the girl's intelligence quotient, or IQ. This number (which the little girl may actually be told) is likely to exert appreciable effect upon her future, influencing the way in which her teachers think of her and determining her eligibility for certain privileges. The importance attached to the number is not entirely inappropriate: after all, the score on an intelligence test does predict one's ability to handle school subjects, though it foretells little of success in later life.

The preceding scenario is repeated thousands of times every day, all over the world; and, typically, a good deal of significance is attached to the single score. Of course, different versions of the test are used for various ages and in diverse cultural settings. At times, the test is administered with paper and pencil rather than as an interchange with an examiner. But the broad outlines—an hour's worth of questions yielding one round number—are pretty much the way of intelligence testing the world around.

Many observers are not happy with this state of affairs. There must be more to intelligence than short answers to short questions—answers that predict academic success; and yet, in the absence of a better way of thinking about intelligence, and of better ways to assess an individual's capabilities, this scenario is destined to be repeated universally for the foreseeable future.

But what if one were to let one's imagination wander freely, to consider the wider range of performances that are in fact valued throughout the world? Consider, for example, the twelve-year-old male Puluwat in the Caroline Islands, who has been selected by his elders to learn how to become a master sailor. Under the tutelage of master navigators, he will learn to combine knowledge of sailing, stars, and geography so as to find his way around hundreds of islands. Consider the fifteen-year-old Iranian youth who has committed to heart the entire Koran and mastered the Arabic language. Now he is being sent to a holy city, to work closely for the next several years with an ayatollah, who will prepare him to be a teacher and religious leader. Or, consider the fourteen-year-old adolescent in Paris, who has learned how to program a computer and is beginning to compose works of music with the aid of a synthesizer.

A moment's reflection reveals that each of these individuals is attaining a high level of competence in a challenging field and should, by any reasonable definition of the term, be viewed as exhibiting intelligent behavior. Yet it should be equally clear that current methods of assessing the intellect are not sufficiently well honed to allow assessment of an individual's potentials or achievements in navigating by the stars, mastering a foreign tongue, or composing with a computer. The problem lies less in the technology of testing than in the ways in which we customarily think about the intellect and in our ingrained views of intelligence. Only if we expand and reformulate our view of what counts as human intellect will we be able to devise more appropriate ways of assessing it and more effective ways of educating it.

Around the world many individuals involved in education are reaching similar conclusions. There is interest in new programs (some of them grandiose) which seek to develop human intelligence for a whole culture, to train individuals in such general skills as "anticipatory learning," to help individuals to realize their human potential. Intriguing experiments, ranging from the Suzuki method of training violin to the LOGO method of introducing the fundamentals of computer programming, seek to elicit accomplished performances from young children.* Some of these experiments have had demonstrated success, while others are still in the pilot phase. Yet it is probably just to say that the successes as well as the failures have occurred in the absence of an adequate framework for thinking about intelligences. Certainly in no case does there exist a view of intelligence which incorporates the range of abilities I have just surveyed. To arrive at such a formulation is the purpose of the present book.

In the chapters that follow, I outline a new theory of human intellectual competences. This theory challenges the classical view of intelligence that most of us have absorbed explicitly (from psychology or education texts) or implicitly (by living in a culture with a strong but possibly circumscribed view of intelligence). So that the new features of this theory can be more readily identified, I will in these introductory pages consider some facts of the traditional view: where it came from, why it has become entrenched, what are some of the outstanding issues that remain to be resolved. Only then will I turn to the characteristics of the revisionist theory that I am propounding here.

For well over two thousand years, at least since the rise of the Greek city-state, a certain set of ideas has dominated discussions of the human condition in our civilization. This collection of ideas stresses the existence and the importance of mental powers—capacities that have been variously termed *rationality*, *intelligence*, or the deployment of *mind*. The unending search for an essence of humanity has led, with seeming ineluctability, to a focus upon our species's quest for knowledge; and those capacities that figure in knowing have been especially valued. Whether it be Plato's philosopher-king, the Hebrew prophet, the literate scribe in a medieval monastery, or the scientist in a laboratory, the individual capable of using his† mental powers has been singled out. Socrates' "Know thyself," Aristotle's "All men by Nature

---

*The sources for all quotations, research findings, and allied factual information will be found in the notes beginning on page 395.

†For ease of exposition, the pronoun "he" will be used in its generic sense throughout this book.

desire to know," and Descartes's "I think: therefore I am" provide epigraphs that frame an entire civilization.

Even in that dark millennium that intervened between Classical times and the Renaissance, the ascendancy of intellectual factors was rarely challenged. Early in the medieval period, St. Augustine, the very father of faith, declared:

The prime author and mover of the universe is intelligence. Therefore, the final cause of the universe must be the good of the intelligence and that is truth. . . . Of all human pursuits, the pursuit of wisdom is the most perfect, the most sublime, the most useful, and the most agreeable. The most perfect, because in so far as a man gives himself up to the pursuit of wisdom, to that extent he enjoys already some portion of true happiness.

At the height of the Middle Ages, Dante put forth his view that "the proper function of the human race, taken in the aggregate, is to actualize continually the entire capacity possible to the intellect, primarily in speculation, then through its extension and for its sake, secondarily in action." And then, at the dawn of the Renaissance, a century before Descartes's time, Francis Bacon described the English ship in New Atlantis which comes upon a Utopian island whose chief institution is a great establishment devoted to scientific research. The ruler of this realm declares to visiting travelers:

I will give the greatest jewel I have. For I will impart unto thee, for the love of God and men, a relation of the true state of Solomon's house. . . . The end of our foundation is the knowledge of causes, and secret motions of things; and the enlarging of the bounds of human empire, to the effecting of all things possible.

Of course, esteem for knowledge—and for those who appear to possess it—is not the only theme that haunts what we have come to term (somewhat inexactly) the "Western world." The virtues of feeling, faith, and courage have also been leitmotifs over the centuries and, in fact, have sometimes (if not always justifiably) been contrasted with the quest for knowledge. What is instructive is that, even when faith or love is extolled above all else, each is typically opposed to the powers of reason. In a parallel vein, when leaders of a totalitarian bent have sought to remake their societies in the light of a new vision, they have typically "put away" those rationalists or intellectuals whom they could not co-opt—once again paying a kind of perverse compliment to the powers of reason.

Reason, intelligence, logic, knowledge are not synonymous; and much of this book constitutes an effort to tease out the various skills and capacities that have too easily been combined under the rubric of "the mental." But, first, I must introduce a different kind of distinction—a contrast between two attitudes toward mind which have competed and alternated across the centuries. Adopting the appealing distinction of the Greek poet Archilochus, one can contrast those who view all intellect as a piece (let us dub them the "hedgehogs"), with those who favor its fragmentation into several components (the "foxes"). The hedgehogs not only believe in a singular, inviolable capacity which is the special property of human beings: often, as a corollary, they impose the conditions that each individual is born with a certain amount of intelligence, and that we individuals can in fact be rank-ordered in terms of our God-given intellect or I.Q. So entrenched is this way of thinking—and talking—that most of us lapse readily into rankings of individuals as more or less "smart," "bright," "clever," or "intelligent."

An equally venerable tradition of the West glorifies the numerous distinct functions or parts of the mind. In Classical times, it was common to differentiate between reason, will, and feeling. Medieval thinkers had their trivium of grammar, logic, and rhetoric, and their quadrivium of mathematics, geometry, astronomy, and music. As the science of psychology was launched, an even larger array of human mental abilities or faculties was posited. (Franz Joseph Gall, whom I shall formally introduce later, nominated 37 human faculties or powers of the mind; J. P. Guilford, a contemporary figure, favors 120 vectors of mind.) Some of the foxes also tend to the innate and rank-ordering cast of thought, but one can find many among them who believe in the altering (and ameliorating) effects of environment and training.

Dating back many centuries, debate between the hedgehogs and the foxes continues into our own time. In the area of brain study, there have been the *localizers*, who believe that different portions of the nervous system mediate diverse intellectual capacities; and these localizers have been arrayed against the *holists*, who deem major intellectual functions to be the property of the brain as a whole. In the area of intelligence testing, an interminable debate has raged between those (following Charles Spearman) who believe in a general factor of intellect; and those (following L. L. Thurstone) who posit a family of primary mental abilities, with none pre-eminent among them. In the area of child development, there has been vigorous debate between those who postulate general structures of the mind (like Jean Piaget) and those who believe in a large and relatively unconnected set of mental skills

7

(the environmental-learning school). Echoes in other disciplines are quite audible.

Thus, against a shared belief, over the centuries, in the primacy of intellectual powers, there is continuing debate about the propriety of parceling intellect into parts. As it happens, some long-standing is-sues in our cultural tradition show no signs of resolution. I doubt that topics like free will or the conflict between faith and reason will ever be resolved to everyone's satisfaction. But, in other cases, there may be hope for progress. Sometimes progress occurs as a consequence of logi-cal clarification, as for instance, when a fallacy is exposed. (No one continues in the mistaken belief that the distorted faces in El Greco's portraits were due to an astigmatic condition, once it has been ex-plained that astigmatism would not lead to the painting of elongated faces. An astigmatic painter would *perceive* the faces on his canvas (and in the everyday world) to be elongated; but, in fact, these faces would appear completely normal to non-astigmatic eyes.) Sometimes progress results from dramatic scientific findings (the discoveries of Copernicus and Kepler radically changed our view about the architecture of the universe). And sometimes progress comes about when a large body of information is woven together in a convincing tapestry of argument (as happened when, in the course of introducing his theory of evolution, Charles Darwin reviewed masses of evidence about the development and differentiation of species).

The time may be at hand for some clarification about the structure of human intellectual competence. In the present case, there is neither a single scientific breakthrough, nor the discovery of an egregious logi-cal blunder, but rather the confluence of a large body of evidence from a variety of sources. Such a confluence, which has been gathering with even greater force over the past few decades, seems to be recognized (at least in peripheral vision) by those concerned with human cognition. But the lines of convergence have rarely, if ever, been focused on di-rectly and systematically examined in one place; and they certainly have not been shared with the wider public. Such confrontation and collation are the twin purposes of this book.

In what follows, I argue that there is persuasive evidence for the existence of several *relatively autonomous* human intellectual compe-tences, abbreviated hereafter as "human intelligences." These are the "frames of mind" of my title. The exact nature and breadth of each intellectual "frame" has not so far been satisfactorily established, nor has the precise number of intelligences been fixed. But the conviction that there exist at least some intelligences, that these are relatively independent of one another, and that they can be fashioned and combined in a multiplicity of adaptive ways by individuals and cultures, seems to me to be increasingly difficult to deny.

Previous efforts (and there have been many) to establish independent intelligences have been unconvincing, chiefly because they rely on only one or, at the most, two lines of evidence. Separate "minds" or "faculties" have been posited solely on the basis of logical analysis, solely on the history of educational disciplines, solely on the results of intelligence testing, or solely on the insights obtained from brain study. These solitary efforts have rarely yielded the same list of competences and have thereby made a claim for multiple intelligences seem that much less tenable.

My procedure is quite different. In formulating my brief on behalf of multiple intelligences, I have reviewed evidence from a large and hitherto unrelated group of sources: studies of prodigies, gifted individuals, brain-damaged patients, *idiots savants*, normal children, normal adults, experts in different lines of work, and individuals from diverse cultures. A preliminary list of candidate intelligences has been bolstered (and, to my mind, partially validated) by converging evidence from these diverse sources. I have become convinced of the existence of an intelligence to the extent that it can be found in relative isolation in special populations (or absent in isolation in otherwise normal populations); to the extent that it may become highly developed in specific individuals or in specific cultures; and to the extent that psychometricians, experimental researchers, and/or experts in particular disciplines can posit core abilities that, in effect, define the intelligence. Absence of some or all of these indices, of course eliminates a candidate intelligence. In ordinary life, as I will show, these intelligences typically work in harmony, and so their autonomy may be invisible. But when the appropriate observational lenses are donned, the peculiar nature of each intelligence emerges with sufficient (and often surprising) clarity.

The major assignment in this book, then, is to make the case for the existence of multiple intelligences (later abbreviated as "M.I."). Whether or not the case for specific intelligences proves persuasive, I shall at least have gathered between two covers several bodies of knowledge that have hitherto lived in relative segregation. In addition, however, this volume has a number of other, and not wholly subsidiary, purposes—some primarily scientific, others distinctly practical.

First of all, I seek to expand the purviews of cognitive and developmental psychology (the two areas to which, as a researcher, I feel the closest). The expansion that I favor looks, in one direction, toward the biological and evolutionary roots of cognition and, in the other direction, toward cultural variations in cognitive competence. To my mind, visits to the "lab" of the brain scientist and to the "field" of an exotic culture should become part of the training of individuals interested in cognition and development.

Second, I wish to examine the educational implications of a theory of multiple intelligences. In my view, it should be possible to identify an individual's intellectual profile (or proclivities) at an early age and then draw upon this knowledge to enhance that person's educational opportunities and options. One could channel individuals with unusual talents into special programs, even as one could devise prosthetics and special enrichment programs for individuals presenting an atypical or a dysfunctional profile of intellectual competences.

Third, I hope that this inquiry will inspire educationally oriented anthropologists to develop a model of how intellectual competences may be fostered in various cultural settings. Only through such efforts will it be possible to determine whether theories of learning and teaching travel readily across national boundaries or must be continually refashioned in light of the particularities of each culture.

Finally—this is the most important, but also the most difficult, challenge—I hope that the point of view that I articulate here may prove of genuine utility to those policy makers and practitioners charged with "the development of other individuals." Training and heightening of intellect is certainly "in the international air": the World Bank's report on Human Development, the Club of Rome's essay on anticipatory learning, and the Venezuelan Project on Human Intelligence are but three recent visible examples. Too often practitioners involved in efforts of this sort have embraced flawed theories of intelligence or cognition and have, in the process, supported programs that have accomplished little or even proved counterproductive. To aid such individuals, I have developed a framework that, building on the theory of multiple intelligences, can be applied to any educational situation. If the framework put forth here is adopted, it may at least discourage those interventions that seem doomed to failure and encourage those that have a chance for success.

I regard the present effort as a contribution to the emerging science of cognition. To a considerable extent, I am summarizing the work of other scholars; but, to a certain extent (and I intend to make clear where), I am proposing a new orientation. Some of the claims are controversial, and I expect that experts versed in cognitive science will eventually have their say as well. Part II, the "heart" of the book, con-

sists of a description of several intellectual competences of whose existence I feel reasonably certain. But, as befits a potential contribution to
science, I shall first (in chapter 2) review other efforts to characterize
intellectual profiles and then, after putting forth the evidence in support of my theory, will (in chapter 11) subject that point of view to
lines of criticism. As part of my mission to broaden the study of cognition, I adopt a biological and crosscultural perspective throughout part
II and also devote a separate chapter each to the biological bases of
cognition (chapter 3) and to cultural variations in education (chapter
13). Finally, given the "applied" agenda I have just sketched, I shall in
the concluding chapters of the book address more directly questions of
education and policy.

A word, finally, about the title of this chapter. As I have indicated,
the idea of multiple intelligences is an old one, and I can scarcely claim
any great originality for attempting to revive it once more. Even so, by
featuring the word *idea* I want to underscore that the notion of multiple intelligences is hardly a proven scientific fact: it is, at most, an idea
that has recently regained the right to be discussed seriously. Given the
ambition and scope of this book, it is inevitable that this idea will
harbor many shortcomings. What I hope to establish is that "multiple
intelligences" is an idea whose time has come.

2

Intelligence:
Earlier Views

As a schoolboy growing up in the latter part of the eighteenth century, Franz Joseph Gall observed a relationship between certain mental characteristics of his schoolmates and the shapes of their heads. For instance, he noted that those boys with prominent eyes tended to have good memories. He clung to this idea as he became a physician and scientist and, some years later, placed it at the center of a discipline called "phrenology" which aspired to be a science.

The key idea of phrenology is simple. Human skulls differ from one another, and their variations reflect differences in the size and the shape of the brain. Different areas of the brain, in turn, subserve discrete functions; and so, by carefully examining the skull configurations of an individual, an expert should be able to determine the strengths, the weaknesses, and the idiosyncracies of his or her mental profile.

Gall's list of powers and "organs" of the mind, as modified by his colleague, Joseph Spurzheim, was a mixed bag. Featured were some thirty-seven different powers which included affective faculties, such as amativeness, philoprogenitiveness, and secretiveness; sentiments like hope, reverence, and self-esteem; reflective powers and perceptual capacities, including language, tune (for music), as well as sensitivity to such visual properties as shape and color.

It should come as no surprise (at least to observers of best-sellers over the years) that the phrenology of Gall and Spurzheim achieved enormous popularity in Europe and the United States during the early part of the nineteenth century. The simple doctrine had intrinsic appeal, and every individual could "play the game." The popularity of the aspiring science was strengthened by the fact that it was endorsed by many scientists of the day.

Of course, armed with hindsight, one can readily spot the flaws in the phrenological doctrine. We know, for example, that the sheer size of the brain has no clear-cut correlation with an individual's intellect; in fact, individuals with very small brains, such as Walt Whitman and Anatole France, have achieved great success, even as individuals with massive brains are sometimes idiots and all too often decidedly unremarkable. Moreover, the size and configuration of the skull itself proves an inexact measure of the important configurations of the human cortex.

Nonetheless, even as it would be unpardonable to overlook the flaws in Gall's claims, it would be equally fallacious to dismiss them entirely. Gall, after all, was among the first modern scientists to stress that different parts of the brain mediate different functions; the fact that we are not yet able to pinpoint specifically the relationship between size, shape, and function should by no means be taken as proof that we will never be able to do so. Moreover, Gall proposed other pregnant ideas, among them this fascinating claim: there do not exist general mental powers, such as perception, memory, and attention; but, rather, there exist different forms of perception, memory, and the like for *each* of the several intellectual faculties, such as language, music, or vision. Though seldom taken seriously throughout most of the history of psychology, this idea proves to be highly suggestive and may well be correct.

The century following Gall's original claims has seen repeated oscillations between a belief in localization of function and a skepticism about this entire line of brain-behavior correlations: in fact, this oscillation continues to plague us today. The first dubious voices were raised in the decades following Gall's original publications in the early 1800s: scholars like Pierre Flourens showed, by extirpating different parts of the brain of an animal and then observing its new behavior, that some of Gall's claims could not be supported. But then a strong chorus of support came in the 1860s, when the French surgeon and anthropologist Pierre-Paul Broca demonstrated, for the first time, an indisputable relationship between a specific brain lesion and a particular cognitive impairment. In particular, Broca amassed evidence that a lesion in a certain area of the left anterior portion of the human cortex caused aphasia, the breakdown of linguistic capacities. This dramatic demonstration was followed in succeeding years by ample documentation that various lesions in the left hemisphere could impair particular linguistic functions along specifiable lines. One lesion would reliably impair reading, while another would compromise naming or repetition. Localization of function, if not phrenology, once more carried the day.

Attempts to relate the brain to mental function or, for that matter, to uncover the physical roots of mental functions antedated the nineteenth century. The Egyptians had located thought in the heart and judgment in the head or kidneys. Pythagoras and Plato had held the mind to be in the brain. Analogously, Aristotle thought that the seat of life is in the heart, while Descartes placed the soul in the pineal gland. Scientists of the nineteenth century were not the first to try to break down the range of human intellectual abilities (though a list of thirty-seven was on the longish side). Plato and Aristotle had certainly been interested in varieties of rational thought and forms of knowledge. During the Middle Ages, scholars dwelled upon the trivium and the quadrivium, those realms of knowledge which every educated person mastered. The Hindu Upanishads actually describe seven kinds of knowledge. What the nineteenth century ushered in were highly specific claims about the profile of human mental capacities and, eventually, empirically based efforts in the clinic and the experimental laboratory to relate specific areas of the brain to particular cognitive functions.

Psychology Proper

Efforts to set up psychology as a science began in earnest in the latter half of the nineteenth century, with scholars like Wilhelm Wundt in Germany and William James in America providing a rationale and leading the way. Because the history of pre-scientific psychology was entangled with philosophy rather than with medicine, and because the first psychologists themselves were eager to define their discipline as separate from physiology and neurology, there was relatively little contact between the new breed of psychologists and the individuals who were conducting experiments with the human brain. Perhaps as a result, the categories of mentation that interested psychologists proved to be remote from those that had engaged students of the brain. Rather than thinking (like Gall) in terms of particular mental contents (like language, music, or various forms of visual perception), psychologists searched (and have continued to search) for the laws of broad, "horizontal" mental faculties—abilities like memory, perception, attention, association, and learning; these faculties were thought to operate equivalently—in fact, blindly—across diverse contents, independent of the particular sensory modality or the type of ideational content involved in the domain. In fact, such work continues to this day and makes remarkably little contact with findings emanating from the brain sciences.

Thus, one strand of scientific psychology has searched for the most general laws of human knowing—what might today be called the principles of human information processing. An equally energetic area of study has searched for individual differences—the distinctive profiles of abilities (and disabilities) in individuals. The British polymath Sir Francis Galton was instrumental in launching this field of inquiry a century ago. Given his particular interest in genius, eminence, and other notable forms of accomplishment, Galton developed statistical methods that made it possible to rank human beings in terms of their physical and intellectual powers and to correlate such measures with one another. These tools enabled him to verify a suspected link between genealogical lineage and professional accomplishment.

In fact, if one were going to measure individuals, one needed numerous dimensions and tasks on which to measure and compare. It was only a matter of time before psychologists devised various tests and began to rank human beings by comparing performances on these measures. At first, the prevailing wisdom held that powers of intellect could be estimated adequately by various tasks of sensory discrimination—for example, the ability to distinguish among lights, among weights, or among tones. Galton, in fact, believed that more refined and learned individuals would be characterized by especially keen sensory capacities. But gradually (for a variety of reasons) the scientific community concluded that one would have to look principally at more complex or "molar" capacities, such as those involving language and abstraction, if one wished to gain a more accurate assessment of human intellectual powers. The chief worker in this area was the Frenchman Alfred Binet. At the beginning of the twentieth century, with his colleague Théodore Simon, Binet devised the first tests of intelligence in order to sift out retarded children and to place other children at their appropriate grade level.

Within the scientific community and the larger society, excitement over intelligence testing was at least as pronounced and was much

15

more prolonged than had been the enthusiasm about phrenology almost a century earlier. The tasks and tests were soon available for widespread use: the mania for evaluating people for specific purposes—be it school, the military, placement in industrial organizations, or even social companionship—fueled the excitement over intelligence testing. At least until recent years, most psychologists would agree with the assessment that intelligence testing was psychology's greatest achievement, its chief claim to social utility, and an important scientific discovery in its own right. They might even applaud the British psychologist H. J. Eysenck's conclusion that the concept of intelligence "constitutes a true scientific paradigm in the Kuhnian* sense."

The tale describing the rise of the I.Q. test, and the various debates that have raged about it, has been retold so many times that I am relieved of the necessity to relate the sound and fury once again. Most scholars within psychology, and nearly all scholars outside the field, are now convinced that enthusiasm over intelligence tests has been excessive, and that there are numerous limitations in the instruments themselves and in the uses to which they can (and should) be put. Among other considerations, the tasks are definitely skewed in favor of individuals in societies with schooling and particularly in favor of individuals who are accustomed to taking paper-and-pencil tests, featuring clearly delineated answers. As I have noted, the tests have predictive power for success in schooling, but relatively little predictive power outside the school context, especially when more potent factors like social and economic background have been taken into account. Too much of a hullabaloo over the possible heritability of I.Q. has been sustained over the past few decades; and while few authorities would go so far as to claim that the I.Q. is in no degree inherited, extreme claims on heritability within and across races have been discredited.

Still, one long-standing debate within the area of intelligence testing must be briefly rehearsed here. On one side are arrayed those individuals influenced by the British educational psychologist Charles Spearman—in my terms, a "hedgehog"—who believe in the existence of "g"—a general overriding factor of intelligence which is measured by every task in an intelligence test. On the other side are supporters of the American psychometrician and "fox" L. L. Thurstone, who believe in the existence of a small set of primary mental faculties that are relatively independent of one another and are measured by different tasks.

---

*Eysenck refers here to Thomas Kuhn, a contemporary philosopher who defines sciences in terms of their central assumptions and procedures, or "paradigms."

Thurstone, in fact, nominated seven such factors—verbal comprehension, word fluency, numerical fluency, spatial visualization, associative memory, perceptual speed, and reasoning. (Other less widely quoted scholars posit a far higher number of independent factors.)

Most important to stress is that neither side has been able to gain an upper hand. That is because the issues surrounding the interpretation of intelligence scores turn out to be mathematical in nature and not susceptible to empirical resolution. Thus, given the same set of data, it is possible, using one set of factor-analytic procedures, to come up with a picture that supports the idea of a "g" factor; using another equally valid method of statistical analysis, it is possible to support the notion of a family of relatively discrete mental abilities. As Stephen Jay Gould has shown in his recent book, *The Mismeasure of Man*, there is nothing intrinsically superior about either of these mathematical measures. When it comes to the interpretation of intelligence testing, we are faced with an issue of taste or preference rather than one on which scientific closure is likely to be reached.

Piaget

It is from an individual originally trained in the I.Q. tradition that we have obtained a view of intellect which has, in many quarters, replaced the vogue of intelligence testing. The Swiss psychologist, Jean Piaget, began his career around 1920 as a researcher working in Simon's laboratory and soon became particularly interested in the errors children make when tackling items on an intelligence test. Piaget came to believe that it is not the accuracy of the child's response that is important, but rather the lines of reasoning the child invokes: these can be most clearly seen by focusing on the assumptions and the chains of reasoning that spawn erroneous conclusions. So, for example, it was not revealing in itself to discover that most four-year-olds think that a hammer is more like a nail than like a screwdriver; what was important is that children reach this conclusion because their view of similarity reflects physical co-occurrence (hammers are found in the vicinity of nails) rather than membership in the same hierarchical category (tools).

Piaget himself never undertook a critique of the intelligence-testing movement; but in looking at the scientific moves he made, one can gain a feeling for some of the inadequacies of the Binet-Simon program. First of all, the I.Q. movement is blindly empirical. It is based

17

simply on tests with some predictive power about success in school and, only marginally, on a theory of how the mind works. There is no view of process, of how one goes about solving a problem: there is simply the issue of whether one arrives at a correct answer. For another thing, the tasks featured in the I.Q. test are decidedly microscopic, are often unrelated to one another, and seemingly represent a "shotgun" approach to the assessment of human intellect. The tasks are remote, in many cases, from everyday life. They rely heavily upon language and upon a person's skill in defining words, in knowing facts about the world, in finding connections (and differences) among verbal concepts.

Much of the information probed for in intelligence tests reflects knowledge gained from living in a specific social and educational milieu. For instance, the ability to define *tort* or to identify the author of the *Iliad* is highly reflective of the kind of school one attends or the tastes of one's family. In contrast, intelligence tests rarely assess skill in assimilating new information or in solving new problems. This bias toward "crystallized" rather than "fluid" knowledge can have astounding consequences. An individual can lose his entire frontal lobes, in the process becoming a radically different person, unable to display any initiative or to solve new problems—and yet may continue to exhibit an I.Q. close to genius level. Moreover, the intelligence test reveals little about an individual's potential for further growth. Two individuals can receive the same I.Q. score; yet one may turn out to be capable of a tremendous spurt in intellectual attainment, while another may be displaying the very height of his intellectual powers. To put it in the terms of the Soviet psychologist Lev Vygotsky, intelligence tests fail to yield any indication of an individual's "zone of potential [or, "proximal"] development."

With such critical considerations at least implicitly in mind, Piaget developed over several decades a radically different and extremely powerful view of human cognition. In his view, all study of human thought must begin by positing an individual who is attempting to make sense of the world. The individual is continually constructing hypotheses and thereby attempting to generate knowledge: he is trying to figure out the nature of material objects in the world, how they interact with one another, as well as the nature of persons in the world, their motivations and their behavior. Ultimately he must piece them all together into a sensible story, a coherent account of the nature of the physical and the social worlds.

Initially, the baby makes sense of the world, primarily through his reflexes, his sensory perceptions, and his physical actions upon the world. After a year or two, he arrives at a "practical" or "sensori-motor" knowledge of the world of objects, as they exist in time and space. Equipped with this knowledge, he can make his way satisfactorily in his environment and can appreciate that an object continues to exist in space and time even when it is out of view. Next the toddler goes on to develop *interiorized actions* or *mental operations*. These are actions that can potentially be performed upon the world of objects; but, owing to a newly emerging capacity, these actions need only be performed cerebrally, within the head, perhaps through imagery. So, for example, to proceed from his destination to a familiar starting point, the child does not have to try out various routes: he can simply calculate that, by reversing his steps, he will return to his origin. At the same time, the child also becomes capable of symbol use: now he can use various images or elements—such as words, gestures, or pictures—to stand for "real life" objects in the world, and can become skilled in deploying various *symbol systems*, like language or drawing.

These evolving capacities of *interiorization* and *symbolization* reach a high point around the age of seven or eight when the child becomes capable of *concrete operations*. Armed with this new set of capacities, the child is now able to reason systematically about the world of objects, number, time, space, causality, and the like. No longer confined simply to acting in a physically appropriate manner with objects, the child can now appreciate the relations that obtain among a series of actions upon objects. So he understands that objects can be rearranged and still remain the same quantity; that a material can be changed in shape without the mass being thereby affected; that a scene can be viewed from a different perspective and still contain the same elements.

According to Piaget, a final stage of development comes into being during early adolescence. Now capable of *formal operations*, the youth is able to reason about the world not only through actions or single symbols, but rather by figuring out the implications that obtain among a set of related propositions. The adolescent becomes able to think in a completely logical fashion: now resembling a working scientist, he can express hypotheses in propositions, test them, and revise the propositions in the light of the results of such experimentation. These abilities in hand (or in head), the youth has achieved the end-state of adult human cognition. He is now capable of that form of logical-rational thought which is prized in the West and epitomized by mathematicians and scientists. Of course, the individual can go on to make further discoveries but will no longer undergo any further qualitative changes in his thinking.

This sprint through Piaget's principal precepts highlights some of the strengths and the weaknesses of his formulation. On the positive side, Piaget has taken children seriously; he has posed to them problems of importance (particularly ones drawn from the scientific realm) and has adduced evidence that, at each stage, the same underlying organized structure can be discerned across a wide range of mental operations. For instance, in Piaget's view, the "concrete-operational" child is capable of handling a gamut of tasks having to do with conservation of number, causality, quantity, volume, and the like, because they all draw upon the same core mental structures. Similarly, equipped with formal operations, the adolescent displays a structured whole of operations so that he can now reason logically about any set of propositions posed to him. Unlike the architects of intelligence testing, Piaget has also taken seriously the list of issues that philosophers, and most especially Immanuel Kant, deemed central to human intellect, including the basic categories of time, space, number, and causality: At the same time, Piaget has avoided forms of knowledge that are simply memorized (like word definitions) or restricted to certain cultural groups (such as those that favor "high" art). Wittingly or not, Piaget has limned a brilliant portrait of that form of human intellectual growth which is valued most highly by the Western scientific and philosophical traditions.

But these undeniable strengths, which have made Piaget *the* theorist of cognitive development, cohabit with certain weaknesses that have become increasingly clear over the past two decades. First of all, while Piaget has painted a redoubtable picture of development, it is still only one sort of development. Centered on the intellectual agenda addressed by the young scientist, Piaget's model of development assumes relatively less importance in non-Western and pre-literate contexts and may, in fact, be applicable only to a minority of individuals, even in the West. The steps entailed in achieving other forms of competence—those of an artist, a lawyer, an athlete, or a political leader—are ignored in Piaget's monolithic emphasis upon a certain form of thinking.

Of course, Piaget's perspective might be limited, yet totally accurate within its own restricted domain. Alas, a generation of empirical researchers who have looked closely at Piaget's claims, have found otherwise. While the broad outlines of development as sketched by Piaget remain of interest, many of the specific details are simply not correct. Individual stages are achieved in a far more continuous and gradual fashion than Piaget indicated; in fact, one finds little of the discontinuity that he claimed (and that made his theoretical claims particularly riveting). Thus, most tasks claimed to entail concrete operations can be solved by children in the pre-operational years, once various adjustments have been introduced into the experimental paradigm. For example, there is now evidence that children can conserve number, classify consistently, and abandon egocentrism as early as the age of three—findings in no way predicted (or even allowed) by Piaget's theory.

Another claim central to Piaget's theory has also fallen on hard times. He contended that the various operations that he had uncovered could be applied to any manner of content. (In this, he resembled the proponents of "horizontal faculties" who believe in all-encompassing processes like perception or memory.) In reality, however, Piaget's operations emerge in a much more piecemeal fashion, proving effective with certain materials or contents, while failing to be invoked (or being invoked improperly) with other materials. Thus, for example, a child who exhibits the operation of conservation with some materials will fail to conserve with other materials. Piaget was aware that operations would not crystallize instantaneously: he even invented a "fudge factor"—called *décalage*—which allowed the same underlying operation to emerge at somewhat different times with different materials. But what has happened is that *décalage* has, in fact, become the rule in studies of cognitive development. Rather than a whole series of abilities coalescing at about the same time (as Piaget would have it), theoretically related abilities turn out to emerge at disparate points in time.

One confronts other limitations as well. Despite his skepticism about I.Q. items couched in language, Piaget's tasks themselves are usually conveyed verbally. And when they have been posed nonlinguistically, the results are often different from those obtained in Genevan laboratories. While Piaget's tasks are more molar and complex than those favored in intelligence tests, many still end up fairly remote from the kind of thinking in which most individuals engage during their normal daily lives. Piaget's tasks continue to be drawn from the benches and blackboards of a laboratory scientist. Finally, somewhat surprisingly, while his picture of the active, exploring child strikes a responsive chord, Piaget tells us little about creativity at the forefront of the sciences, let alone about the originality that is most prized in the arts or other realms of human creativity. Over and above its failure to convey the universal pattern of cognitive growth which all normal children are alleged to traverse, Piaget's scheme—restricted at its mature end to the classroom exercises of a high-school science class—emerges as even less relevant to that discovery of new phenomena or that positing of new problems which many consider central in the life of the mind. Piaget's scheme may well be the best that we have, but its deficiencies are becoming all too evident.

The Information-Processing Approach

If intelligence testing was the vogue forty years ago, and Piagetian theory the rage twenty years ago, a new form of study, often called "information-processing psychology" or "cognitive science," is currently enjoying hegemony among students of the mind. The information-processing psychologist uses the methods devised by experimental psychologists over the past century in order to investigate tasks of the sort that Piaget and other more molar cognitive theorists have been employing. As an example, a researcher working in the information-processing paradigm seeks to provide a second-by-second (or even a millisecond by millisecond) "microgenetic" picture of the mental steps involved as a child solves (or fails to solve) a conservation problem. The process begins with information delivered to eye or ear and only concludes when an answer has been issued by mouth or hand. Rather than simply describing two or three basic stages found at different ages, and the strategies favored at each point, as Piaget would do, the information-processing psychologist attempts to describe in the finest detail all steps used by a given child. In fact, an ultimate goal of information-processing psychology is to describe the steps so exhaustively and scrupulously that an individual's performance can be simulated on a computer. Such a descriptive *tour de force* involves detailed analysis of the task itself, as well as painstaking analysis of the subject's thoughts and behavior.

In its focus on the details of processing, and in its illumination of the microstructure of a task, information-processing intelligence theory is an advance over earlier lines of study. We now have available a much more dynamic view of what happens in the course of problem solving: included is a picture of the informational "intake" or access mechanisms; the forms of immediate and short-term retention which hold onto information until it can be encoded in memory; various recoding and transforming operations which can be imposed upon the newly acquired information. Moreover, there is the suggestive notion of executive functions, "meta-components" or other higher-order control mechanisms, whose mission it is to determine which problems ought to be tackled, which goals sought, which operations applied, and in which order. Throughout, one encounters the healthy, if somewhat unexamined, American emphasis on mechanics: on what is done, in what order, by what mechanism, in order to yield a particular effect or result.

Information-processing psychology, then, represents progress along certain—but not, in my view, all—lines. In opposition to the Piagetian paradigm, for example, information-processing psychology lacks an articulated theory within which different forms of cognition can be convincingly related to (or distinguished from) one another. Ofttimes, a survey of the literature suggests the existence of a thousand expert information processors carrying out one or another operation without any particular connection to the others. But, like Piaget, information-processing psychologies sometimes commit the opposite sin as well: one encounters the blithe notion that a single, highly general problem-solving mechanism can be brought to bear willy-nilly on the full range of human problems. While in theory the idea of a single "horizontal" problem-solving apparatus is attractive, in fact the carefully selected problems to which it is said to apply turn out to be disturbingly similar to one another. Thus, the claim that we use the same problem-solving apparatus across the board becomes vacuous. In fact, in common with Piagetian psychology, nearly all the problems examined by information-processing psychologists prove to be of the logical-mathematical sort. The prototypical problems—solving logical theorems, carrying out geometric proofs, playing a game of chess—might well have been borrowed directly form Piaget's archive of pivotal intellectual tasks.

As information-processing psychology is still in its infancy, it is perhaps unfair to criticize it for not having solved major outstanding issues in the area of intelligence. Moreover, recent flirtation with the "intelligence-testing" industry has infused with new life this somewhat discredited branch, as researchers like Robert Sternberg have attempted to identify the operations involved in the solution of standard intelligent-test items. Yet, to my mind, the excessively mechanistic computer-driven model for thinking and the penchant for scientifically oriented test problems foreshadow certain long-term problems with this approach. For one thing, like most previous approaches to intelligence, the information-processing tack is studiously non- (if not anti-) biological, making little contact with what is known about the operation of the nervous system. For another, there is as yet relatively little interest in the open-ended creativity that is crucial at the highest levels of human intellectual achievement. The problems posed characteristically feature a single solution or small set of solutions, and there is scant attention to problems with an indefinite range of solutions, let alone the generation of new problems.

Finally, a more serious objection. At present, there seems to be no procedure by which to adjudicate among the principal debates within the area of information-processing psychology. Is there a central executive or not? Are there general problem-solving skills or just skills specific to particular domains? What elements change with development—the number and size of storage areas, the kinds of strategy available, or the efficiency with which operations are carried out? The information-processing psychologists could retort, "This criticism is true at present but will become less true as we accrue more data. When we succeed in producing a sufficiently rich set of computer simulations, we will determine *which* simulation most closely mimics the thoughts and behavior of human beings."

But as I see it, it is far too easy to spin out simulations that can support rival lines of argument, or to counter an apparent refutation of a model simply by effecting minor adjustments in a task. Should one psychologist claim that short-term memory may contain more than the reported "magic number" of seven chunks, a defender of the classic position can simply count the chunks differently or claim that what had been four chunks have been "re-chunked" into two. More generally, unless one can envision a decisive test between one information-processing approach and another, one is faced with the likelihood that there will be as many convincing information-flow box diagrams as there are ingenious researchers.

The "Symbol Systems" Approach

Investigations that accentuate one view of human intellect naturally breed a counter movement. As we have seen, the I.Q., the Piagetian, and the information-processing approaches all focus on a certain kind of logical or linguistic problem solving; all ignore biology; all fail to come to grips with the higher levels of creativity; and all are insensitive to the range of roles highlighted in human society. Consequently, these facts have engendered an alternative point of view that focuses precisely upon these neglected areas.

24

I cannot write about this fledgling movement in a disinterested way becaue it is closest to my own work and my own beliefs. It is perhaps best to regard this final section as an introduction to the argument being developed throughout the remainder of the book, rather than as a mere conclusion to the survey undertaken in this chapter. As a "symbol" of this "move," I shall adopt the collaborative "we," in describing the principal features of this approach.

For much of the twentieth century, philosophers have displayed a particular interest in human symbolic capacities. According to such influential thinkers as Ernst Cassirer, Susanne Langer, and Alfred North Whitehead, the ability of human beings to use various symbolic vehicles in expressing and communicating meanings distinguishes human beings sharply from other organisms. Symbol use has been key in the evolution of human nature, giving rise to myth, language, art, science; it has also been central in the highest creative achievements of human beings, all of which exploit the human symbolic faculty.

We may speak of two "paradigm" shifts in philosophy. Initially, the philosophical interest of Classical times in objects of the physical world was replaced by that preoccupation with the mind and its objects which we associate with Hume, Kant, and other Enlightenment thinkers. In the twentieth century, however, the focus has shifted once again, this time to the actual symbolic vehicles of thought. Thus, much of contemporary work in philosophy is directed toward an understanding of language, mathematics, visual arts, gestures, and other human symbols.

We can observe the same trends at work in psychology. There, too, we discern a shift from external behavior to the activities and products of human minds and, specifically, to the various symbolic vehicles in which human individuals traffic. Rather than considering symbolic vehicles (or the media by which they are transmitted) as transparent means by which the same contents are presented, a number of researchers—including David Feldman, David Olson, Gavriel Salomon, and myself—have elected to take human symbol systems as a primary focus of attention. In our view, much of what is distinctive about human cognition and information processing involves the deployment of these various symbol systems. It is at least an open question, an empirical issue, whether operation of one symbol system such as language involves the same abilities and processes as such cognate systems as music, gesture, mathematics, or pictures. It is equally open whether information encountered in one medium (say, film) is the "same" information when transmitted by another medium (say, books).

In adopting this symbolic perspective, my colleagues and I do not propose to throw away the Piagetian baby with the bath water. Rather, we seek to use the methods and the overall schemes fashioned by Piaget and to focus them not merely on the linguistic, logical, and numerical symbols of classic Piagetian theory, but rather upon a full range of symbol systems encompassing musical, bodily, spatial, and even personal symbol systems. The challenge, as we see it, is to compose a developmental portrait of each of these forms of symbolic competence and to determine empirically which connections or distinctions might obtain across them.

The problem of reconciling a pluralistic approach to cognition with Piaget's unilineal developmental scheme has been well addressed by David Feldman. According to this educationally oriented developmental psychologist, cognitive accomplishments may occur in a range of domains. Certain domains, such as the logical-mathematical one studied by Piaget, are *universal*. They must be (and are) confronted and mastered by individuals all over the world, simply by virtue of their membership in the same species and the resultant need to cope with that species' physical and social environment. Other domains are restricted to *certain cultures*. For example, the capacity to read is important in many cultures but unknown (or minimally valued) in others. Unless one lives in a culture where this domain is featured, one will make little or no progress in it. Still other domains are restricted to pockets within a culture. For example, map making is important in some literate subcultures but not in others. One also encounters domains that are highly idiosyncratic. Chess playing, the mastery of the Japanese game of go, expertise in crossword puzzles, are not essential in any division of society, and yet some individuals realize tremendous achievements in those domains, within a particular culture.

Finally, arrayed at the opposite extreme from universal domains are *unique* domains, areas of skill in which initially only one or a tiny handful of individuals make progress. One might think of the innovative scientist or artist as working in a unique domain, a domain of which he or she is currently the only denizen. What is particularly fascinating is that, eventually, unique domains may become so well explored and articulated by an individual or a small group that they become accessible to other individuals. Many scientific or artistic breakthroughs, such as the calculus or the theory of evolution, initially began as unique domains but now can be mastered by large segments of a culture. And perhaps the same thing occurred in the remote past in such cultural domains as map making or reading.

A focus on the mastery of domains entails certain assumptions.

One belief is that, within each domain, there exists a series of steps or stages, ranging from the level of rank novice, through apprentice or journeyman's status, to the status of expert or master. Irrespective of domains, there should (in proper Piagetian fashion) be a stagelike sequence through which any individual must pass. However, individuals differ greatly from one another in the speed with which they pass through these domains; and, *contra* Piaget, success at negotiating one domain entails no necessary correlation with speed or success in negotiating other domains. Domains may be cordoned off from one another in this sense. Moreover, progress in a domain does not depend entirely on the solitary individual's actions within his world. Rather, much of the information about the domain is better thought of as contained within the culture itself, for it is the culture that defines the stages and fixes the limits of individual achievement. One must conceive of the individual *and* his culture as embodying a certain stage sequence, with much of the information essential for development inhering in the culture itself rather than simply inside the individual's skull.

This focus on an individual's progress through a domain has stimulated Feldman to confront the phenomenon of the child prodigy. The prodigy may be thought of as an individual who passes through one or more domains with tremendous rapidity, exhibiting a speed that seems to render him qualitatively different from other individuals. In Feldman's view, the mere existence of a prodigy represents a remarkable "co-incidence" of a number of factors—among them an initial, possibly inborn proclivity, considerable pressure from parents and family, excellent teachers, high motivation, and, perhaps most important, a culture in which that proclivity will have a chance to flower. In monitoring the prodigy as he advances, one glimpses a "fast-forward" picture of what is involved in all educational processes. Unlike the Piagetian individual advancing chiefly by himself along a path available to humans the world over, the prodigy is a fascinating amalgam of the highest amounts of natural proclivity with the greatest amounts of stimulation and structure as provided by his own society.

A concern with prodigies well illustrates certain central features of this new approach to intellectual development. First of all, the very existence of prodigies poses a problem that cannot be handled by Piagetian theory: how an individual can be precocious in just one area of development. (I might note parenthetically that none of the other approaches reviewed here can deal adequately with prodigious behavior either.) Second, a survey of prodigies provides support for the notion of particular symbolic domains, since prodigious behavior is characteristically found in certain domains (mathematics, chess playing), while rarely if ever in other ones (literary skill). Study of prodigious achievement also provides support for the Piagetian belief in specific stage sequences, since the progress of prodigies can be well described in terms of negotiation of a set of steps or stages. And, because prodigious accomplishment is not possible without extensive environmental support, focus on the prodigy also highlights the contributions of the society. Finally, through attention to unusual populations like prodigies, investigators of various forms of intelligence have the opportunity to probe the nature and the operation of certain intellectual competences in pristine form.

Not surprisingly, each of the aforementioned researchers working in the symbol systems tradition exhibits a somewhat different focus. For instance, Gavriel Salomon, an educational psychologist working in Israel, has focused particularly on the media of transmission: he studies the *modus operandi* of television, books, and film and the ways in which the various symbol systems of the cultures are picked up and transmitted by these media. Moreover, he has tackled the question of which "prostheses" might enable individuals to acquire information more readily from the various media. David Olson, a cognitive developmental psychologist at the Ontario Institute for Studies on Education, pioneered in this area by showing that, even in a task as simple as constructing a diagonal, the medium of presentation exerts a profound influence on a child's performance. Recently, Olson has focused more on the role of the symbol systems of literacy. He has accrued evidence that individuals reared in a society where literacy is highlighted, learn (and reason) differently from those who employ other kinds of symbol systems in nonschooled settings.

In work at Harvard Project Zero, my colleagues and I have sought to uncover the fine structure of development within each particular symbol system. We have sought to ascertain whether certain common processes may cut across diverse symbol systems, or whether, alternatively, each symbol system is better described as having its own developmental course. Then, in complementary research at the Boston Veterans Administration Medical Center, my colleagues and I posed the opposite question. In which ways do the various human symbolic capacities break down under specific conditions of brain damage? Drawing on information from the developmental and the neuropsychological perspectives, we have striven to arrive at a more satisfactory notion of the structure and organization of human symbolic functioning. Our goal has been to arrive at the "natural kinds" of symbol systems: the families of symbol systems which hang together (or fall apart), and the ways they might be represented in the human nervous system.

To my mind (and here I do not presume to speak for others in the symbol systems movement), a pivotal issue concerns the definition and delineation of particular symbolic domains. Proceeding in terms of logical considerations, one can effect discriminations among specific symbol systems. This is what Nelson Goodman and other philosophers have elected to do. One can also adopt a historical or a cultural view, simply taking as given the list of particular symbol systems or domains that a culture has chosen to exploit for educational or communicational purposes. Following this line of argument, one refers to map making or chess playing, history or geography, as domains, just because they have been so designated by the culture as a whole. One can also adopt the empirically ordered approach of intelligence testers: here one simply ascertains which symbolic tasks correlate statistically, and assumes that these reflect the same underlying competence. In following this path, one is restricted by the nature of the tasks used. Hence, one may well come up with a misleading correlation, particularly if one happens to have used an idiosyncratic collection of tasks.

Finally, one can assume the approach of the neuropsychologist, who looks at which symbolic capacities break down together under conditions of brain damage, and hypothesizes that these reflect the same natural kind. Even this approach (to which I am personally wedded) has its pitfalls, however. For one thing, physical proximity in the nervous system may not reflect similar neural mechanisms. Highly different functions might be carried out in neighboring regions of the cortex. For another, the way in which cultures "mold" or "exploit" raw computational capacities may influence the organization of capacities; and it may be the case that across different cultures, one encounters different pattens of breakdown—as happens, for example, when cultures have evolved radically different forms of reading, one involving pictographs, another based upon character-sound correspondence. The lesion that causes reading disturbance in one culture (say, Italy) produces no disturbance in a culture where reading proceeds by a different mechanism (say, Japan).

There are other difficulties with a neuropsychological approach. Even though breakdowns provide valuable insight into organization of intact capacities, one cannot blithely assume that breakdown directly unmasks organization. The ways a radio breaks down (for example, through destruction of a plug) do not necessarily tell you how best to describe the ordinary operation of the radio. After all, while you can

29

stop the radio by pulling out the plug, this information is irrelevant for understanding the actual mechanical and electrical workings of the apparatus.

In view of these and other limitations in each "window" upon symbolic functioning, I have taken a determinedly catholic approach in what follows. I have surveyed information from a wide range of sources—including developmental data, psychometric findings, descriptions of special populations, such as *idiots savants* and prodigies— all in an effort to arrive at an optimal description of each domain of cognition and symbolization. Nonetheless, every researcher has a bias; and in my own case, I believe that the most valuable (and least misleading) information is likely to come from a deep knowledge of the nervous system: how it is organized, how it develops, how it breaks down. Findings from the brain, in my view, serve as the court of last resort, the ultimate arbiter among competing accounts of cognition. Therefore, before embarking upon my study of different intelligences, I shall survey some relevant highlights of recent work in the biological sciences.

3

Biological
Foundations of
Intelligence

The Phenomena to Be Explained

A comprehensive science of life must account for the nature, as well as the variety, of human intellectual competences. In view of the spectacular progress of recent decades in such areas as biochemistry, genetics, and neurophysiology, there is every reason to believe that the biological sciences will eventually be able to offer a cogent account of these intellectual phenomena. Indeed, it is high time that our understanding of human intellect be informed by the findings that have accrued in the biological sciences since the time of Franz Joseph Gall. And yet, because psychologists and biologists inhabit different environments, the task of marshaling biology to explain human intelligence has barely begun.

As I read current findings in the brain and biological sciences, they bear with particular force on two issues that concern us here. The first issue involves the *flexibility of human development*. The principal tension here centers on the extent to which the intellectual potentials or capacities of an individual or a group can be altered by various interventions. From one point of view, development may be viewed as relatively locked-in, preordained, alterable only in particulars. From an

31

opposing perspective, there is far more malleability or plasticity in development, with appropriate interventions at crucial times yielding an organism with a far different range and depth of capacities (and limitations). Also pertinent to the issue of flexibility, are the related questions of the kinds of intervention that are most effective, their timing, the role of critical periods during which pivotal alterations can be brought about. Only if such issues are resolved will it be possible to determine which educational interventions are most effective in allowing individuals to achieve their full intellectual potentials.

The second issue is the *identity*, or *nature, of the intellectual capacities* that human beings can develop. From one point of view, which I associated earlier with the hedgehog, human beings possess extremely general powers, all-purpose information-processing mechanisms which can be put to a large, or perhaps even an infinite, number of uses. From an opposite perspective, that more reminiscent of the fox, human beings (like other species) have a proclivity to execute certain specifiable intellectual operations, while proving incapable of performing other intellectual operations. An allied issue concerns the extent to which different portions of the nervous system are, in fact, committed to carrying out particular intellectual functions, as opposed to being available for a wide range of operations. It proves possible to analyze this issue of identity at various levels, ranging from the functions of specific cells, at one extreme, to the functions of each half of the brain, on the other. Finally, as part of this concern with identity, the biologist needs to account for those capacities (like language) which seem to evolve to a high degree in all normal individuals, as against other capacities (like music) where striking differences in individual achievement are far more prevalent.

Taken together, these sets of questions add up to a search for general principles that govern the nature and the development of human intellectual capacities, and that determine how these are organized, tapped, and transformed over a lifetime. Much current work in the biological sciences strikes me as relevant to these issues, though often it has not been conceived along these lines. Here I attempt to mine those lodes of research which seem most relevant to a student of the human mind.

In my view, the preponderance of evidence points to the following conclusions. There is considerable plasticity and flexibility in human growth, especially during the early months of life. Still, even that plasticity is modulated by strong genetic constraints which operate from the beginning and which guide development along some paths rather that along others. As for the issue of identity, evidence is accumulating that human beings are predisposed to carry out certain specific intellectual operations whose nature can be inferred from careful observation and experimentation. Educational efforts must build upon a knowledge of these intellectual proclivities and their points of maximum flexibility and adaptability.

These, then, are some conclusions at which one may arrive after weighing the relevant biological evidence. For individuals already familiar with the findings of the biological sciences, as well as for those who have little tolerance for reports from the "harder" sciences, it is possible at this point in the narrative to move directly to chapter 4, where I introduce the criteria for an intelligence. Those with an interest in the details which undergird the foregoing conclusions are invited to enter the realm of genetics.

Lessons from Genetics

Once one has elected to peer through the biologist's lens, an initial concern with genetics is virtually inevitable (and certainly proper). Moreover, given the incredible strides made in genetics, since the "code was cracked" by James Watson and Francis Crick some thirty years ago, it is not surprising that psychologists have searched—in the composition of DNA, RNA, and their fascinating interaction—for *the* answer to puzzles about intellect. Unfortunately, however, lessons from this line of study are far from direct.

To be sure, the geneticists' discoveries must form the point of departure for any biological study. After all, we are living organisms; and, in one sense, everything that we will ever achieve has been coded in our genetic material. Moreover, the distinction between the genotype—the organism's makeup as determined by the genetic contributions of each parent—and the phenotype—the organism's observable characteristics as expressed within a given environment—is fundamental to consideration of any individual's behavioral and intellectual profile. Equally fundamental is the notion of variation: because of the huge number of genes contributed by each parent and the innumerable ways in which they can be combined, we need not worry that any two individuals (except identical twins) will unduly resemble one another, or that any two individuals will exhibit identical profiles.

33

Genetics has made its greatest progress in accounting for simple traits in simple organisms. We know a great deal about the genetic basis for structures and behaviors in the fruit fly; and through studies of inheritance patterns, we have gained insight into the transmission of specific human pathologies like sickle cell anemia, hemophilia, and colorblindness. But when it comes to more complex human abilities—the capacities to solve equations, to appreciate or create music, to master languages—we are still woefully ignorant about the genetic component and its phenotypical expression. First of all, these abilities cannot be studied experimentally in the laboratory. Furthermore, rather than being related to a specific gene or a small set of genes, any complex trait reflects many genes, a fair number of which will be polymorphic (allowing a number of different realizations across a range of environments). Indeed, when it comes to capacities as broad (and vague) as human intelligences, it is questionable whether one ought to speak of "traits" at all.

Those scholars of a geneticist bent have, of course, speculated about what a talent might be. According to one such account certain combinations of genes may be correlated with one another, and these in turn may cause the production of enzymes that affect specific structures in one region of the brain. As a result of enzyme action, these structures might become larger, feature more connections, or promote more inhibition, any one of which possibilities might culminate in a greater potential for high achievement. But the very fact that these speculations involve so many hypothetical steps indicates how far they are from being established facts. We do not even know whether those individuals who have a talent (or, for that matter, a glaring defect) reflect an inherited tendency to form certain neural connections (which would then be found in others who are closely related); or whether they simply represent one tail of a randomly generated distribution (in which case they could equally well arise in any two unrelated individuals).

Probably the most reliable clues to the genetics of human talents come from studies of twins. By comparing identical twins with fraternal twins, or identical twins reared apart with those reared together, we can gain some purchase on which traits are most subject to hereditary influences. Still, scientists eyeing the same set of data—and not even disputing the data—can reach widely divergent conclusions about heritability. Simply on the basis of certain mathematical and scientific assumptions, some scientists would place the heritability of intelligence (as measured by I.Q. tests) as high as 80 percent. In other words, these authorities would claim that up to 80 percent of the variability in intelligence scores in that population can be ascribed to one's genetic background. Other scientists pondering the same data but operating on different assumptions would estimate heritability as less than 20 percent or even zero. Naturally, most estimates run somewhere in between, with 30 percent to 50 percent being commonly cited. There is considerable agreement that physical traits are most straightforwardly genetic, that aspects of temperament are also largely genetic; but that when one comes to aspects of cognitive style or personality, the case for high heritability is far less convincing.

The genetic literature provides few unequivocal answers to questions that preoccupy a student of intelligence. Nonetheless, there are useful concepts that might inform our investigation. Let's begin with the well-documented fact that, as a result of their genetic makeup, certain individuals are "at risk" for a given disease (like hemophilia) or neurological condition (like severe retardation). This fact does not in itself certify that they will get the disease; factors of probability as well as accidents of environment or special treatment also play their role. This fact suggests only that, other things being equal, these individuals are more likely to contract the disease than is someone without this hereditary disposition.

By analogy, it may be useful to consider certain individuals as "at promise" for the flowering of a certain talent. Again, this diagnosis does not ensure that they will develop the talent: one will not become a great chess player, or even a "patzer" in the absence of a chess board. But given an environment where chess is played, and some stimulation, individuals of promise have a special proclivity for acquiring the skill rapidly and reaching a high level of competence. Being at promise is a *sine qua non* for becoming a prodigy; even so, thanks to certain "hot house" training methods, such as the Suzuki Violin Talent Education Program, even an individual with apparently modest genetic promise may make remarkable strides in a short time.

Another suggestive line of speculation concerns the variety of traits and behavior of which human beings are capable. In a large and heterogeneous population like ours, with considerable intermarriage, one encounters a wide variety of traits; but over time, extreme traits tend to become invisible or to disappear altogether. In contrast, certain populations (for example, those in isolated South Sea islands) have lived as a single group for thousands of years and have avoided any kind of intermingling with other groups. These latter populations will exhibit *genetic drift*: through processes of natural selection, they will come to possess a genetic pool that may be distinctly different from that of other populations.

It is not always possible to separate out the purely genetic factors from those reflecting an unusual natural environment or an exotic cultural system. Yet, according to the virologist Carleton Gajdusek, who has studied many primitive societies, populations subjected to genetic drift often exhibit a remarkable set of characteristics, including unusual diseases, immunities, physical traits, behavioral patterns, and customs. It becomes crucial to record these factors before they have disappeared, or become invisible, owing to the demise of the group or to its extensive intermingling with other populations. Only by careful documentation of these groups will it become possible to determine the full range of human abilities. Indeed, once these groups have disappeared, we may not even be able to envision that they could have been capable of the actions, skills, or traits that they in fact exhibited. But once we have established that some group—in fact, that any human being—has exhibited a certain competence, we can look for—and attempt to foster—that capacity in other members of the species—our species. (An opposite course can be pursued in the case of undesirable traits or competences.) To be sure, we can never definitively establish that a given trait has a genetic component, but that determination actually proves irrelevant to our present concern: documentation of the varieties of human nature.

Consider this perspective in another way. Our genetic heritage is so variegated that one can postulate all kinds of abilities and skills (as well as maladies and infirmities) that have not yet emerged, or that we have not yet come to know about. Given genetic engineering, countless other possibilities arise as well. An individual with a clever imagination might well be able to anticipate some of these possibilities. However, it is a far more prudent research strategy to sample widely among human beings of diverse stock and to determine which competences they have in fact achieved. Studies of remote and isolated groups—the prize for the geneticist—prove extremely valuable for psychologists as well. The broader the sampling of human beings, the more likely that any list of the range of human intelligences will be comprehensive and accurate.

The Neurobiological Perspective

While genetics still proves to be of limited utility for the student of intelligence, a review of neurobiology—including the specialities of neuroanatomy, neurophysiology, and neuropsychology—promises to bear much richer fruit. Knowledge of the nervous system is accumulating as rapidly as knowledge of genetics, and the findings are much closer, so to speak, to phenomena of cognition and the mind.

CANALIZATION VERSUS PLASTICITY

A study of neurobiology bears critically on the two central issues with which I am concerned in this chapter. We can ferret out general principles, as well as specific nuances, concerning the flexibility of development and the identity of human competences. In this survey, I shall begin by considering the issue of flexibility, and particularly those findings that document the relative plasticity of the nervous system during the early phases of development. Following the review of flexibility, I shall turn to those lines of research that help illuminate the abilities and operations of which human beings are capable. Though my concern throughout this volume will fall on the capacities of human beings, and the extent to which they can be developed and educated through appropriate interventions, most of the findings that I review will, in fact, be drawn from research with animals, invertebrates as well as vertebrates. And in this effort, I have been helped in particular by two lines of work that have deepened our understanding of the principles of development: the work of David Hubel, Torsten Wiesel, and their co-workers on the development of the visual system in mammals; and the works of Fernando Notebohm, Peter Marler, Mark Konishi, and their co-workers on the development of singing capacities in birds. While the transfer from animal to human populations, must be made cautiously, particularly in the intellectual realm, findings in these areas are far too suggestive to be ignored.

A key concept for the understanding of neural growth and development is *canalization*. First posited by C. H. Waddington, a geneticist at Edinburgh University, canalization refers to the tendency of any organic system (like the nervous system) to follow certain developmental paths rather than others. Indeed, the nervous system grows in an exquisitely timed and elegantly programmed fashion. The origins of cells in the fledgling neural tube, and their migration to regions where they will eventually constitute the brain and spinal chord, can be observed with predictable regularity within and, to some extent, even across species. Far from representing a random or accidental collection, the neural connections that are actually effected reflect the highest degree of biochemical control. One beholds a stunning epigenetic sequence where each step in the process lays the groundwork for, and facilitates the unfolding of, the next.

To be sure, the development of any system also reflects environmental influences: if, through experimental intervention, one alters the chemical balance, one can affect the migration of particular cells or even cause one cell to carry out the function ordinarily assumed by another. Yet according to Waddington, it proves surprisingly difficult to divert such patterns from what appears to be their prescribed developmental goals—in the present case, an adequately functioning nervous system. As Waddington put it, "it is quite difficult to persuade the developing system not to finish up by producing its normal end result." Even if one seeks to block or otherwise to divert the expected patterns, the organism will tend to find a way to finish up in its "normal" status; if thwarted, it will not return to its point of origin but will rather make its peace at a later point in the developmental course.

So far my description of the development of the nervous system has stressed strict, genetically programmed mechanisms. This is appropriate. And yet an equally amazing facet of biological development is its flexibility, or, to adopt the more technical epithet, its *plasticity*. An organism exhibits plasticity in a number of ways. To begin with, there are certain developmental periods where a relatively wide range of environments can each bring about the proper effects. (For example, if a human infant is swaddled for most of the first year of life, it will still walk normally during the second year.) Moreover, in the event that the young organism is deprived or damaged in a significant way, it may often exhibit great recuperative powers. Indeed, in general, this plasticity proves greater at the earliest points in development. For example, even if a human infant loses the dominant of its two cerebral hemispheres, it will still learn to speak. But there is a point at which the Rubicon is crossed, and plasticity is permanently on the wane. The adolescent or the adult who loses a hemisphere will be severely impaired.

Yet even these generalizations about plasticity must be qualified. First of all, sometimes early injury or deprivation can have extremely severe results. (Failure to use one eye during the first months of life infirms the possibility of binocular vision.) Second, certain abilities or skills prove robust, even in the face of an adult injury, thus suggesting a residual plasticity which endures throughout much of the life cycle. Some adults recover the ability to talk despite massive injury to the left (or dominant) hemisphere of the brain, and many recover the use of paralyzed limbs. Overall, the notion of plasticity cannot be considered apart from the timing of a particular manipulation or intervention and from the nature of the behavioral competence involved.

Plasticity is limited in other ways as well. Reflecting their behaviorist heritage, some psychologists have been prone to assume that most any organism can, given proper training, learn to do most anything. Searches for "horizontal" "Laws of Learning" have often reflected this faith. Similar claims have been made about human beings, such as the suggestion that anything can be learned at any age, in some useful form. More recent studies have come down, however, in harsh opposition to this optimistic cast of mind. An emerging consensus insists that each species—including ours—is specially "prepared" to acquire certain kinds of information, even as it proves extremely difficult, if not impossible, for that organism to master other kinds of information.

A few examples of this "preparedness" and "counter preparedness" will be helpful. We know that many birds are capable of learning songs, and some can eventually produce a great variety of songs. And yet female sparrows may be so carefully "pretuned" that they are sensitive only to the particular dialect sung by males in their own region. Rats can learn very quickly to run or jump to escape shock but only with greatest difficulty to press a lever in order to effect the same escape. Moreover, there are even limitations to the jumping mechanism. While jumping to avoid a shock seems to be a "natural" or "prepared" response, if the rat must jump in a box with a closed lid, learning will be extremely slow. The ease with which all normal (and many subnormal) individuals master natural language (despite its apparent complexity) suggests that the species as a whole is specially prepared to acquire facility in this realm. By the same token, the difficulties most humans exhibit in learning to reason logically—particularly when propositions are presented in an abstract form—suggests no special preparedness in this area and perhaps even a predisposition to attend to the concrete specifics of a situation *rather than* to its purely logical implications. While no one understands the reasons for selective preparedness, it may be that certain neural centers can be readily triggered, stimulated, programmed, and/or inhibited, while others prove far more difficult to activate or inhibit.

In the light of these general remarks about plasticity in behavior, we are now in a position to look more closely at evidence pertaining to the degree of determinedness (or flexibility) which characterizes the developing organism. Our survey will consider the particulars of plasticity around the time of birth, the effects of various early experiences on subsequent development, and the possibility that various kinds of learning can be understood at the neurological or the biochemical level.

Principles of Plasticity during Early Life. While the particulars concerning each species differ, research on plasticity in early life has yielded a number of principles that seem reasonably robust. A first principle enunciates the maximum flexibility encountered early in life. Consider one example, which can stand for many others in the literature. As explained by W. Maxwell Cowan, neurobiologist at the Salk Institute, both the forebrain and the neural part of the eye develop out of the head end of the neural plate. If, at an early stage in development, one removes a small piece of ectodermal tissue, neighboring cells proliferate, and the development of both the brain and the eye should proceed normally. But if the same operation is performed a little later, there is a permanent defect either in the forebrain or in the eye; the actual damage depends on the particular piece of tissue that has been removed. Such progressive "blocking out" leads to the determination of increasingly precise regions of the brain. Studies by other neurobiologists, such as Patricia Goldman, confirm that, during the earliest period of life, the nervous system can adapt flexibly to severe injury or experimental alteration. For some time thereafter, the nervous system may devise an alternative route or connection which may prove adequate; but if the injury or alteration occurs too late during the developmental process, the relevant cells will either connect randomly or atrophy altogether.

A second, related principle underscores the importance of so-called *critical periods* during the process of development. For example, in the cat, there is a critical period in visual development from the third to the fifth week postnatally. If, during this time, one eye is deprived of form or light, then the central connections of the eye change and the ill-seeing eye will be suppressed from functioning. Such interference seems to be permanent. As a general point, it seems that the most vulnerable time for an organism occurs during these sensitive periods. Irreversible damage to the central nervous system seems particularly likely to occur in the wake of even mild restrictions during such a critical period. Conversely, rapid development will occur if the proper conditions obtain during the critical period.

According to a third principle, the degree of flexibility differs across the region of the nervous system with which one is concerned. Regions that develop later in childhood, such as the frontal lobes or the corpus callosum, turn out to be more malleable than those that have developed in the first days and weeks of life, such as a primary sensory cortex. The surprising degree of *uncommittedness* which characterizes regions like the corpus callosum seems to reflect both the need for a high degree of modifiability for certain cortical connections and also the importance of specific postnatal experiences in determining the kinds of connection which will ultimately be made. Indeed, when it comes to the most complex of human capacities, such as language, the individual can withstand even massive damage, including the removal of an entire hemisphere, during the first few years of life and still acquire the ability to speak in a reasonably normal fashion: this recovery suggests that large portions of the cortex remain uncommitted (and thus available for diverse uses) during early childhood.

A fourth principle concerns those factors that mediate or modulate development. An organism will fail to develop normally unless it undergoes certain experiences. Thus, the cat's visual system will not develop normally—and parts of it will actually atrophy—if the animal is not exposed to patterned light after birth. Moreover, the cat must be exposed to a variegated environment, permitted to use both eyes, and move about its environment. If exposed to horizontal patterns only, the cells destined to carry out vertical processing will either atrophy or be taken over for other functions. If the cat is allowed to use only one eye, those cells dedicated to binocular vision will degenerate. And if the cat does not move actively in its environment—for example, if it is passively transported through a patterned environment—it will also fail to develop a normal visual system. It seems that the neural system that mediates vision exhibits a scheduled plan for development that "expects" visual inputs of certain sorts during sensitive periods. If proper stimulation is lacking, or if inappropriate stimulation is supplied, the usual developmental goals will not be achieved, and the animal will fail to function properly in its environment.

A final principle treats the long-term effects of injury to the nervous system. While some injuries exert immediate and evident effects, others may be invisible at first. Suppose, for example, that a region of the brain which is destined later in development to assume an important function, happens to be injured at an early point in life. It may well be that the consequences of the injury will not be observed for some time. Thus, injuries to the frontal lobes in primates may not be detected during the first years of life but may become all too manifest at a later time when the animal is expected to carry out those complex and organized forms of behavior that are ordinarily mediated by the frontal lobes. Early brain injury may also stimulate certain anatomical reorganizations which ultimately prove counterproductive. For instance, connections may be formed that allow the animal to carry out tasks crucial at the present time, but that prove useless for the emergence of needed skills at a later time. In such cases, the tendency of the nervous system to canalize may actually have maladaptive long-term consequences.

Consideration of these five principles should confirm that any simple verdict on the issue of determination versus flexibility is impossible. Strong pressures favor each factor, and both therefore exert considerable influence on the development of the young organism. Determination (or canalization) helps to ensure that most organisms will be able to carry out the functions of the species in the normal way; flexibility (or plasticity) allows for adaptability to changing circumstances, including anomalous environments or early injuries. Clearly, if one must sustain an injury, it is better to have it early; but probably every deviation from the normal developmental path exacts its cost.

Early Experience. Up to this point, I have considered chiefly the effects of specific kinds of experience (such as exposure to certain kinds of stripes) upon relatively circumscribed regions of the brain (most notably, the visual system). But psychologists and neurologists have also examined the question of more general effects of stimulation, or deprivation, on the overall functioning of organisms.

Pioneering studies come from Mark Rosenzweig and his colleagues at the University of California at Berkeley. Beginning in the early 1960s, the Rosenzweig group raised animals (chiefly rats) in environments that were enriched: these environments featured numerous other rats as well as various "toys," such as ladders and wheels. A comparable set of rats were raised in an "impoverished environment," which contained enough food but no special features. The "enriched rats" performed better on various behavioral tasks and were also trimmer than their well-fed but duller peers. After eighty days in these contrasting environments, all the rats were sacrificed and their brains subjected to analysis. The crucial findings: the cerebral cortexes of the enriched rats weighed 4 percent more than the cortexes of the impoverished (though fatter) rats. More crucially, the largest increase in brain weight occurred in those portions of the brain that serve visual perception, presumably the portions that had been particularly stimulated in the enriched environment.

Numerous studies with rats and other species have confirmed that an enriched environment produces more elaborate behavior as well as palpable changes in brain size. Effects can be surprisingly specific. The Rosenzweig team has shown that if you provide a richer experience to only one half of the brain, only that half exhibits changes in cell structure. William Greenough has demonstrated that, in animals raised in complex environments, one finds larger nerve cells in some brain areas, as well as more synapses, synaptic connections, and other dendritic connections. As he summarizes it, "the gross regional size changes that accompany differences in experience are associated with changes at the neuronal level in the number, pattern, and qualities of synaptic connections."

Other intriguing and highly specific brain changes have been claimed. As part of his studies of the songs of male canaries, Fernando Nottebohm has correlated the size of two nuclei in the bird's brain with the appearance of singing. He finds that, during the most productive vocal periods, these two nuclei may become double the size they reach during the least productive period, during the summer molt. Then, when the brain grows larger in the fall, new nerve fibers develop, fresh synapses are formed, and accordingly, a larger song repertoire once again emerges. Apparently, in birds, the learning (or relearning) of a motor activity translates directly into the size of the relevant nuclei, the number of neurons, and the extent of connections among them.

To my knowledge, scientists have hesitated to speculate in print about similar changes in brain size accompanying (or causing) the diverse ability profiles in human beings. In the absence of suitable experimental methods, such prudence seems proper. But it is worth citing the observation of two talented neuroanatomists, O. and A. Vogt. For many years, the Vogts conducted neuroanatomical studies of the brains of many individuals, including talented artists. One painter whose brain they observed turned out to have a very large fourth layer of cells in his visual cortex; and a musician with perfect pitch from early childhood had an analogously large region of cells in his auditory cortex. As hypotheses of this sort become more respectable, and as non-invasive methods for studying brain size, shape, and processing routes become more widely utilized, I would not be surprised to find contemporary support for these ancient phrenological themes.

But bigger is not always better, and vast numbers of cells or fibers are not always virtues in themselves. Indeed, one of the most fascinating findings of recent years in neurobiology supports this cautionary note. Initially, the nervous system produces a great excess of neuronal fibers; a significant portion of the developmental process involves the pruning, or atrophying, of excessive connections which do not appear to be necessary and may, in fact, be injurious to normal function. The most critical interpretations along these lines have been made by two French scientists, Jean-Pierre Changeux and Antoine Danchin. These researchers have noted that, in diverse regions of the brain, there are many more neurons initially than will eventually survive. A period of "selective cell death" occurs, usually at about the time when the population of neurons are forming synaptic connections with their designated targets. The death may involve anywhere from 15 percent to 85 percent of the initial neuronal population.

Why should there be a large excess of initial connections; and why should certain connections endure, while others atrophy? There is speculation that early excessive "sprouting" reflects (or better, "constitutes") the flexibility of the period of growth. This normal feature of development also has adaptive advantages. If some damage occurs during a time when excessive connections are available, the chances are greater that the organism will survive despite injury. In support of this notion, a tremendous growth in cell connections occurs immediately after a lesion, with sometimes as much as six weeks' worth of growth occurring in seventy-two hours. Analogously, if one eye is removed at birth, the death of retinal ganglion cells, which would ordinarily occur in the first two postnatal weeks, is markedly reduced.

There are other possible reasons for this proliferation of cell processes and synapses. During this period of richness, there appears to be intense competition among the cells, with those that are most effective in forming connections of the appropriate strength and specificity proving most likely to survive. Perhaps, in time-honored Darwinian fashion, this proliferation may entail a kind of competition, allowing the most fit or appropriate of the organism's nerve fibers to prevail.

An excess of nerve fibers in early development may well lead to the transient appearance of functional and behavioral properties associated with the excess connections. And here one may encounter U-shaped phenomena, where the behavior of the immature organism (the left arm of the U) bears a striking resemblance to behavior ordinarily found only among adult organisms (the right arm of the U). Quite possibly, certain early reflexes in humans—like swimming or walking—reflect a proliferation of connections which temporarily allow certain precocious behavior. It is also possible that the tremendously rapid learning of which young organisms are capable, particularly during certain critical periods, may be related to an excess of connections, some of which will soon be pruned or eliminated. For instance, in human beings, the density of synapses increases sharply during the first months of life, reaches a maximum at the ages of one to two (roughly 50 percent above the adult mean density), declines between the ages of two and sixteen, and then remains relatively constant until the age of seventy-two. More than one scientist has speculated that the extremely rapid learning of the young child (for example, in the area of language) may reflect an exploitation of the large number of synapses available at that time.

And after the pruning has occurred? We may have here a functional definition of maturity—that time when excess cells have been eliminated and the originally targeted connections have been effected. The flexibility of youth seems at an end. Through survival of the fittest, the number of neurons has now been adjusted to match the size of the field that they are designed to innervate. (If a new target like an extra limb is surgically added, the number of neurons will not decline as precipitously; there is now additional space in which the synapses can be formed.) The critical period apparently ends when the process of synapse elimination has progressed to the point where few, if any, synapses are still capable of competitive interaction. Most scientists feel that there are further neural changes later in life. But, whether with aging there is a gradual decline in synaptic density, progressive reduction in dendritic length and branching, or a more selective loss (being restricted to certain areas of the cortex) is an issue on which scientists are not yet agreed.

Biological Bases of Learning. Understandably, most neurobiological research with implications for human beings has been conducted with primates; and there has been a focus on the principal sensory systems, which presumably work similarly across the biological order. But recently there have been efforts to understand the basis of learning, using species quite remote from man. Because of the suggestiveness of the findings, I quote two samples here.

In my view, a veritable treasure trove of information that has stimulated the thinking of cognitively oriented scholars has been obtained by students of bird song. Although from a different order of animals, bird song involves highly complex activities, which, as it happens, are lateralized to the left portion of the bird's brain and are all mastered in instructive ways during the juvenile period.

In the face of many differences across bird species, a few generalizations seem warranted. Early in the first year of life, the male bird produces a *subsong*—a babbling output which continues for several weeks. This is followed by the period of *plastic song*, a longer interval, where the bird rehearses a large number of the bits of those songs that it will eventually use to communicate its territory to other birds and also to advertise for a mate. This "playful" rehearsal resembles the exploratory activities exhibited by primates in many realms of activity.

Where avian species differ from one another is in the flexibility and the conditions of song learning. Some birds, like the ringdove, will come to sing the song of their species eventually, even in the absence of exposure to the correct model. Some birds, like canaries, require feedback from their own singing, but not exposure to a model. (If such birds are deafened, they fail to master their species' repertoire.) And other birds, like the chaffinch, require exposure to the models supplied by conspecifics, in order to sing an appropriate song. Some birds sing the same songs each year, while others alter their repertoire on an annual basis. (It is clearly vital to understand the biological underpinnings of these "cultural" differences.) But what is striking is that the bird emits during learning far more songs and song bits than it will vocalize during its adult prime. Moreover, birds are oriented to favor the songs from the environment which their species is destined to learn, and (relatively speaking) to ignore songs from other species or even other dialects of their own species.

As I have already noted, the production of song depends upon structures in the left portion of the bird's nervous system. Lesions there prove far more disruptive than lesions in matching areas of the right brain. One can, in fact, produce an aphasia—or amusia—in birds. But the aphasic canary can recover its prior songs because the homologous pathways of the right hemisphere have the potential of being exploited. In this "recovery of function," birds are more fortunate than adult humans.

The learning of bird songs provides one intriguing model for how organisms come to master a highly particular kind of skill through the interplay of environmental stimulation, exploratory practice, and a predisposition to develop certain structures of the nervous system. In my view, it may well prove possible some day to apply some of the principles involved in the learning of bird song to the processes whereby higher organisms (including human beings) come to master the cognitive and symbolic systems of their own cultural milieu. Another quite divergent set of researches, using a simple mollusk called *Aplysia Californica*, promises to cast additional light on the biological bases of learning.

With his colleagues, Eric Kandel of Columbia University has been examining the simplest forms of learning in Aplysia. He has been investigating how this organism, with a relatively small number of neurons, becomes able to habituate to a stimulus (so that it no longer responds after a while), becomes sensitized to a stimulus (so that it can respond even in the presence of diminished stimulation), and becomes classically conditioned (so that it can respond to a learned, or conditioned, stimulus as well as to an unconditioned, or reflexive, stimulus). And he has come up with four major principles.

First of all, elementary aspects of learning are not diffusely distributed in the brain but can rather be localized in the activity of specific nerve cells. Some learned behavior may involve as few as fifty neurons. Second, learning results from an alteration in the synaptic connections between cells: rather than necessarily entailing new synaptic connections, learning and memory customarily result from alteration in the strength of already existing contacts. Third, prolonged and profound changes in synaptic strength can come about through an alteration in the amount of chemical transmitter released at the terminals of neurones—the sites at which cells communicate with other cells. And so, for example, in the course of habituation, each action potential produces progressively less influx of calcium and, hence, less transmitter release than does the preceding action potential. Finally, these simple processes of altering synaptic strengths can be combined to explain how progressively more complex mental processes take place, and thus yield, in Kandel's phrase, a "cellular grammar" underlying various forms of learning. That is, the same processes that explain the simplest form of habituation serve as a kind of alphabet from which one can compose far more complex forms of learning, such as classical conditioning. As Kandel summarizes his findings:

Basic forms of learning, habituation, sensitization, and classical conditioning *select* among a large repertory of pre-existing connections and alter the strength of a subset of this repertory.... An implication of this view is that the potentialities for many behaviors of which an organism is capable are built into the basic scaffolding of the brain and are to that extent under genetic and developmental control.... Environmental factors and learning bring out these latent capabilities by altering the effectiveness of the pre-existing pathways, thereby leading to the expression of new patterns of behavior.

Thanks to Kandel and the lowly mollusk, some of the major forms of learning investigated by psychologists can be described in terms of events occurring at the cellular level, even including certain candidate chemical transactions. The once seemingly unbridgeable gap between behavior and biology seems to have been sealed. The work of Kandel and his associates also casts tantalizing light on those issues of the specifiability of particular competences, which will concern us in the following pages. It seems that the same principles may characterize all neural cells, independent of species membership or form of learning— apparent support for a "horizontal" view of learning. And yet, as Kandel indicates, organisms themselves seem capable of only certain patterns of behavior and not others; and this phenomenon will also have to be accounted for in any biological approach to cognition.

In contrast to the state of affairs in genetics, where links between the mainstream of the science and issues of human cognition were few and speculative, the view from neurobiology has proved far more revealing for our enterprise. Clear principles of plasticity and flexibility, determination and canalization have been uncovered. There is good reason to believe that, with suitable modifications, these principles can apply to the ways in which human beings develop certain cognitive systems, and learn to achieve certain intellectual skills, in the process of following certain paths rather than others. The clear and manifest effects of rich (or impoverished) early experiences on the general functioning of the organism have also been convincingly demonstrated. And we already know from studies of the effects of malnutrition in human beings that analogous effects can occur in our own species, with deleterious consequences for both emotional and cognitive functioning. Finally, through studies of such unlikely populations as song birds and California mollusks, we have received promising insights into the ways in which forms of learning are manifest at the nervous system, cellular and biochemical levels. While there is still an enormous distance between these simple forms of behavior, and the varieties of learning and development of greatest moment to human beings, at least some of the insights gained from these lines of study should eventually prove applicable to the investigation of human learning and mastery.

IDENTIFYING THE ELEMENTS OF THE NERVOUS SYSTEM

Up to this point, I have at times tolerated a convenient fiction: the contention that the nervous system is relatively undifferentiated, and that variation in size, density, and connectivity can be discussed with seeming indifference to where these differences happen to be found. In fact, however, study of the nervous system has revealed an astonishingly highly organized architecture, with incredible specificity in appearance and in organization. Moreover, differences in organization appear to be closely linked to differences in the functions subserved by different portions of the brain. For example, it is clear that the earlier maturing areas of the cortex are involved in *primary* sensory functions (the perception of discrete sights and sounds), while the later maturing *association* sensory cortexes mediate the meanings of the stimuli and effect connections between sensory modalities (for example, associating seen objects with heard names).

For our purposes, the organizational structure of the nervous system can be considered at two separate levels of detail: a fine-grained or molecular structure, and a grosser or molar structure. While this is also a convenient fiction, it is not a frivolous one; it was in fact recognized in the division of the 1981 Nobel Prize between Roger Sperry, in recent years a student of the molar level, and David Hubel and Torsten Wiesel, students of the molecular structure. And it proves highly relevant to our search for the identity of human intellectual functions.

The Molecular Level. According to Vernon Mountcastle, physiologist at Johns Hopkins University, the human cerebral cortex can be viewed as being organized into columns, or modules. These columns, which are vertical to the surface of the cortex, are approximately 3 millimeters long and between .5 and 1 millimeter across. They are increasingly recognized as forming separate anatomical entities which give rise to different quasi-independent functions. In fact, perception and memory may be distributed through the nervous system in the "person" of these special-purpose "cognitive demons."

These columns were first established in the visual cortex. As Hubel and Wiesel put it:

given what has been learned about the primary visual cortex, it is clear that one can consider an elementary piece of cortex to be a block about a millimeter square and two millimeters deep. To know the organization of this chunk of tissue is to know the organization for all of the [visual cortex]; the whole must be mainly an integrated version of this elementary unit.

In light of more recent findings, it seems probable that other sensory areas also consist of such columns; and it has even been proposed that the frontal lobe—the area deemed responsible for more abstract, and less topographically mapped knowledge—has a columnar organization of this sort.

To what sorts of things do these columns—or their constituent cells—respond? In the visual system, they respond to orientation—horizontal, vertical, oblique—and to ocular dominance—different degrees of eye preference. Less thoroughly understood cortical cells in the visual system may also respond to color, direction of movement, and depth. In the somatosensory system, the columns respond to the side of the field which has been stimulated and to the location of receptors in the skin layers. In the frontal lobe, the columns respond to spatial and temporal information concerning objects that have been present in the organism's field. Taken together, sensory and motor areas appear to contain two-dimensional maps of the world they represent. As information on vision or touch or sound is relayed from one

49

cortical area to the next, the map becomes progressively more blurred and the information carried becomes more abstract.

The columns may turn out to be the fundamental unit of organization throughout evolution. Columns have similar size and shape not only within but also across species. Thus, different species of monkeys may have cortexes of different sizes and different numbers of columns, but the actual dimensions of their columns are the same. Patricia Goldman and Martha Constantine-Paton have speculated that, when the number of axons directed in a certain way exceeds a critical number, columns will form as a time-tested and efficient way of filling in the space. Indeed, if one plants an extra eye into a frog during gestation, a column will promptly be set up.

But is the column or module the only way to think of the nervous system? Vernon Mountcastle, whose work led to the discovery of the columnar organization of the nervous system, himself distinguishes between minicolumns (which may have as few as one-hundred cells and, thereby, constitute the irreducibly small processing unit of the neocortex) and the macrocolumn, each packing several hundred minicolumns inside. Proceeding to a grosser level of organization, Francis Crick suggests the existence of larger distinct areas. The owl monkey, for example, has at least eight cortical areas that are primarily visual: all are perceptually distinct with a fairly well-defined boundary. In his opinion, there are perhaps fifty to one-hundred discrete areas in the human cortex. As he puts it somewhat wistfully, "if each area could be clearly stained *postmortem*, so that we could see exactly how many there are, how big each one is, and exactly how it is connected to other areas, we would have made a big step forward." It seems clear at this point that one may divide the nervous system into units of widely different sizes. What is important for our inquiry is that, through the appearance and location of different neural units, nature provides important clues about the identity of its valued processes and functions.

The Molar Level. In speculating about larger areas of the cerebral cortex, we move to what has been called a molar level of brain analysis—a level dealing with regions that can be readily inspected by the naked eye. While molecular studies rely heavily on recordings from single cells, visible only under high powers of magnification, the chief source of information about molarity of mind comes from clinical work with brain-damaged patients.

As a result of stroke, trauma, or other accidents, individuals may suffer damage to extensive but still limited regions of the brain. The frontal lobe of the brain may be destroyed, wholly or partially (unilaterally); there may be a lesion in the temporal lobe or at the temporoparietal juncture. The results of this injury can be seen through radio-logical measures (brain or CAT scans) and can, of course, be examined with great precision in a post-mortem. Here is where the scientific payoff inheres. It becomes possible to correlate the loss of sizeable por-tions of brain tissue—sometimes ones that are sharply delimited, some-times ones dispersed across several regions of the brain—with specific patterns of behavioral and cognitive breakdown.

By far the most excitement has been generated by the discovery that the two halves of the brain do not subserve the same functions. While each hemisphere controls motor and sensory capacities on the opposite side of the body, one side of the brain is clearly dominant: such dominance determines whether an individual is right-handed (in the case of left-brain dominance) or left-handed (in the case of right-brain dominance). More telling for our purposes than this relatively mechanical division of labor, it has now been established beyond rea-sonable doubt that the left hemisphere is dominant for language in most normal right-handed individuals, while the right hemisphere is dominant (though not to the same extent) for visual-spatial functions.

This much is known to all followers of biological science. What is less widely appreciated is that specificity of cognitive function can be tied much more precisely to finer regions of the human cerebral cortex. This state of affairs has been best worked out in the case of language. We find that damage to the frontal lobe—particularly that area called Broca's—results in selective difficulty in producing grammatical speech, against a background of relatively preserved comprehension. Conversely, damage to the temporal lobe (in the area called Wer-nicke's) allows relatively fluent speech, replete with appropriate gram-matical inflections, in the face of distinct difficulty in comprehension of language. Other, even more specific linguistic disorders turn out to be linked to particular regions in the brain: these include selective difficulties in repetition, naming, reading, and writing.

It seems clear, then, that in the normal adult, cognitive and intel-lective functions of distinctiveness can be linked to particular areas of the brain which, in many cases, are morphologically distinct. David Hubel provides impressive testimony in favor this point of view:

We are led to expect each region of the central nervous system has its own special problems that require different solutions. In vision we are concerned with contours and direction and depth. With the auditory system, on the other hand, we can anticipate a galaxy of problems relating to temporal interactions of sounds of different frequencies and it is difficult to imagine the same neural apparatus dealing with all of these phenomena . . . for the major aspects of the brain's operation, no master solution is likely.

Many of the issues raised earlier re-emerge in the context of human cognition. For example, the left hemisphere is "committed" to being the language hemisphere; and yet, if that hemisphere must be removed early in life, most individuals will still acquire relatively normal language. To be sure, there are impairments in the language of a hemispherectomized patient, but it takes fairly subtle testing to reveal them. In other words, plasticity is evident in the acquisition of language, but such flexibility diminishes rapidly after puberty. Even a relatively punctate lesion in the left hemisphere of an adult male over the age of forty is likely to produce a permanent and debilitating aphasia.

The language zones may have been designed over time to serve auditory-oral language, and yet they do not fall into disuse if an individual is deaf. Indeed, the zones that ordinarily subserve language can be mobilized, in instructively different ways, to acquire sign languages or other ersatz communication systems. For instance, deaf children, who do not reside in "signing" households, will on their own, or working in tandem, invent gestural languages: careful analyses by linguists reveal clear-cut analogies between such contrived gestural language and the natural language of hearing children—for example, in the manner of construction of two-word utterances. Thus, there seems to be canalization not only in the exploitation of certain brain regions but also in the functional lines along which a communicative system develops. Finally, if, through severe abuse an individual should be deprived of language until puberty and then given an opportunity to learn to speak, there may be progress in some aspects of language. Yet, in the one case that has been carefully studied, this advance in language apparently occurred through exploitation of right-hemisphere regions. Quite possibly, some sort of critical period for the mobilization of left-hemisphere structures has elapsed, and so the language of this individual turns out to be most deficient in such left-hemisphere aspects as grammar.

Views of Brain Organization

While the story about other higher cognitive functions is not nearly so well understood—nor so clear—as that which obtains for language, there are determinable cortical organizations for other higher mental functions; and these functions, too, can break down along predictable lines. Adducing evidence for these other human intelligences is a task for the succeeding chapters of this book. At this point, however, it becomes germane to review some contrasting opinions about the relationship between intellect and brain organization, as well as certain efforts to relate human cognition to the specific computational capacities represented by the neural columns or regions.

Discussion of the relationship between intellect and the brain has reflected prevailing scientific views about the general organization of the brain. At times when a localizationist view has held sway, there has been a correlative belief that different parts of the brain subserve different cognitive functions. Sometimes, the discussion has focused on "horizontal" faculties—perception is seen as residing in one region, memory in another; though, more frequently, the discussion has centered on specific "vertical" contents—visual processing in the occipital lobe, language in the left temporal and frontal regions. During other scientific eras, the brain has been regarded as a general information-processing mechanism, and as an "equipotential" organ, where functions can be performed and skills represented in any section of the nervous system. At such times intelligence has tended to be regarded, in hedgehog fashion, as a unitary capacity, one linked to the overall mass of usable brain tissue.

Fifty years ago, it appeared as if the holists or "equipotentialists" would carry the day. The influential work of the neuropsychologist Karl Lashley suggested that the amount of intact brain tissue, rather than its particular identity (in terms of fissures and commissures) would determine whether an organism (like a rat) could perform a task. Lashley showed that one could section regions from almost any area of the brain and the rat would still be able to run a maze. While this finding seemed to sound a death knell to localizationist positions, subsequent examination of this research has revealed a basic flaw. As the rat was relying on highly redundant cues from several sensory areas in running the maze, it really did not make much difference which areas of brain were removed, as long as at least some were left. Once investigators began to attend to the specific kinds of cues that were used, and to eliminate redundancies, even quite focal lesions turned out to impair performance.

Parallel trends can be observed in studies of human cognitive processes as well. The "bully" period for the holists, or generalists (like Henry Head and Kurt Goldstein), was half a century ago. Again, intelligence was related to the amount of brain tissue which was spared, rather than to its particular locus. It does, indeed, seem that many human intellectual tasks can be carried out even in the wake of considerable brain damage; but, again, once a task has been examined more carefully, its dependence upon certain key brain areas will ordinarily be demonstrated. Recent studies have revealed that the posterior parietal regions, particularly in the left hemisphere, prove of special importance in the solution of tasks thought to measure "raw" intelligence, such as Raven's progressive matrices. Even in the miasma of intelligence testing, it seems that the nervous system is far from equipotential.

We find, then, an emerging consensus about brain localization. The brain can be divided into specific regions, with each emerging as relatively more important for certain tasks, relatively less important for others. Not all or none, by any means: but with definite gradients of importance. In the same vein, few tasks depend entirely on one region of the brain. Instead, once one examines any reasonably complex task, one discovers inputs from a number of cerebral regions, each making a characteristic contribution. For example, in the case of freehand drawing, certain left-hemisphere structures prove crucial for the providing of details, while right-hemisphere structures are equally necessary for the mastery of the overall contour of the depicted object. Compromise in either half of the brain will result in some impairment, but the *kind* of impairment can only be anticipated once one knows where the brain injury has occurred.

While this description of brain organization would be regarded as reasonable by most workers in neuropsychology, it has yet to exert much impact in cognitive psychology in this country. (Neuropsychology is more widely accepted by cognitivists in Europe, possibly owing to the greater involvement there of medically trained scientific investigators.) Indeed, as we have seen before, most workers in the cognitive area do not yet consider evidence about the organization of the brain relevant to their concerns or feel that neural processes must be made consistent with cognitive accounts, rather than vice versa. To use the jargon, "hardware" is considered irrelevant to "software," "wet" preparations to "dry" behavior. One encounters, in American cognitive circles, continued belief in the existence of extremely general problem-solving capacities, which cut across every manner of content, and which presumably can be subserved by any area of the nervous system. Now even if localization proves to be the most accurate description of the nervous system, it remains possible that there may still be very general problem-solving devices as well as considerable "horizontal" structure—with perception, memory, learning, and the like cutting across heterogenous contents. Nonetheless, it would seem high time for psychologists to take seriously the possibility that the molar—and even the molecular—analyses of the nervous system may have definite implications for cognitive processes.

Approaching cognition from widely divergent perspectives, the philosopher Jerry Fodor, the physiological psychologist Paul Rozin, the neuropsychologist Michael Gazzaniga, and the cognitive psychologist Alan Allport have all endorsed the notion that human cognition consists of a number of "special purpose" cognitive devices, presumably dependent upon neural "hard wiring." There are many differences in emphasis in their accounts, some of which will be reviewed in chapter 11; but for present purposes, the points of consensus can be expressed as follows:

Over the course of evolution, human beings have come to possess a number of special-purpose information-processing devices, often termed "computational mechanisms." Some we share with some animals (face perception), while others prove peculiar to human beings (syntactic parsing). Some of them are decidedly molecular (line detection), while others are far more molar (control of voluntary action).

The operation of these mechanisms may be considered autonomous in two senses. First of all, each mechanism operates according to its own principles and is not "yoked" to any other module. Second, the information-processing devices can operate without being directed to do so, simply in the presence of certain forms of information to be analyzed. Indeed, their operation may not be subject to conscious use and, hence, proves difficult or even impossible to thwart. They may simply be "triggered" by certain events or information in the environment. (In the jargon, they are "cognitively impenetrable" or "encapsulated.") It is equally possible that some may be accessible to conscious use or to voluntary exploitation; and, in fact, the potential to become aware of the operation of one's information-processing system may be a special (and prized) feature of human beings. However, access to the "cognitive unconscious" is not always possible; and even awareness of its operations may not be sufficient to influence its enactment. (Consider what happens when one knows one is looking at, or listening to, an illusion and still remains unable to perceive the stimulus veridically.)

Though, again, there are differences, most exponents of a so-called modular view are not friendly to the notion of a central information-processing mechanism that decides which computer to invoke. Homunculi are not popular. Nor is there much sympathy for the notion of general working memory or storage space which can be equally well used (or borrowed) by the different special-purpose computational mechanisms. Instead, the thrust of this biologically oriented position is that each intellectual mechanism works pretty much under its own steam, using its own peculiar perceptual and mnemonic capacities with little reason (or need) to borrow space from another module. Over the course of evolution, there may well have been borrowing across systems, or even combinations of systems; and many, if not most, mechanisms customarily work together in the execution of complex behavior. But at any one historical moment, one can specify the component processes of each computational mechanism or, if you will, of each form of intelligence.

Readers of these pages will not be surprised to learn of my sympathy for this "modularity" position. As I view the evidence, both the findings from psychologists about the power of different symbol systems, and the findings from neuroscientists about the organization of the human nervous system, support the same picture of human mentation: a mind consists of a number of fairly specific and fairly independent computational mechanisms. Common properties and common regions may well exist, but they are surely not all of the story and may well not even be its most pertinent (and educationally relevant) part.

Grafting this modular analysis onto the more general principles of plasticity and early experience reviewed earlier is a task that has yet to be carried out. It might well be that principles of plasticity pervade the nervous system and can be evoked, independently of which computational mechanism is at issue. Such an outcome would not in itself pose problems for the point of view propounded here. Yet it seems far more likely that each of the intelligences has its own forms of plasticity and its own critical periods: these need not occur at the same time or for the same interval of time or entail the same costs and benefits. Indeed, if I may adopt the perspective termed "heterochrony," different neural systems may develop at different rates or in different ways, depending upon the period of primate evolution in which they began to function and the purposes to which they have been put.

Conclusion

What picture emerges of the human nervous system, in the light of our embarrassingly rapid trek through neurobiology? The plan for ultimate growth is certainly there in the genome; and, even given fairly wide latitude (or stressful circumstances), development is likely to proceed along well-canalized avenues. We could hardly have survived as a species for many thousands of years without a secure likelihood that we would all be able to speak, perceive, and remember many forms of information in relatively similar ways. To be sure, there is clear plasticity in the nervous system as well; and, especially during the early periods of growth, with its sprouting and pruning, there may well be tremendous resilience and adaptability in the system. These, too, aid survival. But that growth by alternative routes which plasticity permits is not always an advantage. Newly contrived connections may well carry out certain processes adequately but prove inadequate for others or entail pernicious long-term effects. Programming, specificity, considerable early flexibility with some costs—such are the general principles of the nervous system that have emerged from our analysis. We can reasonably expect these same principles to apply when we consider how normal human beings come to negotiate various intellectual challenges and to advance in diverse symbolic domains.

We find, from recent work in neurology, increasingly persuasive evidence for functional units in the nervous systems. There are units subserving microscopic abilities in the individual columns of the sensory or frontal areas; and there are much larger units, visible to inspection, which serve more complex and molar human functions, like linguistic or spatial processing. These suggest a biological basis for specialized intelligences. We have seen at the same time, however, that even the most informed scholars of the nervous system differ about the level of modules that are most useful for various scientific or practical purposes. Clearly, Nature cannot hand us a complete answer to the "identities" or the "kinds of cognition" as a reward for our dispassionate investigation of the nervous system *sui generis*.

But building upon the findings from neurobiology, studied in molar as well as molecular terms, we receive a powerful hint about the possible "natural kinds" of human intelligence. We cannot (even should we wish to) neatly factor culture out of this equation, because culture influences every individual (except possibly some freaks) and will, therefore, necessarily color the way that intellectual potentials evolve from the first. But the universal intrusion of culture also confers an advantage upon our analysis. Culture makes it possible for us to examine the development and implementation of intellectual competences from a variety of perspectives: the roles the society values; the pursuits in which individuals achieve expertise; the specification of domains in which individual prodigiousness, retardation, or learning disabilities may be found; and the kinds of transfer of skills which we may expect in educational settings.

Here, then, is the burden of this book: to bring to bear the insights culled from these various windows on cognition, cultural no less than biological; to see which families of intellectual competence, examined together, make the most sense. It remains only to state more explicitly the criteria to be invoked in this synthesizing effort.

4

What Is
an Intelligence?

I HAVE now set the stage for an
introduction of the intelligences. My review of earlier studies of intelligence and cognition has suggested the existence of a number of different intellectual strengths, or competences, each of which may have
its own developmental history. The review of recent work in neurobiology has again suggested the presence of areas in the brain that correspond, at least roughly, to certain forms of cognition; and these same
studies imply a neural organization that proves hospitable to the notion of different modes of information processing. At least in the fields
of psychology and neurobiology, the *Zeitgeist* appears primed for the
identification of several human intellectual competences.

But science can never proceed completely inductively. We might
conduct every conceivable psychological test and experiment, or ferret
out all the neuroanatomical wiring that we desired, and still not have
identified the sought after human intelligences. We confront here a
question not of the certainty of knowledge but, rather, of how knowledge is attained at all. It is necessary to advance a hypothesis, or a
theory, and then to test it. Only as the theory's strengths—and limitations—become known will the plausibility of the original postulation
become evident.

Nor does science ever yield a completely correct and final answer.
There is progress and regress, fit and lack of fit, but never the discov-
ery of the Rosetta stone, the single key to a set of interlocking issues.
This has been true at the most sophisticated levels of physics and

chemistry. It is all the more true—one might say, it is all too true—in the social and behavioral sciences.

And so it becomes necessary to say, once and for all, that there is not, and there can never be, a single irrefutable and universally accepted list of human intelligences. There will never be a master list of three, seven, or three hundred intelligences which can be endorsed by all investigators. We may come closer to this goal if we stick to only one level of analysis (say, neurophysiology) or one goal (say, prediction of success at a technical university); but if we are striving for a decisive theory of the range of human intelligence, we can expect never to complete our search.

Why, then, proceed along this precarious path at all? Because there is a need for a better classification of human intellectual competences than we have now; because there is much recent evidence emerging from scientific research, cross-cultural observations, and educational study which stands in need of review and organization; and perhaps above all, because it seems within our grasp to come up with a list of intellectual strengths which will prove useful for a wide range of researchers and practitioners and will enable them (and *us*) to communicate more effectively about this curiously seductive entity called the intellect. In other words, the synthesis that we seek can never be all things for all people, but it holds promise of providing some things for many interested parties.

Before moving on to the intellectual competences themselves, we must consider two topics. First of all, what are the prerequisites for an intelligence: that is, what are the general desiderata to which a set of intellectual skills ought to conform before that set is worth consideration in the master list of intellectual competences? Second, what are the actual criteria by which we can judge whether a candidate competence, which has passed the "first cut" ought to be invited to join our charmed circle of intelligences? As part and parcel of the list of criteria, it is also important to indicate those factors that suggest we are on the wrong track: that a skill that had appeared as a possible intellectual competence does not qualify; or that a skill that seems very important is being missed by our approach.

Prerequisites of an Intelligence

To my mind, a human intellectual competence must entail a set of skills of problem solving—enabling the individual *to resolve genuine problems or difficulties* that he or she encounters and, when appropriate, to create an effective product—and must also entail the potential for *finding or creating problems*—thereby laying the groundwork for the acquisition of new knowledge. These prerequisites represent my effort to focus on those intellectual strengths that prove of some importance within a cultural context. At the same time, I recognize that the ideal of what is valued will differ markedly, sometimes even radically, across human cultures, within the creation of new products or posing of new questions being of relatively little importance in some settings.

The prerequisites are a way of ensuring that a human intelligence must be genuinely useful and important, at least in certain cultural settings. This criterion alone may disqualify certain capacities that, on other grounds, would meet the criteria that I am about to set. For instance, the ability to recognize faces is a capacity that seems to be relatively autonomous and to be represented in a specific area of the human nervous system. Moreover, it exhibits its own developmental history. And yet, to my knowledge, while severe difficulties in recognizing faces might pose embarrassment for some individuals, this ability does not seem highly valued by cultures. Nor are there ready opportunities for problem finding in the domain of face recognition. Acute use of sensory systems is another obvious candidate for a human intelligence. And when it comes to keen gustatory or olfactory senses, these abilities have little special value across cultures. (I concede that people more involved than I in the culinary life might disagree with this assessment!)

Other abilities that are certainly central in human intercourse also do not qualify. For instance, the abilities used by a scientist, a religious leader, or a politician are of great importance. Yet, because these cultural roles can (by hypothesis) be broken down into collections of particular intellectual competences, they do not themselves qualify as intelligences. From the opposite end of analysis, many skills tested for perennially by psychologists—ranging from recall of nonsense syllables to production of unusual associations—fail to qualify, for they emerge as the contrivances of an experimenter rather than as skills valued by a culture.

There have, of course, been many efforts to nominate and detail essential intelligences, ranging from the medieval trivium and quadrivium to the psychologist Larry Gross's list of five modes of communication (lexical, social-gestural, iconic, logico-mathematical, and musical), the philosopher Paul Hirst's list of seven forms of knowledge (mathematics, physical sciences, interpersonal understanding, religion, literature and the fine arts, morals, and philosophy). On an *a priori* basis, there is nothing wrong with these classifications; and, indeed, they may prove critical for certain purposes. The very difficulty with these lists, however, is that they are *a priori*—an effort by a reflective individual (or a culture) to devise meaningful distinctions among types of knowledge. What I am calling for here are sets of intelligences which meet certain biological and psychological specifications. In the end, the search for an empirically grounded set of faculties may fail; and then we may have to rely once more on *a priori* schemes, such as Hirst's. But the effort should be made to find a firmer foundation for our favorite faculties.

I do not insist that the list of intelligences presented here be exhaustive. I would be astonished if it were. Yet, at the same time, there is something awry about a list that leaves glaring and obvious gaps, or one that fails to generate the vast majority of roles and skills valued by human cultures. Thus, a prerequisite for a theory of multiple intelligences, as a whole, is that it captures a reasonably complete gamut of the kinds of abilities valued by human cultures. We must account for the skills of a shaman and a psychoanalyst as well as of a yogi and a saint.

Criteria of an Intelligence

So much, then, for the prerequisites of this undertaking and onward to criteria, or "signs." Here, I outline those considerations that have weighed most heavily in the present effort, those desiderata on which I have come to rely in an effort to nominate a set of intelligences which seems general and genuinely useful. The very use of the word *signs* signals that this undertaking must be provisional: I do not include something merely because it exhibits one or two of the signs, nor do I exclude a candidate intelligence just because it fails to qualify on each and every account. Rather, the effort is to sample as widely as possible among the various criteria and to include within the ranks of the chosen intelligences those candidates that fare the best. Following the suggestive model of the computer scientist Oliver Selfridge, we might think of these signs as a group of demons, each of which will holler when an intelligence resonates with that demon's "demand characteristics." When enough demons holler, an intelligence is included; when enough of them withhold approbation, the intelligence is, if regrettably, banished from consideration.

Ultimately, it would certainly be desirable to have an algorithm for the selection of an intelligence, such that any trained researcher could determine whether a candidate intelligence met the appropriate criteria. At present, however, it must be admitted that the selection (or rejection) of a candidate intelligence is reminiscent more of an artistic judgment than of a scientific assessment. Borrowing a concept from statistics, one might think of the procedure as a kind of "subjective" factor analysis. Where my procedure does take a scientific turn is in the making public of the grounds for the judgment, so that other investigators can review the evidence and draw their own conclusions.

Here then, in unordered fashion, are the eight "signs" of an intelligence:

POTENTIAL ISOLATION BY BRAIN DAMAGE

To the extent that a particular faculty can be destroyed, or *spared* in isolation, as a result of brain damage, its relative autonomy from other human faculties seems likely. In what follows I rely to a considerable degree on evidence from neuropsychology and, in particular, on that highly revealing experiment in nature—a lesion to a specific area of the brain. The consequences of such brain injury may well constitute the single most instructive line of evidence regarding those distinctive abilities or computations that lie at the core of a human intelligence.

THE EXISTENCE OF IDIOTS SAVANTS, PRODIGIES, AND OTHER EXCEPTIONAL INDIVIDUALS

Second only to brain damage in its persuasiveness is the discovery of an individual who exhibits a highly uneven profile of abilities and deficits. In the case of the prodigy, we encounter an individual who is extremely precocious in one (or, occasionally, more than one) area of human competence. In the case of the *idiot savant* (and other retarded or exceptional individuals, including autistic children), we behold the unique sparing of one particular human ability against a background of mediocre or highly retarded human performances in other domains. Once again, the existence of these populations allows us to observe the human intelligence in relative—even splendid—isolation. To the extent that the condition of the prodigy or the *idiot savant* can be linked to genetic factors, or (through various kinds of non-invasive investigative methods) to specific neural regions, the claim upon a specific intelligence is enhanced. At the same time, the selective absence of an intellectual skill—as may characterize autistic children or youngsters with learning disabilities—provides a confirmation-by-negation of a certain intelligence.

AN IDENTIFIABLE CORE OPERATION OR SET OF OPERATIONS

Central to my notion of an intelligence is the existence of *one or more* basic information-processing operations or mechanisms, which can deal with specific kinds of input. One might go so far as to define a human intelligence as a neural mechanism or computational system which is genetically programmed to be activated or "triggered" by certain kinds of internally or externally presented information. Examples would include sensitivity to pitch relations as one core of musical intelligence, or the ability to imitate movement by others as one core of bodily intelligence.

Given this definition, it becomes crucial to be able to identify these core operations, to locate their neural substrate, and to prove that these "cores" are indeed separate. Simulation on a computer is one promising way of establishing that a core operation exists and can in fact give rise to various intellectual performances. Identification of core operations is at this point still largely a matter of guesswork, but it is no less important on that account. Correlatively, resistance to the detection of core operations is a clue that something is amiss: one may be encountering an amalgam which calls for decomposition in terms of its own constituent intelligences.

A DISTINCTIVE DEVELOPMENTAL HISTORY, ALONG WITH A DEFINABLE SET OF EXPERT "END-STATE" PERFORMANCES

An intelligence should have an identifiable developmental history, through which normal as well as gifted individuals pass in the course of ontogeny. To be sure, the intelligence will not develop in isolation, except in an unusual person; and so it becomes necessary to focus on those roles or situations where the intelligence occupies a central place. In addition, it should prove possible to identify disparate levels of expertise in the development of an intelligence, ranging from the universal beginnings through which every novice passes, to exceedingly high levels of competence, which may be visible only in individuals with unusual talent and/or special forms of training. There may well be distinct critical periods in the developmental history, as well as identifiable milestones, linked either to training or to physical maturation. Identification of the developmental history of the intelligence, and analysis of its susceptibility to modification and training, is of the highest import for educational practitioners.

AN EVOLUTIONARY HISTORY AND EVOLUTIONARY PLAUSIBILITY

All species display areas of intelligence (and ignorance), and human beings are no exception. The roots of our current intelligences reach back millions of years in the history of the species. A specific intelligence becomes more plausible to the extent that one can locate its evolutionary antecedents, including capacities (like bird song or primate social organization) that are shared with other organisms; one must also be on the lookout for specific computational abilities which appear to operate in isolation in other species but have become yoked with one another in human beings. (For example, discrete aspects of musical intelligence may well appear in several species but are only joined in human beings.) Periods of rapid growth in human prehistory, mutations that may have conferred special advantages upon a given population, as well as evolutionary paths that did not flourish, are all grist for a student of multiple intelligences. Yet it must be stressed that this is an area where sheer speculation is especially tempting, and firm facts especially elusive.

SUPPORT FROM EXPERIMENTAL PSYCHOLOGICAL TASKS

Many paradigms favored in experimental psychology illuminate the operation of candidate intelligences. Using the methods of the cognitive psychologist, one can, for example, study details of linguistic or spatial processing with exemplary specificity. The relative autonomy of an intelligence can also be investigated. Especially suggestive are studies of tasks that interfere (or fail to interfere) with one another; tasks that transfer (and those that do not) across different contexts; and the identification of forms of memory, attention, or perception that may be peculiar to one kind of input. Such experimental tests can provide convincing support for the claim that particular abilities are (or are not) manifestations of the same intelligences. To the extent that various specific computational mechanisms—or procedural systems—work together smoothly, experimental psychology can also help demonstrate the ways in which modular or domain-specific abilities may interact in the execution of complex tasks.

BACKGROUND

SUPPORT FROM PSYCHOMETRIC FINDINGS

Outcomes of psychological experiments provide one source of information relevant to intelligences; the outcomes of standard tests (like I.Q. tests) provide another clue. While the tradition of intelligence testing has not emerged as the hero of my earlier discussion, it is clearly relevant to my pursuit here. To the extent that the tasks that purportedly assess one intelligence correlate highly with one another, and less highly with those that purportedly assess other intelligences, my formulation enhances its credibility. To the extent that psychometric results prove unfriendly to my proposed constellation of intelligences, there is cause for concern. It must be noted, however, that intelligence tests do not always test what they are claimed to test. Thus many tasks actually involve the use of more than their targeted ability, while many other tasks can be solved using a variety of means (for example, certain analogies or matrices may be completed by exploiting linguistic, logical, and/or spatial capacities). Also, the stress on paper-and-pencil methods often precludes the proper test of certain abilities, especially those involving active manipulation of the environment or interaction with other individuals. Hence, interpretation of psychometric findings is not always a straightforward matter.

SUSCEPTIBILITY TO ENCODING IN A SYMBOL SYSTEM

Much of human representation and communication of knowledge takes place via symbol systems—culturally contrived systems of meaning which capture important forms of information. Language, picturing, mathematics are but three of the symbol systems that have become important the world over for human survival and human productivity. In my view, one of the features that makes a raw computational capacity useful (and exploitable) by human beings is its susceptibility to marshaling by a cultural symbol system. Viewed from an opposite perspective, symbol systems may have evolved *just in those cases* where there exists a computational capacity ripe for harnessing by the culture. While it may be possible for an intelligence to proceed without its own special symbol system, or without some other culturally devised arena, a primary characteristic of human intelligence may well be its "natural" gravitation toward embodiment in a symbolic system.

These, then, are criteria by which a candidate intelligence can be judged. They will be drawn on repeatedly, as appropriate, in each of the substantive chapters that follows. It is germane here to remark on certain considerations that might cause one to rule out an otherwise plausible candidate intelligence.

Delimiting the Concept of an Intelligence

One group of candidate intelligences includes those that are dictated by common parlance. It may seem, for example, that the *capacity to process auditory sequences* is a strong candidate for an intelligence; indeed, many experimentalists and psychometrians have nominated this capacity. However, studies of the effects of brain damage have repeatedly documented that musical and linguistic strings are processed in different ways and can be compromised by different lesions. Thus, despite the surface appeal of such a skill, it seems preferable not to regard it as a separate intelligence. Other abilities frequently commented upon in specific individuals—for example, remarkable common sense or intuition—might seem to exhibit such signs as "prodigiousness." In this case, however, the categorization seems insufficiently examined. More careful analysis reveals discrete forms of intuition, common sense, or shrewdness in various intellectual domains; intuition in social matters predicts little about intuition in the mechanical or musical realm. Again, a superficially appealing candidate does not qualify.

It is, of course, possible that our list of intelligences is adequate as a baseline of core intellectual abilities, but that certain more general abilities may override, or otherwise regulate, the core intelligences. Among candidates that have frequently been mentioned are a "sense of self," which derives from one's peculiar blend of intelligences; an "executive capacity," which deploys specific intelligences for specific ends; and a synthesizing ability, which draws together conclusions residing in several specific intellectual domains. Beyond challenge, these are important phenomena, which demand to be considered, if not explained. Such discussion, however, is a task best left until later when, having introduced the specific intelligences, I initiate a critique of my own in chapter 11. On the other hand, the question of how specific intelligences come to be linked, supplemented, or balanced to carry out more complex, culturally relevant tasks, is one of the utmost importance, to which I shall devote attention at several points in this book.

Once one has set forth the criteria or signs most crucial for the identification of an intelligence, it is important to state as well what intelligences are *not*. To begin with, intelligences are not equivalent to sensory systems. In no case is an intelligence completely dependent upon a single sensory system, nor has any sensory system been immortalized as an intelligence. The intelligences are by their very nature capable of realization (at least, in part) through more than one sensory system.

Intelligences should be thought of as entities at a certain level of generality, broader than highly specific computational mechanisms (like line detection) while narrower than the most general capacities, like analysis, synthesis, or a sense of self (if any of these can be shown to exist apart from combinations of specific intelligences). Yet it is in the very nature of intelligences that each operates according to its own procedures and has its own biological bases. It is thus a mistake to try to compare intelligences on all particulars; each must be thought of as its own system with its own rules. Here a biological analogy may be useful. Even though the eye, the heart, and the kidneys are all bodily organs, it is a mistake to try to compare these organs in every particular: the same restraint should be observed in the case of intelligences.

Intelligences are not to be thought of in evaluative terms. While the word *intelligence* has in our culture a positive connotation, there is no reason to think that an intelligence must necessarily be put to good purposes. In fact, one can use one's logical-mathematical, linguistic, or personal intelligences for highly nefarious purposes.

Intelligences are best thought of apart from particular programs of action. Of course, intelligences are most readily observed when they are being exploited to carry out one or another program of action. Yet the possession of an intelligence is most accurately thought of as *a potential*: an individual in possession of an intelligence can be said to have no circumstance that prevents him from using that intelligence. Whether he chooses to do so (and to what end he may put that intelligence) fall outside the purview of this book. (See notes to page 68.)

In the study of skills and abilities, it is customary to honor a distinction between *know-how* (tacit knowledge of how to execute something) and *know-that* (propositional knowledge about the actual set of procedures involved in execution). Thus, many of us know how to ride a bicycle but lack the propositional knowledge of how that behavior is carried out. In contrast, many of us have propositional knowledge about how to make a soufflé without knowing how to carry this task through to successful completion. While I hesitate to glorify this rough-and-ready distinction, it is helpful to think of the various intelligences chiefly as *sets of know-how*—procedures for doing things. In fact, a concern with propositional knowledge about intelligences seems to be a particular option followed in some cultures, while of little or no interest in many others.

Conclusion

These remarks and cautionary notes should help to place in proper perspective the various descriptions of specific intelligences which constitute the next part of this book. Naturally, in a book reviewing a whole spectrum of intelligences, it is not possible to devote sufficient attention to any specific one. Indeed, even to treat a single intellectual competence—like language—with sufficient seriousness would require at least one lengthy volume. The most that I can hope to accomplish here is to provide a feeling for each specific intelligence; to convey something of its core operations, to suggest how it unfolds and proceeds at its highest levels, to touch upon its developmental trajectory, and to suggest something of its neurological organization. I shall rely heavily on a few central examples and knowledgeable "guides" in each area and can only offer my impression (and my hope!) that most of the pivotal points could have been equally well conveyed by many other examples or guides. Similarly, I will depend on a few key cultural "roles," each of which utilizes several intelligences but can properly be said to highlight the particular intelligence under study. Some notion of the wider data base on which I am drawing, and of the sources relevant for a fuller inquiry into each intelligence, can be gained from a study of the references for each chapter. But I am painfully aware that a convincing case for each of the candidate intelligences remains the task for other days and other volumes.

A final, crucial point before I turn to the intelligences themselves. There is a universal human temptation to give credence to a word to which we have become attached, perhaps because it has helped us to understand a situation better. As noted at the beginning of this book, *intelligence* is such a word; we use it so often that we have come to believe in its existence, as a genuine tangible, measurable entity, rather than as a convenient way of labeling some phenomena that may (but may well not) exist.

This risk of reification is grave in a work of exposition, especially in one that attempts to introduce novel scientific concepts. I, and sympathetic readers, will be likely to think—and to fall into the habit of saying—that we here behold the "linguistic intelligence," the "interpersonal intelligence," or the "spatial intelligence" at work, and that's that. But it's not. These intelligences are fictions—at most, useful fictions—for discussing processes and abilities that (like all of life) are continuous with one another; Nature brooks no sharp discontinuities of the sort proposed here. Our intelligences are being separately defined and described strictly in order to illuminate scientific issues and to tackle pressing practical problems. It is permissible to lapse into the sin of reifying *so long as we remain aware that this is what we are doing.* And so, as we turn our attention to the specific intelligences, I must repeat that they exist not as physically verifiable entities but only as potentially useful scientific constructs. Since it is language, however, that has led us to (and will continue to dip us into) this morass, it is perhaps fitting to begin the discussion of the particular intelligences by considering the unique powers of the word.

Part II

The Theory

5

Linguistic Intelligence

It is true the white man can fly; he can speak
across the ocean; in works of the body he is indeed greater than we, but he has no songs like
ours, no poets to equal the island singers.

A GILBERT ISLANDER

When . . . writing . . . all the natural instincts are
at work the way some people play a musical instrument without a lesson and, others, even as
children, understand an engine.

LILLIAN HELLMAN, *An Unfinished Woman*

Poetry: Linguistic Intelligence Exemplified

In the early 1940s, Keith Douglas, a young British poet, initiated a
correspondence with T. S. Eliot, already the doyen of poets in England.
Eliot's responses, invariably helpful, are revealing about the considerations at the level of the word which enter into the penning, and the
subsequent revision, of a line of poetry. Warning against the use of
"ineffective adjectives," Eliot criticizes the phrase "impermanent
building": "this impermanence should have been clearly established
earlier in the poem." After the young poet compares himself to a pillar
in a glass house, Eliot asks, "Do you mean that you are also glass?"
Referring to a subsequent comparison of the poet to a mouse, Eliot

73

again detects the apparent inconsistency: "I don't think you should be a pillar and like a mouse in the same stanza." Of the poem as a whole, Eliot offers a more general critique:

I am not sure that its myth is wholly consistent. For instance, toward the end you spoke of exorcising the dead lady in the upper room. One does speak of exorcising ghosts from material houses, but in this case the lady to be exorcised seems to be very much more substantial than the house in which you have set her. That is what I mean by consistent.

In offering such suggestions, Eliot was merely making public some of the processes through which a poet may pass each time he or she writes a poem. We learn from Eliot's own notes of the care he took, and the frequent agony he underwent, in selecting the correct word. For example, in the *Four Quartets,* he tried out the phrases "at dawn," "the first faint light," "after lantern end," "lantern-out," "lantern-down," "lantern-time," "the antelucan dusk," "the antelucan hour," "antelucan dark," before accepting a friend's suggestion of "waning dusk." Many of Eliot's contemporaries in this most introspective century have related similarly fine weighings of alternative wording. For instance, Robert Graves reviewed his efforts to find a substitute for the word "pattern" in the phrase "and fix my mind in a close pattern of doubt." He considered "frame of doubt" (too formal) and "net" (too negative a connotation) before alighting, after a trip to the sea, on the phrase, "and fix my mind in a close caul of doubt." Upon consulting the *Oxford English Dictionary,* Graves found that *caul* bore all the senses he needed: a new cap confirming the glory of a woman; a gossamer web spun by spiders; and a smooth caplike membrane in which a lucky child is sometimes born. Juxtaposed with *close, caul* also furnished pleasing alliteration.

Along similar lines, Stephen Spender recounts how he built a poem upon one of his notebook jottings:

There are some days when the sea lies like a harp stretched flat beneath the cliffs. The waves like wires burn with the sun's copper glow.

He attempted at least twenty versions of these lines in an effort to clarify this scene, to bring out its musical feeling, to realize his "inner image" of the brief life of earth and the death of the sea. Among the efforts were these:

> The waves are wires
> Burning as with the secret songs of fires

> The day burns in the trembling wires
> With a vast music golden in the eyes
>
> The day glows on its trembling wires
> Singing a golden music in the eyes
>
> The day glows on its burning wires
> Like waves of music golden to the eyes
>
> Afternoon burns upon the wires
> Lines of music, dazzling the eyes
>
> Afternoon gilds its tingling wires
> To a visual silent music of the eyes

Each of these stabs presented problems. For instance, in the first, the direct statement, "waves are wires" creates an image that is not quite fitting, because it is overstated; in Spender's view, the poet must avoid stating his vision too overtly. In the sixth attempt, "visual silent music of the eyes" mixes too many figures of speech in a phrase that is itself somewhat awkward. Spender's final version places the images within an appropriately expansive context:

> There are some days the happy ocean lies
> Like an unfingered harp, below the land.
>
> Afternoon gilds all the silent wires
> Into a burning music of the eyes.

While the overall effect, with its intimation of Homer and of Blake, is perhaps not as strikingly original as that wrought by some of their earlier attempts, the final version does capture, with fidelity and clarity, Spender's underlying impulse, his initial vision.

In the poet's struggles over the wording of a line or a stanza, one sees at work some central aspects of linguistic intelligence. The poet must be superlatively sensitive to the shades of meanings of a word; indeed, rather than shaving off connotations, he must try to preserve as many of the sought-after meanings as possible. This is why *caul* was the most desirable of the choices considered by Graves. Moreover, the meanings of the words cannot be considered in isolation. Since every word assesses its own penumbras of meaning, the poet must make sure that the senses of a word in one line of the poem do not clash with those aroused by the occurrence of a second word in another line. This is why Eliot warns against the co-occurrence of "pillar" and "mouse" in the same stanza and challenges the exorcising of a lady, rather than a ghostly house. Finally, the words must capture as faithfully as possible the emotions or images that have animated the initial desire to compose. Spender's alternative verses may be striking or pleasurable, but if they do not convey the vision that he initially had, they fail as poetry—or, to put it another way, they can become the basis of a new poem, one that the poet had not initially intended to write.

In discussing the meanings or connotations of words, we find ourselves in the area of *semantics*, that examination of meaning which is universally considered central to language. Eliot once observed that the logic of the poet is as severe, though differently placed, as the logic of a scientist. He also noted that the arrangement of imagery requires "just as much fundamental brainwork as the arrangement of an argument." Where the scientist's logic requires sensitivity to the implications of one proposition (or law) for another, the poet's logic centers around a sensitivity to shadings of meaning, and what they imply (or preclude) for neighboring words. Even as one could not hope to be a scientist without appreciating the laws of logical deduction, one cannot aspire to be a poet without sensitivity to the interaction among linguistic connotations.

But other domains of language, as laid out by linguists, are also of singular importance for the aspiring poet. The poet must have keen sensitivity to *phonology*: the sounds of words and their musical interactions upon one another. The central metrical aspects of poetry clearly depend upon this auditory sensitivity, and poets have often noted their reliance on aural properties. W. H. Auden declared, "I like hanging around words, listening to what they say." Herbert Read, another poet of the Eliot generation, indicates that, "in the degree that they are poetic . . . words are automatic associations of an aural rather than a visual nature." And Graves's *close caul* had to work as sound just as much as it had to work semantically.

A mastery of *syntax*, the rules governing ordering of words and their inflections, is another *sine qua non* of poetry. The poet must understand, intuitively, the rules of constructing phrases as well as the occasions on which it is permissible to flaunt syntax, to juxtapose words that, according to ordinary grammatical principles, should not occur together. And, finally, the poet must appreciate the *pragmatic* functions, the uses to which language can be put: he must be aware of the different poetic speech acts, ranging from the lyric of love to the epic of description, from the directness of an order to the subtleties of a plea.

Because this mastery of language is so central, so defining of the poet's calling, it is the love of language, and the eagerness to explore its every vein, that most clearly mark the young poet. Fascination with language, technical facility with words, rather than the desire to express ideas, are hallmarks of the future poet. Though it is probably not a strict requirement, the ability readily to pick up and remember phrases, especially those favored by other poets, is an invaluable stock-in-trade for the poet. The critic Helen Vendler recalls sitting in on the poetry writing classes of Robert Lowell, where this leading American poet effortlessly recalled the verses of the great poets of the past, occasionally (and always intentionally) improving a line that he felt inadequate. Beholding this linguistic facility, Vendler remarks, "made one feel like a rather backward evolutionary form confronted by an unknown but superior species." This species—the poet—possesses a relation to words beyond our ordinary powers, a repository, as it were, of all the uses to which particular words have been put in previous poems. That knowledge of the history of language use prepares—or frees—the poet to attempt certain combinations of his own as he constructs an original poem. It is through such fresh combinations of words, as Northrop Frye insists, that we have our only way of creating new worlds.

The Core Operations of Language

In the poet, then, one sees at work with special clarity the core operations of language. A sensitivity to the meaning of words, whereby an individual appreciates the subtle shades of difference between spilling ink "intentionally," "deliberately," or "on purpose." A sensitivity to the order among words—the capacity to follow rules of grammar, and, on carefully selected occasions, to violate them. At a somewhat more sensory level—a sensitivity to the sounds, rhythms, inflections, and meters of words—that ability which can make even poetry in a foreign tongue beautiful to hear. And a sensitivity to the different functions of language—its potential to excite, convince, stimulate, convey information, or simply to please.

But most of us are not poets—not even of amateur standing—and still we possess these sensitivities in significant degrees. Indeed, one could not appreciate poetry without at least a tacit command of these aspects of language. More, one could not hope to proceed with any efficacy in the world without considerable command of the linguistic tetrad of phonology, syntax, semantics, and pragmatics. Linguistic competence is, in fact, the intelligence—the intellectual competence—that seems most widely and most democratically shared across the human species. Whereas the musician or the visual artist—not to mention the mathematician or the gymnast—exhibit abilities that seem remote from, and even mysterious to, the average person, the poet seems simply to have developed to a superlatively keen degree capacities that all normal—and perhaps even many subnormal—individuals have within their grasp. Thus, the poet can serve as a reliable guide, or as an apt introduction, to the domain of linguistic intelligence.

But for those among us who are not practicing poets, what are some of the other major uses to which language can be put? Of numerous candidates, I would single out four aspects of linguistic knowledge that have proved of striking importance in human society. First of all, there is the rhetorical aspect of language—the ability to use language to convince other individuals of a course of action. This is the ability that political leaders and legal experts have developed to the highest degree, but that every three-year-old desirous of a second helping of cake has already begun to cultivate. Second of all, there is the mnemonic potential of language—the capacity to use this tool to help one remember information, ranging from lists of possessions to rules of a game, from directions for finding one's way to procedures for operating a new machine.

A third aspect of language is its role in explanation. Much of teaching and learning occurs through language—at one time, principally through oral instructions, employing verse, collections of adages, or simple explanations; and now, increasingly, through the word in its written form. A compelling example of this aspect can be found in the sciences. Despite the evident importance of logical-mathematical reasoning and symbol systems, language remains the optimal means for conveying the basic concepts in textbooks. In addition, language supplies the metaphors that are crucial for launching and for explaining a new scientific development.

Finally, there is the potential of language to explain its own activities—the ability to use language to reflect upon language, to engage in "metalinguistic" analysis. We can see intimations of this capacity in the youngest child who says, "Did you mean X or Y?"—thereby directing his addressor to reflect upon a prior use of language. Far more striking instances of metalinguistic sophistication have emerged in our own century—in fact, in the past thirty years. Thanks to the revolution in the study of language sparked by the linguist Noam Chomsky, we have gained a firmer understanding of what language is and how it works, as well as some bold hypotheses about the place of language in the sphere of human activities. While a concern with this form of propositional knowledge (know-that) about language seems more prevalent in our culture than in many others, interest in language-as-a-system is by no means restricted to Western or other scientifically oriented cultures.

To convey the flavor of these different faces of language is the chief burden of this chapter. We turn our attention first to language because it is a pre-eminent instance of human intelligence. It also has been the most thoroughly studied intelligence, and so we find ourselves on relatively firmer ground in reviewing the development of linguistic intelligence and in discoursing on the breakdown, under conditions of brain damage, of linguistic capacities. Relevant information has also been secured on the evolutionary course of human language, its cross-cultural manifestations, and its relation to the other human intelligences. Accordingly, in reviewing the current knowledge base about linguistic intelligence, I seek not only to summarize the state of the art in this particular sphere of human competence but also to suggest the kinds of analysis which I hope will be available in the future for each of the remaining intelligences.

The Development of Linguistic Skills

The roots of spoken language can be found in the child's babbling during the opening months of life. Indeed, even deaf youngsters begin to babble early in life; and during the first months, all infants will issue those sounds found in linguistic stocks remote from their home tongue. But by the beginning of the second year, linguistic activity is different: it involves (in English-speaking lands) the punctate utterance of single words: "Mommy," "doggy," "cookie," and, before long, the concatenation of pairs of words into meaningful phrases: "eat cookie," "byebye Mommy," "baby cry." Let another year pass, and the three-year-old is uttering strings of considerably greater complexity, including questions, "When I get up?"; negations, "I no want to go to sleep"; and sentences with clauses, "Have milk before lunch, please?" And by the age of four or five, the child has corrected the minor syntactic infelicities in these sentences and can speak with considerable fluency in ways that closely approximate adult syntax.

Moreover, sweetening this list of accomplishments, children at these tender ages transcend mundane expression. Average four-year-olds are able to come up with appealing figures of speech (comparing a foot falling asleep to bubbling ginger ale); tell short stories about their own adventures and those of characters whom they have invented; alter their speech register depending upon whether they are addressing adults, peers, or toddlers younger than themselves; and even engage in simple metalinguistic banter: "What does X mean?", "Should I say X or Y?", "Why didn't you say X when you mentioned Y?" In short, the skills of the four- or five-year-old put to shame any computer program for language. Not even the most skilled linguists in the world have been able to write the rules that account for the form (and the meanings) of the utterances of childhood.

This much on linguistic development is fact, not disputed (so far as I am aware) by any scholar. Somewhat more controversial, but rather widely accepted, is the claim that linguistic mastery involves special processes of acquisition, ones apart from those entailed in other intellectual spheres. The most vigorous and most persuasive spokesman for this proposition is Noam Chomsky, who claims that children must be born with considerable "innate knowledge" about the rules and forms of language and must possess as part of their birthright specific hypotheses about how to decode and speak their language or any "natural language." Chomsky's claims grow out of the fact that it is difficult to explain how language can be acquired so rapidly and so accurately despite the impurity of speech samples that the child hears, and at a time when children's other problem-solving skills seem relatively underdeveloped. Other scholars, such as Kenneth Wexler and Peter Culicover, have made the further claim that children would not be able to learn language at all if they did not make certain initial assumptions about how the code must—and must not—operate, such assumptions presumably being built into the nervous system.

All normal children, and a large proportion of retarded ones as well, learn language according to the outlined scheme, usually within a few years. This fact gives comfort to those scholars who want to argue that language is a special process, operating according to its own rules, and at the same time poses difficulties for those scholars who want to argue (as did Piaget) that the acquisition of language simply invokes general psychological processes. It may well be that both sides have a point. The syntactic and phonological processes appear to be special, probably specific to human beings, and unfolding with relatively scant need for support from environmental factors. Other aspects of language, however, such as the semantic and pragmatic domains, may well exploit more general human information-processing mechanisms and are less strictly or exclusively tied to a "language organ." In terms of my "criteria" for an intelligence, we might say that syntax and phonology lie close to the core of linguistic intelligence while semantics and pragmatics include inputs from other intelligences (such as logical-mathematical and personal intelligences).

Even though the processes described here pertain to all children, there are clearly vast individual differences. These are found in the kinds of words that children first utter (some children first issue names of things, while other children, avoiding nouns, favor exclamations); the extent to which children slavishly imitate the signals emitted by their elders (some do, others hardly mimic at all); and, not least, the rapidity and skill with which children master the central aspects of language.

Young Jean-Paul Sartre was extremely precocious in these regards. The future author was so skilled at mimicking adults, including their style and register of talk, that by age five he could enchant audiences with his linguistic fluency. Shortly thereafter, he began to write, soon completing whole books. He found his fullest identity in writing, in expressing himself with his pen, entirely apart from whether his words were even read by others.

> By writing I was existing. . . . My pen raced away so fast that often my wrist ached. I would throw the filled notebooks on the floor, I would eventually forget about them, they would disappear. . . . I wrote in order to write. I don't regret it; had I been read, I would have tried to please [as he did in his earlier oral performances]. I would have become a wonder again. Being clandestine I was true. [At age 9]

Here, then, was a child who discovered his considerable powers in the relentless exercising of his linguistic intelligence.

The Development of the Writer

By writing a great deal, and by realizing himself most fully as a young writer, Sartre was forging the path common to those who end up as authors, be they poets, essayists, or novelists. In this, as in every intellectual realm, practice is the *sine qua non* of eventual success. Writers speak of their skill as a muscle that demands daily exercise—*no day without a line* is their byword, just as it was Sartre's.

In recollecting their own development, many writers have been able to illuminate the important positive factors as well as the pitfalls that threaten to ensnare the aspiring young writer. Auden argues that, in a young writer, promise inheres neither in originality of ideas nor in the power of emotions, but rather in technical skill with language. He draws an instructive analogy to a lad courting:

> In the first stages of his development, before he had found his distinctive style, the poet is, as it were, engaged to language, and like any other young man who is courting, it is right and proper that he should play the chivalrous servant, carry parcels, submit to tests and humiliations, wait hours at street corners, and defer to his beloved's slightest whims, but once he has proved his love and has been accepted, then it is another matter. Once he is married, he must be master in his own house and be responsible for their relationship.

Another crucial early component of mastery, according to Spender, is sheer memory for experiences:

> Memory exercised in a particular way is the natural gift of poetic genius. The poet, above all else, is a person who never forgets certain sense impressions which he has experienced and which he can relive again and again as though with all their original freshness. . . . It therefore is not surprising that although I have no memory for telephone numbers, addresses, faces, and where I have put this morning's correspondence, I have a perfect memory for the sensation of certain experiences which are crystallized for me around certain associations. I could demonstrate this from my own life by the overwhelming nature of associations which, suddenly aroused, have carried me back so completely into the past, particularly into my childhood, that I have lost all sense of the present time and place.

The young poet generally begins his self-education by reading other poets and by imitating their voices as best he can. Such an imitation of the form and style of a master is proper, and perhaps even necessary, so long as it does not ultimately stifle the development of one's own poetic voice. But there are numerous signs of poetic immaturity at this time, including an excessive imitation of the model; stating one's emotion, tension, or idea too often or too readily; rigid adherence to a given rhyme scheme or metric pattern; too self-conscious an effort to play with sounds and meanings. An effort to be pretty or aesthetically "proper" is also suspect; rather than being presented overtly to the reader, these attributes of beauty and form should emerge from the total experience of reading a work.

According to Auden, such an "undeveloped" poet may reveal himself in at least three ways. He may come off as bored; he may be in a hurry and therefore write poetry that is technically slipshod or carelessly expressed (witness Keith Douglas's youthful verses); or he may produce work that seems deliberately false or tawdry. In Auden's view, such "trash" results when a person is trying to achieve through poetry what can be achieved only by personal actions, by study, or by prayer. Adolescents prove particularly guilty of these flaws: if they have talent, and have found that poetry can indeed express something, they may fall prey to the mistaken inference that every idea can be expressed through the medium of verse.

On the road to poetic maturity, young poets often set for themselves a number of poetic tasks, such as the writing of a poem for an occasion. Fledgling poets can vary the degree of difficulty in assignments: for instance, some assignments are carried out simply to master a certain form. Auden indicates the point (and the limitation) of such exercises: "It would take an immense effort . . . to write half a dozen rhopalic hexameters in English but it is virtually certain that the result would have no poetic merit." Following such rugged drill, it is often desirable to set oneself a somewhat simpler task. At such times, previously mastered skills can be drawn on automatically, and the words may flow. Thornton Wilder comments, "I believe that the practice of writing consists in more and more relegating all that schematic operation to the subconscious." Walter Jackson Bate records what happened when Keats lowered his ambition temporarily: "If he turned temporarily to a less ambitious poem in a different form, the gate would quickly open and he would find himself not only writing with remarkable fluency but also incorporating, with rapid and effortless abundance, features of idiom and versification that had been part of the conception of the earlier, more demanding work." In fact, through practice the poet ultimately attains such fluency that, like Auden or the "possessed poet" Sue Lenier, he or she may be able to write verse virtually on command, with the same facility as others speak prose. At such time, the danger, paradoxically, becomes excessively ready production, which may keep one mired at the level of superficial glibness rather than ever-increasing profundity.

In the end, of course, the writer who would be a poetic master must find the right framework for expressing his words and ideas. As the poet Karl Shapiro once declared,

Genius in poetry is probably only the intuitive knowledge of form. The dictionary contains all words and a textbook on verse contains all meters, but nothing can tell the poet which words to choose and in what rhythms to let them fall, except his own intuitive knowledge of form.

The Brain and Language

Future writers are those individuals in whom the linguistic intelligence has flowered through work and, perhaps as well, through the luck of the genetic draw. Other individuals, less happily, may exhibit peculiar difficulties with language. Sometimes the costs are not severe: Albert Einstein is said to have begun to speak very late; but, if anything, his initial reticence may have allowed him to view and conceptualize the world in a less conventionalized way. Many children, otherwise normal or close to normal, demonstrate selective difficulties in the learning of language. Sometimes the difficulty seems to inhere chiefly in auditory discrimination: because these children experience difficulty in decoding a rapid string of phonemes, they not only have problems in comprehension but may also articulate improperly. The ability to process linguistic messages rapidly—a prerequisite for the understanding of normal speech—seems to depend upon an intact left temporal lobe; and so injuries to, or the abnormal development of, this neural zone generally suffice to produce language impairments.

Even as many children exhibit selective difficulties in the phonological aspects of language, one also encounters children impaired in other linguistic components. Some children show insensitivity to syntactic factors: given sentences to imitate, they are forced to effect simplifications of the following sort:

Target Sentence	Impaired Imitation
They won't play with me.	They no/not play with me.
I can't sing.	I no can sing.
He doesn't have money.	He no have money.
She isn't very old.	She not very old.

It is striking that such children prove quite normal in solving all manner of problems providing that the oral-aural channels of presentation can be bypassed.

In contrast to those children who are relatively normal, except for selective difficulty in language tasks, many otherwise disturbed children exhibit language that has been selectively spared. I have already noted that many retarded children display a surprising ability to master language—particularly its core phonological and syntactic aspects—though they may have relatively little of significance to utter. Even more striking are those rare children who, despite retardation or autism, prove able to read at an astonishingly early age. While reading normally begins at the ages of five or six, these "hyperlexic" children are often able to decode texts as early as two or three. In fact, the very children who have little meaningful conversation (and are often restricted to echoing) will, when they enter a room, seize any reading material and begin to read aloud in a ritualistic fashion. The reading is so compulsive that it is hard to stop; it proceeds by the child's disregarding semantic information, indifferent to whether the materials are drawn from a primer, a technical journal, or a collection of nonsense. At times, hyperlexia occurs with other symptoms of the *idiot savant* or the autistic child. For example, one hyperlexic child studied by Fritz Dreifuss and Charles Mehegan could immediately tell the day of the week of remote historical dates, while another showed an excellent memory for numbers.

In normal right-handed individuals, as I have already noted, language is intimately tied to the operation of certain areas in the left hemisphere of the brain. Accordingly, the question arises about the fate of language in young individuals in whom major areas of the left hemisphere have had to be excised for therapeutic reasons. Generally, if areas as large as an entire hemisphere of the brain are removed during the first year of life, a child will be able to speak quite well. Apparently, early in life the brain is sufficiently plastic (or equipotential) and language sufficiently important that language will develop in the right hemisphere, even at the cost of compromising those visual and spatial functions that would normally be localized there.

It must be pointed out, however, that this assumption of language functions by the right hemisphere is not without costs. Careful examination of such children reveals that they utilize linguistic strategies that are different from those of individuals (normal or abnormal) who employ the normal language areas in the left hemisphere. Specifically, individuals dependent upon the analytic mechanisms of the right hemisphere proceed almost entirely from semantic information: they decode sentences in the light of meanings of the principal lexical items, while proving unable to utilize cues of syntax. Only those children whose language exploits left hemisphere structures prove able to pay attention to syntactic cues such as word order. Thus, both left and right hemidecorticates are able to understand sentences whose meaning can be inferred simply from a knowledge of the meaning of substantives:

The cat was struck by the truck.
The cheese was eaten by the mouse.

85

But only the individual with an intact left hemisphere can decode sentences where the critical difference in meaning inheres wholly in syntactic cues:

The truck was hit by the bus.
The bus was hit by the truck.

It also seems that children without a left hemisphere are inferior to those lacking a right hemisphere in tasks of speech production and vocabulary comprehension and, overall, may learn language more slowly.

As I observed in chapter 3, the canalization that governs the process of language acquisition is confirmed by examinations of other unusual populations. Deaf children of hearing parents will, on their own, develop simple gesture languages which exhibit the most pivotal features of natural language. In these spontaneously developing gesture languages, one finds manifestations of the basic syntactic and semantic properties exhibited in the earliest oral utterances of hearing children. From a less happy vantage point, there is the recently documented case of Genie, a child who was abused to such an extent during the opening decade of life that she never learned to speak. Freed at last from her cruel imprisonment, Genie began to speak during the second decade of her life. She acquired vocabulary quite readily and was able to classify objects properly, but she showed marked and continuing difficulty in using syntax and was reduced to communication primarily through single words. Most tellingly, her linguistic processing seemed to be mediated by the right cerebral hemisphere. In a single case study, one can never be certain of the reasons for a particular pattern of brain lateralization. But it seems reasonable to conjecture that the tendency for lateralization of language to the left hemisphere may weaken with age, possibly because of the passage of a critical period for language acquisition. As a consequence, the individual who must learn language after puberty may be limited to those mechanisms mediated by the right hemisphere.

With young children, we confront a system still in the course of development and, as a consequence, a system exhibiting considerable (though by no means total) flexibility in the manner of neural localization and the mode of realization. With age, however, a far greater degree of localization of language function becomes the rule. This trend means, first, that in normal right-handed individuals, specific forms of disability will prove consequent upon specific lesions in critical areas of the left hemisphere; and, second, that the possibilities for complete recovery (or takeover) of these functions by other regions of the brain becomes much slighter.

A century of study of the linguistic consequences of unilateral injury to the brain provides powerful lines of evidence in support of the analysis of language functions I have put forth here. Specifically, one can specify lesions that cause particular difficulties in phonological discrimination and production, in the pragmatic uses of speech, and, most critically, in the semantic and syntactic aspects of language. Moreover, each of these aspects of language can be destroyed in relative isolation: one can confront individuals whose syntax is impaired but whose pragmatic and semantic systems are relatively preserved, even as one can encounter individuals whose ordinary communicative language is largely vitiated in the face of selective preservation of their syntactic powers.

Why this picture of astonishing specificity and localization? Part of the answer lies, no doubt, in the histories (and mysteries) of the evolution of the language faculty—an issue that has fascinated scholars for many centuries, but whose full lines of explanation remain obscured forever, buried as they are in fossils or prehistory, if not in the Tower of Babel. Some of the mechanisms are shared with other organisms— for example, the detection of phoneme boundaries occurs in similar fashion in other mammals, such as the chinchillla: other processes, such as syntax, seem clearly restricted to human beings. Some linguistic mechanisms are located in quite punctate regions of the brain—for example, the syntactic processes mediated by the so-called Broca's area; others are much more widely dispersed in the left hemisphere of the brain—for example, the semantic system; still others seem crucially dependent upon right hemisphere structures, such as the pragmatic functions of language. What does seem clear, however, is that, with age, these functions become increasingly focalized in normal right-handed individuals:* the more complex interactions that characterize our daily linguistic intercourse depend upon a seamless flow of information among these crucial linguistic regions.

Nowhere is this interaction more telling than in the decoding of written language. It has been established convincingly that written language "piggybacks" upon oral language, in the sense that it is not possible to continue reading normally if one's oral-auditory language areas have been destroyed. (This loss of reading skill occurs even in individuals who read fluently without subvocalization or lip move-

---

* For reasons that are not understood, language functions seem more strongly localized to the left hemisphere in males than in females.

ments.) Yet, while aphasia almost always entails reading difficulty, the extent of difficulty will depend on the kind of literacy present. What proves instructive are the different ways in which reading may be represented in the nervous system, depending upon the code favored by a particular culture. In the phonologically based systems of the West, reading relies particularly on those areas of the brain that process linguistic sounds; but in those systems (in the Orient) where ideographic reading is preferred, reading is more crucially dependent upon those centers that interpret pictorial materials. (This dependence may also obtain for those deaf individuals who have learned to read.) Finally, in the case of the Japanese, who have both a syllabary reading system (*kana*) and an ideographic system (*kanji*), two mechanisms for reading are housed in the same individual. Thus, one kind of lesion will cause relatively greater injury to the decoding of *kana* symbols, while another will wreak its havoc particularly on the decoding of *kanji* symbols.

As these mechanisms have become better understood, certain pedagogical implications have followed. We now have insights about how one might go about teaching the reading of various codes to otherwise normal children who, for one or another reason, have difficulty in mastering the prevalent code of their culture. Given that it is possible to learn to read by at least two alternative routes, children with a specific learning disability ought to be able to exploit the "other route" and thus to master the principle of written scripts, if not the particular written script that happens to be favored by their culture. And, in fact, ideographically based systems have proved effective with children who exhibit particular problems in mastering a phonologically based system of literacy.

While evidence from brain damage confers a "face validity" upon the analysis of the components of language faculty I have proposed, we must still address its implications for the existence of language as a separate, semi-autonomous faculty—in our terms, a separate intelligence. Here the evidence is somewhat less decisive. It seems clear that, in the face of a significant aphasia, there may be some impairment of more general intellectual capacities, particularly the ability to form concepts, to classify properly, and to solve abstraction problems, such as those featured in many tests of nonverbal intelligence. In that sense, at least, it is difficult to have a full-fledged compromise of one's language area in the face of otherwise unimpaired comprehension and reasoning skills.

Nonetheless, in my view, the preponderance of evidence does support the notion of linguistic intelligence as being an intelligence apart. In fact, it may be the intelligence for which evidence across the full range of criteria sketched in chapter 4 is most persuasive. For one thing, there are clearly individuals who are highly, even grossly aphasic, who can perform very well—within the normal range—on cognitive tasks that are not tied specifically to language. Aphasic patients have lost their abilities to be authors (alas, highly developed skills serve as no guarantor against the ravages of brain disease); and yet severely aphasic patients have retained their abilities to be musicians, visual artists, or engineers. Clearly, this selective sparing of occupational skills would be impossible were language indissolubly melded to other forms of intellect.

Thus, in its strictest sense, when one focuses on phonological, syntactic, and certain semantic properties, language emerges as a relatively autonomous intelligence. But once one encompasses broader aspects, such as pragmatic functions, the picture of linguistic autonomy becomes less convincing. Indeed, it appears that individuals with a severe aphasia often have a preserved ability to appreciate and carry out various kinds of communicative acts, while individuals with preserved syntactic and semantic capacities may, as a consequence of injury to their nondominant hemispheres, exhibit gross abnormalities in communicating their intentions and in understanding the intentions and motivations of others. Even as research suggests the separability of pragmatics as a distinct aspect of language, it confirms its neurological dissociation from the "hard core" of language abilities. Perhaps this state of affairs exists because "speech act" or "communicative act" aspects of language are most clearly shared with other primates and, accordingly, least tied to the evolution of a separate language faculty housed in certain regions of the left hemispheres of human beings. By the same token, and perhaps relatedly, sensitivity to narrative, including the ability to communicate what has happened in a series of episodes, seems more closely tied to the pragmatic functions of language (and thus proves more fragile in cases of right-hemisphere disease) than to the core syntactic, phonological, and semantic functions I have described.

As already noted, even a slight aphasia proves sufficient to destroy an individual's literary talent. Yet a study of the way in which language breaks down under conditions of brain damage proves surprisingly suggestive for a student of the literary imagination. It turns out that the linguistic signal can be impoverished in characteristic ways, dependent upon the particular nature of brain injury. In the form of aphasia associated with a Broca's area lesion, the language signal is heavy in substantives and simple propositions, while displaying little inflection or modification—a kind of caricature of the style of Ernest Hemingway. In the case of that aphasia associated with a Wernicke's area lesion, the language signal is replete with complex syntactic forms and a variety of inflections, but often the substantive message is difficult to extract—a kind of caricature of the style of William Faulkner. (Other linguistic aberrations, like *idioglossa*, where one invents one's own patois, and schizophrenic language are also syntactically wild.) Finally, in anomic aphasia, following a lesion in the angular gyrus, the speech signal is devoid of names but filled with "things," "stuff," "kind of," and other circumlocutions—the kind of circumstantial speech frequent in a character out of Damon Runyan, but completely remote from the poet who cherishes *le mot juste*. It would be ludicrous to trace the sources of these distinctive styles to particular regions of the brain; and yet the fact that brain injury can consign an individual to certain stylistic traits which the creative writer *deliberately* selects provides a perverse confirmation of the neurological reality of different modes of expression.

Until only a few years ago, it was generally believed that the two halves of the brain were anatomically indistinguishable from one another. This fact gave comfort to those who wanted to believe in the nonlocalization position, with its corollary assumption that the human brain is equipotential for language. Recent findings have not supported this point of view. It has now been amply documented that the two hemispheres are not anatomically identical, and that, in the large majority of individuals, the language areas in the left temporal lobes are larger than the homologous areas in the right temporal lobes. Other important asymmetries between the hemispheres became evident, once people started to look for them. Armed with this unexpected information, evolutionarily oriented scholars have begun to investigate cranial endocasts and have demonstrated that such asymmetry, which is not evident in monkeys, can be traced back at least as far as Neanderthal man (thirty thousand to one hundred thousand years ago) and may be present as well in the great apes. It seems reasonable to infer, then, that the intellectual capacities for language go back quite a way before history began to be recorded. Notations have been found from thirty thousand years ago, suggesting at least the beginnings of writing systems, though the actual invention of a phonetic script goes back only a few thousand years.

In defiance of "gradual evolution," some eminent scholars, such as the linguist Noam Chomsky, and the anthropologist Claude Lévi-Strauss, believe that all of language had to be acquired at a single moment in time. To my mind, it seems more likely that human linguistic competence results from a coming together of a number of discrete systems, whose evolutionary history dates back many thousands of years. Quite possibly, various pragmatic features of human language evolved from those emotional expressions and gestural capacities (pointing, beckoning) that we share with apes. There may also be certain formal or structural features that reflect or build upon musical capacities of the sort evinced by far more remote species, such as birds. Such cognitive abilities as classification of objects and the capacity to associate a name or sign with an object also seem of ancient origin: these may facilitate that provocative mastery of languagelike systems recently reported in a number of chimpanzees.

Where humans seem unique is in the presence of a supralaryngeal vocal tract that is capable of distinct articulation, and in the evolution of neural mechanisms that make use of the pre-adapted properties of this vocal tract for rapidly induced speech. When sound distinctions can be made and understood rapidly enough, it proves possible to squash individual sounds together into syllable-sized units: the use of speech for rapid communication follows. According to Philip Lieberman, chief proponent of this view of the evolution of language, all of the components for language were present in Neanderthal man, and possibly even in Australopithecus, except for the appropriate vocal tract. It is this latest evolution that has made possible the emergence of rapid linguistic communication, with its profound cultural consequences.

Cross-Cultural Linguistic Variations

Once language took off, it exhibited numerous functions. Something of the variety can be seen by considering just a few of the ways in which individuals from diverse cultures have used language and some of the ways in which cultures have rewarded those individuals who have excelled at such uses. Perhaps most astounding are the abilities displayed by certain bards to sing huge bodies of verse, often nightly, to appreciative audiences. As demonstrated by the folklorist Millman Parry, and his student A. B. Lord, these singers of tales, these contemporary Homers, can create thousands of verses, in part because they have mastered certain frames, or schemes, into which they can place varying specific contents and which they have learned to combine in diverse ways to fashion ever novel epics.

The fact that, like all complex human creations, oral verses can be analyzed into component parts should in no way detract from this achievement. First of all, the sheer mnemonic demands for learning these formulas, and the rules for their concatenation, are formidable: they are in no way inferior to the prowess of the chess master, who knows fifty thousand or more basic patterns, or of the mathematician, who can carry in his head hundreds or even thousands of proofs. In each case, these patterns or schemas are sensible, not meaningless, and this meaningfulness certainly aids in recall; and yet the ability to have so many of them at one's cerebral fingertips is no mean accomplishment. Moreover, these abilities may be particularly elaborated in individuals who are illiterate. In this regard, one may note E. F. Dube's recent finding that illiterate Africans were more successful at remembering stories than either schooled Africans or schooled New Yorkers.

The ability to retain information like lengthy verbal lists, long a favorite testing area for Western psychologists, is another form of linguistic intelligence that has ben especially valued in traditional pre-literate societies. In his book *Naven*, Gregory Bateson reports that an erudite Iatmul male will know between ten thousand and twenty thousand clan names. While techniques are used to recall these names (for example, arrangement in pairs that sound alike), and each name has at least a "leaven of meaning," the actual accomplishment remains staggering. We see intimations of this ability in earlier epochs in our own civilization: during Classical and medieval times, elaborate systems for aiding memory were devised, including number lists, intricate images, spatial codes, zodiac systems, and astrological schemes.

While the person who could remember well was once at a tremendous premium, the advent of literacy, and the possibility of writing down information in books available for ready consultation, made the possession of a powerful verbal memory less vital. Later, printing rendered this aspect of linguistic intelligence even less valuable. And yet these abilities continue to be cultivated in some circles. K. Anders Ericcson and William Chase have recently demonstrated that memory for a string of digits can be lengthened from the canonical seven to eighty or even more by a regimen of drill in which the chunks to be recalled become ever larger. After all, we all know it is easier to remember the list

1 4 9 2 1 0 6 6 1 7 7 6 2 0 0 1 1 9 8 4

once it is seen as a collection of memorable dates in the Anglo-American experience. Memory books and mnemonists remain popular. Finally, in a few fields, a keen verbal memory sets one apart. The philosopher Susanne Langer introspects:

> My verbal memory is like flypaper. That is both good and bad because one's mind becomes filled with irrelevant as well as useful things. For instance, I still remember any number of rhymes from advertisements that I saw in my childhood and these pop into my head at the most unexpected and ridiculous moments. At the same time, however, I remember reams of the fine poetry that I've read over the years and that is a delight to recall. Though my verbal memory may be exceptional, my visual memory is unfortunately far from good. . . . A poor visual memory is a particular handicap in handling source materials in research. That's why I have to keep the elaborately cross-indexed system of file cards.

The recollection of large amounts of information is a tremendously important gift in preliterate cultures. Individuals are often singled out because they have this ability and *rites de passage* are sometimes so devised as to identify the individuals with this treasured power. Naturally these powers can be developed and cultivated, but it is obviously a great help if one can remember such lists with seeming effortlessness, as was the case with the mnemonist studied by Alexander Luria and, to a lessers extent, with humanistic scholars like Susanne Langer.

Sometimes this recall ability is valued for its own sake, but ofttimes it is coupled with the ability to relate words to other kinds of symbols, such as numbers or pictures. We encounter here the rise of certain arcane codes, verbal in the first instance, which individuals can use in games requiring high skills. The abilities that allow a Westerner to solve a crossword or an acrostic puzzle may be akin to the abilities, in other cultures, to pun readily or to invent and master nonsensical or recondite languages. Verbal dueling is often valued. For instance, among the Chamula of Chiapas, Mexico, a player will initiate a phrase that has an apparent as well as a hidden meaning (usually sexual); his opponent has to reply with a phrase that features a minimal sound shift from the first and also has a hidden meaning. If he cannot come up with a suitable response, he loses. For example:

Boy I (challenging) ak'bun avis
                   Give me your sister.
Boy II (responding) ak'bo avis
                   Give it to your sister.

Oratorical contests in which individuals compete by choosing appropriate items from a traditional repertoire of sayings or songs has been described for a number of societies. In a way that would have delighted William James (who was always searching for a "moral equivalent" to war), competitive speech making has replaced warfare, among the Maori, as a way of demonstrating the superiority of one's group. And as if to underscore the importance of ways of speaking, Tzeltal (a Mayan language) features over four hundred terms referring to language use.

Over and above these relatively casual uses of language, the peaks of political power have often been reserved for those individuals who exhibit unusual rhetorical powers. It is surely no accident that a number of the most outstanding leaders in contemporary Africa and Asia have been individuals who have won wide acclaim in rhetoric and whose poetry is often recited. Such poetry, like proverbs, has often been used as a memorable way to disseminate crucial information. Rhetorical finesse is part of the upbringing of aristocrats in a traditional castelike system, even as it may prove to be a significant survival skill among lower echelons of a society. A traditional source of prestige among elder males is their knowledge of the meanings of proverbs and traditional phrases which may still be opaque to less venerable members of the society. Indeed, among the Kpelle of Liberia, there is a patois, "deep Kpelle"—a complex language replete with proverbs, which may defy interpretation by the younger members of the culture. Furthermore, in a number of traditional societies, the ability to wax eloquent about one's own case often provides a decisive edge in "court speech."

Among the Tshidi of Botswana, the effective power of a chief is determined by his performances in public debates, which are carefully analyzed afterward by members of the group. We can see manifestations of these values in certain pockets of our own civilization—for example, among public school graduates in England or among individuals from the southern regions of the United States, where training in political rhetoric is still valued in childhood, and where well-honed skills are displayed up to old age. And, in fact, the roots of this esteem can be traced back within our own society to Greek times, where political power was regularly held by those individuals who had superior linguistic skills. According to Eric Havelock, who studied the oral culture of that time:

within limits, the community's leadership lay with those who had a superior ear and rhythmic aptitude, which would be demonstrable in epic hexameter. It would also however show itself in the ability to compose *rhemata*—effective sayings which used other devices besides the metrical, such as assonance and parallelism. Again, the good performer at a banquet would be estimated not exclusively as an entertainer but as a natural leader of man ... the effective judge or even general tended to be the man with the superior oral memory.... The general effect was to put a great premium upon the intelligence in Greek social transactions and to identify intelligence with power. By intelligence we specially mean a superior memory and a superior sense of verbal rhythm.

It would be a mistake to designate our society as one in which the powers of language have been gradually downplayed (witness the political effectiveness of skilled speakers like Franklin Roosevelt, John Kennedy, or more recently, Ronald Reagan). Yet, on a comparative basis, it does seem that language is less highly valued in our society. Logical-mathematical forms of intelligence, of relatively little moment elsewhere, are certainly as esteemed as language. Also, while the emphasis in traditional cultures still falls very much on oral language, rhetoric, and word play, our culture places *relatively* greater emphasis on the written word—on securing information from reading and on expressing oneself properly through the written word.

While oral and written forms of language doubtless draw on some of the same capacities, specific additional skills are needed to express oneself appropriately in writing. The individual must learn to supply that context that in spoken communication is evident from nonlinguistic sources (like gestures, tone of voice, and the surrounding situations); one must be able to indicate through words alone just what point one wishes to make. These challenges often elude individuals when they are first attempting to write. As an individual becomes more skilled in one means of expression, it may well become more difficult for him or her to excel in the other (although there are always impressive exceptions, like Winston Churchill and Charles de Gaulle).

The construction of a lengthy work—a novel, a history, a textbook—poses organizational challenges that are different from those entailed in shorter linguistic entities, like a letter or poem, and in spoken performances, be they brief speeches, lengthy orations, or recitations of oral verse. Whereas the emphasis in a poem falls on the choice of every word and on the delivery, within a relatively compact set of lines, of one or a small number of messages, the emphasis in a novel necessarily falls on the conveying of a larger collection of ideas and themes, which may bear a complex relationship to one another. Choice of word remains important, to be sure, but proves less at a premium than the successful communication of a set of ideas, themes, moods, or scenes. Of course, some novelists (like Joyce, Nabokov, or Updike) exhibit the poet's obsession with lexical choice, while others (like Balzac or Dostoevsky) are far more immersed in themes and ideas.

Language as a Tool

For the most part, I have focused on those domains of expertise in which language itself is at the fore. Whether it be the penning of a poem or the winning of a verbal joust, the precise choice of words proves important, if not all important. But in most societies, for most of the time, and most strikingly in a complex society such as ours, language is as often as not a tool—a means for accomplishing one's business—rather than the central focus of attention.

A few examples. Scientists certainly rely on language for communicating their findings to others. Moreover, as I have noted, breakthroughs in science are often presented in terms of revealing figures of speech or through well-organized essays. Still, the focus here falls not on the language *per se* but rather on the communication of ideas that could certainly have been conveyed in other words (no need to endure Spenderlike agonies) and, ultimately, may be quite adequately expressed in pictures, diagrams, equations, or other symbols. Freud may have initially required the metaphor of a willful rider upon a horse in order to convey the relationship between the ego and the id; Darwin may have been helped by the metaphor of "a race for survival"; but ultimately their conceptions can be appreciated by individuals who have never read a word by these scholars and have never even been exposed to the original verbal formulation of the concepts.

At first glance, other scholars, such as historians or literary critics, may seem far more dependent upon language, not only as a source of what they study, but also as a means for conveying their conclusions. And, as a practical matter, scholars in the humanities do attend much more closely to words in the texts they study, in the writings of their colleagues, and in their own manuscripts. Yet, even here, the use of language is best viewed as a vital, perhaps irreplaceable, means but still not the essence of the work being accomplished. The goal of the scholar is to describe with accuracy a problem or a situation that he has elected to study; and to convince others that his vision, his interpretation of the situation, is appropriate and accurate. The humanist is tied closely to evidence—facts, records, artifacts, findings of predecessors;

and if his case strays too far from what has been proposed by others, he may well not be taken seriously. But the particular format of his final product is not fixed, and once his viewpoint or conclusion has been gotten across, the particular lexical choices made by the scholar recede in importance, leaving the message to speak for itself. We cannot brook any substitute for the verses of T. S. Eliot, but we can readily enough assimilate the points of his criticism without reading his essays (though in the case of Eliot, much of the power of what he says does inhere in his unusually felicitous phrasing).

Finally, the expressive writer—the novelist, the essayist. Surely here, the particular choice of words is of crucial importance, and we would not readily accept a "trot" for the writings of Tolstoy or Flaubert, Emerson or Montaigne. Yet the purpose does seem to be different, or at least different in emphasis, from that of the poet. For, what the writer of fiction wants most critically, as Henry James once put it, is to wrest the essence, the real truth, "the fatal futility of fact," from "clumsy life." The narrative writer witnesses or envisions an experience or a set of experiences, an emotion or a set of emotions; and his goal is to convey these to the reader as completely and effectively as possible. Once this has been conveyed, the actual words used become less important—though surely they remain a significant proportion of the pleasure of the message, "of language calling attention to itself." Whereas the meaning of the poem continues to inhere in its words, the meaning of a novel is much less tied to these words: that translation that is virtually impossible to carry out faithfully for poems is done without excessive difficulty for most novels—though not for all, and with greatest difficulty, for those written by poets.

Conclusion

While language can be conveyed through gesture, and through writing, it remains at its core a product of the vocal tract and a message to the human ear. Understanding of the evolution of human language, and its current representation in the human brain, is likely to fall wide of the mark if it minimizes the integral tie between human language and the auditory-oral tract. At the same time a student of language who focuses only upon this anatomical arrangement may miss the amazing flexibility of language, the variety of ways in which humans—skilled as well as impaired—have exploited their linguistic heritage for communicative and expressive purposes.

My belief in the centrality of the auditory—and oral—elements in language has motivated my focus upon the poet as the user of language *par excellence* and my citation of the evidence from aphasia as a strong argument in favor of the autonomy of language. To the extent that language were to be considered a visual medium, it would flow much more directly into spatial forms of intelligence; that this is not the case is underscored by the fact that reading is invariably disturbed by injury to the language system, while, amazingly, this linguistic decoding capacity proves robust despite massive injury to the visual-spatial centers of the brain.

And yet I have taken care not to term this capacity as an *auditory-oral* form of intelligence. There are two reasons. First of all, the fact that deaf individuals can acquire natural language—and can also devise or master gestural systems—serves as decisive proof that linguistic intelligence is not simply a form of auditory intelligence. Second, there is another form of intelligence, with a history of equal longevity, and an autonomy of equal persuasiveness, which is also tied to the auditory-oral tract. I refer, of course, to the musical intelligence—the abilities of individuals to discern *meaning* and *importance* in sets of pitches rhythmically arranged and also to produce such metrically arranged pitch sequences as a means of communicating with other individuals. These capacities also rely heavily on auditory-oral abilities—indeed, they prove even less susceptible to visual translation than does language; and yet counter to intuition, musical abilities are mediated by separate parts of the nervous system and consist of separate sets of competence.

Buried far back in evolution, music and language may have arisen from a common expressive medium. But whether that speculation has any merit, it seems clear that they have taken separate courses over many thousands of years and are now harnessed to different purposes. What they share is an existence that is not closely tied to the world of physical objects (in contrast to spatial and logical-mathematical forms of intelligence), and an essence that is equally remote from the world of other persons (as manifest in various forms of personal intelligence). And so, in taking the measure of another autonomous intellectual competence, I turn to the nature and operation of musical intelligence.

6

Musical
Intelligence

[Music is] the corporealization of the intelligence
that is in sound.

HOENE WRONSKY

O F ALL the gifts with which in-
dividuals may be endowed, none emerges earlier than musical talent.
Though speculation on this matter has been rife, it remains uncertain
just why musical talent emerges so early, and what the nature of this
gift might be. A study of musical intelligence may help us understand
the special flavor of music and at the same time illuminate its relation
to other forms of human intellect.

Some feeling for the range and sources of early musical gifts can
be gleaned by attending a hypothetical musical audition in which the
performers are three preschool children. The first child plays a Bach
suite for solo violin with technical accuracy as well as considerable
feeling. The second child performs a complete aria from a Mozart opera
after hearing it sung but a single time. The third child sits down at the
piano and plays a simple minuet which he himself has composed.
Three performances by three musical prodigies.

But have they all arrived at these heights of youthful talent by the
same routes? Not necessarily. The first child could be a Japanese
youngster who has participated since age two in the Suzuki Talent
Education program and has, like thousands of her peers, mastered the

99

essentials of a string instrument by the time she enters school. The second child could be a victim of autism, a youngster who can barely communicate with anyone else and who is severely disturbed in several affective and cognitive spheres; still he exhibits an isolated sparing of musical intelligence, such that he can sing back flawlessly any piece he hears. The third could be a young child raised in a musical family who has begun to pick out tunes on his own—a throwback to the precocious young Mozart, Mendelssohn, or Saint-Saens.

Enough children exemplifying each of these patterns have been observed so that we can say with confidence that these performances are genuine phenomena. One can exhibit musical precocity as a result of involvement in a superbly designed instructional regime, by virtue of life in a household filled with music, or despite (or as part of) a crippling malady. Underlying each of these performances, there may well be a core talent, one that has been inherited; but, clearly, other factors are also at work. At the very least, the extent to which the talent is expressed publicly will depend upon the milieu in which one lives.

But these early performances, however charming, mark the barest beginning. Each of these children may go on to achieve a high degree of musical competence, but it is equally possible that one or another will not realize such heights. Accordingly, just as I first introduced linguistic intelligence through the perspective of the poet, I will begin by examining instances of unambiguous musical accomplishment in adulthood—those skills most lavishly found among individuals who make their livelihood as composers. Having presented an "end-state" of musical intelligence, I will then describe some of the core abilities that underlie musical competence in ordinary individuals—those abilities of a relatively microscopic sort, as well as those that involve larger passages of music. In an effort to gain further purchase on the kinds of talent exhibited by our opening trio of children, I will consider aspects of normal development as well as the training of musical skills. As a complement, I will also investigate musical breakdown and, in the course of this discussion, touch upon the brain organization that makes possible musical achievement. Finally, having surveyed the evidence for an autonomous musical intelligence, in our own and other cultures, I shall in conclusion consider some of the ways in which musical intelligence has—and can—interact with other human intellectual competences.

Composing

The twentieth-century American composer Roger Sessions has provided a revealing account of what it is like to compose a piece of music. As
he explains it, a composer can be readily identified by the fact that he
constantly has "tones in his head"—that is, he is always, somewhere
near the surface of his consciousness, hearing tones, rhythms, and larger musical patterns. While many of these patterns are worth little musically and may, in fact, be wholly derivative, it is the composer's lot
constantly to be monitoring and reworking these patterns.

Composing begins at the moment when these ideas begin to crystallize and to assume a significant shape. The pregnant musical image
can be anything from the simplest melodic, rhythmic, or harmonic
fragment to something considerably more elaborate; but in any event,
the idea seizes the composer's attention, and his musical imagination
begins to work upon it.

In what direction will the idea be taken? As Sessions describes it,
the initial idea harbors many implications. Often it stimulates something contrasting or complementary, though the two motifs will remain part of the same overall design. All the ideas that succeed the
initial one will bear some relationship to it, at least until that idea has
either been completed or abandoned. At the same time, the composer is
nearly always certain which elements belong to an elaboration of the
original idea and which do not:

Assuming, as I am doing, that the conception is adequately strong and firmly
established, it will govern every move that the composer makes from this point
on. . . . Choices are made within a specific framework which, as it grows, exerts
an ever greater influence on what is to come.

For the outside world this process may seem mysterious, but for
the composer it has a compelling logic of its own:

What I have called logical musical thinking is the consequential working out of
a sustained musical impulse, pursuing a result constantly implicit in it. It is not
in any sense a shrewd calculation of what should . . . happen next. The aural
imagination is simply the working of the composer's ear, fully reliable and
sure of its direction as it must be, in the service of a clearly envisaged
conception.

In these efforts, the composer relies on the aforementioned technique
of contrast, but also on other dictates of his ear—passages associated
with the original idea, passages that articulate or place into proper

proportion the elements of the initial idea. Working with tones, rhythms, and, above all, an overall sense of form and movement, the composer must decide how much sheer repetition, and which harmonic, melodic, rhythmic, or contrapuntal variations, are necessary to realize his conception.

Other composers echo this description of the processes in which they are engaged. In his account, Aaron Copland indicates that composing is as natural as eating or sleeping: "It is something that the composer happens to have been born to do; and because of that it loses the character of a special virtue in the composer's eyes." Wagner said he composed like a cow producing milk, whereas Saint-Saens likened the process to an apple tree producing apples. The sole element of mystery, in Copland's view, is the source of an initial musical idea: as he sees it, themes initially come to the composer as a gift from heaven, much like automatic writing. And that is the reason many composers keep a notebook around. Once the idea has come, the process of development and elaboration follows with surprising naturalness, eventually with inevitability, thanks in part to the many techniques available as well as to the accessibility of structural forms or "schemes" that have evolved over the years. As Arnold Schoenberg puts it, "Whatever happens in a piece of music is nothing but the endless reshaping of a basic shape. Or, in other words, there is nothing in a piece of music but what comes from the theme, springs from it, and can be traced back to it."

What is the source of that musical repository from which the musical ideas come? Another twentieth-century American composer, Harold Shapero, helps us to understand the musical lexicon:

The musical mind is concerned predominantly with the mechanisms of tonal memory. Before it has absorbed a considerable variety of tonal experiences, it cannot begin to function in a creative way. . . . The musical memory, where its physiological functions are intact, functions indiscriminately; a great percentage of what is heard becomes submerged in the unconscious and is subject to literal recall.

But the materials exploited by the composer are treated differently:

The creative portion of the musical mind . . . operates selectively, and the tonal material which it offers up has been metamorphized and has become identifiable from the material which was originally absorbed. In the metamorphosis . . . the original tonal memory has been compounded with remembered emotional experiences and it is this act of the creative unconscious which renders more than an acoustical series of tones.

Even as we find consensus among articulate composers about the naturalness of the act of composition, (if not about the source of the germinal idea), there is considerable agreement about what music is not. Sessions goes to great pains to indicate that language plays no role in the act of composition. Once when stuck in the middle of composition, he was able to describe the source of his difficulty to a young friend. But this was a wholly different medium from the one in which the composer must work:

I would like to point out that at no time in the course of the actual process of composition were words involved. . . . In no way, however, did these words [told to the friend] help me—nor could they have helped me—to find the precise pattern that I was seeking. . . . I was trying hard to find the proper words with which to describe a sequence of thought that was carried on in the musical medium itself—by which I mean sounds and rhythms, heard to be sure in imagination, but nevertheless heard accurately and vividly.

Igor Stravinsky goes a step further: as he indicated in conversations with Robert Craft, composing is doing, not thinking. It occurs not by acts of thought or will: it is accomplished naturally. And Arnold Schoenberg quotes with approval Schopenhauer's view, "The composer reveals the inmost essence of the world and utters the most profound vision in a language which his reason does not understand, just as a magnetic somnambulist gives disclosures about things which she has no idea of when awake," even as he castigates that philosopher of music, "when he tries to translate details of this language which *the reason does not understand* into our terms" (italics in original). In Schoenberg's view, it is the musical material that must be dealt with: "I don't believe a composer can compose if you give him numbers instead of tones"—this from the individual who has been accused of expelling melody and converting all music to a numerical manipulation system.

For those of us who do not readily compose music—who are excluded from that small minority of mankind "whose minds secrete music"—these processes necessarily have a remote air. We can perhaps identify somewhat more easily with one who performs works written by other individuals—such as an instrumentalist or a singer—or with one charged with interpretation, like a conductor. Yet, in Aaron Copland's view, the skills involved in listening to music have a clear link to those involved in musical creation. As Copland puts it, "The intelligent listener must be prepared to increase his awareness of the musical material and what happens to it. He must hear the melodies, the rhythms, the harmonies, and the tone colors in a more conscious fashion. But above all he must, in order to follow the line of the composer's thought, know something of the principles of musical form." The musicologist Edward T. Cone suggests, "active listening is, after all a kind of vicarious performance, effected, as Sessions puts it, by 'inwardly reproducing the music.'" In Cone's view, the performer's assignment follows from this prescription: an adequate performance can be best achieved by discovering and making clear the rhythmic life of a composition. Composer and listener come together in full circle in Stravinsky's remark about his intended audience:

When I compose something, I cannot conceive that it should fail to be recognized for what it is and understood. I use the language of music and my statement in grammar will be clear to the musician who has followed music up to where my contemporaries and I have brought it.

There are several roles that musically inclined individuals can assume, ranging from the avant-garde composer who attempts to create a new idiom, to the fledgling listener who is trying to make sense of nursery rhymes (or other "primer level" music). There may well be a hierarchy of difficulty involved in various roles, with performing exacting more demands than listening does, and composing making more profound (or at least different) demands than performing. It is also probable that certain kinds of music—such as the classical forms under discussion here—are less accessible than folk or musical forms. Yet, there is also a core set of abilities crucial to all participation in the musical experience of a culture. These core abilities should be found in any normal individual brought into regular contact with any kind of music. To the identification of such core musical abilities, I now turn.

The Components of Musical Intelligence

There is relatively little dispute about the principal constituent elements of music, though experts will differ on the precise definition of each aspect. Most central are *pitch* (or melody) and *rhythm*: sounds emitted at certain auditory frequencies and grouped according to a prescribed system. Pitch is more central in certain cultures—for example, those Oriental societies that make use of tiny quarter-tone intervals; while rhythm is correlatively emphasized in sub-Saharan Africa, where the rhythmic ratios can reach a dizzying metrical complexity. Part of the organization of music is horizontal—the relations among the pitches as they unfold over time; and part is vertical, the effects produced when two or more sounds are emitted at the same time, giving rise to a harmonic or a dissonant sound. Next in importance only to pitch and rhythm is *timbre*—the characteristic qualities of a tone.

These central elements—these "cores" of music—raise the question of the role of audition in the definition of music. There is no question that the auditory sense is crucial to all musical participation: any argument to the contrary would be fatuous. Yet it is equally clear that at least one central aspect of music—rhythmic organization—can exist apart from any auditory realization. It is, in fact, the rhythmic aspects of music that are cited by deaf individuals as their entry point to musical experiences. Some composers, such as Scriabin, have underscored the importance of this aspect of music, by "translating" their works into rhythmic series of colored forms; and other composers, such as Stravinsky, have stressed the significance of seeing music performed, whether by an orchestra or a dance troupe. Thus, it is probably fair to say that certain aspects of the musical experience are accessible even to those individuals who (for one or another reason) cannot appreciate its auditory aspects.

Many experts have gone on to place the affective aspects of music close to its core. On Roger Sessions's account, "music is controlled movement of sound in time. . . . It is made by humans who want it, enjoy it, and even love it." Arnold Schoenberg, hardly known for his sentimentality, put it this way:

Music is a succession of tones and tone combinations so organized as to have an agreeable impression on the ear and its impression on the intelligence is comprehensible. . . . These impressions have the power to influence occult parts of our soul and of our sentimental spheres and . . . this influence makes us live in a dreamland of fulfilled desires or in a dreamed hell.

In alluding to affect and pleasure, we encounter what may be the central puzzle surrounding music. From the point of view of "hard" positivistic science, it would seem preferable to describe music purely in terms of objective, physical terms: to stress the pitch and rhythmic aspects of music, perhaps recognizing the timbre and the permissible compositional forms; but taking care to avoid the pathetic fallacy, where explanatory power is granted to an object because of the effects it may induce in someone else. Indeed, attempts over the centuries to associate music with mathematics seem a concerted effort to underscore the rationality (if not to deny the emotional powers) of music. Yet hardly anyone who has been intimately associated with music can forbear to mention its emotional implications: the effects it has upon indi-

viduals; the sometimes deliberate attempts by composers (or performers) to mimic or communicate certain emotions; or, to put it in its most
sophisticated terms, the claim that, if music does not in itself convey
emotions or affects, it captures the *forms* of these feelings. Testimony
can be found wherever one looks. Socrates recognized early the links
between specific musical modes and different human character traits,
associating the Ionian and Lydian modes with indolence and softness,
the Dorian and Phrygian modes with courage and determination. Sessions seems to favor this way of speaking:

Music cannot express fear, which is certainly an authentic emotion. But its
movement, in tones, accents, and rhythmic design, can be restless, sharply
agitated, violent, and even suspenseful. . . . It cannot express despair, but it can
move slowly, in a prevailingly downward direction; its texture can become
heavy and, as we are wont to say, dark—or it can vanish entirely.

And even Stravinsky, who in a famous remark once challenged
this way of thinking ("Music is powerless to express anything"), later
went on to recant: "Today I would put it the other way around. Music
expresses itself. . . . A composer works in the embodiment of his feelings and, of course, it may be considered as expressing or symbolizing
them." Turning to the experimental laboratory, the psychologist Paul
Vitz has demonstrated in a number of studies that higher tones evoke a
more positive affect in listeners. And even "cold-hearted" performers
have confirmed this link: it is commonly reported that performers are
so deeply affected by a given composition that they request to have it
played at their funeral. The virtual unanimity of this testimony suggests that when scientists finally unravel the neurological underpinnings of music—the reasons for its effects, its appeal, its longevity—
they will be providing an explanation of how emotional and motivational factors are intertwined with purely perceptual ones.

Bearing these core abilities in mind, psychologists have attempted
to examine the mechanism by which musical patterns are perceived.
For some time, one could discern two radically different approaches to
the psychological investigation of music. The more prevalent school
has taken what might be called a "bottom-up" approach, examining the
ways in which individuals process the building blocks of music: single
tones, elementary rhythmic patterns, and other units that allow ready
presentation to experimental subjects and are devoid of the contextual
information encountered in performances of works of music. Subjects
are asked to indicate which of two tones is higher, whether two rhythmic patterns are the same, whether two tones are played by the same

instrument. The precision with which these studies can be carried out makes them appealing to experimental investigators. Yet musicians have often questioned the relevance of findings obtained with such artificial patterns for the larger musical entities typically encountered by human beings.

This skepticism about the possibility of building up to music from its component parts accounts for the appeal of a "top-down" approach to musical perception, where one presents to subjects musical pieces or, at least, healthy musical segments. In such studies, one typically examines reactions to more global properties of music (does it get faster or slower, louder or softer?) and also to metaphoric characterizations of the music (is it heavy or light, triumphant or tragic, crowded or sparse?). What this approach gains in face validity, it typically sacrifices in terms of experimental control and susceptibility to analysis.

It is perhaps inevitable and, to most minds, entirely desirable that a "middle ground" approach has recently come to the fore. The goal here is to sample musical entities that are large enough to bear a non-superficial resemblance to genuine musical (as opposed to simple acoustic) entities, yet sufficiently susceptible to analysis to permit systematic experimental manipulations. Research in this vein has generally involved the presentation to subjects of short pieces, or incomplete fragments of pieces, that have a clear key or a clear rhythm. Subjects are asked to compare completions with one another, to group together pieces in the same key or rhythm patterns, or to fashion their own completions.

Such research reveals that all but the most naïve (or most disabled) subjects appreciate something of the structure of music. That is, given a piece in a certain key, they can judge which sort of ending is more appropriate, which sort is less appropriate; hearing a piece in a certain rhythm, they can group it together with others of similar rhythm or, again, complete the rhythm appropriately. Individuals with a modest amount of musical training or sensitivity are able to appreciate the relationships that obtain within a key—to know that the dominant or the subdominant enjoy a privileged relationship to the tonic—and which keys are musically close to one another so that a modulation between them is appropriate. Such individuals are also sensitive to the properties of a musical contour, appreciating, for example, when one phrase displays a contour that is the converse of a previous phrase. Scales are recognized as a series of tones with a definite structure, and there are expectations about leading tones, resting tones, cadences, and other fixtures of musical compositions. At the most general level, individuals appear to have "schemas" or "frames" for hearing music—expectations about what a well-structured phrase or section of a piece should be—as well as at least a nascent ability to complete a segment in a way that makes musical sense.

An analogy to language may not be out of place here. Just as one can tease apart a series of levels of language—from the basic phonological level, through a sensitivity to word order and word meaning, to the ability to appreciate larger entities, like stories—so, too, in the realm of music, it is possible to examine sensitivity to individual tones or phrases, but also to look at how these fit together into larger musical structures which exhibit their own rules of organization. And just as these different levels of analysis can—and should—be brought to bear in apprehending a literary work like a poem or novel, so, too, the apprehension of musical works requires the ability to make the local analysis of the "bottom-up" camp as well as the "top-down" schematizations of the Gestalt school. Increasingly, researchers in music are avoiding the Scylla of total concern with detail and ornamentation, and the Charybdis of attention only to overall form, in favor of analyses that take into account aspects at each of these levels and strive for an integration in the Final Analysis. Perhaps in the future, individuals charged with assessing promise in the musical domain will be able to draw on findings from this eclectic approach to musical competence.

The Development of Musical Competence

In Europe during the early years of the century, there was a fair amount of interest in the development of artistic abilities in children, including the growth of musical competence. My opening vignette would have seemed entirely fitting in Vienna seventy-five years ago. For reasons that one could speculate about, this interest rarely crossed the Atlantic. Therefore, little has been firmly established about the normal development of musical competence in our society or, for that matter, about the development of such competence in any culture.

Nonetheless, at least a rough-and-ready portrait of early musical competence can be proposed. During infancy, normal children sing as well as babble: they can emit individual sounds, produce undulating patterns, and even imitate prosodic patterns and tones sung by others with better than random accuracy. In fact, it has recently been claimed by Mechthild Papoušek and Hanus Papoušek that infants as young as two months are able to match the pitch, loudness, and melodic contour of their mother's songs, and that infants at four months can match rhythmic structure as well. These authorities claim that infants are especially predisposed to pick up these aspects of music—far more than they are sensitive to the core properties of speech—and that they can also engage in sound play that clearly exhibits creative, or generative, properties.

In the middle of the second year of life, children effect an important transition in their musical lives. For the first time, they begin on their own to emit series of punctate tones that explore various small intervals; seconds, minor thirds, major thirds, and fourths. They invent spontaneous songs that prove difficult to notate; and, before long, they begin to produce small sections ("characteristic bits") of familiar songs heard around them—such as the "EI–EI–O" from "Old MacDonald" or "All fall down" from "Ring around the Rosie." For a year or so, there exists a tension between the spontaneous songs and the production of "characteristic bits" from familiar tunes; but, by the age of three or four, the melodies of the dominant culture have won out, and the production of spontaneous songs and of exploratory sound play generally wanes.

Much more so than in language, one encounters striking individual differences in young children as they learn to sing. Some can match large segments of a song by the age of two or three (in this they are reminiscent of our autistic child); many others can emit only the grossest approximations of pitch at this time (rhythm and words generally pose less of a challenge) and may still have difficulty in producing accurate melodic contours at the age of five or six. Still, it seems fair to say that by school age, most children in our culture have a schema of what a song should be like and can produce a reasonably accurate facsimile of the tunes commonly heard around them.

Except among children with unusual musical talent or exceptional opportunities, there is little further musical development after the school years begin. To be sure, the musical repertoire expands, and individuals can sing songs with greater accuracy and expressivity. There is also some increase in knowledge about music, as many individuals become able to read music, to comment critically upon performances, and to employ musical-critical categories, such as "sonata form" or "duple meter." But whereas, in the case of language, there is considerable emphasis in the school on further linguistic attainments, music occupies a relatively low niche in our culture, and so musical illiteracy is acceptable.

Once one casts a comparative glance around the globe, a far wider

109

variety of musical trajectories becomes manifest. At one extreme are the Anang of Nigeria. Infants scarcely a week old are introduced to music and dancing by their mothers. Fathers fashion small drums for their children. When they reach the age of two, children join groups where they learn many basic cultural skills, including singing, dancing, and playing of instruments. By the age of five, the young Anang can sing hundreds of songs, play several percussion instruments, and perform dozens of intricate dance movements. Among the Venda of Northern Transvaal, young children start with motor response to music and don't even try to sing. The Griots, traditional musicians of Senegambia, require an apprenticeship of several years. In some cultures, wide individual differences are recognized: for example, among the Ewe of Ghana, less talented persons are made to lie on the ground, while a musical master sits astride them and beats rhythms into their body and their soul. In contrast, the aforementioned Anang claim that all individuals are musically proficient; and the anthropologists who studied this group claim never to have encountered in it a "non-musical" member. In some contemporary cultures, musical competence is highly prized: in China, Japan, and Hungary, for example, children are expected to gain proficiency in singing and, if possible, in instrumental performance as well.

Our understanding of levels of musical competence has been significantly enhanced by Jeanne Bamberger, a musician and developmental psychologist at the Massachusetts Institute of Technology. Bamberger has sought to analyze musical development along the lines of Piaget's studies of logical thought, but has insisted that musical thinking involves its own rules and constraints and cannot simply be assimilated to linguistic or logical-mathematical thinking. Pursuing one line of study, she has demonstrated forms of conservation that exist in the realm of music but are not interchangeable with the classical forms of physical conservation: For example, a young child will confuse a tone with the particular bell from which it is made, and will not appreciate that many bells can produce the same tone or that a bell that is moved will retain its sound. On the other hand, the young child may also recognize that no two performances of a song are exactly identical. Such demonstrations underscore the fact that the concept "same" bears a different meaning in music than it does in the mathematical sphere.

Bamberger has called attention to two contrasting ways of processing music, which correspond roughly to "know-how" versus "know-that." In a *figural* approach, the child attends chiefly to the global features of a melodic fragment—whether it gets louder or softer, faster or slower—and to the "felt" features of groupings—whether a set of tones appears to belong together and to be separated in time from its neighbors. The approach is intuitive, based solely on what is heard irrespective of any theoretical knowledge about music. In contrast, the individual with a *formal mode* of thought can conceptualize his musical experience in a principled manner. Equipped with propositional knowledge about music as a system, he understands what occurs on a measure-by-measure basis and can analyze passages in terms of their time signature. Thus, he can appreciate (and notate) a passage in terms of the number of beats per measure and the occurrence of particular rhythmic patterns against this metrical background.

Ultimately, any individual in our culture who would wish to gain musical competence should master formal musical analysis and representation; but at least initially, this move to the level of "knowledge about music" may involve a cost. Certain important aspects of music that are "naturally" perceived according to the initial "figural" mode of processing may be at least temporarily obscured ("wiped out") as an individual attempts to assess and classify everything according to a formal mode of analysis—to superimpose propositional knowledge upon figural intuitions.

Indeed, the clash between figural and formal modes of processing may even occasion a crisis in the lives of young musicians. According to Bamberger, children treated by their communities as prodigies often advance quite far on the basis of figural apprehension of music. At a certain point, however, it becomes important for them to supplement their intuitive understanding with a more systematic knowledge of music lore and law. This bringing-to-consciousness of what was previously assumed (or ignored) can be unsettling for youngsters, particularly for ones who have depended simply upon their intuition, and who may have a resistance to propositional (linguistic or mathematical) characterizations of musical events. The so-called midlife crisis occurs in the lives of prodigies in adolescence, somewhere between the ages of fourteen and eighteen. If this crisis is not successfully negotiated, it may ultimately prompt the child to cease altogether participating in musical life.

One can posit a pattern of growth for the young musical performer. Up till the age of eight or nine, in a manner reminiscent of the young literary Sartre, the child proceeds on the basis of sheer talent and energy: he learns pieces readily because of his sensitive musical ear and memory, gains applause for his technical skill, but essentially does not expend undue effort. A period of more sustained skill building commences around the age of nine or so, when the child must begin to practice seriously, even to the extent that it may interfere with his school and his friendships. This may, in fact, occasion an initial "crisis" as the child starts to realize that other values may have to be suspended if his musical career is to be pursued. The second and more pivotal crisis occurs in early adolescence. In addition to confronting the clash between figural and formal ways of knowing, the youth must ask whether he actually wishes to devote his life to music. Earlier, he has been an (often willing) vessel in the grasp of ambitious parents and teachers; now he must ponder whether he himself wants to pursue this calling, whether he wants to use music to express to others what is most important in his own existence, whether he is willing to sacrifice his other pleasures and possibilities for an uncertain future where luck and extra-musical factors (like interpersonal skills) may well prove decisive.

In speaking of musically talented children, I am concerned with a tiny group of children who have been singled out by their families and their communities. It is not known to what extent this number could be significantly increased were values and training methods to change. Still, my opening vignettes offer suggestive clues.

In Japan, the great master Suzuki has shown that large numbers of individuals can learn to play musical instruments extremely well (according to Western standards) even at an early age. To be sure, most of these individuals do not go on to become concert musicians—a result that does not disturb Suzuki, who sees his goal as the training of character, not of virtuoso performance. Suzuki's population may be, to some extent, self-selected. Still, the astonishing performances by large numbers of Japanese children—and by "Suzuki-style youngsters" in other cultural settings as well—indicates that such fluency is a reasonable target for a much larger proportion of the population than is currently the case in the United States. The existence of accomplished singing skill in certain cultural groups (Hungarians influenced by the Kodaly method, or members of the Anang tribe in Nigeria) and of comparably high-quality instrumental performances among Russian Jewish violinists or Balinese gamelon players suggests that musical achievement is not strictly a reflection of inborn ability but is susceptible to cultural stimulation and training.

On the other hand, if there is any area of human achievement in which it pays to have adequate or lavish genetic background, music would be a formidable contender. The extent to which music runs in families—like the Bach, Mozart, or Haydn households—is one possible line of evidence; but nongenetic factors (such as value systems or training procedures) might be equally responsible in such cases. Probably a more persuasive line of evidence comes from those children who, in the absence of a hospitable family environment, present themselves initially as able to sing very well, to recognize and recall numerous tunes, to pick out melodies on a piano or other instrument. Even the slightest musical stimulation becomes a crystallizing experience. Moreover, once exposed to formal training, these same children appear to pick up requisite skills with great rapidity—as Vygotsky would put it, they exhibit a large zone of potential (or proximal) development. It seems reasonable to regard this ability as the manifestation of a considerable genetic proclivity to hear accurately, to remember, master (and, eventually, produce) musical sequences. And it would seem that both our autistic child and our young composer display considerable genetic potential in the area of music.

A particularly dramatic instance of a talent that announced itself to the world can be found in the saga of the renowned twentieth-century pianist Arthur Rubinstein. Rubinstein came from a family none of whom, in his own words "had the slightest musical gift." As a toddler in Poland, he loved all manner of sounds, including factory sirens, the singing of old Jewish peddlers, and the chants of ice cream sellers. While he refused to speak, he was always willing to sing and thereby created quite a sensation at home. In fact, his abilities soon degenerated into a sport, where everyone tried to reach him by songs, and he himself came to recognize people by their tunes.

Then, when he had attained the advanced age of three, his parents bought a piano so that the older children in the family could have lessons. Though not studying piano himself, Rubinstein reports:

The drawing room became my paradise. . . . Half in fun, half in earnest, I learned to know the keys by their names and with my back to the piano I would call the notes of any chord, even the most dissonant one. From then on it became mere "child's play" to master the intricacies of the keyboard, and I was soon able to play first with one hand, later with both, any tune that caught my ear . . . All this, of course, could not fail to impress my family—none of whom, I must now admit, including grandparents, uncles, aunts, had the slightest musical gift. . . . By the time I was three and a half years old my fixation was so obvious that my family decided to do something about this talent of mine.

The Rubinsteins in fact took their young prodigy to meet Joseph Joachim, the most celebrated violinist of the nineteenth century, who proclaimed that young Arthur might one day become a great musician, because his talent was extraordinary.

Even given generous dollops of talent, musical achievement need not follow. For every ten musical prodigies (with the presumptive in-born talent), there are several failed prodigies, some of whom ceased music altogether, others of whom tried but failed to reach the heights of musical achievement. (Even Rubinstein had to confront several crises regarding his own talent and will to make music.) Issues of motivation, personality, and character are generally singled out as decisive here—though luck certainly contributes as well. A musician in our culture must be more than simply technically proficient. One must be able to interpret music, to glean the composer's intentions, to realize and project one's own interpretations, to be a convincing performer. As Rudolf Serkin, one of the leading pianists of our day, has put it:

> Ivan Galamian [the leading violin teacher of the middle twentieth century] believes in taking them young, at 10 or 12. So do I. At that age you can already tell the talent, but not . . . character or personality. If they have personality they will develop into quite something. If not, at least they will play well.

Nearly all composers begin as performers, though some performers begin to compose during the first decade of their lives. (Composing at the level of a world-class artist seems to require at least ten years to flower—no matter how gifted one is.) Why a small percentage of performers become composers has not been much studied, though there are presumably positive (proclivity and skill) as well as negative (shyness, awkwardness) factors that prompt one decision rather than the other. In my own cursory study of this question, I uncovered one common theme. Individuals who later became composers (rather than, or in addition to, performers) found themselves by the age of ten or eleven, experimenting with pieces that they were performing, rewriting them, changing them, turning them into something other than they were—in a word, *de*composing them. Indeed, sometimes this discovery occurs even earlier. Igor Stravinsky recalls trying to pick out at the piano the intervals he had heard "as soon as I could reach the piano—but found other intervals in the process that I liked better, which already made me a composer." For the future composers, like Stravinsky, pleasure came increasingly from what changes they could effect rather than simply from performing the piece literally as well as it could be performed.

In all probability, issues of personality figure crucially here. The sources of pleasure for composition are different from those surrounding performance—the need to create and dissect, to compose and decompose arises from different motivations than the desire to perform or simply to interpret. Composers may resemble poets in the sudden apprehension of the initial germinal ideas, the need to explore and realize them, and the intertwining of emotional and conceptual aspects.

My discussion has been partial to Western civilization in the period following the Renaissance. Cults of performer and composer were far less prevalent in the medieval era; and, indeed, the line between composing and performing does not exist in many cultures. Performers *are* the interpreters and composers; they constantly make small changes in the works that they perform, so that they ultimately build up an *oeuvre*; but they do not self-consciously set themselves off from others as "composers." Indeed, cross-cultural studies suggest a stunning range of attitudes toward the creation of music, with the Congo Basongye feeling uncomfortable with any personal role in the creation of new music; the Plains Indians willing to claim credit for a composition, so long as it was conceived during a vision quest; and the Greenland Eskimos actually judging the results of a fight among men in terms of which antagonist can compose the songs that best convey his side in a dispute. We simply do not know whether individuals in other cultures feel as Beatle John Lennon did during early childhood:

> People like me are aware of their so-called genius at ten, eight, nine . . . I always wondered, "Why has nobody discovered me? In school, didn't they see that I'm more clever than anybody in this school? That the teachers are stupid, too? That all they had was information that I didn't need." It was obvious to me. Why didn't they put me in art school? Why didn't they train me? I was different, I was always different, Why didn't anybody notice me?

Evolutionary and Neurological Facets of Music

The evolutionary origins of music are wrapped in mystery. Many scholars suspect that linguistic and musical expression and communication had common origins and, in fact, split off from one another several hundred thousand, or perhaps even a million, years ago. There is evidence of musical instruments dating back to the Stone Age and much presumptive evidence about the role of music in organizing work groups, hunting parties, and religious rites; but, in this area, theories are all too easy to fabricate and too difficult to discredit.

Still, in studying the ontogenesis of music, we possess at least one advantage not available in questions concerning language. While ties

115

between human language and other forms of animal communication seem to be limited and controversial, there is at least one instance in the animal kingdom whose parallels to human music are difficult to ignore. That is bird song.

As I noted in discussions of the biological underpinnings of intelligence, much has recently been discovered about the development of song in birds. For present purposes, I wish to stress the following aspects. First of all, one observes a wide range of developmental patterns of bird song, with some species being restricted to a single song learned by all birds, even those that are deaf; other species feature a range of songs and dialects, depending clearly on environmental stimulation of specifiable sorts. We find among birds a remarkable mix of innate and environmental factors. And these can be subjected to that systematic experimentation that is impermissible in the case of human capacities.

Within these different trajectories, there is a prescribed path to development of the final song, beginning with *subsong*, passing through *plastic song*, until the species song or songs are finally achieved. This process bears nontrivial and perhaps striking parallels to the steps through which young children pass as they first babble and then explore fragments from the songs of their environments. To be sure, the ultimate output of human singers is much vaster and more varied than even the most impressive bird repertoire; and this discontinuity between the two vocalizing species needs to be kept in mind. All the same, suggestive analogies in the development of singing should stimulate experimentation that may illuminate more general aspects of musical perception and performance.

But without question, the most intriguing aspect of bird song from the point of view of a study of human intelligence is its representation in the nervous system. Bird song turns out to be one of the few instances of a skill that is regularly lateralized in the animal kingdom— in this case, in the left part of the avian nervous system. A lesion there will destroy bird song, whereas comparable lesions in the right half of the brain exert much less debilitating effects. Moreover, it is possible to examine the bird's brain and to find clear indices to the nature and the richness of songs. Even within a species, birds differ in whether they have a well or a sparsely stacked "library of songs," and this information is "legible" in the avian brain. The stock of song changes across seasons, and this alteration can actually be observed by inspecting the expansion or the shrinkage of the relevant nuclei during different seasons. Thus, while the purposes of bird song are very different from

116

those of human song ("bird songs are promise of music, but it takes a human being to keep them"), the mechanism by which certain core musical components are organized may well prove analogous to those exhibited by human beings.

Whether there is, in fact, some direct phylogenetic link between human and bird music proves difficult to determine. Birds are sufficiently remote from human beings to make the wholly separate invention of avian and human auditory-oral activity more than just an idle possibility. Perhaps surprisingly, primates exhibit nothing similar to bird song; but individuals in many species do issue sounds that are expressive and can be understood by conspecifics. It seems more likely that in human song we witness the bringing together of a number of abilities—some of which (for example, imitation of vocalic targets) may exist in other forms in other species; others of which (for example, sensitivity to relative as well as absolute pitch, or the ability to appreciate various kinds of musical transformation) are unique to our own.

The temptations are considerable to draw analogies between human music and language. Even in a work devoted to establishing the autonomy of these realms, I have not refrained from drawing such parallels in order to convey a point. It is therefore important to stress the experimental support for this proposed separation. Investigators working with both normal and brain-damaged humans have demonstrated beyond a reasonable doubt that the processes and mechanisms subserving human music and language are distinctive from one another.

One line of evidence in favor of this dissociation has been summarized by Diana Deutsch, a student of the perception of music whose work falls largely in the "bottom-up" tradition. Deutsch has shown that, counter to what had been believed by many psychologists of perception, the mechanisms by which pitch is apprehended and stored are different from the mechanisms that process other sounds, particularly those of language. Convincing documentation comes from studies in which individuals are given a set of tones to remember and then presented with various interfering material. If the interfering material is other tones, recall for the initial set is drastically interfered with (40 percent error in one study). If, however, the interposed material is verbal—lists of numbers, for example—individuals can handle even large amounts of interference without material effect on the memory for pitch (2 percent error in the same study). What makes this finding particularly compelling is that it surprised the subjects themselves. Apparently, individuals expect that the verbal material will interfere with the melodic material and are frankly incredulous when they are so little affected.

This specialness of musical perception is confirmed dramatically by studies of individuals whose brains have been damaged as a result of stroke or other kinds of trauma. To be sure, there are cases in which individuals who have become aphasic have also exhibited diminished musical ability; but the key finding of this research is that one can suffer significant aphasia without any discernible musical impairment, even as one can become disabled musically while still retaining one's fundamental linguistic competences.

The facts are as follows: Whereas linguistic abilities are lateralized almost exclusively to the left hemisphere in normal right-handed individuals, the majority of musical capacities, including the central capacity of sensitivity to pitch, are localized in most normal individuals in the right hemisphere. Thus, injury to the right frontal and temporal lobes causes pronounced difficulties in discriminating tones and in reproducing them correctly, even as injuries in the homologous areas in the left hemisphere (which cause devastating difficulties in natural language) generally leave musical abilities relatively unimpaired. Appreciation of music also seems to be compromised by right hemisphere disease. (As the names promise, amusia is a disorder distinct from aphasia.)

Once one dons a fine lens, a far more complicated picture emerges, one interestingly more diverse than that found in the case of language. While the syndromes of language seem to be uniform, even across cultures, a great variety of musical syndromes can be found even within the same population. Accordingly, while some composers (like Maurice Ravel) have become amusic following the onset of aphasia, other composers have succeeded in continuing to compose despite a significant aphasia. The Russian composer, Shebalin, proved able to compose very competently despite a severe Wernicke's aphasia; and several other composers, including one whom I studied with my colleagues, retained their composing prowess. Similarly, while the ability to perceive and criticize musical performances seems to rely on right hemisphere structures, certain musicians have exhibited difficulties following injury to the left temporal lobe.

Yet another fascinating wrinkle has been recently uncovered. In most tests with normal individuals, musical abilities turn out to be lateralized to the right hemisphere. For example, in tests of dichotic listening, individuals prove better able to process words and consonants presented to the right ear (left hemisphere), while more successful at processing musical tones (and often other environmental noises as well) when these have been presented to the right hemisphere. But there is a complicating factor. When these, or more challenging tasks, are posed to individuals with musical training, there are increasing left hemisphere, and decreasing right hemisphere, effects. Specifically, the more musical training the individual has, the more likely he will draw at least partially upon the left hemisphere mechanisms in solving a task that the novice tackles primarily through the use of right hemisphere mechanisms.

An image of musical competence crossing the corpus callosum as training accrues must not be taken too far. For one thing, it is not found with every musical skill: for instance, Harold Gordon found that even musicians performed chord analysis with the right, rather than with the left, hemisphere. For another, it is not exactly clear *why* increasing left hemisphere effects are found with training. While the actual processing of music may change loci, it is also possible that the mere affixing of verbal labels to musical fragments brings about *apparent* left hemisphere dominance for musical analysis. Trained musicians may be able to use "formal" linguistic classifications as aids where untrained subjects must fall back on purely figural processing capacities.

What must be stressed in this review, however, is the surprising variety of neural representations of musical ability found in human beings. In my own view, this range rests on at least two factors. First of all, there is the tremendous range of types and degrees of musical skill found in the human population; since individuals differ so much in what they can do, it is conceivable that the nervous system can offer a plurality of mechanisms for carrying out these performances. Second, and relatedly, individuals may make their initial encounter with music through different media and modalities and, even more so, continue to encounter music in idiosyncratic fashion. Thus, while every normal individual is exposed to natural language primarily through listening to others speak, humans can encounter music through many channels: singing, playing instruments by hand, inserting instruments into the mouth, reading of musical notation, listening to records, watching dances, or the like. Even as the way in which written language is represented neurally reflects the kind of script used in one's culture, the various ways in which music can be processed cortically probably reflect the wealth of ways in which humans have found to make and absorb music.

Given the apparently greater variability in brain representation, how does this affect my claim that music qualifies as an autonomous intellectual competence? To my mind, the variation in representation does not compromise my argument. So long as music is represented *with some localization* in an individual, it is not relevant that one individual's localization is not identical to another's (after all, if one includes left-handers, the variety of linguistic localization proves much greater than if one ignores them). Second, what is really crucial is whether other abilities predictably occur together with music, such that when musical ability is destroyed, so are the others. So far as I am aware, none of the claims with respect to musical breakdown suggest any systematic connection with other faculties (such as linguistic, numerical, or spatial processing): music seems, in this regard, *sui generis*, just like natural language.

Finally, I believe that, in the last analysis, there may be considerable underlying regularity in musical representation across individuals. The equation for explaining that uniformity may be complicated, having to take into account the means by which music is initially encountered and learned, the degree and type of training an individual has, the kinds of musical tasks that person is called upon to perform. Given this variety , we may need to examine large numbers of individuals before the genuine uniformities become evident. Perhaps once we have refined the proper analytic tools for studying various forms of musical competence, we may find that it is even more lateralized and localized than human language. Indeed, recent studies converge on the right anterior portions of the brain with such predictability as to suggest that this region may assume for music the same centrality as the left temporal lobe occupies in the linguistic sphere.

Unusual Musical Talents

Patterns of unique breakdown of musical ability provide one strong line of evidence for the autonomy of musical intelligence. Its selective preservation or early appearance in otherwise unremarkable individuals is another line. I have already suggested that unusual musical aptitude is a regular concomitant of certain anomalies, such as autism. Indeed, the literature is filled with accounts of astonishing musical and acoustical feats carried out by autistic youngsters. There have also been more than a few *idiots savants* with unusual musical skills. One such child named Harriet was able to play "Happy Birthday" in the style of various composers, including Mozart, Beethoven, Verdi, and Schubert. That this was not rote familiarity was suggested by the fact that she could recognize a version that her physician had contrived in the style of Haydn. Harriet exerted her musical passions in other ways—for example, knowing the personal history of every member of the Boston Symphony Orchestra. At the age of three, her mother called her by playing incomplete melodies, which the child would then complete with the appropriate tone in the proper octave. Other children described in the literature have been able to remember hundreds of tunes or pick out familiar melodies on a variety of instruments.

While the retarded or autistic child may cling to music because it represents a relative island of preservation in a sea of impairments, there are also more positive signs of isolation, where an otherwise normal child simply displays a precocious ability in the musical sphere. Tales abound about young artists. One composer recalls, "I can never understand how anyone could have difficulty recognizing tones and deciphering musical patterns. It's something I've been doing since the age of three at least." Igor Stravinsky was apparently able to remember the first music that he ever heard:

A bristling fife-and-drum marine band from the marine barracks near our house. . . . This music, and that of the full band which accompanied the Horse Guards, penetrated my nursery every day, and the sound of it, especially of the tuba and the piccolos and drums, was the pleasure of my childhood. . . . The noises of wheels and horses and the shots and whipcracks of coachmen must have penetrated my earliest dreams: they are, at any rate, my first memory of the street of childhood.

Stravinsky recalls that when he was two, some nearby country-women had sung an attractive and restful song on their way home from the fields in the evening. When his parents asked him what he had heard, "I said I had seen the peasants and I had heard them sing, and I sang what they had sung. Everyone was astonished and impressed at this recital and I heard my father remark that I had a wonderful ear." Yet, as we have seen, even the most gifted young child will take about ten years to achieve those levels of performance or composition that we associate with mastery of the musical realm.

A different set of prized musical capacities may be gleaned from scattered studies of musical performance in other cultural settings. In traditional cultures, one generally finds far less of an emphasis on the individual performance or on an innovative departure from cultural

121

norms, far more of a treasuring of individuals who have mastered the genres of their culture and can elaborate upon them in appealing ways. One finds in pre-literate cultures individuals with prodigious memories for tunes, memories that rival those displayed elsewhere with stories. (Indeed, musical gifts are often equated with memory for lyrics.) Equipped with basic schemas, such individuals have the option of combining portions of chants in countless ways that give pleasure and prove appropriate to the circumstance for which they have been contrived.

The properties valued in diverse cultures will also determine which youngsters are picked out to participate actively in the musical life of the community. Thus, where rhythmic, dance, or group participation in music is at a premium, individuals with gifts in these areas will be especially esteemed. And sometimes factors that we would consider decidedly nonmusical, such as a visually attractive performance, are considered at a premium.

There are also instructive adaptations to limited cultural resources. For example, in *Naven*, Gregory Bateson relates the following anecdote: Two individuals were playing flutes, neither of which had stops. It was not possible to play the whole tune on a single instrument. So the performers contrived to alternate pitches between them, so that all the tones in the tune could be emitted at the proper time.

Relation to Other Intellectual Competences

The various lines of evidence that I have reviewed in this chapter suggest that, like language, music is a separate intellectual competence, one that is also not dependent upon physical objects in the world. As is the case with language, musical facility can be elaborated to a considerable degree simply through exploration and exploitation of the oral-aural channel. In fact, it scarcely seems an accident that the two intellectual competences that, from the earliest period of development, can proceed without relation to physical objects, both rely on the oral-auditory system; though, as it turns out, they do so in neurologically distinct ways.

But, in closing, it is equally important to note important and integral links that obtain between music and other spheres of intellect. Richard Wagner located music centrally in his *Gesamtkunstwerk* ("pan-artistic work"), and that placement was not altogether an arrogance: in fact, music does relate in a variety of ways to the range of human symbol systems and intellectual competences. Moreover, precisely because it is not used for explicit communication, or for other evident survival purposes, its continuing centrality in human experience constitutes a challenging puzzle. The anthropologist Lévi-Strauss is scarcely alone among scientists in claiming that if we can explain music, we may find the key for all of human thought—or in implying that failure to take music seriously weakens any account of the human condition.

Many composers, Sessions among them, have stressed the close ties that exist between music and bodily or gestural language. On some analyses, music itself is best thought of as an extended gesture—a kind of movement or direction that is carried out, at least implicitly, with the body. Echoing this sentiment, Stravinsky has insisted that music must be *seen* to be properly assimilated: thus, he was partial to the ballet as a mode of performance and always insisted that one observe instrumentalists when they were performing a piece. Young children certainly relate music and body movement naturally, finding it virtually impossible to sing without engaging in some accompanying physical activity; most accounts of the evolution of music tie it closely to primordial dance; many of the most effective methods of teaching music attempt to integrate voice, hand, and body. Indeed, it is probably only in recent times and in Western civilization, that the performance and appreciation of music, quite apart from movement of the body, has become just the pursuit of a tiny "vocal" minority.

Ties between music and spatial intelligence are less immediately evident but, quite possibly, no less genuine. The localization of musical capacities in the right hemisphere has suggested that certain musical abilities may be closely tied to spatial capacities. Indeed, the psychologist Lauren Harris quotes claims to the effect that composers are dependent upon powerful spatial abilities, which are required to posit, appreciate, and revise the complex architectonic of a composition. And he speculates that the dearth of female composers may be due not to any difficulty with musical processing *per se* (witness the relatively large number of female singers and performers) but rather to the relatively poorer performances in spatial tasks exhibited by females.

Recently, an intriguing possible analogue between musical and spatial abilities has come to light. Arthur Lintgen, a physician in Philadelphia, has astonished onlookers by his ability to recognize musical pieces simply by studying the pattern of grooves on a phonograph record. No claims for magic here. According to Lintgen, phonographic grooves vary in their spacing and contours depending on the dynamics and frequency of the music. For instance, grooves containing soft passages look black or dark gray, while the grooves turn silvery as the music becomes louder or more complicated. Lintgen performs his stunt by correlating vast knowledge of the sound properties of classical music with the distinctive pattern of grooves on records, including ones that he has never seen recorded before. For our purposes, the relevant aspect of Lintgen's demonstration is the implication that music has some analogues in other sensory systems; perhaps, then, a deaf person can come to appreciate at least certain aspects of music by studying these patterns (though presumably not so much as a blind person who is able to "feel" a piece of sculpture). And in cultures where non-auditory aspects of music contribute to its effect, at least these features can be appreciated by those individuals who, for one or another reason, are deaf to tone.

I have already noted the universally acknowledged connection between musical performance and the feeling life of persons; and since feelings occupy a central role in the personal intelligences, some further comments may be in order here. Music can serve as a way of capturing feelings, knowledge about feelings, or knowledge about the forms of feeling, communicating them from the performer or the creator to the attentive listener. The neurology that permits or facilitates this association has by no means been worked out. Still, it is perhaps worth speculating that musical competence depends not upon cortical analytic mechanisms alone, but also upon those subcortical structures deemed central to feeling and to motivation. Individuals with damage to the subcortical areas, or with disconnection between cortical and subcortical areas, are often described as being flat and devoid of affect; and while it has not been commented upon in the neurological literature, it is my observation that such individuals seem rarely to have any interest in or attraction to music. Quite instructively, one individual with extensive right hemisphere damage remained able to teach music and even to write books about it, but lost the ability and the desire to compose. According to his own introspection, he could no longer retain the feeling of the whole piece, nor a sense of what worked and what did not work. Another musician with right hemisphere disease lost all aesthetic feelings associated with his performances. Perhaps these feeling aspects of music prove especially brittle in the instance of damage to the right hemisphere structures, whether they be cortical or subcortical.

Much of the discussion in this chapter has been centered around an implicit comparison between music and language; and it has been important for my claim of autonomous intellectual competences to show that musical intelligence has its own developmental trajectory as well as its own neurological representation, lest it be swallowed up by the omnivorous jaws of human language. Still, I would be derelict if I did not note the continuing efforts on the part of musicologists, and also of well-informed musicians like Leonard Bernstein, to search for nontrivial parallels between music and language. Recently, these efforts have centered about attempts to apply at least parts of Noam Chomsky's analysis of the generative structure of language to the generative aspects of musical perception and production. These commentators are quick to point out that not all aspects of language are directly analogous to music: for example, the whole semantic aspect of language is radically underdeveloped in music; and the notion of strict rules of "grammaticality" is once again extraneous in music, where violations are often prized. Still, if these caveats are borne in mind, there do seem to be nontrivial parallels in the modes of analysis which seem appropriate for natural language, on the one hand, and for Western classical music (1700–1900), on the other. But whether these parallels occur chiefly (or even solely) at the level of formal analysis, or whether they also obtain with respect to the fundamental modes of information processing featured in these two intellectual spheres, has by no means been resolved.

I have saved until last that area of intellectual competence that, in popular lore, has been most closely tied to music—the mathematical sphere. Dating back to the Classical discoveries of Pythagoras, the links between music and mathematics have attracted the imagination of reflective individuals. In medieval times (and in many non-Western cultures), the careful study of music shared many features with the practice of mathematics, such as an interest in proportions, special ratios, recurring patterns, and other detectable series. Until the time of Palestrina and Lasso, in the sixteenth century, mathematical aspects of music remained central, though there was less overt discussion than before about the numerical or mathematical substrata of music. As harmonic concerns gained in ascendancy, the mathematical aspects of music became less apparent. Once again, however, in the twentieth century—first, in the wake of twelve-tone music, and more recently, because of the widespread use of computers—the relationship between musical and mathematical competences has been widely pondered.

In my own view, there are clearly musical, if not "high math," elements in music: these should not be minimized. In order to appreci-

125

ate the operation of rhythms in musical work, an individual must have some basic numerical competence. Performances require a sensitivity to regularity and ratios that can sometimes be quite complex. But this remains mathematical thinking only at a relatively basic level.

When it comes to an appreciation of basic musical structures, and of how they can be repeated, transformed, embedded, or otherwise played off one against another, one encounters mathematical thought at a somewhat higher scale. The parallels have impressed at least some musicians. Stravinsky comments:

[Musical form] is at any rate far closer to mathematics than to literature . . . certainly to something like mathematical thinking and mathematical relationships . . . Musical form is mathematical because it is ideal, and form is always ideal . . . though it may be mathematical, the composer must not seek mathematical formula.

I know . . . that these discoveries are abstract in a similar sense.

A sensitivity to mathematical patterns and regularities has characterized many composers, ranging from Bach to Schumann, who have given vent to this interest, sometimes overtly, sometimes through a kind of playful exploration of possibilities. (Mozart even composed music according to the roll of dice.)

Evidently, there is no problem in finding at least superficial links between aspects of music and properties of other intellectual systems. My own hunch is that such analogies can probably be found between any two intelligences, and that, in fact, one of the great pleasures in any intellectual realm inheres in an exploration of its relationship to other spheres of intelligence. As an aesthetic form, music lends itself especially well to playful exploration with other modes of intelligence and symbolization, particularly in the hands (or ears) of highly creative individuals. Yet, according to my own analysis, the core operations of music do not bear intimate connections to the core operations in other areas; and therefore, music deserves to be considered as an autonomous intellectual realm. In fact, this autonomy should be underscored as we look more closely in the next chapter at those forms of intelligence whose connection to music has most often been alleged—logical and mathematical forms of thought.

In my own view, the task in which musicians are engaged differs fundamentally from that which preoccupies the pure mathematician. The mathematician is interested in forms for their own sake, in their own implications, apart from any realization in a particular medium or from any particular communicative purpose. He may choose to analyze

126

music and even have gifts for doing so; but from the mathematical point of view, music is just another pattern. For the musician, however, the patterned elements must appear in sounds; and they are finally and firmly put together in certain ways not by virtue of formal consideration, but because they have expressive power and effects. Despite his earlier remarks, Stravinsky contends that "music and mathematics are not alike." The mathematician G. H. Hardy had these differences in mind when he pointed out that it was music which could stimulate emotions, accelerate the pulse, cure the course of asthma, induce epilepsy, or calm an infant. The formal patterns that are a mathematician's *raison d'être* are for musicians a helpful, but not essential ingredient for the expressive purposes to which their own capacities are regularly marshaled.

7

Logical-
Mathematical
Intelligence

Piaget's Portrait of Logical-Mathematical Thought

Piaget was fond of relating an anecdote about a child who grew up to be an accomplished mathematician. One day the future mathematician confronted a set of objects lying before him and decided to count them. He determined that there were ten objects. He then pointed to each of the objects, but in a different order, and found that—lo and behold!— there were again ten; the child repeated this procedure several times, with growing excitement, as he came to understand—once and for all—that the number 10 was far from an arbitrary outcome of this repetitive exercise. The number referred to the aggregate of elements, no matter how they happened to be acknowledged in the sequence, just so long as each of them was taken into account once and once only. Through this playful dubbing of a group of objects, the youngster had (as all of us have at one time or another) arrived at a fundamental insight about the realm of number.

In contrast to linguistic and musical capacities, the competence that I am terming "logical-mathematical intelligence" does not have its origins in the auditory-oral sphere. Instead, this form of thought can be traced to a confrontation with the world of objects. For it is in confronting objects, in ordering and reordering them, and in assessing their quantity, that the young child gains his or her initial and most fundamental knowledge about the logical-mathematical realm. From this preliminary point, logical-mathematical intelligence rapidly becomes remote from the world of material objects. By a sequence to be described in this chapter, the individual becomes more able to appreciate the actions that one can perform upon objects, the relations that obtain among those actions, the statements (or propositions) that one can make about actual or potential actions, and the relationships among those statements. Over the course of development, one proceeds from objects to statements, from actions to the relations among actions, from the realm of the sensori-motor to the realm of pure abstraction—ultimately, to the heights of logic and science. The chain is long and complex, but it need not be mysterious: the roots of the highest regions of logical, mathematical, and scientific thought can be found in the simple actions of young children upon the physical objects in their worlds.

In describing the early development of language abilities, I found myself drawing on the works of numerous scholars. When it comes to the ontogenesis and development of logical-mathematical thought, one scholar's work is pre-eminent. Accordingly, in what follows, I build upon the path-breaking research of the Swiss developmental psychologist Jean Piaget.

In Piaget's view, all knowledge—and in particular, the logical-mathematical understanding which constituted his primary focus—derives in the first instance from one's actions upon the world. Accordingly, the study of thought should (indeed, must) begin in the nursery. Here one beholds the infant exploring every manner of objects—nipples, rattles, mobiles, and cups—and, soon enough, coming to form expectations about how these objects will behave under diverse circumstances. For many months, the child's knowledge of these objects and of the simple causal connections that exist among them is tied completely to his moment-to-moment experience with them; and so, when they disappear from sight, they no longer occupy his consciousness. Only after the first eighteen months of life does the child come fully to appreciate that objects will continue to exist even when they have been removed from his time-and-space frame. This attainment of a sense of *object permanence*—that objects have an existence apart from one's particular actions upon them at a given moment—proves to be a crucial cornerstone for later mental development.

Once the child appreciates the permanence of objects, he can think of and refer to them even in their absence. He also becomes able to appreciate the similarities among certain objects—for instance, the fact that all cups (despite differences in size and color) belong to the same class. In fact, within a matter of months, the child becomes able to effect groupings on this basis: he can put together all the trucks, all the yellow cars, all the baby's toys—though as a young toddler, he does this only fitfully and only if he is in a cooperative mood.

The ability to group together objects serves as a "public manifestation" of the child's emerging knowledge that certain objects possess specifiable properties in common. It signals, if you like, the recognition of a *class* or *set*. However, for a few years, such a recognition lacks a quantitative aspect. The child is aware that there are larger and smaller piles, more or fewer coins or M & M's; but these understandings remain at best approximate. True enough, the child may have a mastery of *very small* quantities—two and three objects—which he (like some birds and certain primates) can recognize by simple inspection. But he lacks the crucial understanding that there exists a regular number system, with each number signifying one more (+1) than the previous one, and that any set of objects has a single, unambiguous quantity. This failure to *conserve number* is borne out by the fragility of "counts" in the face of competing cues. For instance, the child who beholds two arrays of M & M's, one covering a wider space than the other, is likely to conclude that the more widely dispersed pile contains more candies, even if in fact, the other (denser) heap is the more numerous. Except for very small amounts, sheer quantitative estimates are still overwhelmed by perceptually seductive cues, such as density or spatial extension.

Often at this age, the child can count—that is, he can recite the rote number series. But until the age of four or five, this rote performance—essentially a manifestation of linguistic intelligence—remains removed from his simple estimates of small sets of objects and from his ability to assess the numerosity of a larger array. But then pivotal events ensue. The child learns that the number series can be mapped onto arrays of objects; if he says a single number after pointing to a single object and repeats this process with each succeeding "numerlog" in the series, he can make an accurate assessment of the number of objects in an array. The first object touched is number 1, the second is number 2, the third is number 3, and so forth. The child of four or five has come to realize that the final number in this oral recitation is also the totality (the cardinal quantity) of objects in an array.

Finally, by the age of six or seven, the child has reached the level of Piaget's young mathematician-to-be. Confronted by two arrays, the child can count the number of entities (M & M's or balls) in each, compare the totals, and determine which (if either) contains the greater amount. No longer is he likely to err, for instance, by confusing spatial extent with quantity, or to reach a wrong total because he fails to coordinate his pointing with his numerical recitation. Indeed, he has arrived at a relatively foolproof method of assessing quantity and has, at the same time, gained a reasonable grasp of what quantity means.

The processes involved in mastering such equivalences play an important role in Piaget's view of intelligence. In equating two arrays on the basis of number, the child has, in effect, created two mental sets or mental images—two arrays. He is then capable of an action of comparison—contrasting the number in one set to the number in another, even if the sets are not identical in appearance, and even (for that matter) if they are not both available for inspection.

Once such actions of comparing have been mastered, the child can undertake additional operations. He can add the same number of elements to both; and the result of these two adding operations will yield identical sums. He can subtract equal amounts and again confirm equivalence. More complex operations become possible. Beginning with non-equivalent amounts, he can add to each the same quantity, secure in the knowledge that non-equivalence will be preserved. On his own (or with help), the child can evolve the understandings needed for the gamut of basic numerical operations: adding, subtracting, multiplying, and dividing. And by the same token, he *should* be able to call upon these operations in negotiating the tasks of daily life—buying goods at the store; trading with friends; following cooking recipes; playing marbles, balls, cards, or computer games.

The actions just described may be—and at first generally are—performed physically upon the material world: that is, the child actually manipulates the candies or marbles as he is engaged in numerical operations. Similarly, other elementary forms of logical-mathematical intelligence—for example, the child's initial appreciation of causal relations and his first efforts to classify objects consistently—are also manifest at first through observation and manipulation of physical objects. In short, according to this analysis, the basis for all logical-mathematical forms of intelligence inheres initially in the handling of objects.

Such actions can, however, also be conducted mentally, inside one's head. And after a time, the actions in fact become *internalized*. The child need not touch the objects himself; he can simply make the required comparisons, additions, or deletions "in his head" and, all the same, arrive at the correct answer. ("If I were to add two objects to the pile, I would have . . . ," he reasons to himself.) Moreover, these mental operations become increasingly certain: no longer does the child merely suspect that two different orders of counting will yield ten objects—he is now certain that they will. Logical necessity comes to attend these operations, as the child is now dealing with necessary truths, not merely with empirical discoveries. Deductions, tautologies, syllogisms, and the like are true, not just because they happen to confirm a state of affairs in the world, but also because certain rules of logic must apply: two piles remain the same, not because a count reveals them to be identical, but rather because "you haven't added or taken anything away, and therefore, they *must* remain the same." Yet, for the period under discussion (roughly the ages of seven to ten), these actions— whether physical or mental—remain restricted to physical objects, which at least potentially can be manipulated. Hence, Piaget terms them "concrete" operations.

Further cognitive growth is essential before the child reaches the next—and for Piaget—the final stage of mental development. During the early years of adolescence, at least in the Western societies studied by Piagetians, the normal child becomes capable of *formal* mental operations. Now he can operate not only upon objects themselves, and not only upon mental images or models of these objects, but also upon words, symbols, or strings of symbols (like equations) that stand for objects, and for actions upon objects. He is able to state a set of hypotheses and to infer the consequences of each. Where once his physical actions transformed objects, now mental operations transform sets of symbols. Where once the child added balls to each pile, and confidently declared that the totals remained the same, now the child adds symbols to each side of an algebraic equation, secure in the knowledge that equivalence has been preserved. These symbol-manipulating capacities prove "of the essence" in higher branches of mathematics, with the symbols standing for objects, relations, functions, or other operations. The symbols to be manipulated may also be words, as in the case of syllogistic reasoning, scientific hypothesis formation, and other formal procedures.

While the performing of operations upon equations will be familiar to anyone who recalls school mathematics, the use of logical reasoning in the verbal sphere needs to be distinguished from the rhetorical language that we encountered earlier. One can, of course, make logical inferences that are consistent with common sense. The same rules of reasoning can be equally well applied, however, to apparently unrelated statements. Thus given the assertion, "If it is winter, my name is Frederick," and the fact, "It is winter," one can infer that one's name is indeed Frederick. But the procedure does not work in reverse. Knowledge that one's name is Frederick in no way justifies the inference that it is winter. That inference would be valid only if one had been given the assertion, "If my name is Frederick, it is winter." Such sets of phrases, which delight logicians almost as much as they infuriate the rest of us, serve as a reminder that operations of logic can be (and routinely are) carried out quite apart from common-sense applications of ordinary language. Indeed, only when the statements are treated like elements—or objects—to be manipulated (rather than as meaningful utterances to be pondered) will the correct inferences be drawn.

Note that, in these cases, the kinds of operation carried out earlier with objects themselves have now resurfaced with reference to symbols—numbers or words—that can substitute for the objects and events encountered in real life. Even a three-year-old can appreciate that if you pull lever A, event B will follow; but the parallel inference on the purely symbolic plane takes several years to evolve. Such "second-level" and "higher-level" operations become possible only during adolescence (and if luck and brain cells hold out, afterward as well). And they may sometimes attain such complexity that even otherwise highly competent individuals cannot follow all the processes of reasoning in the chain.

The sequence of development outlined here—Piaget's account of the passage from sensori-motor actions to concrete to formal operations—is the best worked-out trajectory of growth in all of developmental psychology. While many parts of it are susceptible to criticism, it remains the account of development against which all other formulations continue to be judged. I have traced its path with regard to a single topic—the understanding of number and of number-related operations; but to suggest that the sequence is limited to numerical understanding would be a gross error. Indeed, the state of affairs is precisely the opposite: according to Piaget this developmental sequence obtains in *all* domains of development, including those Kantian categories of special interest to him—time, space, and causality. Piaget's fundamental stages of development are like giant cognitive waves, which spontaneously spread their principal ways of knowing across all im-

133

portant domains of cognition. For Piaget, logical-mathematical thought is the glue that holds together all cognition.

My major bone of contention with Piaget has already been revealed in earlier chapters. In my view, Piaget has painted a brilliant portrait of development in one domain—that of logical-mathematical thought—but has erroneously assumed that it pertains to other areas, ranging from musical intelligence to the interpersonal domain. Much of this book is an effort to call attention to the divergent considerations relevant to an understanding of the developmental course in more remote domains of intellect. For present purposes, however, this particular quarrel with Piaget can be suspended: we are now confronting development in that domain where Piaget's work remains supremely germane.

Still, there are problems with the Piagetian perspective here as well. It has been well documented by now that development in the logical-mathematical domain is less regular, lock-step and stagelike than Piaget would have wished. Stages prove far more gradual and heterogeneous. Moreover, children show some signs of operational intelligence far earlier than Piaget had thought, while they fail to exhibit comprehensive formal-operational thought even at the very height of their intellectual powers. The Piagetian picture of higher operational thought also applies principally to the mainstream of Western middle-class development: it is less relevant to individuals drawn from traditional or nonliterate cultures and also explains little about original research or path-breaking scientific work.

What I wish to stress here is that Piaget did pose the right questions and achieve the crucial insights about the main factors involved in logical-mathematical development. He shrewdly discerned the origins of logical-mathematical intelligence in the child's actions upon the physical world; the crucial importance of the discovery of number; the gradual transition from physical manipulation of objects to interiorized transformations of actions; the significance of relations among actions themselves; and the special nature of higher tiers of development, where the individual begins to work with hypothetical statements and to explore the relationships and implications which obtain among those statements. To be sure, the realms of number, mathematics, logic, and science are not coextensive with one another, and, reflecting the views of many scholars, this chapter will treat differences in accent and coloration across these facets of logical-mathematical intellect. But that they do form a family of interrelated competences seems to me true: one of Piaget's enduring contributions is to have suggested some of the integrating links.

Other scholars in the areas of mathematics, logic, and science have also discerned and stressed the links between these domains of knowledge. The mathematician Brian Rotman indicates that "the whole of contemporary mathematics takes for granted and rests on the notion of counting . . . on the interpretation that occurs in the message 1, 2, 3." The great eighteenth-century mathematician Leonhard Euler underscored the importance of number as a basis for mathematical development:

The properties of the numbers known today have been mostly discovered by observation and discovered long before their truth has been confirmed by rigid demonstrations. . . . We should use such discovery as an opportunity to investigate more exactly the properties discovered and to prove or disprove them; in both cases we may learn something useful.

Willard Quine, perhaps the pre-eminent logician of the past half-century, indicates that logic is involved with statements, while mathematics deals with abstract, nonlinguistic entities, but that at its "higher reaches" logic leads by natural stages into mathematics. To be sure, numbers compose but a small part of mathematics at its highest levels: mathematicians are interested more in general concepts than in specific calculations, seeking in fact to formulate rules that can apply to the widest possible range of problems. But, as Whitehead and Russell sought to show, underlying even the most complex mathematical statements, one can find simple logical properties—the sorts of intuition that the child is beginning to display as his operational thinking unfolds.

As Russell himself observed, logic and mathematics have had different histories but, in modern times, have moved closer together: "The consequence is that it has now become wholly impossible to draw a line between the two: in fact the two are one. They differ as boy and man: logic is the youth of mathematics and mathematics is the manhood of logic."

Whatever the views of the experts in these particular disciplines, then, it seems legitimate from the psychological point of view to speak of a family of interlocking capacities. Beginning with observations and objects in the material world, the individual moves toward increasingly abstract formal systems, whose interconnections become matters of logic rather than of empirical observation. Whitehead put it succinctly, "So long as you are dealing with pure mathematics, you are in the realm of complete and absolute abstraction." Indeed, the mathematician ends up working within a world of invented objects and concepts which may have no direct parallel in every-day reality, even as the logician's primary interests fall on the relationships among statements rather than on the relation of those statements to the world of empirical fact. It is primarily the scientist who retains the direct tie to the world of practice:

he must come up with statements, models, and theories which, in addition to being logically consistent and susceptible to mathematical treatment, must also bear a justifiable and continuing relationship to facts which have been (and will be) discovered about the world. However, even these characterizations must be tempered. A scientific theory will often persist despite its inconsistency with certain empirical facts; and mathematical truths can themselves be altered, based upon new discoveries, in view of new demands placed on the characteristics of mathematical systems.

The Work of the Mathematician

While the products fashioned by individuals gifted in language and music are readily available to a wide public, the situation with mathematics is at the opposite extreme. Except for a few initiates, most of us can only admire from afar the ideas and works of mathematicians. Andrew Gleason, a leading contemporary mathematician, develops a telling figure of speech to portray this lamentable state of affairs:

It is notoriously difficult to convey a proper impression of the frontiers of mathematics to non-specialists. . . . Topology, the study of how space is organized, is like the great temples of some religions. That is to say, those uninitiated into its mysteries can view it only from the outside.

Michael Polanyi, eminent scientist and philosopher, confessed that he himself lacked the necessary intellectual equipment to master many contemporary aspects of mathematics which those within the tribe would consider (as mathematicians are fond of saying) relatively trivial. One can glimpse the kinds of demand made in mathematical thinking by noting the difficulties in decoding this English sentence:

We cannot prove the statement which is arrived at by substituting for the variable in the statement form, "we cannot prove the statement which is arrived at by substituting in the statement form the name of the statement form in question," the name of the statement form in question.

As Polanyi suggests, understanding this sentence may well require the setting up of a string of symbols and then carrying out a set of operations upon these symbols. Clearly, the comprehension of certain strings of the symbols of language requires more than simple competence in linguistic syntax and semantics (though, it may be properly pointed out, such competences are a prerequisite for "solving" a sentence of this sort).

In attempting to gain further insight into the thought processes of mathematicians, I (like many others) have found especially helpful the introspections of Henri Poincaré, one of the leading mathematicians in the world at the turn of the century. Poincaré raised the intriguing question why, if mathematics only involves the rules of logic, which are presumably accepted by all normal minds, anyone should have difficulty in understanding mathematics. To suggest an answer, he asks us to imagine a long series of syllogisms, where the conclusion of each one serves as the premise for the next. Because some time will elapse between the moment when we encounter a proposition at the conclusion of one syllogism, and the time when we re-encounter it as the premise in the next syllogism, it is possible that several links of the chain may have unrolled—or we may have forgotten the proposition or changed it in some unrecognized way.

If this ability to recall and use a proposition were the *sine qua non* of mathematical intelligence, then (Poincaré reasons) the mathematician would need to have a very sure memory or prodigious powers of attention. But many individuals skilled in math stand out neither for mnemonic nor for attentional powers, while a far larger group of individuals with keen memories or superb attentional span display little aptitude for mathematics. The reason the mathematician's memory does not fail him in a difficult piece of reasoning, Poincaré testifies, is because it is guided by reasoning:

> A mathematical demonstration is not simply a single juxtaposition of syllogisms, it is syllogisms placed in a certain order, and the order in which these elements are placed is much more important than the elements themselves. If I have the feeling, the intuition, so to speak, of this order, so as to perceive at a glance the reasoning as a whole, I need no longer fear lest I forget one of the elements, for each of them will take its allotted place in the array, and that without any effort of memory on my part.

Poincaré distinguishes, then, between two abilities. One is sheer memory for steps in a chain of reasoning, which might well suffice for the recall of certain proofs. The other ability—and, in his view, by far the more important one—is an appreciation of the nature of the links between the propositions. If these links have been appreciated, the exact identity of the steps in the proof becomes less important, because, if necessary, they can be reconstructed or even reinvented. We can observe this ability at work simply by trying to re-create Poincaré's own reasoning as just presented. If the drift of the argument has been grasped, its re-creation proves a relatively simple matter. If one has not grasped the reasoning, however, one is consigned to falling back on literal verbal memory, which, even if it rescues an individual on a given occasion, is unlikely to exhibit much staying power.

While the mental powers central to any field are spread out unequally within the population, there are few fields of endeavor where the extremes are so great, and the importance of generous initial endowment so patent. As Poincaré points out, the capacity to follow the chain of reasoning is not that elusive, but the ability to invent significant new mathematics is rare:

Anyone could make new combinations with mathematical entities . . . to create consists precisely in not making useless combinations and in making those which are useful, and which are only a small minority: invention is discernment, choice. . . . Among chosen combinations the most fertile will often be those formed of elements drawn from domains which are far apart.

According to Alfred Adler, a mathematician who has introspected tellingly upon the trials and the triumphs of his field,

Almost no one is capable of doing significant mathematics. There is no acceptably good mathematics. Each generation has its few great mathematicians and mathematics would not even notice the absence of the others. In mathematics, those with true genius are discovered virtually immediately and (in comparison with other disciplines) there is little energy wasted in jealousy, bitterness, or reservation, because the characteristics of the mathematically blessed are so evident.

What characterizes those with mathematical gifts? According to Adler, the powers of mathematicians rarely extend beyond the boundary of the discipline. Mathematicians are seldom talented in finance or the law. What characterizes the individual is a love of dealing with abstraction, "the exploration, under the pressure of powerful implosive forces, of difficult problems for whose validity and importance the explorer is eventually held accountable by reality." The mathematician must be absolutely rigorous and perennially skeptical: no fact can be accepted unless it has been proved rigorously by steps that are derived from universally accepted first principles. Mathematics allows great speculative freedom—one can create any kind of system that one wants; but in the end, every mathematical theory must be relevant to physical reality, either in a straightforward manner or by relevance to the main body of mathematics, which in turn has direct physical implications. What sustains and motivates the mathematician is the belief that he may be able to create a result that is entirely new, one that changes forever the way that others think about the mathematical order: "A great new mathematical edifice is a triumph that whispers of immortality." Adler's sentiments echo those of a renowned mathematician of an earlier generation, G. H. Hardy:

> It is undeniable that a gift for mathematics is one of the most specialized talents and that mathematicians as a class are not particularly distinguished for general ability or versatility. . . . If a man is in any sense a real mathematician, then it is a hundred to one that his mathematics will be far better than anything else he can do and . . . he would be silly if he surrendered any decent opportunity of exercising his one talent in order to do any undistinguished work in other fields.

Like a painter or a poet, a mathematician is a maker of patterns; but the special characteristics of mathematical patterns are that they are more likely to be permanent because they are made with ideas: "A mathematician has no materials to work with, and so his patterns are likely to last longer, since ideas erase less well than words do," comments Hardy.

Quite possibly, the most central and least replaceable feature of the mathematician's gift is the ability to handle skillfully long chains of reasoning. If a biologist were to study the locomotive processes of an amoeba and then try to apply his conclusions to successive levels of the animal kingdom, ending up with a theory of human walking, we might think him eccentric. Yet, as Andrew Gleason has pointed out, the mathematician regularly does just this sort of thing. He applies in very complicated contexts theories that were derived in very simple ones; and he generally expects that the results will be valid, not merely in outline, but in detail. Initially, this prosecution of an extended line of reasoning may be intuitive. Many mathematicians report that they sense a solution, or a direction, long before they have worked out each step in detail. Stanislaw Ulam, a contemporary mathematician, reports, "If one wants to do something original, it is no longer a case of syllogism chains. One is only occasionally aware of something in the brain which acts as a summarizer or totalizer of the process going on and that probably consists of many parts acting simultaneously." Poincaré speaks of mathematicians who "are guided by intuition and, at first

stroke, make quick, but sometimes precarious conquests, like bold cav-
alry men of the advance guard." But eventually, if the mathematics is
to convince others, it must be worked out in precise detail, with nary
an error in definition or in chain of reasoning; and this Apollonian
aspect is essential to the performance of the mathematician. In fact,
either errors of omission (forgetting a step) or of commission (making
some assumption that is unnecessary) can destroy the value of a mathematical contribution.

The launching of a field of study—of, if you will, a science of
mathematics—occurs when the findings of each generation build upon
those of the last. In earlier times, it was possible for an educated person
to follow mathematical thinking pretty much up to the contemporary
moment; but for at least a century, this has not been possible. (It is
notable that while the cultural domains that invoke different intelligences all continue to develop, few, if any, have evolved in so arcane a
way as has logical-mathematical thought). In fact, in a manner paralleling the individual developmental pattern I have sketched, mathematics
has become increasingly abstract with the years.

Alfred Adler traces this course. The first abstraction is the idea of
number itself, and the idea that different quantities can be distinguished
from one another on that basis. Every human culture has made this
step. Next comes the creation of *algebra*, where numbers are regarded as
a system, and one can introduce variables to take the place of particular
numbers. The variables, in turn, are simply specialized cases of the
more generalized dimension of mathematical *functions*, where one variable has a systematic relation to another variable. These functions need
not be restricted to real values, such as lengths or widths, but can
confer meaning upon other functions, upon functions of functions,
and upon even longer strings of reference as well.

In short, as Adler indicates, by abstracting and generalizing first
the concept of number, then the concept of the variable, and finally
that of the function, it is possible to arrive at an extremely abstract and
general level of thought. Naturally, with each further step in the ladder of abstraction, some individuals will find the sequence too difficult, too painful, or insufficiently rewarding and hence will "drop
out." It ought to be pointed out that there is also in mathematics a
powerful pull toward finding simpler expressions and for returning to
the fundamental notions of numbers. Therefore, there may be a place
in the discipline of mathematics for individuals who are not especially
gifted in following through these long chains of reasoning or these
increasingly abstract tiers of analysis.

To choose life as a mathematician would seem a difficult move. It is not surprising that mathematicians seem (to an outsider) to be chosen by their precocious skills in the numerical realms and by their singular passion for abstraction. The world of the mathematician is a world apart, and one must be ascetic to derive sustenance from it. The imperative to concentrate energies for many hours on seemingly intractable problems is the norm, and casual contacts with other individuals cannot be allowed to attain much importance. Language is also not much help. One is on one's own with pencil and paper and one's own mind. One must think very hard; and, thus, one often suffers severe strain, if not a breakdown. But mathematics can also provide protection against anxiety. As Stanislaw Ulam suggests, "A mathematician finds his own monastic niche and happiness in pursuits that are disconnected from external affairs. In their unhappiness over the world, mathematicians find a self-sufficiency in mathematics."

If the isolation is severe and the concentration demanding and painful, the rewards seem to be of high order indeed. Mathematicians who have introspected about their feelings upon solving a difficult problem regularly stress the exhilaration that accompanies the moment of breakthrough. Sometimes the intuition comes through first, and then one must actually make efforts to work through the details of the solution; at other times, the careful execution of the steps actually suggests the solution; less frequently, intuition and discipline arrive at the same time or work in concert. But whatever its mode, the solving of a difficult and important problem—and this is the only problem that mathematicians feel worthy of their energy (unless it be to demonstrate that a problem cannot in principle be solved)—provides a thrill of a very special sort.

But what excites mathematicians? One obvious source of delight attends the solution of a problem that has long been considered insoluble. Inventing a new field of mathematics, discovering an element in the foundation of mathematics, or finding links between otherwise alien fields of mathematics are certainly other rewards.

In fact, the ability not merely to discover an analogy, but to find an analogy between kinds of analogies, has been singled out as an especial mathematical delight. And it seems that dealing with elements that are counterintuitive provides yet another special kind of gratification for mathematicians. Roaming in the realm of imaginary numbers, irrational numbers, paradoxes, possible and impossible worlds having their own peculiar properties, yields yet other delicacies. It is possibly not an accident that one of the outstanding inventors of a world contrary to fact, Lewis Carroll, was also a first-rate logician and mathematician.

The tribe of mathematicians is sufficiently special (and sufficiently remote) that it is tempting to lump all its members together. However, within the discipline, individuals readily rate and contrast one another. Speed and power of abstraction provide an immediate means of ranking and, quite possibly, the one that matters above all else. It is paradoxical that, in mathematics, there is still no Nobel prize, because it is probably the single human intellectual endeavor in which consensus about distribution of talent is the greatest among its practitioners. But other dimensions as well are often invoked in discussions of mathematical skill. For instance, some mathematicians are much more given to the use and the valuing of intuition, while others extol only systematic proof.

Nowadays, mathematicians are fond of assessing the greatest mathematician of the previous generation—John von Neumann. In such evaluations, relevant criteria include the ability to size up an area and decide whether it harbors interesting problems, the courage to take on difficult and seemingly intractable problems, the ability to think extremely rapidly. In discussing von Neumann, whom he knew well, Ulam comments,

As a mathematician, von Neumann was quick, brilliant, efficient, and enormously broad in scientific interests beyond mathematics itself. He knew his technical abilities; his virtuosity in following complicated reasoning and his insights were supreme; yet he lacked absolute self-confidence. Perhaps he felt that he did not have the power to divine new truths intuitively at the highest level or the gift for a seemingly irrational perception of proofs or formulation of new theorems.... Perhaps it was because on a couple of occasions, he had been anticipated, preceded, or even surpassed by others.

In other words, von Neumann was the master of, but also a little bit the slave to, his own technical skill. Further insight into von Neumann's powers comes from a recollection of Jacob Bronowski, himself trained as a mathematician. Von Neumann was trying to explain a finding to Bronowski, who could not grasp the point:

Oh, no [said von Neumann], you are not seeing it. Your kind of visualizing mind is not right for seeing this. Think of it abstractly. What is happening on this photograph of an explosion is that the first differential coefficient vanishes identically and that is why what becomes visible is the trace of the second differential coefficient.

The engineer Julian Bigelow recalls:

Von Neumann was a fantastic craftsman of theory. . . . He could write a problem out the first time he heard it, with a very good notation to express the problem. . . . He was very careful that what he said and what he wrote down was really exactly what he meant.

According to the historian of mathematics, Steve Heims, this ability to write down a problem in proper notation indicates that, regardless of the content of a problem, von Neumann was immediately concerned with form. Thus he demonstrated a power of intuition denied to his colleagues, one of whom said, "Beyond anyone else, he could almost instantly understand what was involved and show how to prove the theorem in question or to replace it by what was the true theorem." Ulam compares himself to other mathematicians, including, it would seem, von Neumann when he says:

As for myself, I cannot claim that I know much of the technical material of mathematics. What I may have is the feeling for the gist, or maybe only the gist of the gist, in a number of its fields. It is possible to have this knack for guessing or feeling what is likely to be new or already known, or else not known, in some branch of mathematics, where one does not know the details. I think I have the ability to a degree and can often tell whether a theorem is known; i.e., already proved or is new conjecture.

Ulam adds an interesting aside on the relation between this skill and the musical faculty:

I can remember tunes and am able to whistle various melodies rather correctly. But when I try to invent or compose some new "catchy" tune, I find rather impotently that what I do is a trivial combination of what I have heard. This is in complete contrast to mathematics where I believe, with a mere touch, I can always propose something new.

It seems evident that mathematical talent requires the ability to discover a promising idea and then to draw out its implications. Ulam can accomplish this feat readily in mathematics but lacks the ability almost totally in the musical sphere. On the other hand, Arthur Rubinstein, one of our guides to the area of music, utters the opposite complaint: for him, mathematics is "impossible."

At the center of mathematical prowess lies the ability to recognize significant problems and then to solve them. As for what permits recognition of promising problems, mathematicians seem at a loss. The context of discovery remains a mystery, although (as in music) it is clear that some technically gifted individuals are immediately drawn to discovery and have a flair for it, while others of equal (or even greater)

143

technical competence lack this particular bent. In any event, a considerable literature has developed on methods of problem solving. Mathematicians have devised various heuristics which help individuals to solve problems, and informal training in mathematics often involves assimilating and passing on these techniques to the next generation. From students of mathematical problem solving, like George Polya, Herbert Simon, and Allen Newell, one picks up pointers. Mathematicians are advised to generalize—to proceed from the given set of objects in a problem to a larger set which contains the given one. Conversely, mathematicians are also advised to specialize, to pass from a given set of objects to a smaller set, itself contained in the given one; to ferret out analogies, thereby finding a problem or a situation that bears instructive similarities (and differences) from the one under consideration.

Other procedures are frequently mentioned. Faced with a problem too complex or unwieldy to solve, the mathematician is counseled to find a simpler problem within the larger one, to seek a solution to the simpler component, and then to build upon that solution. The student is also advised to propose a possible solution and to work backward to the problem; or to describe the characteristics that a solution should have and then, in turn, to try to attain each of them. Another popular method is indirect proof: one assumes the opposite of what one is trying to prove and ascertains the consequence of that assumption. More specific heuristics exist—and are drawn upon—within particular areas of mathematics. Clearly, since the most interesting problems are difficult to solve, the mathematician who can draw upon these heuristics appropriately and shrewdly is at a decided advantage. Perhaps the ability to learn and to deploy such heuristics—to supplement purely logical considerations with a sense of what might work—helps define the "zone of proximal development" in the aspiring mathematician.

Though many mathematicians highly value their intuition, these explicit methods of problem solving are their stock in trade—what they fall back upon when inspiration and intuition fail. But these heuristics are not exclusively the possession of the mathematician. Indeed, they prove equally useful to individuals involved in problem solving in other areas of life, and serve as one way of connecting the activities of that rare bird—the pure mathematician—to the pursuits of the others. In particular, they help illuminate the lot of the practicing scientist who must also pose and then solve problems in the most efficient and effective way.

The Practice of Science

Certainly, science and mathematics are closely allied. The progress—even the invention—of science has been linked to the status of mathematics during particular historical epochs, and practically every significant mathematical invention has eventually proved useful within the scientific community. To cite just a few examples, the Greek study of conic sections in 200 B.C. made possible Johannes Kepler's laws of planetary motion in 1609. More recently David Hilbert's theory of integral equations was needed for quantum mechanics, and Georg Friedrich Riemann's differential geometry proved basic for the theory of relativity. Indeed, the marked progress of Western science since the seventeenth century can be traced to a significant extent to the invention of differential and integral calculus. Chemistry and physics are concerned with explaining change—the evolution of physical systems—and not the description of steady states. Without the calculus, the process of dealing with such changes could be very difficult because one would have to calculate every tiny step of the process. But with the calculus, it is possible to determine how the change of one quantity relates to other quantities connected to it. It is thus fitting that Newton, one of the inventors of the calculus, had the opportunity to work out the motion of the planets.

The scientist needs mathematics because the body of brute fact is unwieldy: the orderly scheme of abstract relations which he can obtain from mathematics is a chief tool in making some order out of this chaos. Yet the core of the fields of science (for example, physics) and mathematics can be clearly distinguished. While the mathematician is interested in exploring abstract systems for their own sake, the scientist is motivated by a desire to explain physical reality. For him, mathematics is a tool—albeit an indispensable one—for building models and theories that can describe and, eventually, explain the operation of the world—be it the world of material objects (physics and chemistry), of living things (biology), of human beings (social or behavioral sciences), or of the human mind (cognitive science).

In Classical times, science was closely tied with philosophy (from which it took its questions) and with mathematics (whose methods were often devised in the course of attempting to resolve specific questions). With the passage of time, however, the enterprise of science has become increasingly independent, though it continues to cross-fertilize with philosophy and mathematics. Among the factors important in the

145

rise of science as a separate (and, nowadays, increasingly splintered) enterprise have been its dissociation from politics and theology; the increasing reliance on empirical observation, measurement, and crucial experiments designed to test one model or theory against another; and the rise of public (published) scientific reports where claims are written out and procedures detailed, so that other individuals have the opportunity to replicate studies, to criticize them, and to carry out their own further line of investigation in an effort to support, reformulate, or undermine the scientific dogma of their time.

As Piaget noted long ago, the evolution of science here displays certain intriguing parallels with the development in children of logical-mathematical thought. In both cases, we find simple experimentation with objects and the noting of their patterns of interaction and behavior to be the earliest (and most basic) procedure. The practice of making careful measurements, devising statements about the way in which the universe works, and then subjecting these statements to systematic confirmation does not occur until relatively late in the evolution of the individual and at a comparably tardy moment in the evolution of scientific thought.

We can observe as well a series of stages in the advent of modern science. First, early in the seventeenth century, Francis Bacon stressed the importance of systematic accumulation of facts. However, given his ignorance of mathematics and his failure to pose pregnant questions, Bacon's contribution remained more programmatic than substantive. Shortly afterward, Galileo championed the introduction of mathematics into scientific work. He argued against the simple recording of colors, tastes, sounds, and smells and pointed out that these elements would not even exist were it not for the particular sense organs with which individuals happen to be endowed. Yet even Galileo's introduction of structured techniques of measurement into the scientist's arsenal did not suffice to usher in the modern era. To do so was left to Isaac Newton, an incomparable thinker who, in explicit formal operational style, made a comprehensive survey of physical findings and, applying both analysis and synthesis, fitted together the various pieces into a coherent pattern. As the historian of science Herbert Butterfield put it, "One youth who made a comprehensive survey of the field and possessed great elasticity of mind, could place the pieces into the proper pattern with the help of a few intuitions." In a manner that cannot fail to please Piagetians, Newton postulated an absolute framework of time and space, within which physical events unfold according to a set of immutable laws.

Though scientific and mathematical talent may reside in the same individual (for example, in Newton), the motives behind scientists' passions do not much resemble those we encountered in the lives of mathematicians. What seemed, more than anything else, to impel Newton the scientist was desire to find the secrets or *the* secret of nature. Newton himself knew it was too difficult to explain all of nature, but he did share the notion of being an explorer:

I do not know what I may appear to the world; but to myself I seem to have been only like a boy playing on the sea shore and diverting himself and then finding a smoother pebble or a prettier shell than ordinary, while the greater ocean of truth lay all undiscovered before me.

Bronowski comments on the pleasure attending a discovery by the scientist:

When the figures come out right like that, you know as Pythagoras did that a secret of Nature is open in the palm of your hand. A universal law governs the majestic clockwork of the heavens, in which the motion of the moon is one harmonious incident. It is a key that you have put into the lock and turned and nature has yielded in numbers the confirmation of her structure.

The desire to explain nature, rather than to create a consistent abstract world, engenders an instructive tension between pure scientists and pure mathematicians. The mathematician may peer down his nose at scientists for being practical, applied, insufficiently interested in the pursuit of ideas for their own sake. The scientist, in turn, may feel that the mathematician is out of touch with reality and tends to pursue ideas forever even when (or perhaps even especially when) they do not lead anywhere and may not be of practical consequence. These "ideal/real" prejudices aside, the talents rewarded by the two fields also seem different. For the mathematician, it is most important that one recognize patterns wherever they may exist, that one be able to carry out the implications of one's train of thinking wherever they may lead. For the scientist, a healthy planting of one's feet on the ground and perpetual concern with the implication of one's ideas for the physical universe is a needed and useful feature which goes beyond the mathematician's burden. As Einstein, who considered both careers put it, "Truth in physical matters can of course never be founded on mathematical and logical considerations alone." And he reminisced illuminatingly on his own career decision:

The fact that I neglected mathematics to a certain extent had its cause, not merely in my stronger interest in science than in mathematics, but also in the following strange experience. I saw that mathematics was split up into numerous specialties, each of which could easily absorb the short lifetime granted to us. This was obviously due to the fact that my intuition was not strong enough in the field of mathematics . . . In [physics], however, I soon learned to scent out that which was able to lead to fundamentals and to turn aside from everything else, from the multitude of things that clutter up the mind and divert it from the essential.

Just what is the nature of the intuitions that characterize outstanding scientists, ones of the caliber of a Newton and an Einstein? Beginning with an absorbing interest in the objects of the world and how they operate, these individuals eventually enter into a search for a limited set of rules or principles which can help to explain the behavior of objects. The greatest progress is made when disparate elements are linked and a few simple rules can explain observed interactions. Conceding that this ability differs from the analogizing powers of the pure mathematician, Ulam confesses that it is difficult for the mathematician to understand what it means to have an intuition for the behavior of physical phenomena: he suggests, in fact, that few mathematicians actually have this intuition. Werner Heisenberg, himself a Nobel laureate in physics at the age of thirty-two, recalls the physical intuitions of his mentor Niels Bohr, and how they often overran what the latter could prove:

Bohr must surely know that he starts from contradictory assumptions which cannot be correct in their present form. But he has an unerring instinct for using these very assumptions to construct fairly convincing models of atomic processes. Bohr uses classical mechanics or quantum theory that way just as a painter uses his brush and colors. Brushes do not determine the picture, and color is never the full reality, but if he keeps the picture before his mind's eye, the artist can use his brush to convey, however inadequately, his own mental picture to others. Bohr knows precisely how atoms behave during light emission, in chemical processes and in many other phenomena, and this has helped him to form an intuitive picture of the structure of different atoms: it is not at all certain that Bohr himself believes that electrons revolve inside the atom. But he is convinced of the correctness of his picture. The fact that he cannot yet express it by adequate linguistic or mathematical techniques is no disaster. On the contrary, it is a great challenge.

Such faith in the power of one's own intuitions concerning the ultimate nature of physical reality recurs over and over again in the introspections of the physicists. In speaking to Einstein, Heisenberg once said:

I believe, just like you, that the simplicity of natural laws has an objective character, that it is not just the result of thought economy. If nature leads us to mathematical forms of great simplicity and beauty—by forms, I am referring to coherent systems of hypotheses, actions, etc.—to forms that no one has previously encountered, we cannot help think that they are "true," that they reveal a genuine feature of nature. . . . But the mere fact that we could never have arrived at these forms by ourselves, that they were revealed to us by nature, suggests strongly that they must be part of reality itself, not just our thoughts about reality. . . . I am strongly attracted by the simplicity and beauty of the mathematical schemes with which nature presents us. You must have felt this too: the almost frightening simplicity and wholeness of the relationships which nature suddenly spreads out before us and for which none of us was in the least prepared.

It is left to the greatest scientists to pose questions that no one has posed before, and then to arrive at an answer that changes for all time the way in which scientists (and eventually laymen) construe the universe. Einstein's genius lay in his persistent questioning of the absoluteness of time and space. Already as a teenager, Einstein pondered what our experience would be like if we ourselves were operating from the point of view of light, or, to put it more concretely, if we rode on a beam of light. Suppose, he asked, that we were looking at a clock, but were flying away from it at the speed of light. The time on the clock would then be frozen because a new hour could never travel fast enough to catch up with us; on the beam of light, the time of that clock would remain perpetually the same.

Einstein came to think that, as one approximated the speed of light, one became increasingly isolated in his box of time and space and departed increasingly from the norms around him. No longer was there such a thing as universal time: indeed, the experience of time would now become different for the traveler on the beam from what it was for the individual remaining at home. However, one's experiences on the beam of light *are* consistent with each other: the same relations among time, distance, speed, mass, and force that Newton had described continue to obtain on that beam; and they continue to obtain with a similar consistency in the region of the clock. It is just that the actual values produced for time, distance, and the like are no longer identical for both the beam traveler and the individual who has remained in the vicinity of the clock.

To follow through this line of thinking, to reconcile it with findings of the past (like the Michelson-Morley experiment which challenged the existence of the medium of ether) and with hypothetical future experiments, and then to write out the mathematics needed to create a theory of relativity, took Einstein years and constitutes part of

149

the history of our times. What should be remarked upon here is that his scientific originality lay in the boldness of conceiving the problem, in the persistence in carrying it through, with all of its mystifying and unsettling implications, and in the subtlety to appreciate its connection to the most basic questions about the nature and structure of the universe. Einstein required courage to execute this line of thinking on his own for years, despite the fact that it flouted conventional wisdom, and to believe that his resulting description might be truly more simplifying, edifying, and comprehensive (hence more "true") than Newton's universally accepted synthesis of two centuries before.

As the physicist Gerald Holton has persuasively argued, such a program requires more than just technical facility, mathematical acuity, and keen observational powers—though each of these is probably a prerequisite. Scientists are also guided by underlying themes of themata—beliefs about how the universe must work, and basic convictions about how these principles are best revealed. In Einstein's case, the very belief that there will be a few simple laws, that they will unify diverse phenomena, and that there will be no element of chance or indeterminacy in these laws, are part and parcel of his professional code: Einstein is said to have remarked, "God wouldn't have passed up the opportunity to make Nature this simple." Themata such as these may at times be more central to discussion than the objective facts and figures that are the scientist's normal stock in trade. As Holton puts it, "The awareness of themata which are sometimes held with obstinate loyalty help one to explain the character of the discussion between antagonists far better than do scientific content and social surroundings alone."

The discussion of themes situated at the core of a scientist's system brings to the fore a puzzling but central aspect of scientific practice. Even though the scientist's self-image nowadays highlights rigor, systematicity, and objectivity, it seems that, in the final analysis, science itself is virtually a religion, a set of beliefs that scientists embrace with a zealot's conviction. Scientists not only believe in their methods and themes from the depth of their being, but many are also convinced it is their mission to use these tools to explain as much of reality as falls within their power. This conviction is perhaps one of the reasons that the great scientists have typically been concerned with the most cosmic questions, and that, particularly in the latter years of life, they are often given to making pronouncements about philosophical issues, such as the nature of reality or the meaning of life. Even Newton, it has recently been documented, devoted much of his lengthy life to a consideration of diverse aspects of mysticism, metaphysics, and cosmology and put forth many views that would strike us today as medieval, if not wholly bizarre. Underlying this interest, it seems to me, is much the same desire to explain the world which comes through in a more constrained and disciplined fashion in physics. Commentator Frank Manuel has expressed it this way:

> Newton's statement of fundamental religious principles, his interpretation of prophecy, his textual criticism of the historical words of Scripture, his system of world chronology, his cosmological theories, and his Euhemeristic reduction of pagan mythology all bespeak the same mentality and style of thought. As Nature was consonant with itself, so was Isaac Newton's mind. At the height of his powers there was in him a compelling desire to find order and design in what appeared to be chaos, to distill from a vast inchoate mass of materials a few basic principles that would embrace the whole and define the relationships of its component parts. . . . In whatever direction he turned, he was searching for a unifying structure.

Here, certainly, we see divergence from the concerns of most mathematicians, who would just as soon turn their backs on reality as try to encompass, within their equations and theorems all of its complexity and messiness. And this passion for the single unifying explanation may demark a line between the physical sciences and other disciplines as well. While individuals in other sciences are certainly drawn to explanations of their reality—be it biological, social, or cognitive—they are less likely to search for the overall explanations of the essence of life. And others of a strong logical-mathematical ability—for example, chess players—are also unlikely to devote much energy to a search for the secret of the world's powers. Perhaps—though just perhaps—the desire to solve the principal philosophical puzzles of existence is a special feature of the childhood of the young physical scientist.

As a child of four or five, Albert Einstein received a magnetic compass. He was awed by the needle, isolated and unreachable, yet seemingly caught in the grip of an invisible urge that attracted it toward the north. The needle came as a revelation, for it challenged the child's tentative belief in an orderly physical world: "I can still remember—or at least I believe I remember—that this experience made a deep and abiding impression on me." It is risky to make too much of a single childhood memory; and Einstein, ever careful with his thoughts and words, encircles his own uncertainty by the telltale phrase, "I believe I remember." Yet is is instructive to compare Einstein's recollections of a pivotal early experience with those of other individuals in the logical-mathematical field.

An example: our mathematical guide Stanislaw Ulam recalls that, as a young child, he was fascinated by the intricate patterns in an Oriental rug. The resulting visual picture seemed to produce a "melody" with relations among the various parts resonating with one another. Ulam speculates that such patterns feature a kind of inherent mathematical regularity and power to which certain young individuals are particularly sensitive. And such sensitivity may rely in large measure on a kind of keen memory which enables the child to compare a presently perceived pattern—be it primarily visual or merely ordered—with others "operated upon" in the past. As an aside, I might mention that in our observations of young children, my colleagues and I have identified a group of youngsters who are especially attracted to, if not fixated upon, repetitive patterns. Then unaware of Ulam, we nicknamed these children "patterners" and contrasted them with another group, presumably more linguistically oriented, whom we termed "dramatists." Of course, we do not yet know whether children dubbed patterners in their youth are more "at risk" to become mathematicians.

And other childhood attractions for those in the logical-mathematical field? As a youth, Pascal was avid to learn about mathematics but was kept from doing so by his father, who, in fact, forbade him to speak about mathematics.

Pascal, however, began to dream [about] the subject and . . . he used to mark with charcoal the walls of his playroom, seeking a means of making a circle perfectly round and a triangle whose sides and angles were all equal. He discovered these things for himself and then began to seek the relationship which existed between them. He did not know any mathematical terms and so he made up his own. . . . Using these names he made axioms and finally developed perfect demonstrations . . . until he had come to the thirty-second proposition of Euclid.

Bertrand Russell recalls:

I began Euclid, with my brother as my tutor, at the age of eleven. It was one of the great events of my life, as dazzling as first love. I had not imagined that there was anything as delicious in the world. . . . From that moment until . . . I was thirty-eight, it was my chief interest and my chief source of happiness. . . . [mathematics] is not human and has nothing particular to do with this planet or with the whole accidental universe—because like Spinoza's God, it won't love us in return.

Ulam offers one possible account of the course of such passions. At first a young child undergoes some satisfying experiences with numbers; then he experiments further and builds up his store (and memory) of experiences in the numerical and symbolic domains. Eventually the child proceeds beyond his own idiosyncratic (though sometimes universally shared) explorations—his natural mathematical curiosity—to an acquaintance with problems that have in the past challenged mathematicians. If he is to achieve much, he must then spend hours each day thinking about these issues. For the bald fact is that, in mathematics more so than in any other intellectual domain, the years of the third and the fourth decades of life are crucial. The ability to store and manipulate within one's mind during a finite period of time all the variables necessary to make progress on important mathematical problems is one that, for one or another (presumably neurological) reason, proves especially vulnerable to age, even as young an age as thirty or forty. It is a difficult and often tormenting assignment.

Still another childhood journey surrounds the contemporary American philosopher and logician Saul Kripke, reputed to be the most brilliant philosopher of his generation. At age three, young Saul went to see his mother in the kitchen and asked her if God were truly everywhere. Receiving an affirmative answer, he then asked whether he had squeezed part of God out of the kitchen by coming in and taking out some of the space. Befitting a mathematical prodigy, Kripke went forth quickly on his own and had reached the level of algebra by the time he was in fourth grade. For instance, he discovered that, in multiplying the sum of two numbers by the difference between them, he got the same answer as he did when he subtracted the square of the smaller one from the square of the larger number. Once he realized that this pattern applied to any set of numbers, he had arrived at the core of algebra. Kripke once mentioned to his mother that he would have himself invented algebra if it had not already been invented, because he came upon its insights so naturally. This ability to devise areas of study may be common among prodigious young mathematicians. The great Descartes said, "As a young man, when I heard about ingenious inventions, I tried to invent them by myself, even without reading the author."

Such biographical notes confirm that talent in the logical-mathematical sphere announces itself very early. Initially, the individual can proceed rapidly on his own, as it were, almost apart from experience. Perhaps individuals with this general talent might, by an accident of history, be directed randomly to mathematics, logic, or physics. My own guess is that careful study might uncover different "telltale" early experiences in individuals: the physicists may be especially intrigued by physical objects and their operations: the mathematician may be immersed in patterns *per se*: the philosopher will be intrigued by paradoxes, by questions about ultimate reality, and by the relationships among propositions. Of course, whether this affinity is in itself accidental, or whether each individual gravitates toward those objects or elements for which he has certain proclivities, is a riddle I had better leave to someone of a more decidedly logical-mathematical bent.

Whatever the precocity of the young logician-mathematician, it is crucial that he advance quickly in his field. As we have seen, the best years for productivity in these fields are before the age of forty, maybe even before the age of thirty; and while solid work can be conducted after that time, it seems relatively rare. G. H. Hardy says, "I write about mathematics because, like any other mathematician who has passed sixty, I have no longer the freshness of mind, the energy, or the patience to carry on effectively with my proper job." I. I. Rabi, Nobel laureate physicist, observes that younger individuals carry the baton in his field because they have vast physical energy. Queried about what age physicists tend to run down, he says:

> It very much depends on the individual. . . . I've seen people run down at thirty, at forty, at fifty. I think it must be basically neurological or physiological. The mind ceases to operate with the same richness and association. The information retrieval part sort of goes, along with the interconnections. I know that when I was in my late teens and early twenties the world was just a Roman candle—rockets all the time. . . . You lose that sort of thing as time goes on. . . . physics is an otherworld thing, it requires a taste for things unseen, even unheard of—a high degree of abstraction. . . . These faculties die off somehow when you grow up. . . . Profound curiosity happens when children are young. I think physicists are the Peter Pans of the human race. . . . Once you are sophisticated, you know too much—far too much. [Wolfgang] Pauli once said to me, "I know a great deal. I know too much. I am a quantum ancient."

In mathematics, the situation may be even more severe. Alfred Adler says that the major work of most mathematicians is over by the age of twenty-five or thirty. If little has been accomplished by that time, little is likely to be accomplished in the future. Productivity drops off with each decade, and what is known with difficulty by the teacher is picked up easily, sometimes even effortlessly, by the students. This leads to a kind of poignant technological unemployment, where even the greatest mathematicians are doomed, like young swimmers or runners, to spending most of their self-conscious lives burdened with the knowledge that they have passed their primes. This situation contrasts with that found in many humanistic areas of scholarship, where major works typically appear during the fifth, the sixth, or the seventh decades of life.

154

Mathematical Talent in Isolation

As we have seen, the ability to calculate rapidly is at best an accidental advantage for mathematicians: certainly it is far from central to their talent, which must be of a more general and abstract variety. There are, however, selected individuals who have an ability to calculate enormously well, and one can see in them a portion of logical-mathematical ability operating in relatively autonomous form.

Probably the chief examples of this profile are *idiots savants*, individuals who, with meager or even retarded abilities in most areas, display from early childhood an ability to calculate very rapidly and very accurately. The human calculator has learned a set of tricks: he can add large numbers in his head, commit to memory long sequences of numbers, perhaps state the day of the week for any randomly chosen date in the last three centuries. It must be stressed that these individuals typically are not interested in discovering new problems, or in solving venerable old ones, or even in observing how other people have solved them. *Idiots savants* do not seek to use mathematics to help them in other areas of daily life or to tackle scientific puzzles: instead, they have mastered a series of maneuvers that enable them to stand out—like freaks. There are exceptions—the mathematician Karl Friedrich Gauss and the astronomer Truman Safford were outstanding calculators; but, in general, this talent is most salient in otherwise unremarkable persons.

In most cases, the *idiot savant* appears to have a genuine calculating ability, one that sets him apart from an early age. For example, an institutionalized child named Obadiah taught himself at the age of six to add, subtract, multiply, and divide. George, a calendar calculator, was discovered poring over the perpetual calendar in an almanac at age six and, almost from the beginning, proved completely accurate in his calendar calculation. L., an eleven-year-old who was studied by the neurologist Kurt Goldstein, was able to remember virtually endless series, such as railroad timetables and newspaper financial columns. From an early age, this youngster had delighted in counting objects and had shown remarkable interest in all aspects of numbers and of musical sounds. In other cases, however, there seems to have been no great skill or promise to begin with: rather, being relatively more skilled at this particular pursuit than at others, an otherwise hapless individual invested considerable energy in achieving one particular island of superiority over other individuals. Should this speculation be valid, it might be possible to take individuals with otherwise crippling deficits and train them to achieve such mathematical facility. My own guess, however, is that early arithmetical or calendrical prodigiousness is based upon the relative sparing or proliferation of certain brain areas; like hyperlexia, it represents an automatic, impossible-to-stop process, rather than one that comes about because of excessive application in a casually chosen domain of potential expertise.

Even as certain individuals appear blessed with at least one core component of logical-mathematical aptitude, those of otherwise normal abilities show selective weakness in the numerical realm. Some of these may well have a selective numerical difficulty, akin to the difficulties exhibited by many children with written language (dyslexics) and by a far smaller number, with spoken language (dysphasics).

The most intriguing manifestation of this disability occurs in individuals diagnosed as having the developmental Gerstmann syndrome. Patterned after an adult syndrome of the same name, youngsters with this condition exhibit isolated impairment in learning arithmetic, along with difficulties in recognizing and identifying fingers and in distinguishing their left from right. Though there may be selective problems in writing or spelling, language is normal in these children: this is how we know they are not generally retarded. Neurologists have speculated that these individuals have a deficiency in those regions—the association cortexes in the posterior areas of the dominant hemisphere—that are involved in recognizing ordered arrays and patterns in the visual sphere. According to the prevailing analysis, such selective difficulty with order (especially of a visual-spatial sort) can at one swoop bring about problems in finger recognition, left-right orientation, and numerical calculation. The fact that most children begin their numerical calculations by using fingers confers an especially intriguing flavor upon this exotic syndrome.

There may be other children who also exhibit selective difficulties in logical-mathematical thinking. In those cases where the problem is not simply (or complexly) motivational, the difficulty may inhere in understanding principles of causality or strings of logical implication, which become vital in mathematics, once one has passed the stage of simple counting and elementary calculation. As the educator John Holt has questioned, somewhat plaintively, "What must it be like to have so little idea of the way the world works, so little feeling for the regularity, the orderliness, the sensibleness of things?" Stranded at the opposite end of the continuum from the future physicists, such youngsters not only have no desire to find out the secrets of the world's orderliness, but may not even detect such order as does manifestly exist (for others).

In comparison with language, and even with music, we know little about the evolutionary antecedents of numerical ability and a comparatively minimal amount about its organization in the brain of the normal human adult of today. There are certainly, in other animals, precursors of numerical ability: these include the abilities of birds to recognize arrays of up to six or seven objects reliably; the instinctive ability of bees to calculate distances and directions by observing the dance of their conspecifics; the capacity of primates to master small numbers and also to make simple estimates of probability. Calendars and other notational systems go back at least thirty thousand years, well before the existence of written language: the former way of ordering one's life was certainly available to individuals during the later Stone Age. Our ancestors must have possessed the principal insight of number as an endless sequence, where one could continually add one to make a larger unit; thus, they were not restricted to the small set of perceptibly accessible numbers that seems to be the limit for infrahuman organisms.

As for the organization of numerical abilities in the brain, there are clearly individuals who lose the ability to calculate while remaining linguistically intact, as well as a far larger set of cases of individuals who are aphasic but can still make change, play games requiring calculation, and manage their financial affairs. As was the case with language and music, language and calculation, at even the most elementary level, prove to be quite separate. Moreover, as evidence accumulates, we are finding (shades of music once again!) that important aspects of numerical ability are normally represented in the right hemisphere. Most observers agree that there can be a breakdown of separate arithmetical abilities: comprehending numerical symbols; appreciating the meaning of signs referring to numerical operations; understanding the underlying quantities and operations themselves (apart from the symbols that designate them). The ability to read and produce the signs of mathematics is more often a left hemisphere function, while the understanding of numerical relations and concepts seems to entail right hemisphere involvement. Elementary difficulties in language can impair the understanding of number terms, even as impairments in spatial orientation can render inoperative the ability to use paper and pencil to carry out sums or geometrical demonstrations. Deficits in planning, secondary to frontal lobe lesions, prove crippling in dealing with problems that have many steps.

Despite this variety, there is a fragile consensus that a certain area of the brain—the left parietal lobes, and the temporal and occipital association areas contiguous to them—may assume a particular importance in matters of logic and math. It is from lesions in this area of the angular gyrus that one gets the original adult version of the Gerstmann syndrome—a condition in which calculation, drawing, left-right orientation, and finger knowledge are supposed to break down in relative isolation of other cognitive faculties. A. R. Luria adds that lesions in this area may also reduce the ability to orient oneself in space and to understand certain grammatical structures, such as prepositional phrases and passive constructions.

I deliberately employ the phrase "fragile consensus." In my own view, firm evidence has yet to be established that this area of the brain plays the crucial role in logical-mathematical thought. Regions in the parietal area may be important in many individuals: but an equally persuasive case can be made that, in other individuals or with respect to other operations, structures in the frontal lobes or elsewhere in the right hemisphere can compromise key logical-mathematical functions.

I wish to propose a different account of the neurological organization underlying logical-mathematical operations. In my view, certain neural centers may well be important for specific logical-mathematical operations, such as the ones I have cited. But these centers do not seem as indispensable for logic and mathematical thought as certain areas in the temporal and the frontal lobes appear to be in language or music. There is, in other words, considerably more flexibility in the human brain in the way that such operations and logical implications can be carried out.

A solution lies, I think, in the work of Piaget. The ability to carry out logical-mathematical operations commences in the most general actions of infancy, develops gradually over the first decade or two of life, and involves a number of neural centers that work in concert. Despite focal damage, it is usually the case that these operations can nonetheless be carried out—because the operations inhere not in a given center but in a generalized and highly redundant form of neural organization. Logical-mathematical abilities become fragile not principally from focal brain disease but, rather, as a result of more general deteriorating diseases, such as the dementias, where large portions of the nervous system decompose more or less rapidly. I think that the operations studied by Piaget do not exhibit the same degree of neural localization as those that we have examined in other chapters, and that they therefore prove relatively more fragile in the case of general breakdowns of the nervous system. In fact, two recent electrophysiological studies document considerable involvement of both hemi-spheres during the solution of mathematical problems. As one author puts it, "Each task produces a complex, rapidly changing pattern of electrical activity in many areas in front and back of both sides of the brain." In contrast, abilities like language and music remain relatively robust in the case of general breakdowns, provided that certain focal areas have not themselves been especially singled out for destruction.

In sum, there is a rationale to the neural organization of logical-mathematical abilities, but it is a far more general kind of representa-tion than we have hitherto encountered. Wielding Ockham's razor, one could conclude that logical-mathematical ability is not as "pure" or "autonomous" a system as others reviewed here, and perhaps should count not as a single intelligence but as some kind of supra- or more general intelligence. I have at times felt sympathy for this argument and do not want, in these pages, to come off as more definitive than I actually feel. However, in my view, the fact that one can encounter specific and particular breakdowns of logical-mathematical ability, as well as many kinds of extreme precocity, makes the elimination of logical-mathematical intellect far too extreme a scientific maneuver. After all, most of the signs of an "autonomous intelligence" register positively in the case of logical-mathematical thought. Moreover, it is also possible that logical-mathematical competence may simply involve the concatenation of a number of essential, but somewhat redundant systems. Were these to be destroyed discretely and simultaneously (an event that could come about only through impermissible experimental intervention), one would then encounter syndromes focused to the same degree as those in the linguistic and musical realms.

Logic and Mathematics across Cultures

That the concerns of this chapter are not parochial to the West is amply documented by the many systems of number and calculation which have evolved in different corners of the world. From the counting in terms of body parts found among Papuan New Guineans to the use of cowrie shells for market transactions in Africa, we see ample evidence of the agility of the human mind in wedding our natural proclivities to order and count to the carrying out of functions considered important in diverse cultural settings.

Throughout the history of Western anthropology, there has been a running debate between those scholars who discern an essential continuity between Western and other forms of thought, and those who emphasize the "primitiveness" or savagery of the non-Western mind. This controversy shows no signs of abating soon, though claims that the mind of the "savage" is radically different from our own are not made nearly so readily these days as they were some decades ago.

Since mathematics and science are among the proudest achievements of Western society, it is not surprising that the initial claims for "superiority" came in these areas. Considerable energy was invested in determining whether primitive individuals do (or do not) have the same logics that we have; can (or cannot) calculate accurately; have (or lack) a system of explanation which allows experimentation and disproof; and other such conundrums. In general, when Western social scientists imported their methods of testing and searched, in alien lands, for their own modes of thinking, they found little evidence for them. And so, for example, initial transportation of Piagetian tasks to exotic societies revealed that few individuals scored beyond concrete operations; sometimes even the ability to appreciate conservation failed to be exhibited. Conversely, when evidence was accrued about thinking within the culture itself, particularly in tasks that mattered to the inhabitants, alleged differences between primitive and domesticated minds were lessened and, indeed, sometimes the "primitives" came off as superior to the investigators.

One way to enter into this controversy (without being overwhelmed by it) is to think of non-Western societies in terms of the various scholarly roles I have described. When one searches in other traditional cultures for explicit evidence of the mathematician or the scientist, as we know him, there emerges little evidence that such concerns matter. A desire to build up an elaborate abstract system of mathematical relations for its own sake, or to come up with experiments to test a set of propositions about how the world works, does seem to be a concern of the Western world—commencing in Greek times but really launched with a vengeance in the Renaissance (and now spreading rapidly to every corner of the globe). Analogously, the accumulation of vast written records and debates on these topics seems a Western invention of the past few centuries.

When one shifts the focus, however, and seeks the basic operations of mind on which sciences are based, one finds little reason to doubt the basic universality of logical-mathematical thought. To be specific: where there is a market economy, individuals are perfectly capable of bargaining in their own self-interest, in removing items from sale when they will not fetch a good price, and in making trades that are equitable or advantageous. Where it is important to be able to classify objects—be it for botanical or for social reasons—individuals are capable of coming up with elaborate and hierarchically organized systems and of utilizing them appropriately. Where it is desirable to have a calendar that allows one to perform actions on a regular basis, or a mode of calculation that is rapid and reliable (abacus), societies have contrived solutions that are at least as adequate as ours. And while their scientific theories are not propounded in the patois of the West, bushmen of the Kalahari use the same kinds of methods to make needed discoveries. For example, in hunting, they differentiate among those times when they have seen prey with their own eyes; when they have seen the tracks but not the animals themselves; when they have heard of the animals from others; or when one must remain uncertain because one has neither seen them oneself nor talked directly to individuals who have seen them. As Nicholas Blurton-Jones and Melvin Konner conclude in their study of Bushmen hunting:

> The resulting body of knowledge was detailed, wide-ranging, and accurate ... the processes of tracking, specifically, involves patterns of inference, hypothesis-testing and discovery that tax the best inferential and analytical capacities of the human mind. Determining, from tracks, the movements of animals, their timing, whether they are wounded and if so, how, and predicting how far they will go and in which direction and how fast all involved repeated activation of hypotheses, trying them out against new data, integrating them with previous known facts about animal movements, rejecting the ones that do not stand up and finally getting a reasonable fit.

To suggest the ways in which logical-mathematical intelligence has been enculturated, it may be useful to characterize some of the arithmetical systems of pre-literate groups. In many societies, individuals are able to come up with a reasonable estimate of the number of objects, individuals, or organisms in a field—in fact, estimation ability may be astonishingly powerful. Gay and Cole found that Kpelle adults in Liberia succeeded much better than American adults at estimating the number of stones in piles ranging from ten to one hundred stones. In comparison with the algorithms used in the West, systems based on estimating have the advantage that an individual will almost never be wildly off in a calculation. Using our algorithms for calculation, we are more likely to be completely accurate, but also far more likely to come up with a total that is widely off—if, for example, we misalign the columns in a sum or press the wrong buttons on a hand-held calculator.

161

If, in fact, one is looking for instances of highly developed numerical ability in Africa, the best place to look is in a game such as *kala* (also called *malang* or *Oh-War-ree*), a pit and pebbles game considered "the most arithmetical game with a mass following anywhere in the world." The basic idea of this intricate game is to drop seeds *seriatim* in holes around a board and to capture one's opponent's seeds by placing the final seed in one's hand in an opponent's hole that harbors one or two seeds. Observing individuals at play in this game, Cole and his colleagues found that winners used clear and consistent sets of strategies:

> The winning player makes sure he has solid defenses, that he catalogues the possibilities of every move, that he reserves time to himself, that he lures the opponent into making premature captures, that he moves for decisive rather than piecemeal victories, and that he is flexible in redistributing his forces in preparation for new assaults.

Inasmuch as games can last three hundred or more moves, the skilled Kpelle player must wield these strategies with considerable finesse. And indeed excellent players bring honor to their family and may even be commemorated in song.

Some uses of numerical abilities are straightforward, as, for example, in trade or in keeping track of possessions. One also finds, however, mathematical thinking intertwined with religious and mystical pursuits. Among the Jewish people, insights into numerical properties were closely tied to interpretation and, at times, to prophecy. In the Spanish Inquisition, one could receive life imprisonment or even a death sentence if one possessed Arab manuscripts dealing with mathematics: "Mathematicians were denounced as the greatest of all heretics." Medieval Islamic and Christian scholars believed that magic squares (arrays in which all the rows and columns sum to the same total) could ward off the plague or cure sterility; and in many parts of Africa, there is a taboo on counting humans, domestic animals, or valuable possessions. The interrelation between numerical and other symbol systems has also been central to activities of various sects. Medieval Indians substituted evocative words for numbers (moon for one, eyes or arms for two) and wrote their mathematical and astronomical treatises in verse. Even today, the manipulation of elaborate systems in which words and numbers stand for one another, and secret messages can be conveyed through strings of numbers, is a skill cultivated by Islamic scholars.

When it comes to a sensitivity to numerical properties, then, both pre-literate and traditional literate societies recognize these skills as being important. The numerical core of mathematical intelligence seems to be honored universally. Still, a seemingly strong challenge to the rationality of the primitive mind is the evident embracing by individuals of positions that logically are inconsistent with one another, positions that invoke the supernatural as well as the occult. How can individuals who would propose to be rational believe that they can be a cat at the same time as a human, that childbirth is due to the movement of the stars, and the like? Earlier commentators might have been tempted to pounce on (or attempt to deny) this apparent irrationality, but some anthropologists now make a different analytic move. In their view, all peoples—not excluding those in our society—hold on to many beliefs that are nonrational, if not simply irrational. Indeed, it is impossible to exist as a thinking human being without subscribing to many beliefs at least some of which will turn out to be inconsistent with one another. One need think only of the beliefs of our religions; and even the beliefs of science are often inconsistent with one another. (Consider, for example, the belief in scientific themata without any logical reason for them or the belief on the part of physicists in predictability as well as in indeterminacy.)

What is important to note here is that, however strongly they may be held, these beliefs do not actually interfere with how one makes decisions on a practical day-to-day basis. (In fact, if these beliefs do so interfere, one is seen as crazy, irrespective of the society in which one happens to live.) Instead, they are seen as cosmological or metaphysical theories which have to do with the ultimate nature of reality and not with how one grills a piece of meat, gets from one place to another, or strikes a deal with an acquaintance. It is in these every-day sites of reasoning—and not in our cosmologies, be they mythological or scientific—that the daily practices of human beings are carried out.

Even as numerical thinking is readily found across traditional cultures, high levels of logical thinking can also be discerned. In an elegant study of land tenure disputes in the Trobriand Islands, Edwin Hutchins has demonstrated that litigants in a dispute are capable of long and complex chains of reasoning. According to Hutchins's account, every litigant who wants to demonstrate his ownership of a garden must produce a culturally meaningful account of the history of the garden which terminates in the state where the litigant himself has rights to own the garden. He also is well advised to show that there exists no reasonable history of the garden which terminates in his opponent's having a plausible claim to that garden.

In some respects [notes Hutchins] the problem-solving task of the litigant is akin to theorem-proving in mathematics of logic. The cultural code provides the axioms or implicit premises of the system. The historical background of the case, and especially the state in the past at which the litigants agree on the disposition of the garden, provides the explicit premises of the problem. The theorem to be proved is a proposition which represents the litigant's own rights in the land.

In Hutchins's judgment, the model of folk logic which has been developed from purely Western sources proves adequate as an account of the spontaneous chains of reasoning displayed by the Trobriand litigants. To be sure, it is not straight Aristotelian logic, because it contains plausible as well as necessary inferences; but, as Hutchins points out, "so does our own reasoning."

But if, as a result of such studies, the differences in rationality between "us" and "them" have been minimized, there is also a fresh recognition that schooling in general, and literacy in particular, can bring about major changes in the ways in which individuals think about themselves and in how they communicate with other people. As I shall discuss in detail in chapter 13, one learns in school to deal with information outside of the context in which it is generally encountered; to entertain abstract positions and to explore the relations among them on a hypothetical basis; to make sense of a set of ideas, independent of who says them or of the tone of voice in which they are said; to criticize, to detect contradictions, and to try to resolve them. One also acquires a respect for the accumulation of knowledge, for ways to test statements in which one does not have an immediate interest, and for the relationship between bodies of knowledge that might otherwise seem remote from one another. This valuing of abstract concerns, which relate to reality only by a lengthy chain of inference, and a growing familiarity with "objective" writing, reading, and testing eventually spawns a person at home with the principles of science and mathematics and concerned about the extent to which his views and behavior accord with these somewhat esoteric standards.

In many primitive societies, there is little encouragement to ask questions, to challenge the established wisdom, to question magical or mystical explanations. In contrast, the whole thrust in many "schooled" environments is to challenge statements made without evidence, to attempt to reformulate faulty arguments, and even to forge new syntheses on one's own. The end result is a society that cares deeply about the logical, scientific, and mathematical concerns that I have reviewed here, even, it would appear, at the expense of some of the more aesthetic or personal forms of intelligence that I have reviewed elsewhere in this volume.

Mathematics, Science, and the Passage of Time

In treating the effects of schooling and literacy on the attitudes of a population, I touch on an important aspect of logical-mathematical thought that I have so far minimized. While scientists and mathematicians like to think of themselves as concerned with the eternal verities, their pursuits are in fact rapidly developing and have already undergone profound changes. Conceptions of these realms have also changed over the centuries. As Brian Rotman points out, for the Babylonians, mathematics was a way of astronomical reckonings; for the Pythagorian, it was thought of as an embodiment of the universe's harmonies; for scientists of the Renaissance, it became a means of uncovering nature's secrets; for Kant, it was the perfect science whose propositions were constructed in the deepest layer of our rational faculties; while for Frege and Russell, it became the paradigm of clarity against which ambiguities of ordinary language could be judged. These views will no doubt continue to change; in fact, among leading mathematicians, there are profound differences of opinion about the nature of their whole enterprise, which goals are paramount, which methods of discovery are allowable, and which are not.

Science, of course, changes as well. The change is often seen as progress; but after the provocative writings of Thomas Kuhn, commentators are more hesitant to see science as marching in a unilinear path toward final truth. Few would go so far as some Kuhnians have gone, and declare that science is simply the substitute of one world view for another, or, to deny, with Paul Feyerabend, the distinction between science and non-science. But there is considerable recognition that each world view clarifies certain issues while neglecting or obscuring others; and that the goal of a single science—one unified across all fields—is a chimera that one would do well to exorcise. As one investigates particular scientific work, it is important to know who is writing against what, and who is writing for what end. True, within the execution of "normal science" where the basic paradigm can be assumed, there may be less reason to vex over the roots of one's work. And there may be steady progress toward defining the answers to problems within a circumscribed field. But once one has come to recognize that a scientific consensus may be overthrown tomorrow, the changing nature of science becomes simply a fact of life.

Individuals are beneficiaries but also victims of these time changes. A person with one set of skills may be a tremendous mathematician or scientist in one era, because his skills are just what was

165

needed, while proving relatively useless in succeeding (or prior) historical epochs. For instance, the ability to recall vast strings of numbers or to envision complex relations among forms may prove tremendously important in certain mathematical eras while of little use at other times, where books or computers have taken over such mnemonic functions, or where the notion of spatial concepts as integral to mathematics has not been accepted.

This accident of timing was conveyed most poignantly in the case of the Indian Srinivasa Ramanujan, generally considered to be one of the most talented natural mathematicians of recent centuries. Unfortunately Ramanujan came from a rural site where there was no knowledge of modern mathematics. On his own, he had contrived many years of mathematics, well in advance of mathematics as it was then practiced in his own home. Ramanujan finally moved to England, but it was too late for him to contribute to the field as it was practiced in the present century. G. H. Hardy found it fascinating to teach the mathematics of today to someone who had the deepest instincts and insights but had literally never heard of most of the questions being addressed. As he lay dying, Ramanujan told his teacher, Hardy, who had just arrived in a taxicab, that the number 1,729—the number of the cab—was not as Hardy had supposed, a dull one but, rather, the smallest number that could be expressed as the sum of two cubes in two different ways. This was an absolutely amazingly rapid mathematical insight, but not the sort of contribution that was at a premium (or even especially appreciated) in the mathematical circles of twentieth-century Britain. Beyond natural gifts, aspiring mathematicians must be in the right place at the proper time.

Mathematics and science may accumulate and change, but are there not, in these areas, at least some fundamental laws that remain immutable? The renowned American philosopher W. V. Quine has written convincingly on this issue. As he points out, we change our conceptions of history and economics more readily than those of physics, and those more willingly than laws of math and logic:

Mathematics and logic, central as they are to the conceptual scheme, tend to be accorded such immunity, in view of our conservative preference for revision which disturbs the system least; and herein, perhaps, lies the necessity which the laws of mathematics are felt to enjoy.

And yet Quine indicates in each area, including logic and math, there is a constant drift and drive toward simplicity. Accordingly, mathematics and logic themselves will be revised whenever essential simplification of the whole conceptual enterprise of science is likely to result.

If our century is any indicator, change will become ever more rapid. There has been as much science in the past few decades as in all human history before. Moreover, the proliferation of new fields and of hybrid fields and the explosion of new technology, most prominently the computer, make it difficult even to envision the scope of the scientific enterprise in the future or the issues to which logical and mathematical talent may be applied. Certainly, scientists will make even greater use of new technological innovations; and it is a rash person indeed who would doubt that, before long, computers will themselves be contributing to the process, not only by solving problems that would be beyond human energies to tackle "by hand," but also by helping to define what the new problems will be and how they ought to be approached. (Forms of life created by genetic engineering and new robots with personlike qualities may complicate the picture even further.) And perhaps more so than in the past, individuals ignorant of these advances (and of their implications) will be in an unfavorable position to participate productively in the society.

Relation to the Other Intelligences

The drift of our own society, and perhaps of other societies as well, raises sharply the question whether logical-mathematical intelligence may not be in some way more basic than the other intelligences: more basic, in a conceptual sense, as lying at the center of all human intellect; or more basic, in a practical sense, as guiding the course of human history, its concerns, its problems, its possibilities, and—perhaps—its ultimate constructive or destructive fate. It is often said: there is, after all, only one logic, and only those with developed logical-mathematical intelligences can exercise it.

I do not agree. It should be apparent from this chapter that logical-mathematical intelligence has been of singular importance in the history of the West, and its importance shows no sign of diminishing. It has been less important elsewhere, and whether the present "unifying trends" will continue is by no means certain. To my way of thinking, it is far more plausible to think of logical-mathematical skill as one among a set of intelligences—a skill powerfully equipped to handle certain kinds of problem, but one in no sense superior to, or in danger of overwhelming, the others. (Indeed, there are even different logics with contrasting strengths and limitations.) As we have seen in earlier chapters, there is indeed a logic to language and a logic to music; but these logics operate according to their own rules, and even the strongest dosage of mathematical logic into these areas will not change the ways in which their endogenous "logics" work. To be sure, there have been, and will continue to be, productive interactions between logical-mathematical and spatial intelligences in areas like chess, engineering, and architecture; and some of these synergistic applications will be touched upon in the treatment of spatial knowledge in the next chapter.

Beyond question, then, there can be various links between logical-mathematical and the other forms of intelligence that I am examining here. And, as science and mathematics continue to expand, there is every reason to think that even stronger and more extensive bonds will be established with other intellectual domains. But as the definition of these fields changes, one can also raise another question: Does it still make sense to group all of logic and mathematics together, as one form of intelligence, and to set it off sharply from other forms? Only time can tell whether the grouping that I have proposed here has long-term validity. At present, I remain persuaded that the line of development described by Piaget, which begins with an intuition of number and an appreciation of simple cause and effect, can be traced through to the highest reaches of contemporary logic, mathematics, and science.

And what of the tie to music, with which the last chapter concluded? Can it simply be an accident that so many mathematicians and scientists are attracted to music? And what of the striking commonalities among the energizing ideas in areas like music, the visual arts, and mathematics, as conveyed by Douglas Hofstadter in his justifiably acclaimed *Gödel, Escher, Bach?*

A clue to this conundrum comes from the fact that, while mathematically talented individuals are often intrigued by the order or patterning found in apparently remote areas—ranging from G. H. Hardy's fascination with cricket to Herbert Simon's interest in architectural planning—these interests have not been necessarily reciprocated. It is possible to be a gifted sculptor, poet, or musician without having any particular interest in, or knowledge about, that orderliness and system that form the centerpiece of logical-mathematical thinking. What we encounter in these apparent coincidences of fields are simply, but properly, instances of the intelligences of the logician, the scientist, or the mathematician, as they are applied to other domains of experience. There will, of course, be patterns or orders wherever one looks—some trivial, some not; and it is the special genius (or curse) of logicians and mathematicians to discern these patterns wherever they happen to be found.

It may even be the case—as individuals from Plato to Leibniz thought, and as Einstein continued to hope—that these echoing patterns harbor something of the secret of the universe. But perceiving these patterns and making something of them is an example of the logical-mathematical intelligence at work, working well, or working badly, but displaying its own wares. It does not reflect the core operations of other forms of intelligence. It does not tell us what musical or linguistic or bodily intellect is centrally about. To see these other competences at work, we need to look at the kind of novel that a Saul Bellow might write (perhaps about a mathematician), or at the kind of ballet that a Martha Graham might choreograph (perhaps about a set of equations or a proof!). Each intelligence has its own ordering mechanisms, and the way that an intelligence performs its ordering reflects its own principles and its own preferred media. Perhaps in Bali, one or another aesthetic faculty occupies the same apparent superordinate ordering privileges that we in the West are likely to attribute, almost reflexively, to the abilities exhibited by a mathematician or a logician.

8

Spatial
Intelligence

To play chess requires no intelligence at all.
JOSE RAUL CAPABLANCA,
former world chess champion

The Dimensions of Spatial Intelligence

One way to gain a feeling for the core of spatial intelligence is to attempt the tasks devised by investigators of that intelligence. In figure 1, we begin with the simplest task, requiring only that one choose the form identical to a target item:

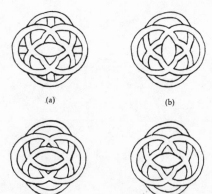

(a)

(b)

(c)

(d)

Target form

FIGURE 1
Instruction: From the array of four, choose that
form that is identical to the target form.

A slightly greater demand is made when one is asked to recognize a particular target item, as viewed from a different angle. In figure 2, the item (or the observer) is assumed to have moved through space:

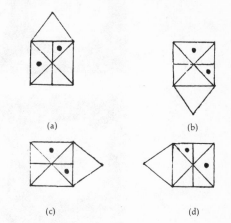

(a)   (b)

(c)   (d)

Target form

FIGURE 2
Instruction: From the array of four, choose that
form which is a rotation of the target form.

A test of spatial ability can offer a greater challenge. For example, in a test item taken from the research of Roger Shepard and Jacqueline Metzler, the target is a depiction of an asymmetric three-dimensional form. The task is for the subject to indicate whether the accompanying form depicts a simple rotation of the target form or is, instead, the reproduction of a different form. In figure 3, I have reproduced three such items: in the first (*a*), the forms are the same but differ by an 80-degree rotation in the picture plane; the forms in the second item (*b*) are again the same form but differ by an 80-degree rotation in depth; in the third item (*c*), the forms are different from each other and cannot be brought into congruence by *any* rotation. Note that, as with the test items in figures 1 and 2, the subject could be requested to draw the required forms, rather than merely to select a single item from a multiple-choice array.

Problems that draw upon spatial capacities can also be couched exclusively in verbal form. For example, take a square piece of paper, fold it in one half, then fold it twice again in half. How many squares exist after this final fold? Or, consider another test: A man and a girl, walking together, step out with their left feet first. The girl walks three paces in the period when the man walks two. At what point will both lift their right feet from the ground simultaneously? Then, to challenge

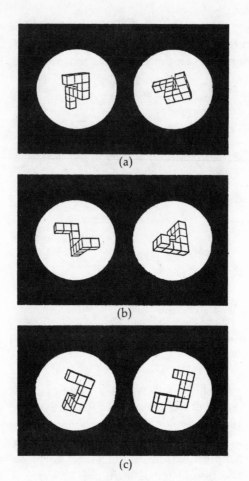

FIGURE 3

Instruction: (For *a, b, c*) Indicate whether the second form in
each pair is a rotation of the first or is a different form.

your thinking powers considerably further, attempt to follow this linguistic description, upon which an explanation of Einstein's theory of
relativity can be constructed:

Imagine a large mass, A, travelling in a straight line through space. The direction of travel is North from South. The mass is surrounded by a huge glass
sphere etched with circles parallel to each other and perpendicular to the line
of travel, like a giant Christmas tree ornament. There exists a second mass, B, in
contact with the glass sphere at one of the etched circles. B's contact with the
sphere is at some point below the largest circle which is the middle circle. Both
Mass A and B are travelling in the same direction. As A and B continue their
motion, B will be continually displaced along the etched circle which is the

172

point of contact with the sphere. Since B is continually displaced, it is actually tracing a spiral path through space-time, time being the North-bound movement. Yet this path when viewed from someone on Mass A from inside the glass sphere, appears to be a circle, not a spiral.

Finally, consider some problems that explicitly call upon the power to create a mental image. First, imagine a horse. Which point is higher, the zenith of the horse's tail, or the lowest part of the horse's head? Imagine an elephant and a mouse. Now imagine the eyelashes of each creature. Which takes longer to bring into sharper focus? Imagine your kitchen sink. Which faucet controls the hot water? Or, to conclude this series, imagine a campus or square with which you are familiar. Time yourself as you scan from one building to the next, and now compare the time elapsed when you scan from one side of the campus (or square) clear across to the other.

By now, you should have an intuitive grasp of the capacities that researchers believe are central to spatial (or as it is often termed, visual-spatial) thinking. Does this family of tasks appear to draw on special cognitive mechanisms? You may also have formed some preliminary opinion on controversial issues: Is there such a discrete capacity as visual or spatial imagery? Can problems that appear to call upon spatial capacities be solved exclusively through verbal or logical-mathematical means? If, for example, you solved the problem of folding paper simply by multiplying $2 \times 2 \times 2$, you are following a logical-mathematical path. You should also have a sense of whether the spatial mode of thinking is natural for you, as it is for many individuals gifted in the arts, in engineering, or in the sciences; or whether it poses undue difficulties for you, as is sometimes the case for individuals with talents in other areas, like music or language.

Central to spatial intelligence are the capacities to perceive the visual world accurately, to perform transformations and modifications upon one's initial perceptions, and to be able to re-create aspects of one's visual experience, even in the absence of relevant physical stimuli. One can be asked to produce forms or simply to manipulate those that have been provided. These abilities are clearly not identical: an individual may be acute, say, in visual perception, while having little ability to draw, imagine, or transform an absent world. Even as musical intelligence consists of rhythmic and pitch abilities which are sometimes dissociated from one another, and as linguistic intelligence consists of syntactic and pragmatic capacities which may also come uncoupled, so, too, spatial intelligence emerges as an amalgam of abilities. All the same, the individual with skills in several of the aforementioned areas is most likely to achieve success in the spatial domain. The fact that practice in one of these areas stimulates development of skills in related ones is another reason that spatial skills can reasonably be considered "of a piece."

A comment is in order concerning the phrase "spatial intelligence." From some points of view, it would be appropriate to propose the descriptor *visual* because, in normal human beings, spatial intelligence is closely tied to, and grows most directly out of, one's observation of the visual world. For the sake of convenience, many examples in this chapter are in fact drawn from the *visual*-spatial realm. But just as linguistic intelligence is not wholly dependent upon the auditory-oral channels and can develop in an individual deprived of these modes of communication, so, too, spatial intelligence can develop (as we shall see) even in an individual who is blind and therefore has no direct access to the visual world. Accordingly, just as I have eschewed the prefix *auditory* in front of musical and linguistic intelligence, it seems preferable to speak of spatial intelligence without linking it inextricably to any particular sensory modality.

As a means of delineating spatial intelligence, we can return to my opening examples. The most elementary operation, upon which other aspects of spatial intelligence rest, is the ability to perceive a form or an object. One can test this ability by multiple-choice questions or by asking an individual to copy a form; copying turns out to be a more demanding assignment, and often latent difficulties in the spatial realm can be detected through errors in a copying task. Analogous tasks can, incidentally, be posed in the tactile modality, for both blind and sighted individuals.

Once one is asked to manipulate the form or the object, appreciating how it will be apprehended from another viewing angle, or how it would look (or feel) were it turned around, one enters fully into the spatial realm, for a manipulation through space has been required. Such tasks of transformation can be demanding, as one is required to "mentally rotate" complex forms through any number of twists and turns. Roger Shepard, one of the leading students of spatial intelligence, has shown the amount of time that it takes to judge whether two forms are in fact identical (as in figure 3) is tied directly to the number of degrees through which one form must be displaced in order to coincide with the other. Given the difficulty of labeling these twisted forms verbally, one is hard pressed to account for this result unless one posits some form of spatial intelligence. In fact, subjects seem to approach this task by attempting to move the form through the requisite number of degrees, as if it existed in real space.

Problems of still greater difficulty can be posed in the "object" or "picture" domain. Indeed, problems in the mathematical branch of topology call precisely for the ability to manipulate complex forms in several dimensions. But when a problem is phrased verbally, a clear option arises to solve the problem strictly through the plane of words, without any resort to the creation of a mental image or "picture in the head." Indeed, each of the problems cited earlier could conceivably be solved strictly in a propositional way. Yet both introspective and experimental evidence suggest that the preferred mode for solution of "imagery problems" is through the positing of an internal mental image which can then be manipulated in ways that parallel operations in the workaday world.

That the ability to solve these problems efficiently is special, apart from straight logical or linguistic ability, has been an article of faith for many years among students of intelligence. One of the individuals who argued strongly for the existence and the independence of spatial ability was the pioneering psychometrician L. L. Thurstone, who saw spatial ability as one of his seven primary factors of intellect. Most students of intelligence testing since Thurstone have reinforced his conclusion that there is something special about spatial ability, though the precise way in which the domain has been carved out has differed across authorities. Thurstone himself divided spatial ability into three components: the ability to recognize the identity of an object when it is seen from different angles; the ability to imagine movement or internal displacement among the parts of a configuration; and the ability to think about those spatial relations in which the body orientation of the observer is an essential part of the problem. Another early worker, Truman Kelley, distinguished between the ability to sense and retain geometric forms, and the capacity mentally to manipulate spatial relationships. A. A. H. El-Koussy, yet another authority, distinguished between two-and three-dimensional spatial aptitude, with each having both static and dynamic aspects. And there have been other typologies as well.

For present purposes, we can bypass the most vociferous discussions among those psychometricians concerned with spatial imagery. The exact number of components and their ideal definition invites a level of specificity beyond the scope of my general survey. The extent to which spatial capacities can be supplanted by verbal ones, possible differences between operations in physical and mental space, and the philosophical ambiguity that surrounds the concept of "mental" imagery can also be left to the experts. It remains for me to lay out those aspects of spatial intelligence that fall most centrally into the competences I am examining here, and to suggest some of the evidence that justifies the positing of a separate domain of intelligence.

We have seen, in the preceding discussion, that spatial intelligence entails a number of loosely related capacities: the ability to recognize instances of the same element; the ability to transform or to recognize a transformation of one element into another; the capacity to conjure up mental imagery and then to transform that imagery; the capacity to produce a graphic likeness of spatial information; and the like. Conceivably, these operations are independent of one another and could develop or break down separately; and yet, just as rhythm and pitch work together in the area of music, so, too, the aforementioned capacities typically occur together in the spatial realm. Indeed, they operate as a family, and use of each operation may well reinforce use of the others.

These spatial capacities can be drawn on in a number of different arenas. They are important for orienting oneself in various locales, ranging from rooms to oceans. They are invoked for the recognition of objects and scenes, both when these are encountered in their original surroundings and when some circumstance of the original presentation has been altered. And they are also utilized when one works with graphic depictions—two dimensional or three-dimensional versions of real-world scenes—as well as other symbols, such as maps, diagrams, or geometrical forms.

Two other uses of spatial capacities prove more abstract and elusive. One involves sensitivity to the various lines of force that enter into a visual or spatial display. I refer here to the feelings of tension, balance, and composition that characterize a painting, a work of sculpture, and many natural elements (like a fire or a waterfall) as well. These facets, which contribute to the power of a display, occupy the attention of artists and viewers of the arts.

A final facet of spatial intelligence grows out of the resemblances that may exist across two seemingly disparate forms, or, for that matter, across two seemingly remote domains of experience. In my view, that metaphoric ability to discern similarities across diverse domains derives in many instances from a manifestation of spatial intelligence. For example, when the gifted essayist Lewis Thomas draws analogies between micro-organisms and an organized human society, depicts the sky as a membrane, or describes mankind as a heap of earth, he is capturing in words a kind of resemblance that may well have occurred to him initially in spatial form. Indeed, underlying many scientific theories are "images" of wide scope: Darwin's vision of the "tree of life," Freud's notion of the unconscious as submerged like an iceberg, John Dalton's view of the atom as a tiny solar system, are the productive figures that give rise to, and help to embody, key scientific conceptions. It is possible that such mental models or images also play a role in more mundane forms of problem solving. In each case, these images have likely arisen in visual form, but each of them could have been created—or appreciated—by an individual who is blind.

While these images are typically seen as helpful aids to thinking, some commentators have gone much farther, deeming visual and spatial imagery as a primary source of thought. An eloquent spokesman for this position is the psychologist of art Rudolf Arnheim. In *Visual Thinking*, Arnheim argues that the most important operations of thinking come directly from our perception of the world, with vision serving as the sensory system *par excellence* which undergirds and constitutes our cognitive processes. As he puts it, "the remarkable mechanisms by which the senses understand the environment are all but identical with the operations described by the psychology of thinking ... truly productive thinking in whatever area of cognition takes place in the realm of imagery." Arnheim is inclined to minimize the role of language in productive thinking: he suggests that unless we can conjure up an image of some process or concept, we will be unable to think clearly about it. An alternative, more catholic view would hold that visual or spatial intelligence contributes to scientific and artistic thought, but does not assume the priority that Arnheim chooses to attribute to it.

On the basis of the present discussion, and in light of many factor analyses of intelligence test results, it seems reasonable to nominate spatial intelligence as a discrete form of intellect, a collection of related skills, perhaps, in fact, that single cluster of abilities which would be most widely conceded by the students of this field. In the view of many, spatial intelligence is the "other intelligence"—the one that should be arrayed against, and be considered equal in importance to, "linguistic intelligence." Dualists speak of two systems of representation—a verbal code and an imagistic code: localizers place the linguistic code in the left hemisphere, the spatial code in the right hemisphere.

Readers of earlier chapters will know that I do not subscribe to such dichotomization of intellect. Still, I would admit that, for most of the tasks used by experimental psychologists, linguistic and spatial intelligences provide the principal sources of storage and solution. Confronted by an item in a standardized test, individuals appear to use words or spatial images to approach the problem and to encode it and may well—though this assumption is far more controversial—also exploit the resources of language and/or imagery to solve the problem. Some of the most convincing demonstrations come from Lee R. Brooks. This investigator varied both the mode of presentation of materials (linguistic or pictorial) and the modes of response (verbal or spatial—for example, pointing on a piece of paper). Through clever manipulations, the various tasks called for using language or for using spatial processing in somewhat different ways—for example, forming a mental image *and* pointing to a mark on a sheet of paper, in the case of the spatial domain; or memorizing a sentence and categorizing the parts of speech of each word, in the case of the linguistic domain. Brooks consistently found subjects impaired in their performances when they had to take in information to produce responses solely in the linguistic or solely in the spatial domain. But when they had the option of taking information in through one modality and then responding through a noncompeting modality, there was no such interference. Just as musical and linguistic processing are carried out by different processing centers and need not interfere with one another, so, too, spatial and linguistic faculties seem able to proceed in relatively independent or complementary fashion.

Development of Spatial Intelligence

Though the centrality of spatial intelligence has long been recognized by researchers who work with adult subjects, relatively little has been definitively established about the development of this set of capacities in children. Just why is not clear. It may be that spatial skills are more difficult to test than linguistic or logical ones; it may also be that students of child development have less intuition for, fewer skills in, or less interest concerning spatial capacities.

An exception is Jean Piaget, who conducted several studies of the development of spatial understanding in children. Nor surprisingly, Piaget saw spatial intelligence as part and parcel of the general portrait of logical growth which he was assembling across his diverse studies. And so, in recounting the course of spatial understanding, Piaget spoke of sensori-motor understanding of space which emerges during infancy. Two abilities are central: the initial appreciation of the trajectories observed in objects and the eventual capacity to find one's way between various locales. At the end of the sensori-motor stage of early childhood, youngsters become capable of mental imagery. They can imagine a scene or an event without having to be there. Piaget traced such mental imagery to the child's earlier experiences of having seen the object of the event itself and at that time exploring it in a sensori-motor manner. Mental imagery was accordingly seen as a kind of *internalized action* or *deferred imitation*, the rough outlines or schemas of actions that had previously been (and could still, in theory, be) carried out in the world. Such imagery remains static during early childhood, however, and children cannot perform mental operations upon it.

Inasmuch as both logical-mathematical and spatial intelligence arise from the child's action upon the world, one may ask whether they in fact entail different forms of intelligence. Even Piaget seems to have sensed that they did. He introduced a distinction between "figurative" knowledge, in which an individual retains the configuration of an object (as in a mental image); and "operative" knowledge, where the emphasis falls upon transforming the configuration (as in the manipulation of such an image). As Piaget saw it, then, the split marked a line between the static configuration and the active operation. For present purposes, one can distinguish instead between relatively static and relatively active forms of spatial knowledge, both of which should fall comfortably under the rubric of spatial intelligence.

Continuing with Piaget's account, the advent of concrete operations at the start of school marks an important turning point in the child's mental development. The child has now become capable of far more active manipulation of images and objects in the spatial realm. Through reversible mental operations, he can now appreciate how objects look to someone situated elsewhere; here we encounter the well-known phenomenon of *decentration* where the child can indicate what a scene would look like to someone seated in another part of the room, or how an object would look if rotated in space. Yet this variety of spatial intelligence is still restricted to concrete situations and events. Only during the formal operation era, at the time of adolescence, can the youth deal with the idea of abstract spaces or with formal rules governing space. Thus, geometry comes to be appreciated by the adolescent (or by the mathematically precocious child), who is newly able to relate the world of figural images to propositional statements, and to reason about the implications of various kinds of transformation.

We thus see a regular progression in the spatial realm, from the

179

infant's ability to move around in space, to the toddler's ability to form static mental images, to the school child's capacity to manipulate such static images, and finally, to the adolescent's capacity to relate spatial relations to propositional accounts. The adolescent, being able to appreciate all possible spatial arrangements, is in a favorable position to join together logical-mathematical and spatial forms of intelligence into a single geometric or scientific system.

As in other areas of study, Piaget provided the first general picture of spatial development, and many of his observations and characterizations have stood the test of time. For the most part, however, he restricted himself to paper and pencil or to desk-top measures of spatial ability, and so largely ignored the child's understanding of the broader spatial environment. There have recently been studies of the child's broader spatial understanding, and these yield intriguing findings. It turns out that children of age three or less can retrace a route that they knew motorically, but have difficulty anticipating what sorts of things they will encounter in regions that they have not themselves visited, but about which they have accrued some independent knowledge (for example, from verbal descriptions or from a visit to a neighboring location). When children do manage to find their way around, landmarks play a central part.

Representing this knowledge poses a whole host of challenges. Even older children have difficulty in capturing, in some other format, their intuitive knowledge of layout. Thus, a five- or a six-year-old may know his way satisfactorily around a layout, even an unfamiliar one: but when asked to describe it in words, or to draw a picture or a map, the child will either fail altogether or will offer an essentially oversimplified and hence unhelpful account (for example, describing the path as a straight line, even though it is in fact convoluted). What proves most difficult for school-age children is to coordinate their knowledge of a spatial layout, as gained from a number of disparate experiences, into a single overall organized framework. Put differently, the children may know their way around many areas in their neighborhood or town and, in fact, never fail to find what they are looking for. Yet they often will lack the capacity to provide a map, a sketch, or an overall verbal account of the relationship among several spots. Representing their piecemeal knowledge in another format or symbol system proves an elusive part of spatial intelligence. Or perhaps one could say: while children's spatial understanding develops apace, the expression of this understanding via another intelligence or symbolic code remains difficult.

Neuropsychological Considerations

If spatial intelligence has been neglected in studies of children, it has certainly partaken of its fair share of the research enterprise in neuropsychology. In fact, with the possible exception of language, there has probably been more established about spatial abilities in the brain than about any other human faculty.

The outcome of this research tradition is clear and persuasive. Just as the left hemisphere of the brain has, over the course of evolution, been selected as the pre-eminent site for linguistic processing, the right hemisphere of the brain, and in particular the posterior portions of the right hemisphere, proves to be the site most crucial for spatial (and visual-spatial) processing. To be sure, the right hemisphere is not quite so decisive in the case of spatial processing as the left hemisphere is for language: for instance, sizable deficits in spatial ability can also follow upon damage to the left posterior regions. But when it comes to finding one's way around a site, to recognizing objects, faces, and scenes, noticing fine details, and many other functions, damage to the right posterior regions is far more likely to cause impairment than damage to any other comparable region in the brain. Moreover, injury to the right hemisphere produces the peculiar phenomenon of neglect, where individuals pay little attention to (or altogether ignore) the left half of space around them. Thus, performance on tasks (or on daily activities) where one must monitor both halves of space poses special problems for people with this condition.

Evidence comes from three principle lines of study. Of foremost importance are clinical studies of individuals who have suffered injury to the brain through stroke or other kinds of trauma. It has been amply documented that lesions to the right parietal regions cause difficulties in visual attention, spatial representation and orientation, imagery production, and memory. The bigger the lesion, the more pronounced the difficulty. Presence of even a small lesion in the left hemisphere, in addition to right hemisphere damage, suffices to devastate an individual's spatial functioning.

A second and closely allied line of evidence comes from the performance of unilaterally brain-injured individuals on standard tests of spatial functioning. From the work of Nelson Butters and his colleagues at the Boston Veterans Administration Medical Center, we have convincing demonstrations of particular difficulties faced by right hemisphere patients in transforming visual arrays; in anticipating how they will appear from other vantage points; in reading a map or finding their way around an unfamiliar space; in encoding and remembering visual and spatial information. This damage rarely impairs linguistic ability (such as the reading of symbols) to a significant extent; left hemisphere dominance for language is sufficiently profound to permit linguistic forms to be apprehended despite massive right hemisphere damage.

Studies in other laboratories have documented further difficulties. Brenda Milner and Doreen Kimura have shown that patients with right temporal excisions are impaired in recognizing overlapping nonsense figures and dot patterns. Elizabeth Warington has documented a difficulty among right hemisphere-injured patients in recognizing familiar objects presented in unusual perspectives; and a number of investigators have noted that right hemisphere patients exhibit particular difficulties in making drawings. The drawings of such patients tend to include details in disparate places, to lack an overall contour, and to feature that neglect of the left half of space which is a peculiar sequel of right hemisphere brain diseases. These drawings reveal an almost exclusive dependence upon propositional knowledge regarding the object (the names of the features of that object) rather than sensitivity to the actual perceived contours of the entities and of the parts to be depicted.

One might question whether such effects of brain damage can be circumvented by linguistic strategies. Right hemisphere patients do indeed try to use language to aid themselves: they will challenge the task, try to reason their way to a solution aloud, or even confabulate answers. But only the most fortunate succeed. Moira Williams relates a poignant anecdote of a world-famous mathematician who had lost most of his right cerebrum as a result of a traffic accident. This individual was given an object-assembly task taken from the standard intelligence battery. Exploiting his preserved linguistic knowledge about principles of spatial relations, the man quipped, "One can always use geometry."

Recently, a fascinating set of difficulties in imagery faced by right hemisphere patients has been documented by Eduardo Bisiach and his colleagues in Milan. It turns out that individuals who exhibit a neglect of the left half of space in ordinary life display much the same symptoms in dealing with mental imagery. That is, these patients prove able to image the right half of objects or scenes, but not the left. This finding was dramatically shown by asking brain-injured individuals to image the famous Duomo Square in the heart of downtown Milan. Told to imagine the square as seen from one vantage point, the patients were able to describe all the objects in the right half of their field, but none in the left half. Then, requested to image while standing at an opposite side, they were able to name the objects seen on the right side (those objects formerly omitted) but not those on the left (those objects formerly listed). A more compelling case for the "psychological reality" of visual imagery would be difficult to envision.

A final source of information about the role of the right hemisphere in the processing of spatial information comes from studies of normal individuals. Subjects are exposed to stimuli either in the right visual field (with connections to the left hemisphere of the brain) or in the left visual field (with connections to the right hemisphere of the brain) and asked to perform various assignments. Findings are confirmatory. In each of these realms, the right hemisphere proves more important for the solution of problems than does the left; though it should be indicated that results are not as dramatic in normal individuals as in those who have sustained injury to the brain.

This picture of right hemisphere involvement in spatial tasks, and particularly the involvement of the parietal lobe, seems firmly established. Indeed, it is my belief that the neural basis for spatial intelligence is more likely to be clarified in the foreseeable future than that underlying any other of the intelligences treated here. We have here a function that, in its simpler guises, is carried out by relatively elementary sensory receptors, and that, even in its more sophisticated forms, is still shared with other organisms to a higher degree than those of, say, logical or linguistic intelligence.

Let us survey the range of findings briefly. From studies at the single-cell level, by researchers like David Hubel and Torsten Wiesel, a great deal has already been established about the perception of lines, angles, edges, and the other building blocks of objects. From studies by Charles Gross, Mortimer Mishkin, and others who record from the inferior temporal regions of the primate brain, we also know a considerable amount about the perception and recognition of entire objects. It appears that inferior temporal neurons participate in coding of the physical attributes of visual stimuli, perhaps by serving as integrators of that information about depth, color, size, and shape which is recorded in the pre-striate cortexes. There is a distance—but a navigable one—between this elementary recognition of objects, and that ability to trace the relationships among objects that proves central in spatial intelligence. Other brain regions will certainly be involved—for instance, the frontal lobes seem crucial for remembering a spatial loca-

183

tion; but the relevant connections can be traced as well. Once this story has been laid out, we may be in a position to explain the operation of spatial intelligence in neuronal terms. And then we can begin to investigate the even more vexed issue of how this form intertwines with those intelligences that are more exclusively the prerogative of *homo sapiens*.

The evolution of spatial intelligence also seems more continuous with processes found in infra-humans than appears to be the case with other intelligences. The group life of many primates—today and millions of years ago—seemed linked to *spatial skills*. On nearly all accounts, spatial intelligence assumed pivotal importance for a roving band, whether it was involved in gathering or in hunting. When individuals needed to traverse wide spaces and return safely to their homes, it was important to have keen spatial intellect—otherwise, the chance of getting lost would be too great. Such skill remains dramatically present in the Arctic today: in the face of near uniformity of landscape, every visual detail must be important, and "Caucasians who have traveled with the Eskimos frequently remark upon their apparently extraordinary ability to find their ways through what appears to be a featureless terrain by remembering visual configuration." The premium on spatial skills may also help to explain why sex differences appear more regularly in tests of spatial intelligence than on most other forms of intelligence. To the extent that hunting and wandering were pre-eminently male preoccupations, there would be more of a selective advantage for males to evolve highly developed visual-spatial abilities, and more likely an early death for those who lacked such skills.

The marshaling of spatial abilities for solving problems has been an interest of comparative psychologists. It is worth recalling the pioneering studies of Wolfgang Köhler with the great apes on Tenerife during the First World War. Köhler was able to show that at least some great apes, and in particular the fabled Sultan, could make tools by combining two or more objects, whose potential visual-spatial integration they were able to anticipate. While interpretation of Köhler's demonstrations is not straightforward, most analysts are comfortable with the notion that the chimpanzees were able to envision—to create an image of—the state of affairs which would obtain were they able, say, to connect two sticks in a certain way. Such insight proved a necessary and often a sufficient precursor for solving a problem and gaining a desired object. We can here see in nonhuman primates an initial manifestation of the kind of spatial intelligence which many humans have brought to an extremely high level of accomplishment. How spatial abilities unite with bodily skill in the area of tool use is an issue which will concern us in the next chapter.

Unusual Forms of Spatial Ability and Disability

Until now, I have spoken of spatial capacities as they develop in normal children and as they are represented in the nervous systems of normal and brain-injured adults. Even though the lines of spatial intelligence are in general regular, there are clear anomalies, and these can sometimes provide fresh insight into spatial intelligence.

The question of blind individuals immediately arises. Certain experiences—such as color—are forever closed to the individual blind from birth, while many others—such as apprehension of perspective—can be grasped only with the greatest difficulty. Nonetheless, research with blind subjects has indicated that spatial knowledge is not totally dependent upon the visual system, and that blind individuals can even appreciate certain aspects of pictures.

A leading student of this issue has been John Kennedy of the University of Toronto. Kennedy and his associates have demonstrated that blind subjects (as well as normal subjects who have been blindfolded) can readily recognize geometrical shapes that have been presented via raised line drawings. The blind individual tends to convert spatial experiences into the number of steps (or finger movements) taken in a certain direction and into the kind of motion needed. Size must be discovered through indirect methods, such as running one's hand along an object: the more movement in time, the larger the object appears to be. The blind individual can exploit cues like straightness, curvature, and prominence of features, to recognize more complex figures (shades of visual imagery measures). In Kennedy's view, there is a perceptual system common to both the tactile and the visual modalities: insights gleaned by normal individuals from a combination of these modalities prove accessible to the blind from the tactile realms alone.

Studies of drawing by Susanna Millar of Oxford University reinforce this picture. Blind children display in their drawings many of the same features and problems exhibited by younger sighted children. For example, blind children are uncertain where and how to place objects on a canvas. Initially, they do not appreciate how to depict the body in two dimensions, nor how to array figures along the bottom of the flat page; but once they appreciate that drawing is possible with a raised line, and that certain experiences known by touch can be realized by such a line, their drawings come to resemble those of sighted subjects. Millar concludes that drawing depends upon the acquisition of rules for which prior visual experience is a facilitating, but not a necessary, condition; the absence of visual feedback during drawing wreaks effects chiefly on the degree of articulation and precision in the drawing.

Gloria Marmor has filled out this picture by showing that blind children are also capable of rotating figures and appreciating mirror images. She concludes:

Without using mental imagery, the early blind appear to organize the attributes of tactile forms into spatial representations that, like visual images, allow all attributes to be entertained simultaneously and are specific enough to make possible mirror image discrimination.

Probably the most dramatic account of spatial abilities in the blind comes from studies by Barbara Landau and her colleagues at the University of Pennsylvania. In one investigation, a congenitally blind two-and-one-half-year-old child proved able to determine the appropriate path between two objects after traveling to each of these objects only from a third location. In order to set the course between objects along a route that she had never herself followed, the child had to be able to detect the distances and the angular relationship of the familiar paths and then derive the angle of the new path from this information. Clearly, her accomplishment indicates that the metric properties of space can be inferred in the absence of visual information. Moreover, the same child seen again at age four was able to use a tactile map in order to find a prize located in the room. Though the child had never before been exposed to a map, she was able immediately to grasp the concept of one, including its arbitrary symbols, and to use it to guide her to the desired location. From such demonstrations, Landau and her colleagues reached a conclusion vital to our own study: spatial representational systems are equally accessible to visual or to tactile experience; and there is not necessarily a privileged relationship between visual input and spatial intelligence.

Individuals with other kinds of pathology do display characteristic deficits in their spatial perception. One such population are females with Turner's syndrome, a condition involving lack of a second x chromosome. While normal in linguistic matters, victims of this condition exhibit spatial problems across the board, ones not reducible simply to problems in visual perception. Individuals with cerebral palsy exhibit disordered eye movements, which in turn lead to difficulties in depth perception and to poor performance on a host of visual-spatial measures. Numerous children who have brain damage also exhibit special difficulties in visual-spatial tasks—for example, in perceiving and understanding the diagonal: there is at least suggestive evidence that some of these individuals suffer from a junior version of a "right hemisphere syndrome."

As for visual imagery, wide individual differences are reported. Indeed, researcher Stephen Kosslyn indicates that he cannot use many individuals as subjects in his studies, for they report absent or very poor visual imagery. In his pioneering investigation of the imagery faculty, Francis Galton found that, when asked to recall the scene of that morning's breakfast, scientists typically reported little or no visual imagery, while individuals of apparently modest intellectual powers often reported detailed concrete imagery. This finding startled Galton, who himself possessed vivid imagery, including an elaborate number-form array in which all the numbers from 0 to 200 were clearly represented. It would also have dismayed E. Titchener, a turn-of-the-century psychologist with a strong belief in the power of imagery. Wrote Titchener:

> The mind, in its ordinary operations, is a fairly complete picture gallery. . . . Whenever I read or hear that somebody has done something modestly, or gravely, or proudly, or humbly, or courteously, I see a visual hint of the modesty or gravity or pride or humility or courtesy. The stately heroine gives me a flash of a tall figure, the only clear part of which is a hand holding up a steely grey skirt; the humble suitor gives me a flash of a bent figure, the only clear part of which is the bowed back, though at times there are hands held deprecatingly before the absent face . . . all the descriptions must be either self-evident or as unreal as a fairy tale.

But the finding of poor imagery would have made sense to novelist Aldous Huxley, who confessed to being a poor visualizer, and conceded that words did not evoke a picture in his mind. Only by an effort of will could he evoke even a faint image. Perhaps this is one reason that Huxley eventually indulged in drugs, an experience that allowed "the untalented visionary" to perceive a reality "no less tremendous, beautiful, and significant than the world *held* by Blake."

In a smattering of otherwise normal individuals, visual and spatial abilities are remarkably developed. For example, the inventor Nikola Tesla "could project before his eyes a picture complete in every detail, of every part of the machine." These pictures were more vivid than any blueprint. Tesla's inner imagery was sufficiently acute that he could build his complex inventions without drawings. Further, he claimed to be able to test his devices in his mind's eye, "by having them run for weeks—after which time he would examine them thoroughly for signs of wear." Artists often stand out for their spatial powers. Thus Rodin was able to represent different parts of the body as projections of interior volumes: "I forced myself to express in each swelling of the torso or the limbs the efflorescence of a muscle or of a bone which lay deep beneath the skin"; while Henry Moore is able to think of the entire sculpture as if it were in his hand:

he thinks of it, whatever its size, as if he were holding it completely enclosed in the hollow of his hand; he mentally visualizes a complex form *from all round itself;* he knows while he looks at one side what the other side is like; he identifies himself with its center of gravity, its mass, its weight; he realizes its volume, as the space that the shape displaces in the air.

At other times, such unusual spatial abilities can be found in individuals who are otherwise retarded. There is an English painter Bryan Pearce, who, despite a subnormal I.Q., can sell his paintings at a high price. There are occasional *idiots savants,* such as the Japanese Yamashita and Yamamura, whose artistic abilities were of a surprisingly high caliber, completely out of kilter with their other meager talents. And most mysteriously, there is the English adolescent Nadia, who, despite a condition of severe autism, was able as a very young child to make drawings of the most remarkable finesse and representational accuracy. (See one of her drawings, done at the age of five, in figure 4, page 189.)

With these *idiots savants* and victims of autism, we encounter once again the flowering of a single intelligence in the face of an otherwise meager array of abilities. Perhaps, in certain cases, this visual or spatial bent can be seen as a compensation, where a relatively preserved ability has been accentuated by the child and his family. In the most extreme cases, such as young Nadia, however, no such explanation suffices. Nadia was drawing like a skilled adolescent by the time she was four or five, and her parents seem not even to have been aware of her talent (which was first noted by her therapist). Nadia had an ability to look at objects, to remember their size, shape, and contour, and to translate these into the appropriate motor pattern, which was quite apart from that found in even the most gifted normal child. Probably

FIGURE 4
Drawing of a horse by the autistic child Nadia at age five.

one component was eidetic imagery—that photographic ability to retain in one's mind's eye the appearance of objects once seen directly.
(Comparison of some of Nadia's drawings with models previously
available to her confirms that she had an ability akin to eidetic imagery.) But the capacity to translate these patterns into the appropriate
motor sequences, and to combine images in diverse and unexpected
ways, clearly goes beyond sheer eidetic skill. In fact, her graphic ability
was so agile that she had no need to draw elements in the same order;
instead, she could proceed, almost at will, from one corner of a drawing to another, apparently confident that she would eventually render
the desired form in the correct way.

At the same time, it seems clear that Nadia's gift was established at
a cost. She lacked the conceptual knowledge requisite to her drawing
skills. She could not perform sorting tasks where she had to put togeth-

189

er items of the same category. Moreover, in her own drawings, she would show little regard for the particular object being depicted. Sometimes she would cease to draw an object right in the middle of its contour or continue to draw right off the page, as if slavishly transcribing a form that she had committed to memory. In addition, she was unable to draw simpler versions of an object and seemed compelled to include every detail in every drawing.

Whether Nadia's profile of abilities is unique to one hapless prodigy, is a question that science is unlikely to be able to answer. The requisite experiments cannot be done. But her drawings stand as an eloquent demonstration of the dissociability of spatial intelligence from other intellectual strengths and of its potential for a singularly high degree of development.

The Uses of Spatial Intelligence

A keenly honed spatial intelligence proves an invaluable asset in our society. In some pursuits, this intelligence is of the essence—for example, for a sculptor or a mathematical topologist. Without a developed spatial intelligence, progress in these domains is difficult to envisage: and there are many other pursuits where spatial intelligence alone might not suffice to produce competence, but where it provides much of the necessary intellectual impetus.

In the sciences, the contribution of spatial intelligence is readily apparent. Einstein had an especially well-developed set of capacities. Like Russell, he became mesmerized in first reading Euclid; and it was to the visual and spatial forms, and their correspondence, that Einstein was most strongly drawn: "His intuitions were deeply rooted in classical geometry. He had a very visual mind. He thought in terms of images—gedanken experiments, or experiments carried out in the mind." It can even be conjectured that his most fundamental insights were derived from spatial models rather than from a purely mathematical line of reasoning. As he put it:

The words of the language, as they are written and spoken, do not seem to play any role in my mechanisms of thought. The psychical entities which seem to serve as elements in thought are certain signs and more or less clear images which can be voluntarily reproduced or combined. . . . The above mentioned elements are, in my case, of visual and some of muscular type.

190

The vivid role of imagery in the solution of problems has often been recounted by scientists and inventors. In one of the most famous of such accounts, the chemist Friedrich Kekulé came across the structure of the benzene ring. He fell asleep and

again the atoms were gamboling before my eyes. . . . My mental eye . . . could not distinguish larger structures . . . all twining and twisting in snake-like motion. But look! What was that? One of the snakes had seized hold of its own tail and the form whirled mockingly before my eyes. As if by a flash of lightning I awoke.

These insights had suggested to Kekulé that organic compounds like benzene are not open structures, but closed rings. And in a moment closer to our own times, the structure of the DNA molecule, as ferreted out by James Watson and Francis Crick, depended critically upon the ability to sketch the various ways in which molecules might be bound with one another. These experiments—sometimes constructed in the scientists' heads, sometimes on paper, and sometimes using an actual three-dimensional model—led in the end to the correct reconstruction of the double helix.

Spatial thinking of the sorts sketched at the beginning of this chapter can participate in the scientific process. Sometimes the actual problem is spatial—as in the case of the building of the DNA models—and so the answer involves thinking (or even direct modeling) in this medium. Sometimes the spatial gift can provide a helpful, though perhaps not a necessary, metaphor or model for the process—as happened when Darwin came to think of the origin of species as an ever-branching tree and of the survival of the fittest as a race among species members.

Progress in science may, in fact, be closely yoked to the development of certain spatial displays. According to E. Ferguson, many of the problems in which scientists and engineers are engaged cannot be described in verbal form. The scientific progress in the Renaissance may have been intimately tied to the recording and conveying of a vast body of knowledge in drawings—as, for instance, in the renowned sketches of Leonardo da Vinci. Instead of memorizing lists of objects or parts (as medieval workers often had to do), aspiring scientists could now study the actual organization of machines and organisms that were not available for inspection. The invention of printing proved as important for the dissemination of these pictures as it had been for the spread of texts. In general, the widespread availability of manuscripts played an important role in the teaching of science and in the promotion of scientific ways of thinking.

Clearly, spatial knowledge can serve a variety of scientific ends, as a useful tool, an aid to thinking, a way of capturing information, a way of formulating problems, or the very means of solving the problem. Perhaps McFarlane Smith is right when he suggests that, after individuals have attained a certain minimal verbal facility, it is skill in spatial ability which determines how far one will progress in the sciences.

It must be stressed that the involvement of spatial reasoning is not uniform across various sciences, arts, and branches of mathematics. Topology exploits spatial thinking to a much greater extent than does algebra. The physical sciences depend upon spatial ability to a greater extent than do the traditional biological or social sciences (where verbal abilities are relatively more important). Individuals with exceptional gifts in the spatial area, such as Leonardo or the contemporary figures Buckminster Fuller and Arthur Loeb, have the option of performing not only in one of these spheres but across a number of them, perhaps excelling in science, engineering, and various of the arts. Ultimately, one who wishes to master these pursuits must learn the "language of space" and "thinking in the spatial medium." Such thinking includes an appreciation that space allows the coexistence of certain structural features, while disallowing others. And, for many,

thinking in three dimensions is like learning a foreign language. The number four is no longer a digit larger than three and less than five, it is the number of vertices as well as the faces of a tetrahedron. Six is the number of edges of a tetrahedron, the number of faces of a cube, or the number of vertices of an octahedron.

If one had to choose a single area to illustrate the centrality of spatial intelligence, chess would suggest itself as a strong candidate. The ability to anticipate moves and their consequences seems closely tied to strong imagery. And, indeed, chess masters have generally had outstanding visual memory—or visual imagination, as they call it. Yet a close examination of these individuals reveals that they possess a special kind of memory.

In a pioneering study nearly a century ago, Alfred Binet, the founder of intelligence testing, examined mnemonic virtuosity in blindfolded chess. This is a form in which, classically, individuals play several games simultaneously against an equal number of opponents. The opponents can each see the relevant board, but the blindfolded chessplayer cannot. His only cue is a recitation of the last move made by his opponent, and on that basis he must make his move.

What do the players themselves say? In Binet's report, we get an initial clue from a Dr. Tarrasch who writes, "Some part of every chess game is played blindfold. For example, any combination of five moves is carried out in one's head—the only difference being that one is sitting in front of the chess board. The sight of the chessman frequently upsets one's calculations." We encounter here evidence that the game is typically represented at a relatively abstract level: the identities of the pieces, let alone their physical attributes, are completely extraneous. What is important is the power of each piece—what it can and cannot do.

In Binet's view, successful blindfold chess depends upon physical endurance, great powers of concentration, scholarship, memory, and imagination. For its practitioners, chess is a completely meaningful enterprise, and so they strive to capture the essence of an encounter on the board. Each game has its own character, its own shape, which impresses itself upon the chess player's sensibility. Says a Mr. Goetz, "I grasp it as a musician grasps harmony in his orchestra.... I am often carried to sum up the character of a position in a general epithet . . . it strikes you as simple and familiar, or as original, exciting and suggestive." So Binet comments, "It is the multitude of suggestions and ideas emanating from a game which makes it interesting and establishes it in memory." The blindfolded player must remember primarily lines of reasoning and strategies. As he tries to recall a given position, he recollects his reasoning at an earlier time, and thus gets on the track of a particular move. He does not remember that move in isolation, but remembers rather that he had a particular plan of attack, and that the move was required to carry out that attack. "The move itself is only the conclusion of an act of thinking; that act itself must first be recaptured." In fact, one method used by players to help themselves is to pursue a different strategy of play in each game, a procedure that helps make each game more distinctive.

What of chess memory? Chess players have fabled memories, particularly of important games in their past. But, again, this memory does not reduce to sheer rote recall. Rather, for the good player, the game has as distinctive and individual a character as a particular play read, movie seen, trip taken. Binet contrasts this memory with that of an *idiot savant*. The *idiot savant* can remember something slavishly; but once it has played out, the memory as a whole vanishes because it harbors no intrinsic significance. In sharp contrast, the memory of the chessplayer proves far more lasting, for it encodes plans and ideas, not rote lists.

Nonetheless, the blindfolded master must somehow keep the board in mind. Here are the introspections of one leading master:

> To envision a position, I keep it before me continuously in all its plasticity. I have a very clear picture of the chessboard in mind, and lest the inner image be disturbed by visual sensations, I close my eyes. Then I people the board with the chessmen. The first of these operations, that is, the attainment of a mental image of the chessboard is the prime essential. Once you can see the board clearly before your closed eyes, it is not difficult to imagine also the pieces, at first in their familiar initial array. Now the game starts.... Right away, it begins to evolve on the chessboard before the mind's eye; it changes the original picture a bit and I try to retain it in its altered condition. My opponent responds, and again the picture changes. I retain the transformations one after the other.

But in Binet's view, the better the player, and the more games in which he is involved, the more abstract is the representation of the game. There is no need for a vivid recall of each of the pieces, let alone of their shape and size; what is needed is a more abstract representation, where the general drift of the game is kept in mind, and an "inner beacon" allows a reconstruction of as much of the game as is needed in order for it to be faithfully followed—no more. Shape and color are unimportant. As Master Tarrasch puts it:

The player absorbed in the strategy of the game does not see a piece of wood with a horse head, but a piece that follows the course prescribed for the knight, that is worth approximately three pawns, that is perhaps at that moment badly placed at the edge of the board, or about to wage a decisive attack, or in danger of being nailed down by an adversary.

Binet concludes that the best players have a visual memory; but it differs profoundly from that of a painter. It lacks the latter's concrete pictorial quality. Though visual, it is abstract; in fact, it is a kind of geometrical memory. We might compare Binet's conclusion with Napoleon's view of conflict. The commander who enters into battle with a detailed image of his battle plan finds the image too difficult to modify quickly to accommodate sudden and unpredictable changes on the battlefield, and thus will make a bad commander. Napoleon, in fact, held that individuals who think only in relation to concrete mental pictures are unfit to command. Here, perhaps, we see a difference between the literal imagery of an *idiot savant* or a Nadia at her easel, and the more abstract intelligence of a chessplayer, a battle commander, or a theoretical physicist. It seems reasonable to underscore the spatial—rather than the purely visual—dimensions of this skill.

Binet's findings have been reinforced by more recent studies. Adrian de Groot and his colleagues in the Hague have shown that chess masters have a remarkable ability to reconstruct a chessboard that they have seen for just a few seconds—providing only that the chessmen on the board were set in a meaningful position. If, however, the chessboard has randomly located figures positioned upon it, the chess master performs no more accurately than a rank novice. This finding indicates precisely that the chess master does not differ qualitatively from other individuals in sheer visual memory for rote configurations; he differs rather in his ability to relate a pattern to one that he has previously encountered, to encode it meaningfully, and to reconstruct it upon that basis. Herbert Simon, a pioneer in artificial intelligence who has collaborated with the de Groot group, believes that chess masters may have mastered fifty thousand or more patterns: it is this remarkable store that allows them to proceed so effectively when they have been exposed to a new board for but a few seconds. But whether the individuals who eventually become chess masters have from the first a special proclivity for appreciating such patterns and then "chunking them" has not been addressed by these researches.

In my own view, the extremely rapid advance made by these few individuals who become chess masters in the first decade of their lives is difficult to explain in any terms other than that of precocious intelligence in one or more relevant spheres. Contrary to Capablanca's whimsical remark, quoted at the beginning of this chapter, spatial and logical-mathematical intelligences are probably the twin contributors, with their relative importance differing across individual situation. What the lore about chess masters reminds us, however, is that sheer visual imaging capacity in itself will not a master make: it is the ability to relate a perceived pattern to past patterns, and to envelop the present position into an overall game plan, that is the true sign of talent at chess.

The Visual-Spatial Arts

While one might underestimate the component of spatial thinking in the sciences, the centrality of spatial thinking in the visual arts is self-evident. The enterprises of painting and sculpture involve an exquisite sensitivity to the visual and spatial world as well as an ability to re-create it in fashioning a work of art. Certain other intellectual compe-tences, such as facility in the control of fine motor movement, contrib-ute as well; but the *sine qua non* of graphic artistry inheres in the spatial realm.

It is not surprising, then, that the shop talk of artists dwells on the qualities of the perceptual world and on how these can best be cap-tured on canvas. In his revealing letters to his brother Theo, Vincent Van Gogh returns repeatedly to his efforts to master these properties. Talking of color, for example, Van Gogh states:

There are effects of color which I but rarely find painted in the Dutch pictures. Yesterday evening, I was busy painting a rather sloping ground in the wood, covered with moldered and dry beech leaves. You cannot imagine any carpet so splendid as that deep brownish-red, in the glow of an autumn eve-ning sun, tempered by the trees. The question was—and I found it very diffi-cult—how to get the depth of color, the enormous force and solidity of that ground. And while painting it I perceived for the first time how much light there was in that darkness, how was one to keep that light and at the same time retain the glow and depth of that rich color.

Elsewhere he talks about more general challenges which he must confront in his work:

There are laws of proportion, of light and shadow, of perspective which one must know in order to be able to draw well; without that knowledge it always remains a fruitless struggle and one never brings forth anything. I shall try this winter to store some capital of anatomy: I may not push it off longer and in the end it would prove expensive, for it would be loss of time.

The twentieth-century architect and artist Le Corbusier talks about the struggle the artist faces in capturing objects:

Our concept of the object comes from a total knowledge of it, a knowledge acquired by the experience of our senses, tactile knowledge, knowledge of its materials, its volume, its profile, of all its properties. And the usual perspective view only acts as the shutter release for the memory of these experiences.

Artists typically begin by mastering techniques developed by their predecessors; and if a technique is not already available, they will try to devise one. Dürer and his contemporaries of the Renaissance were de-termined to master the perspective that had eluded earlier generations. In a famous woodcut, Dürer presented one beguiling solution. The artist depicted in the woodcut marked a square grid on a window and a similar grid on a drawing surface, thereby making it possible to transpose the perspective image as seen through the window square by square directly onto the paper.

Artists must attend as well to the world of individuals. The Renaissance historian of painting Giorgio Vasari said of da Vinci: "Leonardo was so pleased whenever he saw a strange head or beard, or hair of unusual appearance that he would follow such a person a whole day and so learn him by heart, that when he reached home he could draw him as if he were present."

In his description of Michelangelo, Vasari helps us to understand the way in which Leonardo's fellow master attained his skills:

He had a most tenacious memory; he could remember and make use of the works of others when he had only once seen them; while he never repeated anything of his own because he remembered all he had done. . . . In his youth . . . it was proposed that [his friends] should try who could make a figure without any drawing in it, like those things that ignorant fellows draw on the walls. . . . He remembered having seen one of these rude drawings on a wall, and drew it as if he had it in front of him, and so surpassed all the other painters—a difficult thing for a man to do who had such knowledge of drawing.

Now Michelangelo may have been born with such accurate visual recall that he was able without effort to realize and re-create all prior percepts. We have evidence, however, from the artist William Hogarth that one can strive to develop one's perceptual and recall powers:

I therefore endeavored to habituate myself to the exercise of a sort of technical memory and by repeating in my own mind the parts of which objects are composed, I could by degree combine and put them down with my pencil . . . the early habit I thus acquired of retaining it in my mind's eye, without coldly copying it carefully on the spot, whatever I intended to imitate.

And Leonardo himself advised his painting students to contemplate, with a reflective eye, the cracks on an old wall in order to see what pregnant forms they might discover therein.

In any event, such testimony underscores the extent to which the plastic arts begin with a painstaking observation of the every-day world. However, artistic achievement cannot end there, if only because so much of abstract art remains apart from the world of personal experience. And actually, much of painting takes place at a plane remote from sheer duplication. Picasso claims, "Painting is poetry and is always written in verse with plastic rhythms, never in prose. . . . Plastic rhythms are forms that rhyme with one another or supply assonances

197

either with other forms or with the space that surrounds them." According to Rudolf Arnheim, a close student of artistry, both the representational and the abstract artist are concerned with the production of forms whose interactions hold significant meaning for them:

> Just as a chemist "isolates" a substance from combinations that distort his view of its nature and effects, so the work of art purifies significant appearance. It presents abstract themes in their generality, but not reduced to diagrams. The variety of direct experience is reflected in highly complex forms.

Ben Shahn, one of the premier American artists of this century, speaks of the struggle between idea and image: "The idea has to emerge from an image. . . . One thinks of Turner, for this great innovator did manipulate colors and suppress forms to create light." And Sir Herbert Read describes the feat involved in seeing forms—beautiful colors and shapes—rather than physical objects—such as a chair, which is the product of mundane intelligence.

All this testimony underscores that aspect of spatial intelligence which I earlier termed sensitivity to composition. Perhaps, indeed, once one is deeply interested in painting, problems of design, color, form become all important, with the particular subject matter a mere point of departure. In support of this speculation, Picasso stresses the formal element in all graphic art and declares, "Drawing, design, and color are understood and practiced in cubism in the spirit and manner that they are understood and practiced in all other schools." In the last analysis, there is a definite logic in the pursuit of the arts, one that sets it apart from the imitation of nature and places it close to other areas of rigorous investigation. Nearly two centuries ago, the English painter John Constable declared, "Painting is a science, and should be pursued as an inquiry into the laws of nature. Why, then, may not landscape be considered a branch of natural philosophy, of which pictures are but experiments?" Cézanne noted, some years later, "I am going on with my researches." And Clive Bell has suggested:

> Virginia [Woolf] and Picasso belonged to another order of beings: they were a species different from the common; their mental processes were different from ours . . . their standards, too, were of their own creation; yet, spontaneously, we appraised by those standards, which for the moment we not only accepted, but appropriated, whatever they chose to offer. Their conclusions were as satisfying as the conclusions of mathematics, though reached by quite other roads.

Achievements of painting masters, marvelous to behold, are as remote from most of us as the processes used by an outstanding composer or dancer. Somewhat closer to our world are the acitivities of the connoisseur, the individual who looks at and enjoys art, who can make fine discriminations, recognize style, and render evaluations. My own studies have shown that such connoisseurship can be acquired in a modest way even by young children, who can learn to overlook subject matter and attend as well (or instead) to those qualities of brush stroke and texture which often define a master's style.

It would be a grave mistake to assume, however, that connoisseurship develops automatically, or that it does not require well-developed powers. Picasso declared in a taunting spirit:

People say, "I have no ear for music" but they never say "I have no eye for painting" . . . people must be forced to see painting in spite of nature. We always believe that we're looking, right? But it's not true. We're always looking through glasses. People don't like painting. All they want to know is which paintings will be considered good one hundred years from now.

But some individuals do learn the language of connoisseurship; and, happily for us, the British art historian Kenneth Clark has reflected upon some of the key abilities. Even as a young child, he had a special attraction to the arts. Upon entering a gallery, he recalls

immediately I was transported. On either side were screens with paintings of flowers of such ravishing beauty that I was not only struck dumb with delight, I felt that I had entered a new world. In the relationship of the shapes and colors a new order had been revealed to me, a certainty established.

The fact that he was impressed so young is not lost on Clark. He speaks of the pure aesthetic sensation:

I am not so vain as to compare it to an infant musician's immediate understanding of a fugue, or to a youthful mathematician's joy when he first encounters Euclid's proof of the infinity of Prime Numbers. . . . Nevertheless, I think it must be reckoned a freak aptitude of the same kind . . . and in case any psychologist is rash enough to investigate this mysterious branch of the human psyche, I will record the sequel. Fifty-five years later, I was visiting a temple near Kyoto. . . . As I sat on the floor I experienced the clearest recollection of having seen these paintings before and said so to my companion, the official guide from the Foreign Office. "Nooh, Nooh, not possible" [Clark was told].

But, in fact, he was right; they had been exhibited in New York in 1910, and he had remembered the experience.

Clark notes that, from his earliest recollections, he could be moved by a painting, and he also had supreme confidence in his judgment: "it never occurred to me that someone else, with more mature judgment, might feel differently." Still, he had to undergo a long training in order to get to know the painters well, so that he could feel in his bones the differences among them. To look intensely at original drawings by Michaelangelo and Raphael, to decide on one's own which were authentic and which were false, was

the finest training for the eye that any young man could have had. One felt, in all humility, that one was entering into the artist's mind and understanding the implications of his slightest gesture. . . . One could also recognize that most inexplicable of all attributes in a work of art—a sense of form.

Clark describes the task of a connoisseur:

To say whether a picture is, or is not, by Bellini or Botticelli involves a combination of memory, analysis, and sensibility, which is an excellent discipline for both mind and eye. The nearest analogy is the textual criticism which was considered the ultimate end of classical scholarship. . . . In connoisseurship memory of facts and documents is replaced by visual memory . . . of spatial and compositional elements, tone and color. . . . It is an exacting discipline. Also involved is a feeling for the almost indescribable way in which a line evokes a form and for the equally mysterious relationship of tone and color. A serious judgment of authenticity involves one's whole faculties.

Here is a use of spatial intelligence which seems in no way less worthy of awe and emulation than that displayed by the scientist, the architect, the sculptor, or the painter.

The Cultural Perspective

As an intelligence that reaches far back into the past, spatial competence can be readily observed in all known human cultures. To be sure, specific inventions, like geometry or physics, kinetic sculpture or impressionist painting, are restricted to certain societies; but the capacity to make one's way around an intricate environment, to engage in complex arts and crafts, and to play sports and games of various types seems to be found everywhere.

What seems particularly intriguing are the types of spatial intelligence that have been developed in cultures remote from our own. The ability to notice fine details has been brought to an apogee by the Gikwe bushmen of the Kalahari, who can deduce from the spoor of an antelope its size, sex, build, and mood. In the several hundred square miles area where they travel, they know "every bush and stone, every convolution of the ground, and have usually named every place in it where a certain kind of veldt food may grow, even if that place is only a few yards in diameter, or where there is only a patch of tall grass or a bee tree." A keen visual memory is equally highly prized among the Kikuyu in Kenya. As a young child, Jomo Kenyatta was taught how to recognize every head of livestock in his family's herd from its color, markings, and size and type of its horns. Then he was tested: "Two or three herds were mixed, and he [was] expected to select the animals belonging to his own family. Or several animals [were] hidden and [he was] asked to inspect the herd and report the missing members."

Just as they exploit logical-mathematical skills, many games around the world also tap spatial intelligence. Tanzanian children play a game heavily dependent on this ability. Forty-five beans are arranged in nine rows to form a triangle. The beans are numbered in order. While the challenger is not looking, other players remove one bean at a time, working their way up from the base to the apex by taking beans from alternate edges of each row. The challenger has to call out the number name of each bean as it is removed, but remains silent when the first bean in a row is taken. Thus, he is in the position of the blindfolded chess player who must be able to visualize the absent board. The Shongo people of the Congo play a game where complex arrays are drawn in the sand, and the player must copy an array in a single path, without lifting a finger from the sand or retracing any line segment. As in certain games in Western culture, what is at stake here is the ability to use images to plan alternate sets of actions—quite possibly that union of spatial and logical-mathematical skills which we saw at work in chess.

The exploitation of spatial competence for more pragmatic ends is also striking. As I noted earlier, Eskimos have developed a high degree of spatial ability, possibly because of the difficulty of finding their way around their environment. They must be able to detect slight cracks in the ice, because a breaking ice pack could set one adrift in the ocean. Also, to find one's way back to a few houses in the tundra, the hunter must attend to the angle and shape of small drifts of snow; he must be able to judge weather conditions by carefully observing subtle patterns of dark and light on the clouds.

Examples of spatial acuity on the part of certain Eskimos are legendary. For example, Eskimos are said to be able to read as well upside down as right side up, and they can carve complexly designed figures without having to orient them correctly. Eskimos who have never before seen certain equipment are sometimes able to repair it when none of its customary users can: this ability presumably calls for a union of spatial skills with other forms of intelligence.

It might be thought that the Eskimo males would perform particularly well in spatial tasks; but, in fact, skilled performances are found among Eskimo females as well. This finding demonstrates that the sex differences in spatial abilities reported regularly in our western culture can be overcome in certain environments (or, conversely, that the biases in our own environments are producing apparent spatial deficits in females). At least 60 percent of Eskimo youngsters reach as high a score on tests of spatial ability as the top 10 percent of Caucasian children. This heightened ability also generalizes to tests of conceptual ability and to tests measuring visual details.

But I am not dealing here with a feature of climate. Highly developed spatial abilities are also found amongst a radically different population—the Puluwat people of the Caroline Islands in the South Seas. In the case of the Puluwats, the highly developed skill is that of navigation, one found in a minority of individuals who are allowed to sail canoes. Within this well-trained population, there occurs a flowering of skills that has filled Western-trained navigators with awe.

The key to Puluwat navigation can be found in the arrangement of stars in the sky. To navigate among the many islands in their vicinity, the Puluwats must recall the points or directions where certain stars rise and set around the horizon. This knowledge is first committed to memory by rote, but then becomes absorbed into the intuition of the sailor as he spends many months traveling back and forth. Ultimately, the knowledge must be integrated with a variety of factors including the location of the sun; the feeling one experiences in passing over the waves; the alteration of waves with changes in course, wind, and weather; skills in steering and handling the sheet; ability to detect reefs many fathoms down by sudden changes in the color of the water; and the appearance of the waves on the surface. Thomas Gladwin, who studied the system under the guidance of a master sailor, concludes,

No one set of observed phenomena will suffice to guide a sailing craft under all the conditions it will encounter at sea. Many categories of information must be integrated into a system whose diverse elements supplement each other to achieve a satisfactory level of accuracy and reliability.

To achieve this knowledge, the chosen Puluwats must learn much secret lore and negotiate a long series of tests:

The learning job is not complete until the student at his instructor's request can start with any island in the known ocean and rattle off the stars both going and returning between that island and all the others. . . . Armed with this knowledge, the sailor can then start off in a direction so that he will know he will end up in the vicinity of where he wants to go; will be able to keep the canoe steady on its course; and when near the goal have the techniques for locating the distinct island and heading toward it. . . . [The skilled navigator] can also use a star off to one side, adjust his sitting position so that when he is on course the star he has chosen rides near a stay, or perhaps just above an end of the outrigger float. In this way he can sail almost indefinitely without attending to his actual course.

While this sailing appears to be a seamless operation, the journey is actually divided conceptually into a series of segments. The number of star positions that lie between the bearing of the reference island as seen from the island of origin and its bearing as seen from the island of destination determines the number of segments to be negotiated. When the navigator envisions in his mind's eye that the reference island is passing under a particular star, he notes that a certain number of segments have been completed, and that a certain proportion of the voyage has therefore been accomplished. Like the blind individual, the navigator cannot see the islands, but he has learned where they are and how to keep their locations and relations in his mind. Asked where an island is, he can point to it—immediately and accurately.

How do the Puluwat Islanders themselves regard this skill? Apparently they respect their navigators not because they are "intelligent" but just because of what they can do, because of their ability to guide a canoe safely from one island to another. Asked whom they consider "intelligent," the natives are likely to mention statesmen or others who have good judgment. As Gladwin expresses it, "We in the Western world value intelligence highly. For this reason we respect the Puluwat navigator. Puluwatans also respect their navigators, but not primarily because they are intelligent. They respect them because they can navigate." Gladwin warns us, however, not to dismiss these abilities as concrete, primitive, or pre-rational. In his view, "abstract thinking is a pervasive characteristic of Puluwat navigation." In our terms, these Puluwatan navigators exhibit spatial intelligence to a high degree.

The individuals who hold the key to sailing in the Puluwats are the elders, who train the youngsters and who possess the greatest mastery of the navigating art. Similarly, among the Eskimos and numerous other traditional groups, elder individuals are often the repository of knowledge. It is striking that, in the Western context as well, high achievements in the spatial realm are often found amongst older individuals. In the case of painting, for example, Picasso and Titian painted until their nineties; and most of the greatest Western artists were painting as well as ever during the final years of their life. The contemporary sculptor Henry Moore, now in his eighties and a fine exemplar of this longevity, declares:

One does find the greatest artists doing their greatest work as they get older. I think that unlike most arts or sciences, the visual arts are more connected with actual human experience. Painting and sculpture have more to do with the outside world and they are never ending.

We encounter here a paradox. As it happens, on routine tests of visual-spatial thinking, normal adults as they age often exhibit a falling off in their performance, one that has even led to speculation that the right hemisphere is more vulnerable to aging. Yet, at the same time, individuals in whom spatial abilities are prized often perform very well until the end of their lives. My own view is that each form of intelligence has a natural life course: while logical-mathematical thought proves fragile later in life, across all individuals, and bodily-kinesthetic intelligence is also "at risk," at least certain aspects of visual and spatial knowledge prove robust, especially in individuals who have practiced them regularly throughout their lives. There is a sense of the whole, a "gestalt" sensitivity, which is central in spatial intelligence, and which seems to be a reward for aging—a continuing or perhaps even an enhanced capacity to appreciate the whole, to discern patterns even when certain details or fine points may be lost. Perhaps wisdom draws on this sensitivity to patterns, forms, and whole.

With this view of spatial intelligence, we have now encountered a second form of intelligence involved with objects. In contradistinction to logical-mathematical knowledge, which concludes its developmental trajectory with increasing abstraction, spatial intelligence remains tied fundamentally to the concrete world, to the world of objects and their location in a world. Perhaps, indeed, we find here another reason for the "staying power" of this intelligence. There is yet a third form of object-based intelligence, however, to be considered—a form that remains even closer to the individual, in that it inheres in the use of ones body, and one's actions upon the world. We turn in the next chapter to bodily-kinesthetic intelligence.

9

Bodily-
Kinesthetic
Intelligence

OUR Hero Bip hauls his suitcase onto the platform, climbs aboard the train, locates a seat, and then, with considerable strain, shoves his heavy suitcase onto the overhead rack. As the train gathers speed, Bip is tossed about on his seat even as his precariously rested suitcase is thrown out of the overhead rack. Bip manages to catch it and then carefully replaces it upon the shelf. The conductor arrives to gather his ticket. Bip goes through his pockets and, with increasing frustration, turns them inside out, as all the while the moving train continues to toss him about. When he still cannot find his ticket, his search becomes frantic, and he goes through all the compartments of his suitcase.

Next our Hero takes lunch out of his suitcase. He unscrews the cap of his thermos bottle, lifts the cork, pours coffee from the open thermos into the cup, which has earlier served as the cap of the bottle. But, due to the sway of the train, the coffee being poured from the mouth of the thermos never reaches the cup. Instead, the liquid flows in a straight line downward to where the cup was but no longer is. The hapless Bip eventually falls asleep. As the train slows down and comes to a rather abrupt halt, Bip is rudely awakened, apparently jolted by the cessation of the train's movement.

Delineating Bodily-Kinesthetic Intelligence

This little set of events could be a scene spied upon a train or, more likely, a comic skit enacted upon a stage or in a movie house. In actuality, however, it is a mime performance by the great French artist Marcel Marceau, as described by psychologist Marianne Simmel. As Simmel points out, Marceau seems on a superficial level merely to be doing what "real individuals" do all the time, "but he's so funny when he does it." In fact, however, the representation of actors, objects, events, and actions in the absence of the actual physical props amounts to a considerable departure from daily activities. It is up to the mime to create the *appearance* of an object, a person, or an action; and this task requires artful caricature, an exaggeration of movements and reactions, if the components are to be unambiguously recognized and stitched together into a seamless performance. To depict an object, for example, the mime has to delimit, by means of gestures, the shape of an object and to denote, by means of facial expressions and bodily actions, what that object is doing and its effects upon him. An especially talented mime like Marceau is able to create not only personalities (like a bully) and actions (like climbing) but also animals (butterflies), natural phenomena (waves cresting), and even abstract concepts such as freedom or bondage, good or evil, ugliness or beauty. More amazingly, still, he often creates a number of these illusions simultaneously.

The mime is a performer, and an exceedingly rare one, indeed. The intelligences upon which he draws are not widely developed in our culture. Yet, perhaps for that very reason, he indicates in particularly striking form the actions and capacities associated with a highly evolved bodily-kinesthetic (or, for short, bodily) intelligence. Characteristic of such an intelligence is the ability to use one's body in highly differentiated and skilled ways, for expressive as well as goal-directed purposes: these we see as Marceau pretends to run, climb, or prop up a heavy suitcase. Characteristic as well is the capacity to work skillfully with objects, both those that involve the fine motor movements of one's fingers and hands and those that exploit gross motor movements of the body. Again, these can be observed in a Marceau performance, as he delicately unscrews the cap of the thermos or lurches from side to side in the hurtling train. In this chapter, I treat these two capacities—control of one's bodily motions and capacity to handle objects skillfully—as the cores of bodily intelligence. As I have noted in the case of other intelligences, it is possible for these two core elements to exist separately; but in the typical case, skill in the use of the body for functional or expressive purposes tends to go hand in hand with skill in the manipulation of objects.

Given these core components, I will focus upon those individuals—like dancers and swimmers—who develop keen mastery over the motions of their bodies, as well as those individuals—like artisans, ballplayers, and instrumentalists—who are able to manipulate objects with finesse. But I will also consider other individuals in whom use of the body proves central, such as inventors or actors. It is important to stress that, in these latter occupations, other intelligences ordinarily play an important role. For instance, in the case of the actor or the performer, skill in personal intelligences—and also in many cases in musical or linguistic intelligence—is part and parcel of successful performance. Nearly all cultural roles exploit more than one intelligence; at the same time, no performance can come about simply through the exercise of a single intelligence. In fact, even Marcel Marceau's capacity to use his body with such precision may well involve contributions from several intellectual domains.

Skilled use of one's body has been important in the history of the species for thousands, if not millions, of years. In speaking of masterful use of the body, it is natural to think of the Greeks, and there is a sense in which this form of intelligence reached its apogee in the West during the Classical Era. The Greeks revered the beauty of the human form and, by means of their artistic and athletic activities, sought to develop a body that was perfectly proportioned and graceful in movement, balance, and tone. More generally, they sought a harmony between mind and body, with the mind trained to use the body properly, and the body trained to respond to the expressive powers of the mind. But intelligent use of the body can be discerned in other pursuits as well. Turning his attention to physical combat, the novelist Norman Mailer indicates:

There are languages other than words, language of symbol and languages of nature. There are languages of the body. And prize-fighting is one of them. A prizefighter . . . speaks with a command of the body which is as detached, subtle, and comprehensive in its intelligence as any exercise of the mind. [He expresses] himself with wit, style, and an aesthetic flair for surprise when he boxes with his body. Boxing is a dialogue between bodies, [it] is a rapid debate between two sets of intelligences.

A description of use of the body as a form of intelligence may at first jar. There has been a radical disjunction in our recent cultural tradition between the activities of reasoning, on the one hand, and the activities of the manifestly physical part of our nature, as epitomized by our bodies, on the other. This divorce between the "mental" and the "physical" has not infrequently been coupled with a notion that what we do with our bodies is somehow less privileged, less special, than those problem-solving routines carried out chiefly through the use of language, logic, or some other relatively abstract symbolic system.

This sharp distinction between the "reflective" and the "active" is not, however, drawn in many other cultures. This fact should at least give us pause before we conclude that a particular legacy of Western Cartesian thought is a universal imperative. It is also worthy of note that psychologists in recent years have discerned and stressed a close link between the use of the body and the deployment of other cognitive powers. There is a discernible tendency to focus on the cognitive facets as well as the neuropsychological basis of skilled body use, and a clear trend to analogize thought processes with "sheer" physical skills. The insightful British psychologist Sir Frederic Bartlett drew an analogy among various kinds of skills where diverse receptive and performing functions were linked:

> This essential requirement of any performance that can be called skilled becomes much more plain if we look at a few actual instances. The player in a quick ball game; the operator, engaged at his work bench, directing his machine, and using his tools; the surgeon conducting an operation; the physician arriving at a clinical decision—in all these instances and in innumerable other ones that could just as well be used, there is the continuing flow from signals occurring outside the performer and interpreted by him to actions carried out; then on to further signals and more action, up to the culminating point of the achievement of the task, or whatever part of the task is the immediate objective. . . . Skilled performance must all the time submit to receptor control, and must be initiated and directed by the signals which the performer must pick up from his environment, in combination with other signals, internal to his own body, which tell him about his own movements as he makes them.

According to Bartlett's analysis, all skilled performances include a well-honed sense of timing, where each bit of a sequence fits into the stream in an exquisitely placed and elegant way; points of repose or shift, where one phase of the behavior is at an end, and some calibration is necessary before the second one comes into play; a sense of direction, a clear goal to which the sequence has been heading, and a point of no return, where further input of signals no longer produces a result because the final phase of the sequence has already been activated. Bartlett goes beyond the sheer analysis of bodily skill in his intriguing claim that much of what we ordinarily call thinking—routine as well as innovative—partakes of the same principles that have been uncovered in overtly physical manifestations of skill.

From related analyses by other psychologists, we can identify other staples of highly skilled performance. Over the years the highly skilled performer has evolved a family of procedures for translating intention into action. Knowledge of what is coming next allows that overall smoothness of performance which is virtually the hallmark of expertise. The periods of hovering or halting, which call for keen attention to environmental factors, alternate with periods of seamless fluency, where numerous component parts fall readily into place. Programming of actions at a relatively abstract level allows the choice of those particular units of performance which will result in the smoothest possible sequence of activity. It is just because of this mastery of the possible alternatives, the ability to enact the sequence most effective for present purposes, that the expert looks as though he has all the time in the world to do what he wants.

As I have noted, bodily use can itself be differentiated into a variety of forms. Like Marcel Marceau, one may use one's whole body to represent a certain kind of activity—for example, running or falling—chiefly for expressive ends. (In a sport like football or boxing, one tends to use one's whole body or grosser motor actions). Of equal (if not greater) importance in human activity is the elaboration of fine motor movements, the ability to use one's hands and fingers, to carry out delicate movements involving precise control. The act of grasping a small object precisely with opposed thumb and finger—which prosimians cannot execute at all, and which higher primates can do with only modest skill—has been carried to an exquisitely and qualitatively higher level by human beings. A good pianist can produce independent patterns of movement in each hand, sustain different rhythms in each hand, while also using the two hands together to "speak to one another" or to produce a fugal effect. In typing or in shooting, a finger can be moved for just a few milliseconds, or an eye just a few degrees, in order to allow precise attacks or adjustments. And in dance, even the tiniest quiver of a finger may assume importance. As Suzanne Farrell, master ballerina of the New York City Ballet, has declared:

In a performance, when I look and see my little finger out there, I say to myself, "That's for Mr. B." [the noted choreographer George Balanchine]. Maybe nobody in the audience notices it, but he's seen it and appreciates it.

209

The Brain's Role in Bodily Movement

While studies of perception and language have dominated published treatments in neuropsychology, the saga of the brain's role in physical activity proves to be as intriguing as reports about the aphasias or as accounts of the detection of edges, lines, colors, and objects. And, indeed, even as bodily intelligence may have been taken for granted, or minimized in importance by many researchers, motor activity has been considered as a less "high" cortical function than functions subserving "pure" thought. Yet, as Roger Sperry, the doyen of American neuropsychologists, has shrewdly pointed out, one should look upon mental activity as a means to the end of executing actions. Rather than motor activity as a subsidiary form designed to satisfy the demands of the higher centers, one should instead conceptualize cerebration as a means of bringing "into motor behavior additional refinement, increased direction toward distant, future goals and greater overall adaptiveness and survival value."

It is hardly an exaggeration to say that most segments of the body (and the nervous system) participate in one or another way in the execution of motor actions. The various agonist and antagonist muscles, joints, and tendons are involved in the most direct ways. Our kinesthetic sense, which monitors the activity of these regions, allows us to judge the timing, force, and extent of our movements and to make necessary adjustments in the wake of this information. Within the nervous system, large portions of the cerebral cortex, as well as the thalamus, the basal ganglia, and the cerebellum, all feed information to the spinal cord, the way station *en route* to the execution of action. Paradoxically, whereas the cortex serves as the "highest" center in most forms of human activity, it is the relatively lowly basal ganglia and the cerebellum that contain the most abstract and complex forms of "representation of movements"; the motor cortex is more directly tied to the spinal cord and the actual execution of specific muscular movements.

For my purposes it is not necessary to review the mass of information which has been secured about the physical operation of the bodily-kinesthetic systems in human beings, but it is germane to call attention to some general principles that have emerged. To begin with, the operation of the movement system is tremendously complex, calling upon the coordination of a dizzying variety of neural and muscular components in a highly differentiated and integrated fashion. For example, in the movement of the hand to retrieve an element or to throw or catch an object, there is extremely intricate interaction between the eye and the hand, with the feedback from each particular movement allowing more precisely governed subsequent motion. Feedback mechanisms are highly articulated, so that motor movements are subjected to continuous refinement and regulation on the basis of a comparison of the intended goal state and the actual position of the limbs or body parts at a particular moment in time.

In fact, voluntary movements require perpetual comparison of intended actions with the effects actually achieved: there is a continuous feedback of signals from the performance of movements, and this feedback is compared with the visual or the linguistic image that is directing the activity. By the same token, the individual's perception of the world is itself affected by the status of his motor activities: information concerning the position and status of the body itself regulates the way in which subsequent perception of the world takes place. In fact, in the absence of such feedback from motor activity, perception cannot develop in a normal way.

Much voluntary motor activity thus features the subtle interaction between perceptual and motor systems. At least some activity, however, proceeds at so rapid a clip that feedback from perceptual or kinesthetic systems cannot be used. Particularly in the case of overlearned, automatic, highly skilled, or involuntary activities, the whole sequence may be "preprogrammed" so that it can unfold as a seamless unit with only the slightest modifications possible in light of information from the sensory systems. Only such highly programmed sequences will allow activities of the pianist, the typist, or the athlete, each of whom depends upon lengthy sequences of movement that unfold at great speed. Manfred Clynes, a neuroscientist interested in musical performance, points out:

One may decide to move a finger a distance corresponding to one inch or two inches, or to turn the eyes to look at an object say twenty degrees or thirty degrees to the left. In each case, the muscles start, complete and stop the motion in a fraction of a second. . . . The movement is preprogrammed by the brain before it begins. Once such a short movement has begun the decision is merely executed. Within that fraction of a second it takes to execute there is no feedback that can permit one to modify the programmed decision.

Moreover, some of these motor programs may not need to be developed:

Many motor programs are part of a primate's genetic endowment. No sensory feedback or spinal reflex loops are necessary for learning the repertoire

211

of movements. . . . Perceptual and motor systems are no doubt in part "set" by the shaping effect of some aspects of the environment, but the systems that emerge seem to be highly specialized, intrinsically programmed in quite different ways. In short, what is taken for granted without direct evidence in the case of physical growth on the basis of an implicit argument from poverty of the stimulus is also being found in the study of the brain and the nervous system.

While much of the operation of the motor system occurs in similar fashion throughout the primate order, at least one dimension of human motor activity—and perhaps the most important—seems restricted to our species. That is the capacity for dominance—the potential for one half of the body (and one half of the brain) to assume the ascendancy across a range of motor and perceptual activities. There are traces of brain laterality in higher primates: as baboons learn to carry out activities with a high degree of finesse, one limb will tend to become dominant, playing the leading role in both gross and delicate movements, while the other assumes a supporting role. Moreover, this division of labor will be reflected after brain damage, where the "supporting hand" becomes unable to carry out what were formerly "executive roles." But there are apparently no tendencies in baboons or other primates for one specific side of the brain (and the contralateral body side) to become generally dominant. The tendency for left hemisphere dominance in motor activity seems to be a proclivity of human beings, no doubt at least partially under genetic control, and one that in all likelihood is linked to language. Just as most normal individuals will have their language capacities housed in the left hemisphere, so, too, will the left halves of their brains be dominant for motor activity. And, again supporting the genetic argument, left-handedness (or right-brainedness for motor activities) seems to run in families.

Buttressing my claim for a separate bodily intelligence, it turns out that injuries to those zones of the left hemisphere that are dominant for motor activity can produce selective impairment. Neurologists speak of the *apraxias*, a set of related disorders, in which an individual who is physically capable of carrying out a set of motor sequences, and cognitively capable of understanding a request to do so, is nonetheless unable to carry them out in the proper order or in a proper manner. Some apraxias of great specificity have been described: For instance, there are cases of isolated dressing apraxia (impairment in putting on a suit of clothes). More commonly, individuals exhibit *limb-kinetic* apraxia, where they cannot carry out a command with either hand; *ideomotor apraxia*, where they clumsily execute actions and use the body part itself as an object (for example, when pretending to pound a nail, they will ram a fist against a surface rather than represent the absent implement in their grip); or *ideational apraxia*, where individuals exhibit a special difficulty in running through a sequence of actions smoothly and in the correct order. It is of some interest that these various lapses—an inappropriate execution or an omitted action—are also found in normal individuals, particularly when they are operating under pressure.

While these apraxias often occur in conjunction with aphasia, there is considerable evidence that apraxia is not simply a linguistic or a symbolic disorder. Individuals who fail to carry out commands can understand what is called for, even as individuals with severe linguistic comprehension disorders exhibit amazing preservation of the ability to execute certain kinds of command (for example, those involving the movement of the whole torso); moreover, a number of studies have confirmed that the degree of impairment in understanding various symbols does not correlate highly with the ability to carry out voluntary motor actions. Finally, several researchers have documented that individuals who have completely lost their verbal memories nonetheless remain capable of learning and remembering complex motor sequences and patterns of behavior (even when they vehemently deny that they ever have encountered the sequence in question)! All of which adds up to a picture of bodily intelligence as a realm discrete from linguistic, logical, and other so-called higher forms of intellect. There are even occasional patients, otherwise normal, who can carry out virtually no actions at all: these are the isolated apraxics who exhibit, in essentially pure form, an absence of bodily intelligence.

Can intelligence of the body be spared in isolated form as well? Certainly there are neuropsychological patients whose linguistic and logical capacities have been devastated but who show little or no difficulty in carrying out highly skilled motor activities. These patients have not been much studied, perhaps because this symptomatic picture is—to the Western mind—much less surprising than the contrasting capacity to speak or reason in the absence of motor skills. While selective preservation of motor activities has not been much commented upon, one form of preservation related to bodily intelligence is remarkable. Some exceptional youngsters, such as *idiots savants* or autistic children, may be totally cut off from their fellows yet show a preserved interest in, and knowledge of, bodily activities and mechanical devices. In order to evince these forms of understanding, it is probably essential to have preserved bodily and spatial knowledge. The *idiot savant* literature includes the cases of Earl, who on his own figured out how to make a windmill out of a clock; of Mr. A., who was able to wire his stereo, lights, and television to a single switch; and of another similarly impaired youth who designed and built a functional merry-go-round. The clinical psychologist Bernard Rimland relates the story of an autistic youth Joe, who draws on theories of electronics to build devices:

> He recently put together a tape recorder, fluorescent light and a small transistor radio with some other components so that music from the tape was changed to light energy in the light and then back to music in the radio. By passing his hand between the recorder and the light, he could stop the music. He understands the concepts of electronics, astronomy, music, navigation, and mechanics. He knows how things work and is familiar with technical terms. By the age of 12 he could find his way all over the city on his bike with a map and compass. He reads Bowditch on navigation. Joe is supposed to have an IQ of 80. He does assembly work in a Goodwill store.

Perhaps the most famous case of this type is Joey, the "Mechanical Boy," described some years ago by psychoanalyst Bruno Bettelheim. According to Bettelheim's report, Joey was an otherwise hapless autistic youngster who displayed a special interest in machines. Not only did he like to play with machines—taking them apart, putting them together, manipulating all manner of screws, wires, cords—but, most phenomenally, young Joey liked to pretend that he was a machine. Indeed his reality was one of machines. As Bettelheim describes it:

> During Joey's first weeks with us, we watched absorbedly, for example, as he entered the dining room. Laying down an imaginary wire he connected himself with his source of electrical energy. Then he strung the wire from an imaginary outlet to the dining room table to insulate himself, and then plugged himself in. (He had tried to use real wire but this we could not allow.)
> These imaginary electrical connections he had to establish before he could eat, because only the current ran his ingestive apparatus. He performed the ritual with such skill that one had to look twice to be sure there was neither wire nor outlet nor plug. His pantomime was so skilled, and his concentration so contagious, that those who watched him seemed to suspend their own existence and become observers of another reality.

By virtue of his pathetic story (happily Joey eventually improved), this youngster demonstrates that the ability to enact and mime can exist despite a profound communicative deficit. He also underscores the link that I have imputed between the capacity to use one's body in highly skilled ways and the understanding of machinery—for, as suggested, Joey possessed considerable understanding of the nature and operation of a variety of machines, particularly ones that feature whirling motion and climactic destruction. Here, bodily intelligence may well be supplemented by spatial and logical-mathematical forms of understanding.

The Evolution of Bodily Skill

How might refined bodily and mechanical intelligence come about? One set of clues derives from a study of the evolution of cognitive skills. There is essentially no flexible tool use found in animals below the primate order: that is, lower organisms do not use different objects flexibly for the purpose of manipulating the environment. Rather, there is a tendency for each species to use one or two tools, in a highly stereotypical way, with only the appendages of the body—claws, teeth, beaks—used in an instrumental fashion.

Even in the lower primate orders, tool use is infrequent and not particularly generative or innovative. Often objects are thrown around during periods of great excitement but they are not directed toward any utilitarian ends. They are, in fact, simply random components of loud and aggressive agonistic displays whose purpose is to intimidate others.

Yet evolutionary sources document that higher primates have been using simple tools for several million years, and that chimpanzees can achieve some impressive results. A much studied and highly suggestive example of sophisticated primate tool use is termite fishing in chimpanzees. As described by Geza Teleki, this is an activity in which the chimpanzee first uses a finger or a thumb to scrape away a thin layer of soil covering the entrance to a tunnel; then pokes an object into the mouth of the tunnel; pauses while holding the end of the object in one hand; extracts the object with its attached termites; and then picks off the desired termites with lips and teeth while holding the probe in one hand and stabilizing the free end on the other wrist.

Such termite fishing is by no means an easy task. Initially the chimpanzee must find a tunnel. (That one is not easy to find is confirmed by Teleki, who himself engaged in weeks of futile searching for a tunnel until he finally opened one inadvertently.) Next the chimpanzee must select a tool for probing. Again, it may try a number of twigs, vines, or grass stalks before selecting an appropriate probe and, if necessary, modifying it. Modification can consist of trimming away leaves

215

or other projections, or breaking or biting the probe down to suitable size. Again Teleki found that, despite months of observation and imitation, he could never reach the proficiency of a young chimp. In his own view:

selection proficiency is a learned skill which must, like tunnel-locating, entail a considerable amount of trial-and-error behavior backed by long term retention of the results. The retention span may actually cover the lifetime of an individual.

In the fishing stage, the chimpanzee must insert the probe to the right depth (8 to 16 centimeters) with appropriate turns of the wrist so that the probe can navigate the curves of the tunnel. Then the probe must be gently vibrated with the fingers, enough so that the termites will bite onto the probe, but not so much that they will bite right through it. Once they are hooked on, the probe can be extracted from the tunnel, but not too rapidly or clumsily lest the termites be scraped off by the tunnel wall.

Termite fishing is performed differently across diverse chimpanzee groups. Since these groups are close genetically, it is likely that the contrasting practices reflect different social customs. For example, one population uses probes to fish inside the mound, so its probes are relatively short and thin; a second group uses the probe to perforate the mound surface, and so its probes must be relatively strong and rigid. Other "cultural differences" involve the kind of material selected for the probes, whether the tools are obtained near or far from the mound, whether one or both ends of the probe are used, whether the chimpanzees use a power or a precision grip on the tool.

W. C. McGrew has described the acquisition of the skills for termite fishing in the Gombe chimpanzee population in Tanzania. According to his account, infants under the age of two will exhibit all elements of the technique in rudimentary form; they will eat termites, poke on the mound's surface, modify raw materials, and the like. Between two and four years of age, the young chimps spend considerable time climbing about termite mounds, poking into mounds or holes, and snatching their mother's tools. Their sequential integration gradually improves over the period. By the age of four, some individuals may exhibit the polished adult form of the behavior but still will not persist in long feeding bouts. This latter capacity develops by the age of five or six.

As I have noted, it is important for the young primate to sustain a relationship with an adult figure throughout such a learning process.

The young chimpanzee or monkey observes and gains knowledge about the process from seeing others engage in it. By contrast, primates raised with surrogate parents exhibit a different approach to problem solving. While wild monkeys view the situation as a problem where some solution is possible, surrogate-raised monkeys behave as if they lack any consistent strategy or plan. Only naturally reared monkeys apparently understand that their behavior has an effect on the environment, and that they can, to some extent, control events: lack of efficacious models results in learned helplessness. More generally, primates are much more likely to learn use of a tool if they are situated (and play) in proximity to other individuals that are already able to accomplish desirable goals. Primates are much more likely to emit a behavior if they have observed a conspecific carry it out, if a reward (like food) has been obtained, or if the primate just happens to imitate the response and finds that it leads to a desired outcome.

Authorities speculate that at least three sets of factors determine whether a primate will be able to learn to use a tool. First of all, there is sensory-motor maturation, necessary for skill and precision of muscle movement. Second, there is play with environmental objects in casual or problem-solving settings: during play, for example, the chimpanzee learns to use a stick as a functional extension of its arm. Finally, there is response-contingent stimulation, which teaches the young organism that its own behavior can, at least to some extent, control the environment.

Termite fishing is among the most complex form of tool use found among organisms outside the hominoid stock. Other forms of tool use found among primates include the following categories: extension of the user's reach (for example, using a stick to reach food); amplifications of mechanical force that the user exerts on the environment (pounding stones to open nuts or fruits); enhancing of the user's display behavior (for example, brandishing a stick during displays of aggression); or increasing the efficiency with which users can control fluids (for example, using leaves to sponge up water or wipe off blood). While each of these forms has definite adaptive value, most can be arrived at largely through trial-and-error on the part of the organism. Moreover, according to the archaeologist Alexander Marshack, these activities are largely *one-handed:* rather than featuring genuine integration of a more and a less dominant hand, they require essentially one dominant hand, with the secondary hand being used merely to hold or to grasp. There is little of that highly orchestrated alternation in spacing, action, and orientation which characterizes skilled two-hand use

217

in human beings. Impressive as primate tool use is, it still exhibits severe limitations.

Evolution of human beings over the past three or four million years can be described in terms of the increasingly sophisticated use of tools. Two to three million years ago, the tool use by *homo habilis* represented only a modest advance over what primates had been doing for millions of years before. The basic tool kit at this time consisted of rounded stones which were used to bash objects, and rough stones used for chopping. At this time, prehistoric humans began to use stones to bash crude flakes from a pebble. The bashing of stones against one another—with force being transmitted through such object contact—produced stone tools like scrapers with a sharp edge which could be used for cutting. Such tools represented a genuine innovation, for early hominids could use these sharp edges to chop hides and to butcher a carcass.

Such choppers and flakes constituted the basis of tool making until about one and one-half million years ago, when large bifaces or hand axes began to appear. The wielder was *homo erectus,* who employed these axes for finer, more powerful, and more accurate kinds of cutting and splitting. Over the next million years, possibly until forty or fifty thousand years ago, changes in tool use proceeded slowly and gradually. Presumably, the procedures for making tools were passed on through visual observation and gestural imitation, with but slight changes occurring from one generation to another. Perhaps one-half million years ago, men began to hammer stone in order to make finer implements; two-hundred thousand years ago, during the Acheulian period, there was soft hammering of bone for flaking and retouching; and one-hundred thousand years ago, during the Levallois period, there was the first striking of flakes from a prepared core stone, followed by working or touching up the flakes. During this one-million year period, other changes were taking place in humans, as reflected in the steadily increasing size of the brain. Fire came under hominid control; there was collective and brutal big-game hunting, including the massacre of large herds of elephants; individuals erected settlements, including not only hearths but also houses and sitting and working areas. Still, men were probably communicating through gesture and, possibly, simple vocalizations of an emotional sort.

By one-hundred thousand years ago, Neanderthal man, fully human in physique, had appeared in Europe. This powerful and robust individual engaged in running and much combat, as witnessed by the large number of broken bones and healed fractures, presumably received from spear points during close fighting. But there was a tender side to Neanderthal as well. Skulls were placed in niches; individuals were buried, possibly in family plots; and most poignantly, flowers were placed in the graves. Here we see what may well be the first intimations of symbolic behavior oriented toward specific other individuals.

The major explosion in human evolution occurred sometime in the last fifty thousand years, probably thirty-five to forty thousand years ago at the time of Cro-Magnon man. It is difficult to avoid the speculation that the use of productive oral-auditory languages were somehow linked to this explosion, though whether as cause or effect (or both) it is impossible to know. At that time, there emerged clear signs of human symbolic capacities, including pictures (as in the splendid animals and female figures in the Paleolithic caves of southern Europe), notations (as in the calendrical systems found across Europe and Siberia), and, in all likelihood, the ritualistic dances that are sketched on the walls of many of the caves. There was a correlative revolution in the degree of precision of tools, as bone and stone technology was marshaled with increasing effectiveness. In addition to utilitarian purposes, tools were now used to decorate and, most important, to make other tools. By this time, men had knowledge not only of a wide variety of materials but also of diverse types and classes of tools to be made and used for different purposes, including lances, knives, chisels, needles, and tools for scraping, performing, whittling, serving, and pounding. The productive cycle between greater brain size (which allowed better planning and more precise use of tools) and the devising of still better tools conferred a decisive adaptive advantage on individuals who could fashion physical tools and, eventually, those abstract and versatile tools called symbols.

It is almost irresistible to compare the slow evolution of tool use in primates and in hominids with the analogous though far more rapid increase in sophistication found in normal children everywhere: provided such comparison is done cautiously, it can be informative. Susan Parker suggests that the common ancestor of the great apes and humans apparently exhibited those forms of intelligence, found in children aged one to four, that allow the extraction of food with foraging tools; the descendants of the first hominids displayed a higher level of intelligence, found in children of four to six, and could handle more complex tools, such as missiles for throwing and stone tools to be manufactured, and such tasks as animal butchery, food division, and shelter construction. One can discern a progression, then, from the manipulation of objects, associated with the simple circular reactions of the early sensori-motor period to the use of tools for the attainment of goals, which reflects the heights of sensori-motor intelligence, to still more sophisticated capacities to use tools that produce non-direct effects on objects, or to design new tools to meet fresh challenges.

Such a progression, observable in children and to some extent in present-day primates, can in part be inferred from the fossil record. And it is in the light of this recurring sequence that authorities speculate about the role of greater overall brain size and newly emerging brain regions in producing the breakthroughs that made our species what it is. One clear difference must be noted, however. Language use begins relatively early in the life of the young child, long before tool use has achieved a sophisticated level; this is the point where divergence from the evolutionary record is most likely, since most authorities see the evolution of language as following a period characterized by considerable sophistication with tools and by the use of gesturing and "emotional" sounds as the principal means of communication.

The Development of Bodily Intelligence in the Individual

The prehistoric origins of bodily intelligence, and its relation to language and other cognitive functions, may forever be wrapped in uncertainty; but the development of these skills in the human beings of today is a subject on which scientific progress can be made. Though Piaget did not himself view his work in relation to bodily intelligence (he was interested in "headier" issues!), his description of the unfolding of sensori-motor intelligence, in fact, illuminates its initial evolution. One can see in Piaget's description how individuals progress from the simplest reflexes—such as those involved in sucking and looking— to behavioral acts that fall increasingly under the control of environmental variation and individual intentions. One can see formerly isolated events yoked together—such as sucking and looking, or looking and reaching—in order to obtain familiar goals. One can see separate acts combined in novel ways in order to achieve fresh goals—earmarks of the height of object permanence. Finally, as the child begins to operate upon mental representations such as symbols, one can note the same sequence of acts and operations recapitulated in a less public arena. Tool use has now invaded the realm of "pure thought."

A number of students of child development, among them Jerome Bruner and Kurt Fischer, have embraced the idea that the development of skills ought to be conceived of generally, not merely with reference to the bodily activities of infancy, but rather with respect to all manners of cognitive operations. These researchers construe the development of knowledge as a building up of more elaborated and increasingly flexible skills: smoothed-out acts themselves become the subcomponents or constituent acts of ever higher and more complex skills. Thus, for example, the child first combines reaching and looking into grasping; the grasping of single objects evolves into the passing of objects from one hand to the other; the use of sets of objects for daily tasks is transformed into the building of simple structures; such simple structures become combined into more elaborated displays; and so on. Scholars who pursue the idea of knowledge-as-skill recognize the increasing internalization of public action into private thought but insist that every new skill sequence must nonetheless pass through a parallel developmental sequence. In this way, they recall the approach of Frederic Bartlett, who brooked no sharp distinction between physical actions and thinking skills; and they align themselves with contemporary students of human performance, who focus on the development of skills like typing, chess playing, or computer programming, and see each as manifesting increasing mastery of, and smoother coordination among, various types and levels of skill.

There may well be significant continuities between the earliest circular reactions of the infant and the much more elaborated forms of activity that characterize the skilled juggler, typist, chess player, reader, or programmer. Yet the question must be raised whether the acquisition of symbolic competence may, in fact, affect the development of bodily skill in profound ways. When one can state a goal in words, convey instructions verbally, criticize one's own performance, or coach another individual, the methods whereby skills are acquired and combined may take on a different cast. By the same token, mastery of such symbolic functions as representation (denoting an entity, like a person or an object) and expression (communicating a mood, like gaiety or tragedy) provides individuals with the option of mobilizing bodily capacities in order to communicate diverse messages. Perhaps activities of the body operate to some degree independently of these symbolic functions; the fact that symbolic capacities and motor activities can be dissociated from one another as a consequence of neurological disorders is at least suggestive evidence in this regard. Nonetheless, it is my guess that once human symbolic functioning has become a reality, the

221

motor system becomes forever altered: the flowering of symbolization forges a major chasm between bodily intelligence as it is practiced in humans and bodily intelligence as deployed by other animals.

An anecdote related by the neuropsychologist Edith Kaplan proves relevant to this issue. As part of a test of apraxia, Kaplan asked an apraxic patient to pretend "to saw." Afflicted with ideomotor apraxia, this individual proved unable to enact the sawing motion through the representation of the absent implement (holding his clenched hand as if there were a saw in it): instead, in classic apraxic fashion, he treated the hand itself like a saw (moving the edge of the open hand back and forth as if it were itself a saw blade). As Kaplan wanted to ascertain whether the patient could, in fact, carry out the desired motion, she simply asked him to imitate a nonrepresentative act—in this case, that is, to oscillate his hand back and forth as though he were holding an implement, but she did not specify what the implement might be. The patient performed the apparently arbitrary action in an adequate manner. Pleased with this demonstration, Kaplan declared, "See, you're sawing"—only to find that the instant the morpheme "saw" left her lips, the patient's fist opened and reverted to the edge-as-a-blade position. Clearly, in this instance, the symbolic code ("saw") had triumphed over a sheer perceptual-bodily link.

Mature Forms of Bodily Expression

THE DANCE

Of all the uses of the body, none has reached greater heights, or has been more variably deployed by cultures than the dance. Following the helpful discussion of Judith Hanna, a careful student of this medium, we can define dancing as culturally patterned sequences of nonverbal body movements that are purposeful, intentionally rhythmic, and have aesthetic value in the eyes of those for whom the dancer is performing. Dance goes back many thousand of years, in all probability to Paleolithic times, for masked dancing sorcerers and hunters are depicted in the ancient caves of Europe and in the mountain ranges of South Africa. In fact, of all the human activities depicted in the caves, dancing is the second most prominent, right after hunting, with which it may well have been associated.

We do not know all the uses to which dancing has been put, but the anthropological evidence suggests at least the following. Dance can reflect and validate social organization. It can serve as a vehicle of secular or religious expression; as a social diversion or recreational activity; as a psychological outlet and release; as a statement of aesthetic values or an aesthetic value in itself; as a reflection of an economic subsistence pattern, or an economic activity in itself. Dance can serve an educational purpose, in an initiation rite, by acting out transformation through which an individual will eventually pass; it can be used to embody the supernatural, as when medicine men dance to invoke the spirits; it can even be used for sexual selection, in cases where women can discriminate among men in terms of their dance performance and endurance (in the Nuba Tira tribe of the Sudan young women will "throw themselves against the partners they have chosen"). And in many cultures, dance can serve several of these functions, either simultaneously, at different times, or in different milieux.

A feeling for some of the diverse uses of dance can be gained by comparing dance among the Hopi Indians of the American Southwest with dance among Samoans in Polynesia. In both cultures, dance is important, the extent of motion is limited, and supernatural powers are involved. However the aims and the character of the dance differ across these two cultures. Among the Hopi, dance serves to maintain tribal unity, to placate the gods, and to preserve cultural values. Men are the primary performers: for them, dance is a duty, an obligation to the tribe. A good performer is one who remembers the steps, dances energetically but does not covet individual praise. In contrast, in Polynesia the dances are personalized, less conservative, more open to improvisation. Polynesians dance to commemorate events, to entertain, to increase mana, and to propitiate the gods. Both men and women, as well as children, dance; and whether someone becomes a dancer depends upon personal interest, skill, and family tradition. Good performers are those who have individual style and move well. Dance is an area where, in the face of much societal conformity, individualism is tolerated and even encouraged. One might say that among the Hopi, dance serves as a primary area in which the culture's values are expressed; whereas among the Samoans, it provides a kind of counterpoint to the customary rigor of the culture.

Given the great variety of purposes that dance can serve, it is difficult to generalize about its canonical form. Sometimes, indeed, the formal features are less important than the surrounding ambiance or the explicit referential content. Nonetheless, certain features do appear to characterize dance in a range of settings, and these prove most germane to a consideration of how skills are embodied in this form of intelligence.

According to the American dancer and choreographer Paul Taylor, a dancer must learn to execute a dance movement precisely in shape and time. The dancer is concerned with placement, stage spacing, the quality of a leap, the softness of a foot—whether a movement goes out to an audience or spirals into itself. Many movements are possible, ranging from swaying ones to those that are like a piston, from percussive ones to those that are sustained. It is from the combination of these qualities—varied in speed, direction, distance, intensity, spatial relations, and force—that one can discover or constitute a dance vocabulary. In addition to these relatively objective features, the personality of the dancer will inevitably come across in a performance. Traditionally, dance has dealt with the extreme emotions, like joy and grief: but in modern dance it is now customary to attempt to convey more complex emotions like guilt, anguish, or remorse, though, as George Balanchine once remarked wittily, "It is still not possible to depict a mother-in-law in a dance." Music is the most important partner in dance, and the structure of a musical composition will strongly affect the technique in a dance; but inasmuch as dance can also proceed without music, the latter's presence cannot define the dance.

So described, dance may seem a dry and relatively abstract form of communication and expression. And indeed, it is difficult to get dancers (or even dance critics) to characterize their activity in a straightforward and concrete way. Isadora Duncan, pioneer dancer of this century, summed it up in her well-known remark, "If I could tell you what it is, I would not have danced it." Martha Graham, perhaps the premier modern dancer of this century, has made an intriguing observation:

> I have often remarked on the extreme difficulty of having any kind of conversation with most dancers which has any kind of logical cohesiveness— their minds just jump around (maybe like my body)—the logic—such as it is—occurs on the level of motor activity.

Nonetheless, it is typically the concrete and physical aspects of dancing, the use of the body in all kinds of unusual but satisfying ways, that serve initially to attract an individual to the dance. The American dancer and choreographer José Limón recalls:

> As a child in Mexico I had been fascinated—as any child would be—by Spanish jotas, Mexican jarabes, and Indian bailes. Later, across the border, I had seen tap dancers and ballet dancers. Then pure accident brought me to a performance by [the modern dancer] Harald Kreutzberg. I saw the dance as a

vision of ineffable power. A man could, with dignity and a towering majesty, dance.

Sometimes the sheer properties of one's body serve as seducer. Nijinsky, arguably the greatest dancer of the century, already stood out as a ballet student, displaying a technical virtuosity that was completely out of the ordinary. And sometimes it is the mystery of the patterns that are produced. Amy Greenfield, a contemporary dancer, says that when she attended the ballet as a child, she used to shut her eyes and imagine what would come next. If she opened her eyes, and the dancers were where she had imagined them to be, she won.

With males in the West, interest in dance may only emerge much later, presumably because of the cultural taboo with respect to men dancing (Nijinsky was teased for being like a girl: thus, the taboo was not absent in Czarist Russia either!). Perhaps because of this taboo the contemporary choreographers Eric Hawkins and Remy Charlip did not even begin to become involved in dance until they were in college.

Atavistic forces underlie the creation of dance. Dancer and choreographer Alwin Nikolai gives an appealing description of how an idea becomes a dance:

I prefer to drop a simple, single idea into my brain and let it rummage around for several months, with no particular efforts toward consciousness on my part. Then two or three weeks before I begin to choreograph, I attempt to cast up the result of this Rorschach process. Then I like to choreograph swiftly and within a short span of time; I feel that in this outpouring I keep the channels of my subject open.

Another artistic performer, Donald McKayle, recalls that a childhood memory triggered his first dance: a street, a playground of tenement children, ringing with calls and cries, the happy shouts of the young; then a large and looming shadow thrown by a street lamp—the constant specter of fear—"Chickee the cop," and the game became a sordid dance of terror.

At an extreme, dance becomes sheer pattern. It has been said that, just as the ballet-master Balanchine cut the bond between dance and narrative, the contemporary choreographer of modern dance Merce Cunningham has cut the knot between music and dance. Cunningham, in fact, is interested in movement pure and simple; he likes to observe insects under microscopes and animals in zoos. He is one of the prime formalists of the dance, an inveterate investigator of how weight and force interact with time and space, a champion of the idea that dance is an independent art that requires no support from music, no visual background, and no plot. His dances therefore provide an opportunity for one to observe bodily intelligence in its purest form, uncontaminated with representational overlay. But dance can come in many forms. As Mikhail Baryshnikov has commented: "Dancing is like many new languages, all of which expand one's flexibility and range. The dancer, just like the language scholar, needs as many as possible; there are never enough."

OTHER PERFORMING ROLES

The Actor. While the major training in dance is the disciplined use of the body, other roles that also exploit knowledge of the body require additional or different skills. Ron Jenkins describes steps through which one passes (and through which he himself passed) in becoming a Balinese clown. First, it is necessary to achieve high technical proficiency in the dance and in the wearing of the masks. These skills are usually handed down directly and personally from generation to generation, with older performers selecting apprentice-pupils as young as six-year-olds. In learning to be a dancer, one is first grabbed from behind and moved through the proper shapes; in fact, one's limbs are forcibly molded into the canonical stances. Jenkins comments, "I was an awkward student, not nearly as supple as the Balinese children who know the movements before studying dance as a result of watching countless performances since infancy." He was told, "Don't lift your legs so high . . . keep your elbows closer to your chest." Next, the newly trained dancer turns his attention to other requirements: he must increase his knowledge of texts, of current events, drama, the making and wearing of masks. Beyond these performing prerequisites, the aspiring performer must master personal relationships, getting along with the other individuals in the troupe, so that they can cast one in a proper and flattering role. Jenkins was ultimately given the role of an old man, in which he could exploit his knowledge of comedy and dramatic timing while minimizing his meagre movement technique— and finally, after several months of performing, he was allowed to fashion and dramatize his own stories.

In all forms of performance, but particularly in acting, one's ability to observe carefully and then to re-create scenes in detail is at a premium. Such mimetic ability begins very early, perhaps even in the first days or weeks of life; and by the age of two, every normal child is able to observe scenes or performances by other individuals and re-create on a subsequent occasion at least some of the highlights of the display. It is clear that some children are much better at imitating than are others. These "born mimics," who are perhaps gifted with a high potential in the area of bodily intelligence, can watch a scene but once or twice and pick up the most salient and most individuating features, while other individuals who behold the same scene numerous times still prove far less accurate and acute in their re-creations.

A strong proclivity to imitate and remember displays well may be a desirable or even a necessary stock-in-trade for a future performer but, in itself, does not suffice to produce memorable performances. Other intellectual powers are also at a premium. The acting teacher Richard Boleslavsky stresses the importance of absolute concentration, where one directs all one's attention, as long as one's strength endures, toward defining the desired object. The actor must try to re-create feelings with the aid of unconscious memory:

> We have a special memory for feelings which works unconsciously for itself and by itself. . . . It is in every artist. It is that which makes experience an essential part of our life and craft. All we have to know is how to use it.

Boleslavsky goes on to counsel, "The gift of observation must be cultivated in every part of your body, not only in your sight and memory. . . . Everything registers anatomically somewhere in my brain and through the practice of recalling and reenacting, I am ten times as alert as I was."

Another master acting teacher, Constantin Stanislavski, also underscores the crucial role of emotions in the performance of the actor. The actor must feel the emotion not merely at the time when he is studying the part, but at every time that he is performing it. Stanislavski sees training as a technique for putting the performer into a creative state where the subconscious can function naturally. In his view, such technique bears the same relation to our subconscious creative nature as grammar does to the composition of poetry. As he puts it:

> Some musicians have a power to reconstruct sounds inwardly. They play over in their minds an entire symphony they have just heard. . . . Some painters possess the power of inner vision to such a degree that they can paint portraits of people they have seen but who are no longer alive. . . . Actors have this same kind of power of sight and sound.

On the other hand, some acting techniques de-emphasize the need to re-create the felt mood, and stress instead attention to surface details. In the terms of this study, I might suggest that an "emotion-centered" acting technique highlights the *intra*personal intelligence, while the latter, "surface" form mobilizes *inter*personal intelligence.

For many analysts, the ability to watch, to observe keenly, to imitate and re-create is central in all performing arts. According to John Martin, a student of performance, we are all equipped with a sixth sense of *kinesthesis*—the capacity to act gracefully and to apprehend directly the actions or the dynamic abilities of other people or objects. Martin claims that this process comes to occur automatically. Thus, when we pick up an object that we have not lifted before, we draw on muscle memories of lifting objects of similar bulk and density as a natural mode of anticipating what our body will have to perform. Past experiences of lifting are symbolized in a kinesthetic language, which is drawn on directly by the body, without the need for any other symbolic intervention. By the same token, when we see someone sucking a lemon, we are likely to feel a distinct activity in the mouth and throat as if we were tasting the acid; or when someone cries, we frequently feel a lump rising in our throats.

Martin believes that it is our capacity involuntarily to mimic, to go through the experiences and feelings of others, which allows us to understand and also to participate in art forms. He declares:

> It is the dancer's whole function to lead us into imitating his actions with our faculty for inner mimicry in order that we may experience his feelings. Facts he could tell us, but feelings he cannot convey in any other way than by arousing them in us through sympathetic action.

By the same token, in looking at architecture, we decide whether a proportion is acceptable according to whether we feel in our bodies the mass is supportable by the columns in question or is too heavy for them: "The building becomes for the moment a kind of replica of ourselves and we feel any undue strains as if they were in our bodies."

If Martin is right, and imitation is the central component of kinesthetic thought, then imitative teaching and learning may be the most appropriate way to impart skill in this domain. As we have seen, such methods are sometimes used directly, as in the training of Balinese clowns. Cultural anthropologist Ruth Benedict noted that, in Japan,

> in the traditional teaching of writing ... the instructor took the child's hand and made the ideographs. It was to "give him the feel." The child learned to experience the controlled, rhythmic movements before he could recognize the characters, much less write them. ... The bow, the handling of the chopsticks, shooting an arrow, or tying a pillow on the back in lieu of a baby may all be taught by moving the child's hand and physically placing his body in the correct position.

Similarly, at Balinese cockfights, the spectators' hands often mimic the movements of the fight so closely that one can follow the action just by watching the hands in the air. The fact that some individuals prove skilled at this kind of learning, but that it is accorded a low priority, may help explain why many promising young performers and dancers in our culture become alienated from school at an early age. If anything, the ability to mimic, to imitate faithfully, is often considered a kind of arrogance or a failure to understand, rather than the exercise of another form of cognition which can be highly adaptive.

The interpretation of keen mimetic skill as a failure to understand is, however, not necessarily entirely wrong. A number of comedians who later went on to achieve great success have indicated that their initial impetus for imitating (and making fun of) the teacher came from their genuine difficulties in understanding the point of lessons that they were supposed to be mastering. To be sure, such actors and humorists eventually go on to create full-bodied characters. They do so by filling in superficial outlines of a character; by developing the various situations in which the character customarily finds himself; by touching on the various proclivities, abilities, and deficits of that particular persona himself and, in its highest realization, of all humans. It is through such a process that the great silent clowns of the past—Chaplin, Lloyd, and Keaton—may have passed; and this process may also characterize such contemporary masters of humorous characterizations as Lily Tomlin, Johnny Carson, or Woody Allen.

As we encroach on this fascinating and still dimly understood area, it is worth reminding ourselves that humor and jokes are the exclusive property of human beings. While it is certainly possible to make nonverbal jokes and to act out humorous scenes without words, there is so far no convincing evidence that this sensibility is shared with any other animals. It is tempting to relate humor in part to the mimetic activity on which it frequently (and successfully) draws. Yet this cannot be the whole story, since other primates are certainly able to imitate behavioral sequences; and, in fact, humans often find chimpanzee and other primate imitations very funny. Perhaps it is in the perception (rather than the creation) of these mimetic sequences, and in the perception of their affinity to (and departure from) the original model display, that a key component of the humor response lies. While other primates are horrified by events or scenes that imitate the familiar but are in some way deviant, they do not—so far as we are aware—become amused by our imitating aspects of their experiences nor do they find such mimicry by conspecifics to be funny. Possibly the fact that the previous experience is being *commented upon* makes it alien to animals other than the human being—sometimes called, seriously, the laughing animal.

The Athlete. The dancer and the actor are but two roles in our culture that highlight the intelligence of the body. Others have also been greatly valued by the society. The athlete's ability to excel in grace, power, speed, accuracy, and teamwork not only provides a source of pleasure to the athlete himself but also serves, for countless observers, as a means of entertainment, stimulation, and release.

According to B. Lowe, an observer of sports, certain features typically characterize the talented baseball pitcher. There is control—the ability to throw the ball just where one wants it. There is craft—the knowledge that comes with experience, analytic power, skillful observation, and resourcefulness. There is poise—the ability to apply craft under great pressure and to produce when the need is most pronounced. And there is "stuff"—

> Stuff is the physical element: how hard can he throw, how big is the break on his curve? Stuff is the product of strength and exceptional hair-trigger coordination and seems to be an innate quality, perhaps improvable by practice and technique but not acquirable.

Obviously, bodily endowment is important in these areas. In baseball, for example, the pitcher should be tall, weigh about 240 pounds, and have the speed of a sprinter; an ideal hitter should be cross-dominant, having the dominant eye on the opposite side of the body from the dominant hand to obtain a view of the pitch unobstructed by his nose. Athletes in other sports also benefit from optimal sizes and physical prowess. Less likely to be a part of one's birthright is a well-developed sense of timing: the sense of coordination and rhythm that leads to well-executed and powerful motions. The champion golfer Jack Nicklaus describes this kinesthetic sense:

> Feeling the weight of the clubhead against the tension of the shaft helps me to swing rhythmically. As the backswing progresses I like to feel that clubhead's weight pulling my hands and arms back and up. Starting down I like to feel the weight of the clubhead lagging back—resisting, as my thrusting legs and hips pull my arms and hands down. When I can "wait" for these feelings, I am almost certainly swinging in proper tempo. I am giving myself enough elapsed time to make all the various moves in rhythmical sequence.

While one's sense of timing may seem a direct consequence of one's bodily intelligence, craft may well draw on other intellectual strengths. There is the logical ability to plot a good strategy, the capacity to recognize familiar spatial patterns and to exploit them on the spot, and an interpersonal sense of the personality and the motivation of other players in a game. A description of the hockey player Wayne Gretzky conveys some of these components of craft:

> In front of the net, eyeball to eyeball with the goalie, he will . . . hold the puck one . . . extra instant, upsetting the rhythm of the game and of the goalie's anticipation. . . . Or, in the heat of play, he will release a pass before he appears ready to do so, threading it through a maze of players who are a beat behind him. . . . If there is such a thing as sleight of body he performed it. . . . He sends a pass into a spot behind Goring. Nobody is there yet to receive the puck—but suddenly a teammate arrives to accept it. What seems like either luck or magic is neither. Given the probable movements of the other players, Gretzky knows exactly where his teammate is supposed to be.

While some commentators might think that Gretzky's achievements were effortlessly attained, he himself disagrees:

> Nine out of ten people think what I do is instinct. . . . It isn't. Nobody would ever say a doctor had learned his profession by instinct: yet in my own way I've spent almost as much time studying hockey as a med student puts in studying medicine.

In our culture, the professional athlete is trained in much the same way as an artistic performer and is, in fact, subjected to many of the same pressures and opportunities. Given the highly competitive environment, the achievement of excellence in athletics proves sufficiently elusive that most individuals end up as spectators.

The Inventor. Our discussion of bodily intelligence has focussed on capacities that highlight the use of the body *per se*, with relatively little emphasis on the use of the body, and particularly of the hands, with other materials. Yet, as we have seen, the development of the capacity to manufacture and transform objects, both directly with one's body and through the use of tools, has been especially characteristic of the human species.

Work with relatively small physical objects constitutes a major part of the occupational roles of a great variety of individuals. Most workers deal with one or another kind of object, whether they are hunting, planting, farming, cooking, or toiling in a factory. Sometimes such manipulation of objects becomes routine, while at other times a considerable amount of creativity may be involved. In fact, the engineer, the technician, or the inventor does not merely use materials in culturally established ways but actually rearranges materials in order to create an object better fitted to the task that he is confronting.

231

We return to a question I raised earlier. Do such uses of objects and tools in general, and the devising of new inventions in particular, fall within the purview of bodily intelligence, or are they better viewed through the lens of some other intellectual competence or, perhaps, as an amalgam of several intelligences? In my own view, fine motor bodily intelligence, in combination with spatial capacities, is most strongly entailed in the use of objects and tools. Particularly during the initial use of an object or a tool, the individual should carefully coordinate the information that he can assimilate through his spatial intelligence, with the capacities that he has elaborated through his bodily intelligence. Confined to spatial intelligence, he may understand a mechanism reasonably well and yet have no idea of how actually to manipulate or operate the object in which it is housed; restricted to bodily intelligence, he may be able to execute the appropriate motions yet fail to appreciate the way in which the apparatus or the procedure works and therefore be stymied should he encounter it in a somewhat different setting, format, or situation. Conceptualizing how an object should work is most likely to succeed if the individual has a feeling for the activity of each of its parts and the capacity to envision how they will coordinate within a single mechanism.

When it comes not merely to understanding complex tools or machinery but also to the devising of new inventions, a combination of several intelligences is clearly desirable. In addition to that fusion of bodily and spatial intelligences which may suffice for understanding a common apparatus, the individual will have to use as well his logical-mathematical capacities in order to figure out the precise demands of the task, the procedures that could in principle work, and the necessary and sufficient conditions for the desired product. To the extent that the individual relies on trial and error or approaches the task as an improvising handyman or, to use Lévi-Strauss's term, *bricoleur*, the use of logical-mathematical reasoning will be less crucial.

One can see the role of sheer deduction in invention by considering how John Arnold of the Massachusetts Institute of Technology goes about making a new kind of printing device. Rather than simply building up from printing devices that already exist, he tries to figure out the strictest set of constraints on his product. He concludes that what is basic to any printing device is that it conveys information, transfers it from one form or place to another, renders it visual, and makes multiple copies of the rendering. This analysis is pertinent whether one employs electronic means, photostatic copying, or more traditional ink-type plates and roller. Certainly such an approach, which is remote from that of the handyman, relies heavily on logical-mathematical capacities.

And what of the developmental links between a child's early preoccupations and eventual inventiveness in a highly valued contemporary occupation like engineering? An intriguing set of clues can be found in Tracy Kidder's account of those "whiz-kids" who build new computer hardware. In the case of several of these talented inventors, much time during childhood was spent in the taking apart of mechanical objects. Describing one such worker, Kidder notes, "Like practically everyone else on the team, he started becoming an engineer at about the age of four, picking on ordinary household items such as lamps and clocks and radios. He took them apart whenever his parents weren't looking." This future engineer did not do well in high school or college until he took a course in basic electronics. "I totally crushed [did extremely well in] the course," he remembered. Another member of the computer team was very depressed in school until he discovered that he could take a telephone apart: "This was a fantastic high, something I could get absorbed in and forget that I had other social problems." Such biographical accounts indicate that an interest in manipulation, in putting together (or taking apart), and in the eventual reassembly of objects may play an important formative role in the development of an engineer; such activity may also provide a needed island of reinforcement for an individual who shows scant interest (or skill) in other domains of experience.

Bodily Intelligence in Other Cultures

In our own cultural history, we must go back to Greek times to find a moment "where the human body was considered beautiful, a worthy and loved and equal partner with the soul-mind." In many other cultures, however, the whole area of bodily expression and knowledge continues to assume great importance. Among the Ibo peoples in Nigeria, the strong bodies needed for arduous dancing develop because all individuals travel long distances in great heat, bend to fetch water, wash in a stream, cultivate crops, squat to defecate, and carry heavy loads on the head. Already at an early age, young children begin to participate in such family chores as yam pounding, wood chopping, and transporting heavy burdens. An individual's dance practice begins in his mother's womb, then on her back as she dances. Even before he can walk, the child is encouraged to dance, and youngsters regularly practice. Among the Anang peoples in Nigeria, every individual is expected to be able to dance and sing well, to carve and to weave. The Anang recognize that a very few individuals may have talents superior to their fellows, but they firmly believe that no one lacks the requisite abilities to achieve in these aesthetic domains. As anthropologist John Messenger indicates, "It is obvious that, to the Anang, talent implies the possession of certain capabilities which anyone can develop if he sets out to do so."

Dissemination of demanding bodily skills occurs quite widely in other societies. In *Growing Up in New Guinea*, Margaret Mead relates that every young Manus baby is taken out in a canoe by its mother. If a sudden wind comes, the canoe may swerve and eject mother and child into the sea. The baby has learned how to grip tight, however, and so will not be lost in the sea. By the age of five or six, the child will be able to balance himself and punt the canoe with accuracy; paddle enough to steer through a mild gale; run the canoe accurately under a house without jamming the outrigger; extricate a canoe from a large group of canoes huddled closely together; and bale out a canoe by dipping the bow and stern alternately. Understanding of the sea also includes swimming, diving, proceeding under water, and knowing how to get water out of the nose and throat. The kind of prowess that is possessed by only a tiny minority of seafaring Western children is considered within the competence of the average child in this tribal society.

Bali is perhaps the most outstanding example of a society where individuals devote care to their bodies and end up as graceful, artful individuals. Everyone in this society learns to focus attention on bodily features:

Learning to walk, learning the first appropriate gestures of playing musical instruments, learning to eat and to dance are all accomplished with the teacher behind the pupil, conveying directly by pressure, and almost always with a minimum of words, the gesture to be performed. Under such a system of learning, one can only learn if one is completely relaxed. The Balinese learn virtually nothing from verbal instruction.

Out of this kinesthetic awareness eventually emerges a well-developed sense of balance and fine motor control:

Balinese children spend a great deal of time playing with the joints of their fingers . . . Where an American or a New Guinea native will involve al-

234

most every muscle in his body to pick up a pin, the Balinese merely uses the muscle immediately relevant to the act, leaving the rest of the body undisturbed. . . . The involved muscle does not draw all the others into a unified act but smoothly and simply a few small units are moved—the fingers alone, the hand and forearm alone, or the eyes alone as in the characteristic Balinese habit of slewing the eyes to one side without turning the head. . . . [The Balinese] body flawlessly and quickly attends to the job in hand.

This concern with grace can be found in other contemporary lands—for instance in India, where awkwardness is virtually a sign of immaturity; in Japan, where the tea ceremony or flower arrangement reflect a pervasive concern with delicate form and patterning; and perhaps most fully in Zen Buddhist enclaves, where the reigning desire is to exceed the ordinary limits of one's bodily potential. Whatever the reason, the fact that a Zen master can break bricks barehand or walk on burning coals—more broadly, the master's belief that he can translate an intention directly into action—deserves to be marveled at, even if (or just because) it defies the canons of current scientific explanation.

The Body as Subject and Object

While I have considered a variety of uses to which individuals put their bodily intelligence, the focus in this chapter has been on the body as an object. We have seen how dancers and athletes use their entire bodies as "mere" objects, and noted how inventors and other workers use parts of the body—particularly hands—in order to manipulate, arrange, and transform objects in the world. Described in this vein, bodily intelligence completes a trio of object-related intelligences: logical-mathematical intelligence, which grows out of the patterning of objects into numerical arrays; spatial intelligence, which focuses on the individual's ability to transform objects within his environment and to make his way amidst a world of objects in space; and, bodily intelligence, which, focussing inward, is limited to the exercise of one's own body and, facing outward, entails physical actions on the objects in the world.

But the body is more than simply another machine, indistinguishable from the artificial objects of the world. It is also the vessel of the individual's sense of self, his most personal feelings and aspirations, as well as that entity to which others respond in a special way because of their uniquely human qualities. From the very first, an individual's existence as a human being affects the way that others will treat him; and very soon, the individual comes to think of his own body as special. He comes to form a sense of self which he will perpetually modify, and which will in turn come to influence his thoughts and behavior as he comes to respond to others in his environment in terms of their special traits and behavior. While still poorly understood, the realm of the personal intelligences is clearly of utmost importance to humans, the site of our most awesome accomplishments as well as of our most terrifying tendencies. To this Janus-headed variety of intelligence—partly mired within the inner emotional-affective sphere, partly peering outward to the circle of other people—we must now shift our gaze.

10

The Personal Intelligences

Introduction: The Sense of Self

In 1909, G. Stanley Hall, the psychologist-president of Clark University, invited Sigmund Freud and a few of his colleagues to the United States to deliver some introductory lectures on the recently devised theory of psychoanalysis. It was the first (and, as it turned out, the only) time that Freud traveled to America, and interest in his new theory and method of treatment was keen. Freud presented a masterful set of lectures on the *Origins and Development of Psychoanalysis*, a series that introduced his then controversial theory of the human personality and helped to further the cause of psychoanalysis in the United States, though it left the mainstream psychological establishment, which was about to take a radical behaviorist turn, completely unmoved. With one exception. From Cambridge, Massachusetts, William James, dean of American psychologists and philosophers, already elderly and ill, made the day-long journey to Worcester to hear Freud and to meet the younger scholar from Austria. After the lecture, James went up to Freud and said simply, "The future of psychology belongs to your work." The historian of social science, H. Stuart Hughes, has commented, "There is no more dramatic moment in the intellectual history of our time."

Freud and James represented different historical movements, different philosophical traditions, different programs for psychology.

237

Freud, the pessimistic European intellectual, had chosen to focus on the development of the individual psyche, its battles within the individual's immediate family, the struggle for independence, the manifold anxieties and defenses that attend the human condition. For Freud the key to health was self-knowledge and a willingness to confront the inevitable pains and paradoxes of human existence.

James had considerable sympathy with this analysis, for his own life had featured many of the strains and tensions that Freud graphically described. Yet James also sensed a difference in the emphasis in their respective world views. While praising Freud, he had also pointed out to a confidant, "I hope that Freud and his pupils will push their ideas to the utmost limits, so that we can learn what they are.... It reveals an entirely unsuspected peculiarity in the constitution of human nature." James, in fact, had chosen to embrace a more positively oriented form of psychology, one less circumscribed by the biological imperatives of behavior, more open to the possibilities of change and growth. More so than his Austrian counterpart, the American thinker stressed the importance of relationships with other individuals, as a means of gaining ends, of effecting progress, and of knowing oneself. In a famous phrase, he had commented, "A man has as many social selves as there are individuals who recognize him and carry an image around of him in their mind." Perhaps most important, James was a potent influence on the succeeding generation of social scientists, including James Mark Baldwin and George Herbert Mead, who came to focus on the social origins of knowledge and on the interpersonal nature of an individual's sense of self.

But what united Freud and James, and what set them apart from the mainstream of psychology both on the Continent and in the United States, was a belief in the importance, the centrality, of the individual self—a conviction that psychology must be built around the concept of the person, his personality, his growth, his fate. Moreover, both scholars deemed the capacity for self-growth to be an important one, upon which depended the possibility of coping with one's surroundings. While neither would have used the phrase, I find it reasonable to say that both of these redoubtable psychologists were sympathetic to the idea of "personal intelligences." At the same time, however, their orientations toward such intelligences would have differed. Freud was interested in the self as located in the individual and, as a clinician, was preoccupied with an individual's own knowledge of himself; given this bias, a person's interest in other individuals was justified chiefly as a better means of gaining further understanding of one's own problems, wishes, and anxieties and, ultimately, of achieving one's goals. In contrast, James's interest, and, even more so, the interests of the American social psychologists who succeeded him, fell much more on the individual's relationship to the outside community. Not only did one's knowledge of self come largely from an ever-increasing appreciation of how others thought about the individual; but the purpose of self-knowledge was less to promote one's personal agenda, more to ensure the smooth functioning of the wider community.

In this chapter, I shall examine the development of both of these aspects of human nature. On the one side, there is the development of the internal aspects of a person. The core capacity at work here is *access to one's own feeling life*—one's range of affects or emotions: the capacity instantly to effect discriminations among these feelings and, eventually, to label them, to enmesh them in symbolic codes, to draw upon them as a means of understanding and guiding one's behavior. In its most primitive form, the intrapersonal intelligence amounts to little more than the capacity to distinguish a feeling of pleasure from one of pain and, on the basis of such discrimination, to become more involved in or to withdraw from a situation. At its most advanced level, intrapersonal knowledge allows one to detect and to symbolize complex and highly differentiated sets of feelings. One finds this form of intelligence developed in the novelist (like Proust) who can write introspectively about feelings, in the patient (or the therapist) who comes to attain a deep knowledge of his own feeling life, in the wise elder who draws upon his own wealth of inner experiences in order to advise members of his community.

The other personal intelligence turns outward, to other individuals. The core capacity here is *the ability to notice and make distinctions among other individuals* and, in particular, among their moods, temperaments, motivations, and intentions. Examined in its most elementary form, the interpersonal intelligence entails the capacity of the young child to discriminate among the individuals around him and to detect their various moods. In an advanced form, interpersonal knowledge permits a skilled adult to read the intentions and desires—even when these have been hidden—of many other individuals and, potentially, to act upon this knowledge—for example, by influencing a group of disparate individuals to behave along desired lines. We see highly developed forms of interpersonal intelligence in political and religious leaders (a Mahatma Gandhi or a Lyndon Johnson), in skilled parents and teachers, and in individuals enrolled in the helping professions, be they therapists, counselors, or shamans.

More so than in other realms, one encounters a tremendous variety of forms of interpersonal and intrapersonal intelligence. Indeed, just because each culture has its own symbol systems, its own means for interpreting experiences, the "raw materials" of the personal intelligences quickly get marshaled by systems of meaning that may be quite distinct from one another. Accordingly, while the forms of spatial or bodily-kinesthetic intelligence are readily identified and compared across diverse cultures, the varieties of personal intelligence prove much more distinctive, less comparable, perhaps even unknowable to someone from an alien society.

Even as the symbolization and enculturation of personal intelligences takes many forms, there are also numerous varieties of breakdowns and pathologies. Indeed, breakdown of the personal intelligences necessarily takes different forms, depending on the "normal blend" within each culture: what might be pathological in one setting can be deemed normal in another. Moreover, rather than simply declining in acuity, an intelligence often assumes aberrant and pathological forms, as inappropriate distinctions are made and acted upon. In one sense, this is analogous to what happens in the language domain when individuals suffer from different aphasias: yet for the analogy to be completely valid, the forms of aphasia would have to differ strikingly across cultures.

In view of such distinctions between personal and other forms of intelligence, a question may appropriately be raised: Are the intrapersonal and interpersonal forms of knowing comparable to those faculties of musical, linguistic, or spatial intelligence that have been reviewed in earlier chapters, or has some classificatory error been committed?

In tackling this question, it is important not to gloss over differences between the personal and other forms of intelligence. We have already indicated some. The "natural course" of the personal intelligences is more attenuated than that of other forms, inasmuch as the particular symbolic and interpretive systems of each culture soon come to impose a decisive coloring on these latter forms of information processing. Also, as I have noted, the patterns of development and of breakdown in the personal intelligences turn out to be far more varied than in other intelligences; and there is an especially wide range of end-states.

I have also intimated another difference. Whereas each of our other intelligences has been comfortably discussed independently of the others, I have here linked two forms of intelligence. To be sure each form has its own pull, with the intrapersonal intelligence involved chiefly in an individual's examination and knowledge of his own feelings, while the interpersonal intelligence looks outward, toward the behavior, feelings, and motivations of others. Moreover, as we shall see, each form has its characteristic neurological representation and pattern of breakdown. The reason, then, for treating these together is chiefly expositional. In the course of development, these two forms of knowledge are intimately intermingled in any culture, with knowledge of one's own person perennially dependent upon the ability to apply lessons learned from the observation of other people, while knowledge of others draws upon the internal discriminations the individual routinely makes. Our two forms of personal intelligence could, in fact, be described separately; but to do so would involve unnecessary duplication as well as artificial separation. Under ordinary circumstances, neither form of intelligence can develop without the other.

Other differences surrounding the personal intelligences should be mentioned. For one thing, the sanctions surrounding pathologies in these areas tend to be far stronger than those that greet disorders of the other intelligences. For another, the premium for acting upon one's particular personal intelligence is far greater. While the decision to employ (or not to employ) one's musical or spatial intelligence is not heavily charged, the pressures to employ one's personal intelligences are acute: it is the unusual individual who does not try to deploy his understanding of the personal realm in order to improve his own well-being or his relationship to the community. There is, of course, no guarantee that his form of personal intelligence will prove adequate to this task, or that he will be able to achieve what he wants. Forms of personal intelligences, no less than forms of other intelligences, can misfire or fail in their intent, and "know-that" does not readily or reliably translate into "know-how."

Given such differences, why have I incorporated personal intelligences in my survey? Chiefly because I feel that these forms of knowledge are of tremendous importance in many, if not all, societies in the world—forms that have, however, tended to be ignored or minimized by nearly all students of cognition.* It is not relevant to my inquiry to explore the reasons for this omission. But whatever the reasons, this omission has spawned a view of intellect which is all too partial and makes it difficult to understand the goals of many cultures and the ways in which these goals are achieved.

Moreover, according to our original list of criteria, the personal

---

*But not by all: the redoubtable student of intelligence David Wechsler wrote many years ago about social intelligence.

intelligences pass muster rather well. As I have already intimated, there is an identifiable core to each, a characteristic pattern of development, a number of specifiable end-states, as well as impressive evidence for neurological representation and for discernible patterns of breakdown. Evolutionary evidence is beginning to come forth, and there is good reason to anticipate that we will eventually understand a great deal about the phylogenetic origins of these intelligences. Evidence for exceptional individuals—prodigies or freaks in the personal realms—is less persuasive but by no means lacking. There is less of relevance in the realms of experimental psychology and psychological testing than would be desirable, but this lack is more likely due to the reluctance of "hard-nosed" psychologists to investigate this area than it is due to insuperable difficulties in assessing these forms of knowledge. Last, while one does not ordinarily think of forms of personal knowledge as being encoded in public symbol systems, I deem symbolization to be of the essence in the personal intelligences. Without a symbolic code supplied by the culture, the individual is confonted with only his most elementary and unorganized discrimination of feelings: but armed with such a scheme of interpretation, he has the potential to make sense of the full range of experiences which he and others in his community can undergo. In addition, it seems legitimate to construe rituals, religious codes, mythic and totemic systems as symbolic codes that capture and convey crucial aspects of personal intelligence.

As we shall see, an emerging sense of self proves to be a key element in the realm of the personal intelligences, one of overriding importance to individuals the world over. While a developed sense of self is ordinarily viewed as a quintessential manifestation of intrapersonal intelligence, my own inquiry has led to a different conclusion. The wide variety of "selves" encountered throughout the world suggests that this "sense" is better thought of as an amalgam, one that emerges from a combination or fusion of one's intrapersonal and one's interpersonal knowledge. The overwhelming differences in senses of self around the world reflect the fact that the merger can come about in widely divergent ways, depending on those aspects of the person (and of persons) that happen to be accentuated in different cultures. Accordingly, in what follows, I shall use the term *sense of self* to refer to the balance struck by every individual—and every culture—between the promptings of "inner feelings" and the pressures of "other persons."

Allusion to sense of self suggests a reason that researchers may have hesitated to construe the personal intelligences in cognitive form. A developed sense of self often appears as the highest achievement of human beings, a crowning capacity which supersedes and presides over other more mundane and partial forms of intelligence. It is also that capacity about which individuals have the strongest and most intimate views; thus it becomes a sensitive (as well as an elusive) target to examine. Difficulty of study and a high degree of personal involvement are not, of course, valid reasons to avert the scrutiny of scientific investigation. And it is my hope that, through the kinds of investigation launched in this chapter, one can see that the sense of self, while marvelous, is not immune from study. Instead, it can be traced to two forms of intelligence which every human being has the opportunity to develop and to merge.

In the last analysis, the personal intelligences amount to information-processing capacities—one directed inward, the other outward—which are available to every human infant as part of its species birthright. This fact of life dictates an examination of personal intelligences. The capacity to know oneself and to know others is as inalienable a part of the human condition as is the capacity to know objects or sounds, and it deserves to be investigated no less than these other "less charged" forms. Personal intelligences may not prove completely cognate with the forms of intelligence we have already encountered—but as I pointed out at the start of this inquiry, there is no reason to expect that any pair of intelligences will be completely comparable. What is important is that they should be part of the human intellectual repertoire, and that their origins should take roughly comparable form the world over.

The Development of the Personal Intelligences

Various forms of personal intelligence clearly arise, in the first instance, from the bond between the infant and its caretaker—in almost all cases, the infant and its mother. Evolutionary and cultural history have combined to make this attachment link an indispensable component of normal growth. During the first year of life, the child comes to form a potent tie to the mother, aided by the equally strong attraction that the mother feels toward her offspring. And it is in these strong ties—and the feelings that accompany them—that the origins of personal knowledge can be found.

For a year or so, the tie is at maximum strength, so that the child becomes disturbed when he is suddenly separated from his mother, or when a strange adult is seen as threatening the bond. The child seeks to maintain the positive feeling of well-being and to avoid situations of pain or anxiety. Then gradually the link becomes looser and more flexible, as the child ventures forth from home base, now secure in the knowledge that he can return to find the mother there (and thereby regain feelings of belonging). If for some reason the bond is not permitted to form properly, or if it is broken abruptly and not soon repaired, profound difficulties are signaled for the child. We know both from Harry Harlow's work with motherless monkeys, and from John Bowlby's studies of institutionalized infants, that the lack of an attachment bond can wreak devastating effects on normal development in the present and in succeeding generations. Especially important for our purposes, the absence of such a bond signals difficulty for an individual's eventual ability to know other persons, to rear offspring, and to draw upon this knowledge as he comes to know himself. Thus, the initial tie between infant and caretaker may be looked on as Nature's effort to ensure that the personal intelligences are properly launched.

One can divide the growth of personal knowledge into a number of steps or stages. At each step, it is possible to identify certain features that are important for the development of intrapersonal intelligence, as well as other factors that prove crucial for the growth of interpersonal intelligence. The portrait to be given here necessarily focuses upon the development of personal intelligences within the context of our own society, for it is chiefly this trajectory that has so far been studied. Only later will I be able to touch on some of the features that may characterize personal intelligences in other cultures.

THE INFANT

Though there is no way to place oneself within the infant's skin, it seems likely that, from the earliest days of life, all normal infants experience a range of feelings, a gamut of affects. Observation of infants within and across cultures and comparison of their facial expressions with those of other primates confirm that there is a set of universal facial expressions, displayed by all normal children. The most reasonable inference is that there are bodily (and brain) states associated with these expressions, with infants experiencing phenomenally a range of states of excitement and of pleasure or pain. To be sure, these states are initially *uninterpreted:* the infant has no way of labeling to himself how he is feeling or why he is feeling this way. But the range of bodily states experienced by the infant—the fact that he feels, that he may feel differently on different occasions, and that he can come to correlate feelings with specific experiences—serves to introduce the child to the realm of intrapersonal knowledge. Moreover, these discriminations also constitute the necessary point of departure for the eventual discovery that he is a distinct entity with his own experiences and his unique identity.

Even as the infant is coming to know his own bodily reactions, and to differentiate them one from another, he is also coming to form preliminary distinctions among other individuals and even among the moods displayed by "familiar" others. By two months of age, and perhaps even at birth, the child is already able to discriminate among, and imitate the facial expressions of, other individuals. This capacity suggests a degree of "pre-tunedness" to the feelings and behavior of other individuals that is extraordinary. The child soon distinguishes mother from father, parents from strangers, happy expressions from sad or angry ones. (Indeed, by the age of ten months, the infant's ability to discriminate among different affective expressions already yields distinctive patterns of brain waves.) In addition, the child comes to associate various feelings with particular individuals, experiences, and circumstances. There are already the first signs of empathy. The young child will respond sympathetically when he hears the cry of another infant or sees someone in pain: even though the child may not yet appreciate just *how* the other is feeling, he seems to have a sense that something is not right in the world of the other person. A link amongst familiarity, caring, and altruism has already begun to form.

Thanks to a clever experimental technique devised by Gordon Gallup for studies with primates, we have a way of ascertaining when the human infant first comes to view himself as a separate entity, an incipient person. It is possible, unbeknownst to the child, to place a tiny marker—for example, a daub of rouge—upon his nose and then to study his reactions as he peers at himself in the mirror. During the first year of life, the infant is amused by the rouge marking but apparently simply regards it as an interesting decoration on some *other organism* which he happens to be examining in the mirror. But, during the second year of life, the child comes to react differently when he beholds the alien coloring. Children will touch their own noses and act silly or coy when they encounter this unexpected redness on what they perceive to be their very own anatomy. Awareness of physical separateness and identity are not, of course, the only components of beginning self-knowledge. The child also is starting to react to his own name, to refer to himself by name, to have definite programs and plans that he seeks to carry out, to feel efficacious when he is successful, to experience distress when he violates certain standards that others have set for him or that he has set for himself. All of these components of the initial sense of person* make their initial appearance during the second year of life.

THE CHILD AGED TWO TO FIVE

During the period spanning the ages two to five, the child undergoes a major intellectual revolution, as he becomes able to use various symbols to refer to himself ("me," "my"), to other individuals ("you," "him," "Mum"), ("you afraid," "you sad"), and to his own experiences ("my birthday," "my idea"). Words, pictures, gestures, and numbers are among the multifarious vehicles marshaled in service of coming to know the world symbolically, as well as through direct physical actions upon it and sensory discriminations of it. Even in cultures where there are no personal pronouns, the same kinds of symbolic discrimination are readily made. By the conclusion of this period, the child is in fact a symbolizing creature, able to create and extract meanings on the level of symbol use alone.

The advent of symbol use has enormous implications for the development of the personal intelligences. The child makes an irrevocable transition from the kinds of simple discrimination of his own moods, and those of others that have been possible on an unmediated basis, to a far richer and more elaborated set of discriminations guided by the terminology and the interpretive system of his entire society. No longer must the child rely on preprogrammed discriminations and on his idiosyncratic inferences (if any); instead, the culture makes available to him an entire system of interpretation on which he can draw as he attempts to make sense of the experiences he himself undergoes as well as of those involving others.

One way in which this emerging symbolizing ability is turned toward personal development is through the exploration of different roles visible (and viable) in the community. Through talk, pretend play, gestures, drawing, and the like, the young child tries out facets of the roles of mother and child, doctor and patient, policeman and robber, teacher and pupil, astronaut and Martian. In experimenting with these role fragments, the child comes to know not only which behavior

---

*I use the locution *sense of person* to avoid confusion with the *sense of self* as defined on page 242.

246

is associated with these individuals but also something about how it feels to occupy their characteristic niches. At the same time, children come to correlate the behavior and the states of other persons with their own personal experiences: by identifying what is positive or negative, anxiety provoking or relaxing, powerful or impotent, youngsters effect an important step in defining what they are and what they are not, what they wish to be and what they'd rather avoid. One's sexual identity is an especially important form of self-discrimination which becomes confirmed during this time.

In examining major theoretical accounts of this period of life, we can discern the different paths and patterns associated with the two lines of personal intelligence. Following those authorities who focus primarily on the isolated individual, we see the child as a creature apart, one in the course of delineating his own roles and feeling himself different from others. In the Freudian account, for example, the young child is engaged in battles with others—with his parents, his siblings, his other peers, and even the protagonists of fairy tales—all in an effort to establish his own unique presence and powers. In the suggestive language of Erik Erikson, this is a time marked by struggle between feelings of autonomy and shame and between impulses of initiative and guilt. In Piaget's less affect-laden language, this is a phase of egocentrism when the child is still locked in his own personal conception of the world: not yet able fully to put himself into the place of others, he is restricted to his own self-centered views. He may have knowledge of himself, but it is still rigid and frozen: he can state his name and perhaps recount his physical attributes, but he is not yet sensitive to psychological dimensions, to wants or needs, to the possibility of changing roles or expectations—he remains a singularly one-dimensional creature. Troubled or not, the child of this age is described as an individual apart, one striving to establish his autonomy from others, one relatively insensitive to the world of other individuals.

An instructively different slant can be found in the American "symbolic-interactionist" school of George Herbert Mead and Charles Cooley as well in the Russian "mediationist" accounts of Lev Vygotsky and Alexander Luria. From the perspective of these observers of childhood, the child can come to know himself during this period only through coming to know other individuals. There is, in fact, no knowledge and no sense of person that can be separated from one's ability to know others—what they are like, and how they view you. Thus, according to this account, the young child is an inherently social creature: as such, he looks to others for their interpretive schemes and draws upon these schemes as the preferred—indeed, the sole—means of discovering and gaining an initial understanding of that person within his own skin. Where an *intra*personal-centered view of early childhood begins with an isolated individual who gradually comes to know (and perhaps care) about other persons, the *inter*personal view assumes an orientation toward, and a gradual knowledge of, other individuals as the only available means for eventually discovering the nature of one's own person.

While it is conceivable that only one of these views is correct, it appears far more likely that the two approaches are simply stressing different aspects of personal development. The individual-centered approach recognizes that the child at this stage is beset with strong and often conflicting feelings; these impel him to focus upon his own condition and stimulate the emerging discovery that he is a separate individual. These dawning insights constitute an important model for that introspecting capacity which lies at the core of intrapersonal knowledge. The socially oriented approach recognizes that the child does not develop in isolation: he is inevitably a member of a community, and his notion of what individuals are like cannot develop in a vacuum. True, he has his own affective experiences, but it is the community that provides an essential point of reference and the necessary interpretive schemes for these affects. Accordingly, knowledge of one's place among others can come only from the external community: the child is inextricably impelled to focus on others, as a clue to himself. Stated most strongly, without a community to provide the relevant categories, individuals (like feral children) would never discover that they are "persons."

THE SCHOOL-AGE CHILD

Differentiation between self and others has been pretty well consolidated by the start of school in our society. The child now has attained a first-level social knowledge. He has attained some mastery of a number of different roles adopted by other individuals, as well as an increasingly clear understanding that he is a discrete individual with his own needs, desires, projects, and goals. With the advent of concrete mental operations, the child can also relate in a more flexible manner to other individuals. He has some understanding of reciprocity: he ought to behave toward others in certain ways, so that they are likely to return the favor; he sees things in a certain way because of his own perspective, but he has the potential to don the lens of others and to apprehend both material and personal matters from *their* points of view. To be sure, the suddenness of these insights should not be over-drawn. Clear signs of the decline of egocentrism can be detected during the preschool years, even as other aspects of egocentrism persist throughout life. But it does seem that, by the time of entry to school, a clear line between self and other, between one's perspective and that of other individuals, can already be drawn.

Even as (or perhaps because) features of one's own person become more fixed, the child now has the option of becoming more of a genuinely social creature. He can step beyond his family circle and forge friendships and peer relations with others. He can appreciate how to treat others in a fair manner: in fact, if anything, he pursues justice to a fault, not yet being able to modulate between the individualizing exigencies of different situations. He also is able to acknowledge the simple intentions and motivations of others, less frequently making the mistake of simply projecting his own wishes onto everyone else. In all, the child at this age comes off as an excessively social and norm-governed creature—as one who wants above all else to be a representative (rather than a specially favored or unfairly mistreated) member of the communities in which he lives.

During this latency period (as the psychoanalysts have dubbed it), personal feelings, lusts, and anxieties may for a while appear quiescent. But growth of self-interest and self-knowledge is scarcely stilled. Rather, at this time, the child becomes especially concerned with the acquisition of objective skills, knowledge, competences. In fact, his own definition of self is no longer mired in physical attributes, though it has not yet become focused on psychological features either. For the child of six, seven, or eight, it is the things he can do—and the degree of success with which he can execute them—that constitute a chief locus of self-knowledge. This is the age of the acquisition of competence, the building up of industry: the child is colored by a fear of feeling inadequate, of appearing to be an unskilled self.

MIDDLE CHILDHOOD

During middle childhood, that five-year period between the start of school and the beginning of adolescence, there are continuing trends toward greater social sensitivity, toward a keener sense of another's motivations, and toward a fuller sense of one's own competences and lacks. Children become more deeply invested in friendships and will go to considerable lengths to maintain a personal relationship;

loss of treasured chums proves much more painful. A great deal of energy is devoted toward cementing one's place within a friendship network. These groups or cliques may be structured informally, but sometimes (particularly in the case of boys) they will be as formally ordered as a primate dominance hierarchy. Life is "heady" for those fortunate enough to be included and correspondingly bleak for those who have lowly places in the group or are excluded altogether.

As children invest much effort into maintaining their friendship patterns, they also devote much time to thinking about the interpersonal realm. With this heightened capacity to place oneself into the skin of specific other individuals, as well as of unfamiliar "generalized others," there is the beginning of intriguing recursive forms of personal knowledge. The child can carry on a set of mental manipulations about possible interactions with other individuals: "He thinks that I think that he thinks. . . ." No wonder that such pre-adolescents are able to appreciate more subtle forms of literature and to make (and appreciate) more sophisticated jokes.

Risks at this time include premature judgments of inadequacy or unrealistic assessments of efficacy. Children of this age may acquire feelings of learned helplessness, as they become convinced that there are certain pursuits that they cannot carry out. (For instance, many young girls come to feel that they cannot solve mathematics problems, thus launching a vicious cycle of diminishing expectations and diminishing achievements.) The child may also come to feel quite alone if he is unable to forge effective friendships with other individuals. For the first time, this inability to relate to others may be felt as a distinct failing, one that lowers one's image of oneself. Personal feelings are less transient; and if they are genuinely troubling, they may well come to dominate the child's introspections.

ADOLESCENCE

With the onset of adolescence, personal forms of knowledge take a number of important turns. Moving away somewhat from the frenetic (and somewhat unexamined) social orientation of earlier years, individuals (at least in our society) become far more psychologically attuned. They prove more sensitive to underlying motivations of other individuals, to their hidden desires and fears. Relationships with others are no longer based primarily on the physical rewards that others may supply, but rather on the psychological support and understanding that a sensitive individual can provide. By the same token, the adolescent seeks friends who value him for his own insights, knowledge, and sensitivity, rather than for his strength or material possessions.

Understanding of the social world also becomes much more differentiated. The youth appreciates that any society must have laws in order to function properly, but that these laws should not be blindly obeyed, and that mitigating circumstances should be taken into account. Similarly, justice remains important but cannot be dispensed without taking into account the individualizing factors in a particular dispute or dilemma. Individuals continue to have a desire to be appreciated and loved by others, but there is increasing recognition that total sharing is not possible, and that certain matters must—and perhaps ought to—be kept private.

We see, then, during the turbulent years of adolescence, a maturation of knowledge of one's own person as well as of knowledge of other persons. But at the same time, within many cultures, an even more crucial event is taking place. Adolescence turns out to be that period of life in which individuals must bring together these two forms of personal knowledge into a larger and more organized sense, a sense of identity or (to use the term I shall favor hereafter) a sense of self. As formulated by the psychoanalyst Erik Erikson, an emerging identity entails a complex definition of self, of the sort that might have pleased both Freud and James: the individual arrives at a delineation of roles with which he himself is comfortable in terms of his own feelings and aspirations, and at a formulation that makes sense in terms of the community's overall needs and its specific expectations regarding the individual in question.

This formation of a sense of self is a project—and a process—of the utmost importance. The manner of its execution will determine whether the individual can function effectively within the social context in which he has chosen—or must choose—to live. It is necessary for the individual to come to terms with his own personal feelings, motivations, and desires—including the powerful sexual ones which are his lot for having passed puberty; and so there may well be pressures with which to contend during this stressful period of the life cycle. There may also be considerable pressure—and desire—to think about one's emerging sense of self; and so propositional knowledge about the self becomes an option valued in some cultural settings. Perhaps paradoxically, the pressures surrounding the formation of sense of self will be less acute in cultural milieus where the options facing the individual are fewer: where external social expectations prove to be determinant, and the individual's cherished aspirations may well be relegated to marginal status.

A MATURE SENSE OF SELF

A number of researchers have attempted to describe the later phases of the maturing self. At times, these accounts have centered upon the decisions or the points of tension that must occur in every life. Erikson, for example, speaks of a crisis of intimacy which follows the crisis of identity, as well as of subsequent struggles involved in the issue of generativity in middle age (transmitting values, knowledge, and the possibility of life to the following generation) and in the issue of integrity in old age (Does one's life make sense and cohere? Is one prepared to face death?). Some researchers speak of periods of renewed stress in middle age—when it may be too late to change one's life plan--and in old age—when one must come to grips with declining powers as well as with growing fears and uncertainties. In contrast, other researchers stress processes of continued development, where an individual has the option of becoming increasingly autonomous, integrated, or self-actualized, provided that he can make the correct "moves" and arrive at a suitable stance of accepting what cannot be altered. The end-goal of these developing processes is a self that is highly developed and fully differentiated from others: desirable models would include Socrates, Jesus Christ, Mahatma Gandhi, Eleanor Roosevelt—individuals who appear to have understood much about themselves and about their societies and to have come to terms successfully with the frailties of the human condition, while at the same time inspiring others around them to lead more productive lives.

These views of maturity all highlight a relatively autonomous sense of self, one that places a heavy accent upon intrapersonal features, even when they are marshaled in the service of others. But there is another view which places a far greater emphasis on the formative role of other persons in the sense of self and, consequently, affords little credence to the notion of an autonomous self. According to this point of view, an individual is always and necessarily a set of selves, a group of persons, who perennially reflect the context they happen to inhabit at any particular moment. Rather than a central "core self" which organizes one's thoughts, behavior, and goals, the person is better thought of as a collection of relatively diverse masks, none of which takes precedence over the others, and each of which is simply called into service as needed and retired when the situation no longer requires it and the "scene" moves elsewhere. Here the accent in the "sense of self" falls much more heavily on interpersonal knowledge and know-how.

This point of view, relatively prominent in the disciplines of social psychology and sociology (as against depth psychology), sees as the ultimate determinant of behavior the situation or context in which one is found and the roles that are accordingly demanded. From this point of view, the ability to manipulate the situation to one's own purposes becomes important: notions of achieving an integrated personality or of being true to one's deepest values and standards tend to take a back seat. Other perspectives, developed in other cultures, concede that individuals may have the potential to develop in individualistic ways and to evolve an autonomous sense of self, but explicitly reject this line of development as inimical to a sense of community and to the virtue of selflessness. Given prevailing Western ideals, these may seem less attractive or complete views of human nature; but they are not, therefore, by any means proven false or illegitimate. After all, the purpose of social science is not to prove that one's prejudices are well founded, but rather to come up with that model (or those models) of human behavior which most clearly approximates the actual state of affairs across time and cultural settings.

TUTELAGE IN PERSONAL KNOWLEDGE

Until this point, I have spoken of the development of personal knowledge as a relatively natural process, in which our ingrained proclivities to make discriminations among our own feelings, or to refine our perceptions of others, are gently prodded along one or another path by the prevailing interpretations of our society. In many cases, in fact, the development of personal knowledge can take place without explicit tutelage: one does not need to show an individual overtly how to make such discriminations; one simply allows them to emerge.

But there are cases where far more explicit instruction in the personal realm may appear necessary or advisable. At times, such instruction is at the behest of the society. Through formal tutoring, or through literature, rituals, and other symbolic forms, the culture helps the growing individual to make discriminations about his own feelings or about the other persons in his milieu. As T. S. Eliot once pointed out, "in developing the language, enriching the meaning of words, the [poet] is making possible a much wider range of emotion and perception for other men, because he gives them the speech in which more can be expressed." At other times, the individual himself, desirous of more skills in the personal realm, will seek help in effecting the proper kinds of discrimination. The recourse to therapy in the West may certainly be seen as an effort to train one's ability to make finer and more appropriate discriminations within one's realm of personal feelings and with respect to "reading" the signals of other individuals. By the same token, the enduring popularity of self-help books—not excluding that perennial favorite *How to Win Friends and Influence People*—represents a widely felt need within an "other-directed" society for those skills that will enable one to interpret a social situation correctly and then to initiate the proper moves with respect to it.

Just how instruction in the personal realm should ideally take place is not known. Nor are there reliable measures for determining the extent to which training of personal intelligences has been successful. But it is worth underscoring the point that the education of such emotions and such discriminations clearly involves a cognitive process. To feel a certain way—paranoid, envious, jubilant—is to construe a situation in a certain way, to see something as having a possible effect upon oneself or upon other individuals. One may develop appropriate appraisals, finely honed discriminations, accurate categorizations and classifications of situations; or, less happily, one can make excessively gross discriminations, inappropriate labelings, incorrect inferences, and thus fundamentally misinterpret situations. The less a person understands his own feelings, the more he will fall prey to them. The less a person understands the feelings, the responses, and the behavior of others, the more likely he will interact inappropriately with them and therefore fail to secure his proper place within the larger community.

Certainly societies have differed in the extent to which they highlight these various views and end-states of human growth, in their relative emphases on the individual as against the social self, in their espousals of explicit modes for training personal intelligences. I shall be examining some of these variations more closely when I consider personal knowledge across cultural boundaries. What needs to be stressed at this point is that one can discern the main features of both faces of development—the focus on others and the mastery of the social role, as well as the focus on self and the mastery of one's own personal life—in every normal individual. Emphases may differ, but the fact that one is a unique individual, who still must grow up in a social context—an individual of feelings and striving, who must rely on others to furnish the tasks and to judge one's achievements—is an ineluctable aspect of the human condition and one firmly rooted in our species membership.

The Biological Bases of Personhood

EVOLUTIONARY CONSIDERATIONS

Comparative psychologists are sympathetic to the possibility that even the most treasured facets of human nature may be found, if in somewhat simpler forms, in other animals. In addition to claims for some linguistic ability in chimpanzees, we know that chimpanzees can also recognize that daub of rouge as being on *their* nose (as monkeys cannot). And there is a growing belief that at least primitive forms of consciousness, if not of self-awareness, may be found among higher mammals. Yet all but the most ardent animal lovers would concede that the forms of personal knowledge under discussion here are still restricted to human beings. In any case, the question arises: Which factors in the evolution of our species have spawned the remarkable focus on the person and on other persons that characterizes *homo sapiens*?

Of the numerous factors that have been cited as contributing to human uniqueness, two seem especially closely tied to the rise of personal knowledge—both the individual and the social varieties. The first factor is the prolonged childhood of the primate and, in particular, its close tie to its mother. We know that chimpanzees spend the first five years of their lives in close proximity to their mothers, and that vast amounts of learning take place during this period. The mother provides models that the young offspring can observe, imitate, and retain in memory for subsequent simulation. Equally important, the mother indicates by her behavior *which* sorts of things and events ought to be noted by the young animal, and thereby defines a universe of significant activities and individuals. The mother is the initial, and remains the principal, teacher: she can even instruct the youngster in carrying out novel patterns of behavior—for example, foraging for potatoes—which have only made a recent appearance in certain pockets of the species. So important is this "significant other" during the opening years of life, that when she is injured or otherwise removed from the scene, the normal development of the individual is placed in jeopardy. The focus on a single other individual for so lengthy a time, the fact that one can learn so much from that individual and eventually pass on that acquired knowledge to the next generation, may well constitute a powerful source of the emphasis on the person found in the human species.

A second factor in the evolutionary past of the species is the emergence several million years ago of a culture in which hunting assumed great importance. Whereas foraging, gathering, or the killing of small animals can be carried out alone or informally in the company of one or two others, the hunting, tracking, killing, sharing, and preparation of the meat of larger animals is an activity that inevitably involves the participation and cooperation of a large number of individuals. Groups of humans or of prehumans—presumably males—must learn to work together, to plan, to communicate, and to cooperate, all in order to snare and share the meats of the hunt. Young males must be trained so that they can participate in the hunt; for instance, the boys must learn to track, to distinguish different smells and cries, to control their gestures and synchronize them with specific partners, to build up certain muscles, to aim accurately, to find their ways around strange locales and return to designated spots at the appointed hour. More generally, the existence of the human group becomes closely tied to the lives of the nearby animals on whom the humans become dependent for food, shelter, clothing, and even religious activity.

In light of these requirements for effective hunting, the needs for group cohesion, leadership, organization, and solidarity become relatively easy to understand. Why there should be the emergence of a nuclear family, with the aforementioned strong tie between mother and child, and ties of a different sort between father and child (particularly the young male), is perhaps less evident. It is certainly conceivable that other social arrangements, distinct from a nuclear family with strong parent-offspring ties, could have evolved in societies where hunting was a pivotal activity. Perhaps, in this extremely speculative area, it suffices to point out that the nuclear family provides one highly adaptive solution to a number of issues: the building of strong interpersonal bonds which bolster the solidarity of the wider community; the training of young males to be hunters; the training of females to be householders and future mothers; the guarantee of some stability as far as mating patterns are concerned; the prevention of possibly injurious incest; and the preservation and transmission of various forms of knowledge and wisdom.

Evolutionary clues to the origins of intrapersonal facets of intelligence are more elusive, in part because these forms of knowledge are less readily identified and documented by scientific observers. One factor that may promote a recognition of oneself as a separate entity is the capacity to transcend the mere satisfaction of instinctual drives. Such an option becomes increasingly available to animals that are not perennially involved in the struggle for survival, have a relatively long life, and engage regularly in exploratory activities. Certainly the use of any kind of symbol system—and of language, the pre-eminent symbol system—also promotes this personal variety of intelligence. Intimations of "personhood" become more probable in those animals with proto-symbolic capacities.

The evolutionary origin of the personal intelligences has engaged the speculative powers of some of our leading students of human prehistory. The paleontologist Harry Jerison makes a sharp distinction between the perception of other individuals and the perception of self. In this view, "the perception of others in social roles can often be handled at the level of organization of fixed action patterns"—in other words, as high-level reflexive actions built into the repertoire of the organism. And, indeed, the recognition of conspecifics, including particular relatives, occurs readily in many animal groups. In contrast, Jerison sees the perception of self "as a peculiarly human development of the capacity for creating 'objects' in the real world." Jerison goes on to maintain that knowledge of self may build on our imagery and imaginative powers which allow us to create models of ourselves.

The British psychologist N. K. Humphrey stresses the creative capacities involved in knowledge of the social world. In fact, he makes the bold claim that the chief creative use of human intellect lies not in the traditional areas of art and science but rather in holding society together. He points out that social primates are required to be calculating beings, to take into account the consequences of their own behavior, to calculate the likely behavior of others, to calculate benefits and losses—all in a context where the relevant evidence is ephemeral, likely to change, even as a consequence of their own actions. Only an organism with highly developed cognitive skills can make do in such a context. The requisite abilities have been worked out over the millennia by human beings and passed on with great care and skill from the elder to the younger individuals:

> The outcome has been the gifting of members of the human species with remarkable powers of social foresight and understanding. This social intelligence, developed initially to cope with local problems of inter-personal relationships, has in time found expression in the institutional creations of the "savage mind"—the highly rational structures of kinship, totemism, myth, and religion which characterize primitive societies.

FEELINGS IN ANIMALS

Elusive as the perceptual basis of the personal intelligences may be, the question whether animals experience—and are able to discriminate among—various feeling states, is shrouded in even greater mystery. To my mind, impressive evidence that discrete feeling states may exist in neurally bounded forms comes from the work of John Flynn. This investigator has shown that it is possible to trigger in cats a complex form of affect-laden behavior by direct electrical stimulation of the brain. For instance, even in cats who do not under ordinary circumstances attack mice, one can produce full-blown attack behavior and associated facial expressions simply by stimulating certain brain regions. This means that the "attack system" has evolved to function as a unit; neither experience nor training or learning is required for full and proper firing. We see here evidence that a whole set of behavior patterns, ones presumably accompanied (or even triggered) by specific affective states, can be set off by endogenous (internal) as well as by conventional environmental triggers. Studies inducing (and then suppressing) profound depression in rats by injecting chemicals into the brain provide another line of supporting evidence. Possibly, such "prepackaged" reactive programs are exploited in higher species in more varied, less canalized situations.

In a species closer to human beings, one can see evidence for the origins of a particular emotion. Donald Hebb has demonstrated that a full-blown fear state can be evoked in the chimpanzee, without any need for training or specific prior experience, simply by the presentation of a display significantly at variance from what the animal has previously perceived. In this case, a chimpanzee will become extremely frightened, excited, or anxious when it beholds an inert, mutilated, or dismembered body of another chimpanzee. The precipitating object must be sufficiently divergent from other members of a class to command attention, while still exhibiting enough of its properties to be perceived as a member of the same class. According to Hebb's formulation, the fear originates in the disruption of cerebral activities usually involved in perception: it is distinctive from other emotions by virtue of its accompanying physiological reactions as well as of the processes that tend to restore cerebral equilibrium—for example, flight from the threatening object. Thus, even as young human infants have emotional reactions tied to specific precipitating events, so, too, we find in a closely related species a set of event-related reactions which signal an incipient awareness of the category of individual to which one belongs. That the category is another "person," and that the response is so "severe," provides further suggestive evidence that the origins of personal intelligences can be discerned in species other than our own.

It is important to stress that such organized reactive programs can also be undermined, given certain environmental manipulations. In the monkey, for example, there exists a complex set of affectual systems which surround the development of the attachment link between mother and infant. Under normal rearing conditions, these systems will evolve without a hitch. Yet, thanks to Harry Harlow's pioneering studies of motherless monkeys, we know that the absence of certain stimulating conditions will yield a monkey that is grossly abnormal in the "personal" domain. These monkeys are not able to react appropriately to other monkeys; they cannot assume their proper role in the dominance hierarchies; they cower in fear or aggressively attack in inappropriate situations; and, most tellingly, they prove unable to raise their own offspring, if they are even able to conceive at all. To a certain extent, the effects of motherless rearing are reversible—for example, if younger organisms are allowed to play with and otherwise substitute for the maternal figure; but even such substitution encounters a "statute of limitations," beyond which time the monkey's knowledge of how to relate to conspecifics has been permanently devastated. It is worth underscoring that, while maternal deprivation exerts irrevocable effects on the personal intelligences of the monkeys, it does not exert comparable effects upon other cognitive capacities such as those measured in routine problem-solving tasks. Apparently, even among infrahumans, intellectual competences enjoy a certain autonomy from one another.

Abnormal social reactions can also be caused by surgical interventions in monkeys. In the light of studies by Ronald Myers and his colleagues at the National Institutes of Health, we know that a number of sites in the primate nervous system play crucial roles in the kinds of adequate social behavior that are part and parcel of interpersonal intelligence. Specifically, removal of the prefrontal cortex in juvenile primates causes decreased use of face and voice for communication, alteration in aggressiveness and patterns of grooming, decreased participation in play activity, and frequent sessions of hyperactivity of an aimless variety. Significant social maturation must have occurred for the adverse effects of the prefrontal lobectomy to be felt; this finding suggests that the requisite modulating structures develop gradually during the period of social growth that Harlow and his colleagues have illuminated.

Many of the effects wrought by damage to the prefrontal cortex are also mimicked by lesions in the anterior temporal areas of the cortex. Following lesions in this area, operated animals failed to rejoin their family groups and did not attempt to re-establish their pre-operative dominance status. They also showed a decreased patterning of fa-

259

cial expressions, gestures, and vocalizations. Unlike the frontally injured monkeys, those with temporal lesions were prone to exhibit inappropriate aggressive behavior. In general, Myers concludes, the most readily apparent change in the behavior of the animals with the prefrontal or the anterior temporal lesions was a reduction in those activities which maintain social bonds.

Myers has put forth the provocative suggestion that there may be two distinct neural mechanisms that serve, respectively, the "actual inner feelings" of the monkeys and their abilities to express (or convey) these emotions facially, whether they are actually felt. According to Myers, lesions at the base of the brain can produce a paralysis of the volitional use of the face while leaving intact spontaneous facial expression of an emotional nature. This finding suggests that we may be able to find in infra-human organisms a preliminary and biologically based intimation of the difference between intrapersonal access to feelings (one's inner state) and the ability to express them voluntarily to others (interpersonal communication). Studies conducted by Ross Buck with human beings confirm the existence of distinct neurological systems in human beings for dealing with volitional as opposed to spontaneous expression of emotions: apparently, like other primates, our ability to convey emotions deliberately to others proceeds along a separate track from our spontaneous and involuntary experiencing and expression of emotions.

THE PATHOLOGY OF PERSONHOOD

We see, then, that even in as patent a human domain as the knowledge of self and other individuals, it is possible to find antecedents among our primate brethren. Of the analogies between human interpersonal knowledge and that displayed by other primates, there seems to be little doubt; and while the development of knowledge of one's self seems more peculiarly human, research with chimpanzees provides a helpful perspective on the origins of this most human of capacities. Nonetheless, given the incomparably greater development in human beings of personal forms of knowledge, researchers have naturally been concerned about the fate of personal knowledge—both inner and social—under various conditions of damage to the human brain.

Once again, all indices point to the frontal lobes as the structures of greatest importance in various forms of personal knowledge. Defects in the frontal lobe can interfere with the development of personal forms of knowledge and can cause various pathological forms of intrapersonal and interpersonal knowledge. It has been known for well over a century that destruction of the frontal lobes in an adult exerts only relatively minor effects on that individual's ability to solve problems (such as those featured on a standard intelligence test) but can wreak severe damage on his personality. In brief, the individual who has had major frontal lobe pathology, particularly if it is bilateral, emerges no longer recognizable as the "same person" by those who had known him before.

There may well be more than one syndrome of personal change following injury to the frontal lobes. Frank Benson and Dietrich Blumer suggest that injury to the orbital (lower) area of the frontal lobes is likely to produce hyperactivity, irritability, insouciance, and euphoria; while injury to the convexity (higher regions) of the frontal lobe is more likely to produce indifference, listlessness, slowness, and apathy—a kind of depressive (as opposed to psychopathic) personality. Indeed, among different individuals, one will find varying mixes of these symptoms, quite possibly correlating with the exact site of damage. But what must be stressed is that, in individuals whose cognitive performance—whose other intelligences—seems relatively preserved in a computational sense, a sense of the "same person" is uniformly felt to be absent. No longer does the individual express his earlier sense of purpose, motivation, goals, and desire for contact with others; the individual's reaction to others has been profoundly altered, and his own sense of self seems to have been suspended.

But since this symptom picture might result from significant damage to the brain, independent of the precise site of the lesion, it becomes important to determine whether, in the face of massive brain injury at other sites, the individual might still display a preserved personality, an enduring sense of self. Pertinent to this issue, the Russian neuropsychologist Alexander Luria reported several years ago the fascinating case of "the man with the shattered world." As a young soldier in the Second World War, Zasetsky had suffered a severe battle wound in the left parietal-occipital area of his head—an injury that drastically crippled him across a distressingly full range of conceptual and symbolic faculties. His speech was reduced to the most elementary forms of expression; he could not write a single word or even a single letter; he could not perceive in his right visual field; he could not hammer a nail, carry out simple chores, play a game, find his way outside; he was confused about the order of the seasons, unable to add two numbers, or even to describe a picture.

Yet, according to Luria, Zasetsky maintained something far more

261

precious than these standard intellectual capacities: those person-related functions associated with the frontal lobes. He continued to possess will, desire, sensitivity to experience, and the treasured ability to form and sustain plans and carry actions through as effectively as his condition permitted. Thus, over a twenty-five-year period, Zasetsky worked steadily to improve his own performance. Under Luria's guidance he was able to re-educate himself to read and write. He kept a notebook in which he painstakingly recorded his daily progress. He even proved able to introspect about his condition:

> Words have lost meaning for me or have a meaning that is incomplete and unformed. Every word I hear seems vaguely familiar. . . . as far as my memory is concerned I know a particular word exists, except that it has lost meaning. . . . so I have to limit myself to words that "feel" familiar to me, that have some definite meaning for me.

In contrast to the frontal lobe patients described by Benson and Blumer, one feels that Zasetsky remained fundamentally the same person, who could continue to relate in normal fashion to other individuals.

Why should the frontal lobes have this special status for the individual's sense of person, such that an individual with a spared frontal lobe can continue to have access to his own views of himself, while other individuals with less extensive damage may have totally lost this presence of mind? According to Walle Nauta, a leading neuroanatomist and long-time student of the frontal lobes, the frontal lobes constitute the meeting place *par excellence* for information from the two great functional realms of the brain: the posterior regions, which are involved in the processing of all sensory information (including perception of others); and the limbic systems, where individual motivational and emotional functions are housed, and whence one's internal states are generated). The frontal cortex turns out to be the realm where neural networks representing the individual's inner milieu—his personal feelings, motivations, and subjective knowledge—converge with the system representing the external milieu—the sights, sounds, tastes, and mores of the world as transmitted through diverse sensory modalities. Thus, by virtue of their strategic anatomical location and connections, the frontal lobes have the potential to serve as the major integrating station—and this they do.

At the core of personal knowledge, as represented in the brain and particularly in the frontal lobes, seem to be two kinds of information. One is our ability to know other people—to recognize their faces, their voices, and their persons; to react appropriately to them; to engage in activities with them. The other kind is our sensitivity to our own feelings, our own wants and fears, our own personal histories. As we have seen, intimations of these abilities can be found in the animal kingdom and certainly within the primate order: the recognition of faces and voices, the formation of close ties to other organisms, and the experience of a range of feelings are certainly not the exclusive property of human beings. Moreover, each of these forms can be compromised by experimental surgery. But the ability to link these forms of knowing to symbols, so that we can conceptualize our intuitive knowledge of our self and our more public knowledge of others, emerges as a unique human function. It allows us to formulate theories and beliefs about other individuals and to develop a propositional account of our own person, which I have elsewhere dubbed a "metaphor of the self." In all probability, many areas of the brain (subcortical as well as cortical) participate in the development and elaboration of these forms of personal intelligence; but because of their unique role as an integrating juncture, and because of their relatively late development in the history of the species and of the individual, the frontal lobes play a privileged and irreplaceable role in the forms of intelligence with which we are here concerned.

The status of personal knowledge has also been studied in other pathological populations. Some pathologies may block the development of knowledge of self and others. With respect to young human beings, we find the occasional individual who is autistic: a child who may well have spared computational capacities, particularly in areas like music or mathematics, but whose pathological condition is in fact defined by an inability to communicate with others and by so impaired a sense of self that the child has singular difficulties in deploying the words *I* and *me*. Whatever the problem that devastates the autistic child, it clearly involves difficulties in knowing others and in using this knowledge to know oneself. The aversion of eyes from other individuals serves as an especially poignant symptom of this disorder.

To my knowledge, one does not find *idiots savants* of an opposite type, individuals with an excessively highly developed sense of self. Such knowledge and maturation of self appear to require so extensive an integration of other capacities that the individual would have to be an essentially normal person. Yet is may be worth remarking that, in certain forms of retardation such as Down's syndrome, the ability to forge effective social relationships with others seems relatively well preserved, at least in comparison with more "straightforward" cognitive capacities like language or logic. Whether this form of interpersonal "savvy" translates to insights into one's own condition, to a kind of intrapersonal knowledge, seems highly doubtful. Moreover, in the case of certain disorders, such as that found in the psychopathic personality, the individual may be extremely keenly attuned to the intentions and motivations of others without displaying comparable sensitivity to his own feelings or motives. Finally, it is also possible that some individuals may have excessively precocious or keen knowledge of their own feelings without being able to indicate, or act upon, this knowledge in the presence of others. By definition, this condition would be most difficult for an observer to identify!

One may examine the fate of personal knowledge in individuals who have sustained various focal injuries—for instance, in persons once normal who have become aphasic as a result of damage to the dominant cerebral hemisphere. It might seem that language holds the key to self-knowledge; and that, in the absence of this form of symbolization, the ability to conceive of oneself or to cooperate with other individuals would be seriously, if not fatally, compromised. In fact, however, severe aphasia can be sustained without equally devastating implications for personal knowledge. Among those who have been aphasic but have recovered sufficiently to describe their experiences, we find consistent testimony: while there may have been a diminution of general alertness and considerable depression about his condition, the individual in no way felt himself to be be a different person. He recognized his own needs, wants, and desires and tried as best he could to achieve them. Family members (and physicians) generally concur that, given the severity of the impairment, the aphasic's ability to relate to other individuals and to reflect upon his own condition survives surprisingly well.

As if to reinforce this point, an instructively different symptomatic picture is found amongst individuals who have sustained unilateral damage to the right (nondominant or minor) hemisphere. In these patients, language is ostensibly intact, and so one might expect an unimpaired ability to make discriminations with respect to oneself and other persons. In fact, in sheer capacity to banter, such patients may superficially appear to have remained the same person. But it generally takes merely a few minutes of discussion to confirm that the ability to deal with others has been maintained chiefly, if not exclusively, at a verbal level, and that there exists a large, perhaps insurmountable gap between the former personality and the present modes of relating to others. Ties to others appear very superficial, and remarks do not seem to emerge from the same individual that had thrived prior to the onset of the brain insult. There are, moreover, little sense of drive, meager signs of plans for recovery, scant eagerness to form or to reaffirm personal relationships. The patient may announce that he is fine (reflecting the denial of illness often associated with the condition), and that he is going to return to work the next day; but he will, in fact, sit for hours near a doorway without moving. Perhaps, indeed, the lack of awareness of their actual condition is a major factor in the poor recovery typically found in patients with injury to the right hemisphere—even as the often surprisingly good recovery of skills in the aphasic patient reflects the preserved sense of self and initiative, along with a concomitant awareness of lingering deficits.

Further perspectives on personal knowledge can be obtained from studies of other patient populations. In patients with Alzheimer's disease—a form of presenile dementia—the breakdown of computational capacities—particularly in the spatial, the logical, and the linguistic realms—is often severe. Yet, at the same time, the patient will remain well groomed, socially appropriate, and continually apologetic about errors that he makes. It is as if the patient felt his powers waning, was aware of this decline, and was distraught at the failure to circumvent his difficulties but would not vent his frustration in a publicly hostile way. My interpretation of this strange and disquieting set of affairs is that the patient's frontal lobes remain relatively preserved during the early stages of this form of presenile dementia: Alzheimer's disease actually attacks the posterior brain zones with special ferocity. In contrast, patients with Pick's disease—another variety of presenile dementia, which is much more frontally oriented—show a rapid loss of social appropriateness, a symptom picture more reminiscent of the irascible forms of frontal lobe pathology.

ALTERATIONS IN PERSONAL KNOWLEDGE

So far, I have considered pathologies that in some way diminish personal knowledge. It is also possible to look at individuals whose personal knowledge has been altered—rather than actually reduced—by a neurological disorder. Patients who suffer from temporal lobe epilepsy prove particularly instructive in this regard. Such patients come to exhibit somewhat different personalities: their own view of the world changes, often profoundly. Whatever their previous personal orientation, they tend to become introspective, given to writing extensive tracts, increasingly tending toward the study of philosophy and religion and the relentless pondering of deep questions. There may be considerable rage, which can erupt at any time, but in the same individual, there is an intensification of ethical and religious feeling which may give rise to a desire to be excessively good, careful, and God fearing. In addition, there may be a viscosity in these patients, in that they seek to form excessively close ties to others and prove unable to "let go" in a personal encounter. It is risky to compare epilepsy directly with destruction of brain tissue, because the condition entails an abnormal firing of nervous tissue rather than the massive destruction of neurons. Yet the fact that the individual's personality constellation and his way of relating to others may be significantly affected by this condition—even as performances on measures of language and other standard cognitive measures may remain just as before—provides additional suggestive evidence that personal intelligences are a domain apart.

Perhaps even two domains apart. Based on extensive work with temporal lobe epileptic patients, David Bear has recently put forth some intriguing notions about two forms of behavioral breakdown and their neuroanatomical substrates. One set of cortical regions, located in the dorsal (parietal) region of the cortex, seems critical for surveillance, attention, and arousal: its injury results in indifference and in the *loss of a sense of caring about one's own person*. A contrasting set of cortical regions, located in the ventral (temporal) regions of the cortex, seems critical for the identification of stimuli, for new learning, and for appropriate emotional responding. Lesions in this latter area produce *a lack of concern with external stimuli* and, accordingly, inappropriate emission of sexual or aggressive responses toward other individuals, with scant consideration of the previously learned consequences of such flagrant displays. While Bear's scheme has not been developed specifically to deal with the varieties of personal intelligence introduced here, one can readily draw suggestive parallels between these forms of impairment and our pair of personal intelligences.

Probably the most dramatic discovery in neuroscience of the past generation also proves relevant to my topic. As is known by virtually every scanner of the Sunday supplements (and by readers of chapter 3 as well), it is now possible through surgical procedures to disconnect the two halves of the brain and to test each separately. In addition to providing further confirmatory evidence that the left hemisphere is dominant for linguistic functioning, and the right for spatial functioning, research with "split-brain patients" has provided suggestive evidence that an individual possesses (at least potentially) more than a single consciousness. Indeed, the individual may harbor two—or even more—consciousnesses, or selves, which, in the wake of the surgical intervention, have become alienated from one another.

Considerable effort is now being invested in characterizing these forms of consciousness, in seeking to discover whether they are both equally subjective or objective, and whether one has some kind of existential or epistemological priority over the other. It may well be that both are involved in emotional processing, with the left hemisphere somewhat more oriented toward euphoria, happiness, and optimism, the right hemisphere toward pessimism, reaction, hostility (this is why destruction of either hemisphere tends to produce the opposite "spared" configuration of traits). It may also be that the consciousness of the left hemisphere is simply more oriented toward words and other discrete symbols and analytic categories, while the right hemisphere is correlatively primed for the emotional, spatial, and interpersonal realms. Perhaps we can find intimations of these two cognitive styles in normal individuals, with individuals who exploit right hemisphere processes being somewhat more humanistically oriented, while those who favor left hemisphere processes being somewhat more sober, scientific, or "straight." Even though these pictures are caricatured, and the brain is far more than two "little selves," one should not minimize the purchase on human intelligences that may eventually be obtained from studies of the sundered hemispheres.

As I have elsewhere criticized those who would too readily dub each hemisphere with a single epithet, I want to underscore the dangers of basing excessive claims about personal intelligence on such a smattering of cues from different patient populations. In candor, the amount of knowledge available about personal intelligences is less, and certainly less compelling, than that available for other, more conventionally computational forms of intelligence, ones less susceptible to cultural canalization. The evidence from different brain-damaged populations can be read in a number of ways, and it is by no means certain whether a contrast between left and right hemisphere lesions, between cortical and subcortical damage, between dorsal and ventral injuries will come closest to cutting the personal intelligences at their proper joints. Still, our discussion clearly suggests that forms of personal intelligence can be destroyed, or spared, in relative isolation from other varieties of cognition: there are highly suggestive hints, in both the evolutionary and the pathological literature, that intrapersonal and interpersonal intelligences can be discriminated from one another. More decisive findings must await the devising of more sensitive measures and the advent of more satisfying descriptions of each form of personal intelligence.

Persons in Other Cultures

Personal intelligences may be rooted in biology, but vast and highly instructive differences in their constitutions can be discerned across cultures. Anthropological explorations have been of fundamental importance in laying out some of the alternatives, in showing how a different balance can be struck between intrapersonal and interpersonal knowledge in various "selves." To convey an initial flavor of the variety, I can do no better than to review Clifford Geertz's sketch of three contrasting concepts of the person which he encountered in a quarter century of fieldwork.

In Java where he worked in the 1950s, Geertz found as lively and persistent a concern with the concept of self as one might encounter among a collection of European intellectuals. As part of a general concern with philosophical issues, even the least prosperous Javanese displays interest in what constitutes a person. In the Javanese view, a person harbors two kinds of contrast. The first obtains between "inside" and "outside." In a manner familiar to Westerners, Javanese isolate the inside "felt realm" of human experience—the flow of subjective feeling which is perceived directly. They contrast this phenomenological immediacy with the "outside world"—the external actions, movements, postures, and speech which in our culture would warm the analytic hearts of strict behaviorists. Rather than being functions of one another, these inside and outside facets are regarded as realms that need to be ordered independently.

The second kind of contrast obtains between "pure" or "civilized," on the one hand, and "rough," "uncivilized," or "vulgar," on the other. The Javanese strive to achieve the pure or civilized form both in the inner realm, through religious discipline, and in the outer realm, through proper etiquette. The ultimate result is a divided conception of the self, "half ungestured feeling and half unfelt gesture." An inner world of quiet emotion and an outer world of shaped behavior confront one another as two distinct realms, which the Javanese must somehow negotiate successfully within a single body and a single life. Certainly, the tension between the two "faces" of personal knowledge is directly confronted in the Javanese context.

What has a philosophical tinge in Java is handled in theatrical terms in Bali. In this enduring Hindu culture, one observes a perpetual attempt to stylize all aspects of personal existence to the point where anything idiosyncratic is muted in favor of the assumption of one's assigned place in the drama of Balinese life. Individuals are conceived of in terms of the masks they wear, the roles that they play in this continuing pageant. People are identified through their roles in a perpetual cast of characters, with current accidental factors subjugated in order to highlight a permanent set of status relations. The big risk, and fear, in such a "presentation of self" is that one's public performance will come apart and one's own personality (as we would call it) will assert itself. As Geertz describes it, "When this occurs, as it sometimes does, the immediacy of the moment is felt with excruciating intensity and men become suddenly and unwillingly creatural." All efforts are maintained vigilantly to protect the stylized self against the threat of immediacy, spontaneity, and brutishness. In this culture, a clear decision has been made to accentuate the interpersonal, and to mute the intrapersonal, forms of self.

The Moroccans whom Geertz came to know in the mid-1960s lived in Sefrou, a small city about twenty miles south of Fez. The town consists of an astounding variety of individuals from different backgrounds (Arabs, Berbers, and Jews) and different professions (tailors, horsemen, and soldiers) reflecting wide differences in wealth, modernity, and migrant status—a swell of humanity reminiscent of a medieval pageant. Perhaps to counter the dangers of anonymity in this variegated assemblage, the Moroccans have adopted a practice, a symbolic means, for identifying one another, called the *nisba*. One's *nisba* is one's attribution—a short label attached to one's name which indicates the region or the group from which one comes. By this mode of identification—"Umar of the Bugadu tribe," "Muhammed from the Sus region"—one becomes known to other individuals. The precise labeling used at any one time may depend upon the context—the smaller the group in which one is presently located, the more precise the labeling; but the practice of identifying an individual in this manner is universal among the denizens of Sefrou.

A *nisba* must be seen as part of a total life picture. One of the most pivotal characteristics of Moroccan society is a strict distinction between the public and the private person. The lively and fluid mosaic of casbah life is carefully segregated from the guarded privacy of the individual's personal concerns. Rather than dividing its diverse society into castes, the Moroccans distinguish the contexts where men are strictly separated from one another (marriage, worship, law, and education) from those more public contexts (work, friendship, trade) where they are variously connected to other individuals. People interact with one another in terms of public categories whose meanings refer to geographical sites, and leave the more personally experienced forms of life to be savored in the privacy of their tents and their temples. Thus, the *nisba* system creates a framework in which persons can be identified in terms of supposedly immanent characteristics (speech, blood, faith) and yet be allowed considerable latitude in their practical relations in public places: what turns out to be permitted is a kind of hyperindividualism in public relations, where almost everything specific can be filled in by the processes of interaction. At the same time, one does not risk the loss of self, which has been carefully set off in the more intimate and insulated activities of procreation and prayer. In the Moroccan setting, then, there is room for cultivation of both intrapersonal and interpersonal intelligences, but the two are never melded into a single integrated self.

Though Geertz's careful and caring descriptions were devoted to another end—an explication of how an anthropologist may understand other peoples through an examination of their symbolic forms—these portraits provide a validation of the distinctions that I have introduced in this chapter. We see here three disparate cultures, spanning half the world, and many centuries of historical evolution, each coping with the same set of constraints: how to confront the feelings, the exigencies, and the idiosyncracies of each individual, on the one hand, and still allow smooth and productive functioning with other members of the community, on the other. Each of the cultures deals with this tension in characteristically distinctive ways: the Javanese, by explicitly positing two distinct realms of existence which each individual must somehow keep in balance; the Balinese, by veering sharply toward the public pole and trying desperately to prevent the "raw" aspects of personality from coming out (except perhaps in the relatively ritualized setting of the cockfight); the Moroccans, by relegating certain portions of one's life exclusively to private expression, thus allowing considerable freedom for the remaining interactions in the public arena.

By these diverse routes, each of these cultures ultimately engenders a person, a sense of self, an idiosyncratic but adaptive amalgam of those aspects of experience that are most purely personal and internal, and of those that govern and maintain one's relation to the outside community. Just how the self will be expressed, just how the balance will be struck, depends on a host of factors, including the history and the values of the culture and, quite possibly, the nature of the ecology and the economy. It is scarcely possible to anticipate the particular forms that conceptions of persons and selves will take in disparate corners of the world. What one can predict, however, is that every culture must somehow come to grips with this ensemble of concerns, and that some nexus between interpersonal and intrapersonal issues will always have to be forged. It follows that the sense of self developed within a given cultural matrix will reflect the synthesis wrought therein between intrapersonal and interpersonal facets of existence.

As one surveys the cultures of the world, one encounters fascinating variations in both interpersonal and intrapersonal forms of intelligence. One also finds varying amounts of emphasis on the personal forms of intelligence *per se*: while, for example, in the Western context, logical-mathematical and linguistic intelligences receive heavy stress, forms of personal intelligence are correlatively emphasized in traditional societies and, even today, in developed societies outside of the West (such as Japan). Short of a Cook's tour of the world's cultures, there is no way fully to portray the range of solutions that have been devised with respect to forms of personal intelligence and to senses of self. It is possible, however, to classify and characterize the various solutions along a number of different dimensions.

Borrowing a distinction from my colleague Harry Lasker, I can begin this survey by distinguishing between two ideal types of society. In a *particle* society like our own, the locus of the self inheres primarily in the specific individual. The individual is seen as having considerable autonomy and as essentially in control of his own fate, which may range from unalloyed triumph to disastrous defeat. There is an associated interest, even a fascination, with the isolated individual person, even as the external environment is seen as providing mere background support or interference. The Western notion of the solitary hero, struggling against the hostile environment and against inimical others, symbolizes a particle existence. It is vividly realized in the French literary tradition:

> The great national literary project. . . . the enterprise construes the self as the locus of all possibilities, avid, unafraid of contradiction (nothing need be lost, everything may be gained) and the exercise of consciousness as a life's highest aim, because only through becoming fully conscious may one be free.

Poaching an analogy from physics, we may contrast the *particle* with the *field* society. In the latter, the locus of attention, power, and control is placed in the hands of other people or even of the society as a whole. Far from accentuating the individual person, with his own goals, wants, and fears, the focus in a field society falls almost entirely on the environment in which one finds oneself. This surrounding context is seen as the determining force in an individual's life, the locus where decisions are actually made; even in cases where an individual comes to stand out, he is seen as being "selected," or as "moved" into a niche, without having a particular say (or even any wish to have a say) concerning his own peculiar fate. For Jean-Paul Sartre, an apostle of the French literary tradition, "Hell is other people." For individuals in a field society, "One's self *is* other people"—and when one's fellows have been shorn away, there is hardly an irreducible core of "self" left.

Nearly all traditional societies and even modern non-Western societies place a much greater weight on "field" factors and are far less likely to attribute significant decisiveness or free will to the individual "particle." Among the Maori of New Zealand, for example, a man's identity is determined by his inherited status and his relationship with his group. Outside of his group, a Maori is no one. Neither suffering nor pleasure come from the inside: instead, they are seen as the result of external forces. Analogously, among the Dinka of Southern Sudan, there is no conception of a mind that stores up one's own experience. Instead, the person is always the object acted upon—for example, by a place. Rather than being an object of study, the world is an active subject whose impact is felt by the passive individual. How different this perspective is from that customarily assumed in a Western particle society. The emphasis on the self as a single atomized particle is a peculiar legacy of Western political, philosophical, and literary traditions, dating back perhaps to Greek times and apparently unrivaled elsewhere in the world. We must be careful not to confuse "our" sense of the person with those senses entertained by other cultures; and we must recognize that, even in Western societies, there are vast individual differences in "field independence" and in judged "loci of control."

In their concern with the realm of the person, the cultures of the world can be arrayed along other instructive dimensions as well. A first consideration is the extent to which these cultures have elaborated an explicit theory of the person. Some societies, such as the Maori of New Zealand, make distinctions only in the language of every-day life. Other groups, such as the Yogas of India, posit a theory of the development of self which is far more complex and differentiated than any embraced in the West. The way in which the realm of the person is carved serves as another useful point of comparison. In traditional China, the mind and physical objects were not set apart. In contrast, among the Ojibwa of the Lake Superior area, the realm of the person is extended to a far wider range of entities, including animals, rocks, and one's own grandmother. Cultures also differ in an instructive manner in those aspects of the person which they choose to value. Among the

Japanese, a style of "minimum message communication" is cultivated. Spurning the "maximum message" of spoken language, the Japanese depend upon subtle nonverbal cues to provide the key to one's true feelings, motivation, and message. The Japanese also cherish and dignify *jikkan*—"real and direct" feelings—and revere the person attuned to his own *jikkan*. Proceeding along a rather different path, the Navajos place a special premium on the ability to be a good listener. Keen listening is seen as the key to proper decision making; those who can listen well are considered to have special gifts.

While cultures differ appreciably in their relative emphasis on the intrapersonal or interpersonal intelligences, one encounters social roles that require a maximum development of both. A particularly stunning example in this regard comes from the Ixils in Guatemala, who consult a shaman, or "daykeeper," for advice and counsel. As described by Benjamin N. and Lore M. Colby, the role of the daykeeper entails an extensive development of both forms of personal knowledge:

He must assess [his patients'] situations, their behavior, their concerns. He must also himself lead an exemplary life, or at least try to. Doing all this requires self analysis as well as an empathic viewpoint for understanding others: it requires an updating, a revising, and a repairing of one's self image: it requires a conceptualization of others which is added to and revised—a conceptualization that includes attributes and relations which one's clients and their families and friends maintain with each other; it requires an understanding of the goals and values that motivate people and of the way in which the context or situation can modify these goals and intentions.

A full consideration of the various roles cherished in diverse societies would doubtless clarify the emphases placed upon differentiated forms of interpersonal and intrapersonal intelligence. Even as the therapist, the religious leader, or the artist in our culture exploits various forms of personal understanding, it is likely that shamans, sorcerers, magicians, fortune tellers, and others of this ilk have a highly differentiated knowledge of the personal realm. In Western society, we have our Rousseau and our Proust, who have cultivated knowledge of self, even as we have artists like Shakespeare, Balzac, or Keats whose knowledge of other persons, whose "negative capability," has been exemplary, and whose ability to place themselves into the skin of others is inspiring. There is every reason to believe that a similar range of skills and roles will be found elsewhere. In any event, it seems parsimonious to assume that, in cultures where social connections are even more important than in our own, the ability to understand other persons and ferret out their motives is certainly at a premium.

Conclusion

In considering those forms of knowledge that revolve about other persons, we have entered a realm where the role of the culture and of historical forces proves especially salient and pervasive. It makes sense of think of some forms of intelligence—for example, those involved in spatial processing—as operating in essentially similar form across diverse cultures, and as relatively resistant to cultural molding; but it is patent that, when it comes to personal knowledge, the culture assumes a determining role. Indeed, it is through the learning—and use—of the symbol system of one's culture that personal intelligences come to assume their characteristic form.

We here encounter factors that have a long evolution. As a species we have reached a unique degree of individualization, one that has culminated in the possibility of a sense of personal identity. As sociologist Thomas Luckmann has pointed out, the emergence of a sense of personal identity is possible only because of the detachment of our species from the situational here-and-now and also from complete absorption in the immediacy of experiences. Owing to this enhanced sense of perspective, we become able to experience our environment through a rich and reasonably stable structure of objects and events. We can go on to integrate sequences of situations into a history of typical events. We can attend to other individuals and recognize the reflection of ourselves in the their behavior and actions. Ultimately, the emerging sense of personal identity mediates between the phylogenetic determinants of human existence and that particular pattern of history which has been made by earlier generations of humans. Because each culture has its own history, its sense of self and of others will necessarily be unique.

In the light of these special circumstances, it is appropriate to question whether personal intelligences—knowledge of self and others—should be conceived of as being at the same level of specificity (and generality) as the other intelligences that we have considered in earlier chapters. Perhaps it makes more sense to think of knowledge of self and others as being a higher level, a more integrated form of intelligence, one more at the behest of the culture and of historical factors, one more truly emergent, one that ultimately comes to control and to regulate more "primary orders" of intelligence.

I doubt that the question of the "specialness" of personal intelligences permits a sharp and decisive response. In some ways, the personal intelligences are as basic and biological as any intelligences considered here: their origins can be discerned in the directly experienced feelings of the individual, in the case of the intrapersonal form, and in the direct perception of significant other individuals, in the case of the interpersonal variety. In these senses, the personal intelligences conform to our working notions of a basic intelligence. Yet it is undoubtedly true that the diverse forms that personal intelligences can eventually assume are among their most outstanding features. And, particularly in the West, it seems reasonable to deem the individual's sense of self as a kind of second-level regulator, an overall metaphor for the rest of the person, and one that can, as part of its "duties," come to understand and to modulate an individual's other capacities. In this sense, then, the personal intelligences may not be directly commensurate with those intelligences that I have treated in earlier chapters.

But it is equally important to stress that this "glorification of the self" is a cultural option, one that has been taken up in contemporary Western circles, but that is in no sense a human imperative. Cultures confront the choice of selecting, as a primary unit of analysis, the individual self, the nuclear family, or a much larger entity (the community or the nation): through this choice, cultures determine (nay, dictate) the extent to which the individual peers inward to himself or gazes outward to others. One reason why we in the West tend to focus, even perseverate, on the *individual* self is because this aspect of existence has—for historical reasons—achieved increasing prominence within our own society. Were we living in a culture in which the focus fell chiefly on other individuals, on interpersonal relations, on the group, or even on the supernatural, we might well not be impaled on the dilemma of the self-as-special. For as we have already seen, any consideration of the "specialness of the self" cannot be undertaken apart from an analysis of the values and interpretive scheme of a particular society.

Nonetheless, if compelled to present a "transcultural" statement about the self, I would offer these remarks. I see the sense of self as an emerging capacity. From one vantage point, it is the natural result of the evolution of intrapersonal knowledge; but this evolution necessarily takes place within an interpreting cultural context, even as it is necessarily channeled by representational capacities which draw on the full gamut of human intelligences. In other words, in my view, every society offers at least a tacit sense of a person or a self, rooted in the individual's own personal knowledge and feelings. However, this sense will inevitably be interpreted and possibly be remade by the individual's relationship to, and knowledge of, other persons and, more generally, by the interpretive schemes supplied by the encompassing culture. Every culture will also engender a mature sense of the person, which will involve some balance between intrapersonal and interpersonal factors. In certain cultures, such as our own, the emphasis on the individual self may become sufficiently extreme that it leads to the appearance of a second-order capacity, which presides over and mediates among the other forms and lines of intelligence. This, then, is a possible outcome of cultural evolution—but an outcome, it must be stressed, that is difficult for us to judge and may be based, at least in part, on an illusory view of the primacy of our own powers and the degree of our own autonomy.

Having now reviewed at considerable length our family of seven intelligences, we might perhaps conceptualize them in broad strokes in the following way. The "object-related" forms of intelligence—spatial, logical-mathematical, bodily-kinesthetic—are subject to one kind of control: that actually exerted by the structure and the functions of the particular objects with which individuals come into contact. Were our physical universe structured differently, these intelligences would presumably assume different forms. Our "object-free" forms of intelligence—language and music—are not fashioned or channeled by the physical world but, instead, reflect the structures of particular languages and musics. They may also reflect features of the auditory and oral systems, though (as we have seen) language and music may each develop, at least to some extent, in the absence of these sensory modalities. Finally, the personal forms of intelligence reflect a set of powerful and competing constraints: the existence of one's own person; the existence of other persons; the culture's presentations and interpretations of selves. There will be universal features of any sense of person or self, but also considerably cultural nuances, reflecting a host of historical and individuating factors.

In reflecting upon the place of personal knowledge in this set of intelligences, I broach the issue of the status of the theory as a scientific enterprise. There are questions to deal with about the particular intelligences as well as about the viability of the enterprise as a whole. While the final critique must be left to others, it seems appropriate at this point for me to articulate some of the most salient difficulties with the theory as well as my own thoughts on how these might best be handled.

11

A Critique of
the Theory
of Multiple
Intelligences

Introduction

In part II, I have put forth a novel theory of intelligences, one designed to provide a positive model of the different intellectual strengths displayed by human beings. For the most part I have proceeded by demonstration: that is, I have introduced each of the intelligences through examples, and have sought to indicate their utility by reviewing the various ways in which these intelligences have been deployed in diverse cultural settings. Many details concerning these intelligences, and their manner of operation, remain to be filled in. Moreover, most of the limitations of the theory have been glossed over or ignored altogether.

In this chapter, I begin the task of examining this new theory with a more critical eye. It is important to consider how the theory stacks up with other competing theories of human cognition: Is it too extreme or too eclectic? What does it accomplish, and what does it omit? How could the theory be expanded to incorporate other facets of our knowledge of human beings? And how could it be made more useful to practitioners and policy makers? This cluster of questions will concern us for the remainder of the book, as I attempt to place the theory of multiple intelligences in a wider context. My concern in this and the next chapter is primarily critical; though in chapter 12, I begin to build a bridge connecting the main lines of this theory to those aspects of education and practice that occupy central stage in the final chapters of the book. For those individuals who are interested chiefly in the application of the theory, it is possible to proceed directly to chapter 13.

In its strong form, multiple intelligence theory posits a small set of human intellectual potentials, perhaps as few as seven in number, of which all individuals are capable by virtue of their membership in the human species. Owing to heredity, early training, or, in all probability, a constant interaction between these factors, some individuals will develop certain intelligences far more than others; but every normal individual should develop each intelligence to some extent, given but a modest opportunity to do so.

In the normal course of events, the intelligences actually interact with, and build upon, one another from the beginning of life. Moreover, as I shall demonstrate in some detail in chapter 12, they are eventually mobilized in the service of diverse social roles and functions. Nonetheless, I believe that, at the core of each intelligence, there exists a computational capacity, or information-processing device, which is unique to that particular intelligence, and upon which are based the more complex realizations and embodiments of that intelligence. Throughout I have tried to suggest what these "core" components might be: phonological and grammatical processing in the case of language; tonal and rhythmic processing in the case of music. For present purposes, however, the idea that each intelligence has one or more "raw" computational cores is more important than the precise delineation of these cores.

I would not wish any reader to take this metaphor of a computational device, or computer, more seriously than it is intended. Certainly, I have no reason to believe that the neural mechanisms in the brain work identically to the electromechanical components of a computer; nor do I have any wish to suggest that my computational devices are engaged in complex decisional processes, about whether a certain signal is (or is not) musical, or grammatical, or personal. Rather, what I want to convey is that the normal human being is so constituted as to be sensitive to certain informational content: when a particular form of information is presented, various mechanisms in the nervous system are triggered to carry out specific operations upon it. And from the repeated use of, elaboration of, and interaction among these various computational devices, eventually flow forms of knowledge that we would readily term "intelligent."

It may seem odd that so venerated a concept as intelligence be thought of as composed of "dumb" mechanisms (that is, ones insensitive to larger meanings, ones that simply operate in quasi-reflexive fashion when stimulated by certain contents or inputs). The philosopher Robert Nozick offers a helpful discussion of this point:

> It is no illuminating explanation of our possession of a trait to attribute it to a little person within us, a psychological homonculus who exercises that very same trait. If there is to be an explanation of how our intelligence functions, it will have to be in terms of factors that, taken individually, themselves are dumb, for example, in terms of a concatenation of simple operations that can be done by a machine. A psychological explanation of creativity will be in terms of parts or processes which aren't themselves creative. . . . The explanation of any valuable trait, feature, or function of the self will be in terms of some other trait, one which does not have precisely that value and probably is not valued . . . so it is not surprising that the explanations are reductionistic, presenting a picture of us as less valuable.

Nonetheless, it is a burden of the following chapters to indicate the ways in which, building upon "dumb" computational capacities, we may still end up with intelligent and even highly creative behavior.

It is best, then, to think of the various intellectual competences introduced here as a set of "natural kinds" of building blocks, out of which productive lines of thought and action are built. Not to push the analogy too far, we might think of the intelligences as elements in a chemical system, basic constituents which can enter into compounds of various sorts and into equations that yield a plethora of processes and products. These intelligences, while initially raw and unmediated, have the potential to be involved in symbol systems, to be enculturated through their implementation in cultural tasks. (Here they differ decisively from their counterparts in other animals.) We can see them operating in isolated fashion, in certain unusual populations and atypical situations; and it is the opportunity to examine these special circumstances systematically that has permitted us to identify the core operations in each domain. But in normal human intercourse, one typically encounters complexes of intelligences functioning together smoothly, even seamlessly in order to execute intricate human activities.

Related Theories

As I noted in the introductory chapters, the idea of multiple intelligences is an old one. Different facets of the mind were recognized even in Greek times; and "faculty psychology" reached its heyday in the early nineteenth century, well before scientific psychology had even gotten underway. It is a further matter of historical record that faculty psychology became almost completely discredited, so much so that it is more likely to appear in a compendium of curiosities than in a textbook of psychological theories. Yet, recently, this approach has experienced a sort of comeback: a number of theorists have put forth points of view that bear at least a family resemblance to the present formulation. Before considering a few of these rejuvenated faculty theories, it is worth considering the factors that have engendered the renaissance of this "modular" view of intellectual capacities.

In its ardor to follow the physical sciences, psychology has searched for the most general laws and processes—capacities that can cut across any manner of content and that can therefore be considered truly fundamental. The most honored figures of the last generation of psychologists—Clark Hull, Kenneth Spence, B. F. Skinner—epitomized this trend. Typically, they searched for the basic laws of sensation, perception, memory, attention, and learning, which, once discovered, were assumed to work equivalently across language and music, across visual and auditory stimuli, across elementary and complex patterns and problems. In its strong "uniformist" version, this search had as its goal a single set of principles—usually laws of association—which were assumed to underlie all of the aforementioned faculties. Under such an analysis, memory was faint perception; learning was enhanced or differentiated perception; and the like.

It is generally agreed that this program of psychology—well motivated though it may have been—has not been notably successful. One rarely hears nowadays of the search for basic all-encompassing psychological laws. Traces of this approach nonetheless are discernible in certain dominant schools of cognitive psychology, those that rely heavily on the model of a general-purpose serial computer. Here one encounters faith in a set of related concepts: *general problem-solving skills*, which can be mobilized for any problem that can be clearly stated; *frame*, *script*, or *schema* analysis, a way of making sense of seemingly diverse elements by viewing them within a structured context, such as the "script" for a familiar set of events; an overall planning or *TOTE* unit which uses feedback to determine whether an intended task has in fact been carried out: a limited *short-term memory capacity*, which can be "used up" by any content; a *central processor*, which initially receives all input; and an *executive*, which determines how the organism should deploy its various capacities in pursuit of a goal. These approaches have, to my mind, been more successful than those of the earlier generation of learning theorists; but they have also proved inadequate and, ofttimes, wrong-headed in their analysis of key psychological processes.

Sharing some of these misgivings, a number of theorists have recently put forth points of view that question the centrality—or, at any rate, the hegemony—of a model that posits general "all-purpose" mechanisms of mind. The British experimental psychologist D. Alan Allport has proposed that the human mind (following the human brain) is best thought of as a large number of independent *production systems:* these computational units operate in parallel (rather than serially) and are each specifically keyed to and activated by a certain kind of information. As he puts it, "Overwhelming evidence has accumulated for the existence of specialized neurones, responding selectively to particular (often quite abstract) invariant properties of the sensory input, as a major design feature of the central nervous system." Key to Allport's formulation is the claim that every production system is *content-dependent:* our cognitive activities are related not to the quantity of information to be processed but, rather, to the presence of particular patterns to which specific neural structures must (and do) resonate.

Allport rejects the need for a central processor in charge of these units. As he sees it, these production systems simply work in parallel, with the ones that fire the most carrying the day. He notes, metaphorically, that control simply passes among systems as the result of something like a discussion among experts (that is, among the various highly sensitized production systems). He finds no need for—not even a rational account of—a central homunculus which would decide what to do. As he asks, "What would the central processor do?"

For the most part, Allport's specialized production systems (and their associated neurons) deal with much finer units of information than do the particular intelligences I posit. Yet, in sympathy with my account, Allport indicates that the modular principle of functionally separable subsystems appears to hold also at a molar level of analysis, one that maps onto such behaviorally relevant systems as language or visual perception. In fact, Allport cites evidence of the breakdown of mental abilities following brain damage as the firmest foundation for the existence of intellectual modules along the lines that I have sketched. Thus, although the theory was put forth for quite separate reasons, the Allport model agrees in major particulars with my own point of view.

In a more extensive discussion, Jerry Fodor, philosopher and psychologist at the Massachusetts Institute of Technology, has eloquently defended the modularity of mind. Drawing most heavily on recent empirical studies of linguistic competence and of visual processing, some of them inspired by his colleague Noam Chomsky, Fodor argues that mental processes are best thought of as independent or "encapsulated" modules, with each operating according to its own rules and exhibiting its own processes. Siding clearly with the faculty psychology views of Franz Joseph Gall (see chapter 2), (and against more recent generations of theorists), Fodor rejects "horizontal processes" like general perception, memory, and judgment, in favor of "vertical modules" like language, visual analysis, or musical processing, each with its characteristic mode of operation. Fodor is not particularly concerned with the precise identity of each module—that is an empirical question; but he puts forth his own hunch that the modules will tend to reflect the different sensory systems, with language constituting a separate module of its own.

Thus far, I sense no fundamental disagreement with Fodor, who in fact posits modules at a level of analysis close to that with which we have been dealing here. But Fodor contends further that only certain portions of cognition can be explained through these relatively encapsulated modules. He sees the need for positing a central "unencapsulated" region of mind, one concerned with the "fixing of beliefs." The central processor has access to the information from the different modules, can compare the various inputs with one another, and can draw on this wealth of data flexibly in order to make decisions and solve problems and do many other things that humans are skilled at doing. The comparisons effected by the central processor allow individuals to make the best hypotheses of what the world is like.

In adopting this point of view, Fodor deviates from a pure modular perspective. Indeed, he indicates that, even as the modular point of view accords with the localized view of the nervous system, the central-processing perspective reflects a more equipotential view of the brain, with diverse areas of the nervous system participating in a wide range of activities and being (at least potentially) in constant communication with one another. Yet Fodor ultimately reaches a conclusion that, though pessimistic from a scientific point of view, aligns his position somewhat closer to my own. Fodor concludes that scientific investigation should be able to illuminate the modules, because they are relatively distinct and so can be subject to controlled experiment, but that the central processor is most probably immune to such study because its lines of information are at once unlimited and totally interconnected. As a practical matter, then, the science of cognition reduces to the study of the individual modules. Even if the central-processing view is valid, says Fodor, we will not be able to incorporate it meaningfully into our science of cognition.

Whether there is the need to posit some central processing mechanism is a complex question which, all agree, cannot yet be adequately resolved. Some authorities sympathetic to a modular point of view, like Zenon Pylyshyn, feel that it is important to make a principled distinction between impenetrable processes (which are impervious to information from other systems) and penetrable processes, which can be influenced by goals, beliefs, inferences, and other forms of knowledge and information. Other researchers, such as Geoffrey Hinton and James Anderson, who have been influenced by a "parallel" model of the operations of the nervous system, see neither the reason nor the use for a hypothetical central processor. Still other researchers equivocate. Michael Gazzaniga and his colleagues maintain, "there are multiple mental systems in the brain, each with the capacity to produce behavior, and each with its own impulses for action, that are not necessarily conversant internally," but go on to propose that the natural language system may eventually exert some kind of control over the other modules. In my own view, which I shall discuss in detail, it is preferable as a research ploy to determine the extent to which all human activities can be thought of as involving the development of, and varied interaction among, the several individual intelligences. In the end, it may even turn out that one can explain high-level processes in either way— that is, through intricate combinations of intelligences or through the positing of some kind of supramodular capacity (with its own genesis and history); but even this ecumenical resolution seems premature.

That points of view similar to multiple intelligence (or M.I.) theory are "in the air" is a source of some encouragement for my own efforts. (There are many competing theories concerning intelligence as well, and some of these will be discussed in chapter 12, following my review of the present theory.) At the same time, it makes it more important to justify some of the particular moves that I have made in putting forth my own theory. It is evident, for example, that the size of the candidate modules can vary widely, from extremely delimited production systems—such as those involved in the perception of a phoneme or the detection of a line—to far more general modules—such as those involved in language or spatial perception. My own feeling is that both the mini- and the maxi-module efforts are equally correct and can be equally justified, but that they serve different purposes.

To the extent that one wants to model faithfully what the nervous system is doing, it is appropriate to focus on the smallest possible modules that can be related to specific behavior. Here the course favored by Allport (or Hinton and Anderson) makes the most sense. On the other hand, if one seeks a framework relevant to educators or policy makers in the field of human development, then it is important to posit modules at the levels of analysis employed in every-day discussion. In this latter instance, the Fodor or Gazzaniga position seems preferable. However, such common-sense categories can only be adopted if they actually emerge, during the course of investigations, as "natural kinds," as legitimate groupings of finer-grained modules; otherwise, arbitrary merging of mini-modules into maxi-modules is simply not justified. Thus, it is of the highest importance that the various mini-modules investigated by researchers like Allport or Hinton in fact seem to coalesce in terms of broader domains: in other words, that various specific perceptual capacities do seem to become part of a more wide-ranging spatial system, even as the various specific linguistic analyzers can validly be spoken of as part of a more general linguistic system. It seems plausible that over the course of millions of years of evolution, such individual production systems have evolved to become part of far wider-ranging and highly intermeshed modules. This happy circumstance can be exploited by those of us interested in positing mental domains that will useful to practitioners concerned with education.

And what of my use of the loaded term "intelligence"? As hinted at earlier, part of the motivation for using this term is my desire to put forth a more viable model of intelligence: I seek to replace the current, largely discredited notion of intelligence as a single inherited trait (or set of traits) which can be reliably assessed through an hour-long interview or a paper and pencil test. But it should be said here as well that nothing much hangs on the particular use of this term, and I would be satisfied to substitute such phrases as "intellectual competences," "thought processes," "cognitive capacities," "cognitive skills," "forms of knowledge," or other cognate mentalistic terminology. What is crucial is not the label but, rather, the conception: that individuals have a number of domains of potential intellectual competence which they are in the position to develop, if they are normal and if the appropriate stimulating factors are available. As normal human beings, we exploit these potentials in dealing with a range of materials and objects, which are given meaning by the situations in which they are employed. In the framework proposed by my colleague Israel Scheffler, intellectual potentials can be realized if preventive circumstances are absent, if the appropriate sequences of experiences are forthcoming, and if there is determination to pursue these lines of growth.

I should note that, in the preceding chapters, I have tended to use examples of the highest forms of realization of an intellectual potential. Accordingly, I have focused on those who "produce" in a realm, and have dwelled upon "high forms of production," such as musical composition or poetic creation. However, the analysis extends readily to perception and appreciation as well as to production, and to diverse forms of art, science, or sense making, be they traditional or innovative, folk culture or high culture. Indeed, these intelligences are routinely seen at work in ordinary activities of nonspecialized individuals, but their most illustrious realizations will be properly noted in those gifted in artistic or scientific production.

Psychological Constructs Not Addressed

There is a final point that should be made before I turn to some of the questions raised by the theory of multiple intelligences. Even if the theory proves well motivated as far as it goes, there are numerous areas of human psychology that it cannot encompass. Included here would be such chapters—or entire textbooks in themselves—that treat social psychology, personality psychology, the psychology of temperament, the psychology of affect or feeling, the development of character. In no sense is the theory of multiple intelligences designed to do away with or supplant these proper subjects of inquiry.

Yet it would be equally misleading to suggest that M.I. theory proceeds on a plane completely removed from these traditional concerns. In fact, the theory cuts across them in at least two ways. First of all, M.I. theory seeks to underscore the extent to which ways of knowing—forms of knowledge—are present in virtually every realm of human existence. Thus far from being divorced from cognition, our capacities to interact with other individuals, to enjoy works of art, or to participate in athletics or dance, each involve highly developed forms of cognition. M.I. theory seeks to establish the pervasiveness of intellectual activities in areas where it has hitherto often been excluded.

M.I. theory may also contribute by suggesting that certain facets of traditional psychology will be properly subsumed within a particular intelligence. According to my analysis, many aspects of social development and social behavior fall under the purview of interpersonal intelligence, just as various aspects of the development of personality, character, and affect can be treated within the purview of intrapersonal intelligence. Just how the lines among these fields could be redrawn— and which aspects of these traditional fields continue to fall outside M.I. theory—is a task that can properly be saved for another day.

Two other perennial concerns of psychology—motivation and attention—have also escaped treatment in my presentation. I have no doubt that these are extremely pivotal aspects of human existence, and that attempts to train any—indeed, all—of the intelligences are likely to come to nought in the absence of proper motivation and sufficiently focused attention. Moreover, my own guess is that mechanisms of motivation and attention will turn out to be rather general: in other words, proper theories of motivation and attention will turn out to have applicability across the several intellectual spheres. Yet it should be evident, even to casual observation, that commitment in one or another intellectual sphere may entail high degrees of motivation or attention, without similar investments being evident in other areas. A youngster may be highly motivated to become a musician, and display superb attentional capacities with regard to instrumental practice while exhibiting neither motivation nor attention in other spheres of life. Thus, even if a general theory of attention or motivation should be forthcoming, it would still have to account for evident differences in the extent to which these vaunted capacities are mobilized in activities representing different intellectual realms.

"Higher-Level" Cognitive Operations

Thus far, in my survey of other areas of psychology, I have been concerned with concepts, and lines of explanation, that may poach upon the intelligences but are not regularly thought of as cognitive in nature. It has seemed possible to discuss these summarily, without placing M.I. theory in serious jeopardy. But more volatile issues arise when we consider certain other aspects of human behavior, more frankly cognitive in nature, which also appear, at first blush, to elude my analytic framework. These are cognitive capacities that seem to be "higher-level"—capacities like common sense, originality, or metaphoric capacity—which clearly make use of mental skills but because of their seemingly broad and general nature seem inexplicable within terms of individual intelligences. In truth, it is by no means evident how each of these terms can be explained within multiple intelligence theory, and, if they cannot, how the theory must be modified if they are to be adequately accounted for. Yet, in a work on this topic, it seems incumbent upon the author to at least reveal his intuitions with respect to these key intellectual functions. I do so here with the understanding that further analyses might well lead in quite different directions.

COMMON SENSE

Perhaps the least problematic "general" cognitive term is *common sense*, which I define as the ability to deal with problems in an intuitive, rapid, and perhaps unexpectedly accurate manner. What has struck me in the analysis of the term *common sense* is that it is customarily invoked with reference to two kinds of individuals: those skillful in the interpersonal domain, and those gifted in the mechanical realm (bodily and spatial in my terms). In contrast, the term *common sense* seems rarely if ever invoked in discussions of individuals skilled in music, math, or purely spatial concerns. One point about common sense, then, is that, far from being common coin, it seems to be applied preferentially to individuals with highly developed skills in one or two areas of intelligence and not in the kind of "across-the-board" manner implied by the term. *Common sense*, in other words, seems cognate to the practical application of a small minority of intelligences.

Nonetheless, I recognize that the term may apply as well to individuals who seem able to plan ahead, to exploit opportunities, to guide their destinies and those of others in a prudent way, uncontaminated by jargon, ideology, or elaborate but possibly irrelevant theories. Such an ability seems less readily accounted for simply as highly developed mechanical or social abilities. Such an individual would seem to be distinguished by the capacity to bring together a wide amount of information and to make it part of a general and effective plan of action.

In order to account for this highly desirable form of competence, it proves necessary to bring to bear a number of other considerations. To begin with, the ability to engage in calculations about the proper ordering and orchestration of multiple lines of activity involves logical-mathematical intelligence. Then, if an individual is to engage in considerable planning about his life (or the lives of others), it is necessary to posit a highly developed intrapersonal intelligence or, more simply, a mature sense of self. Finally, the movement from the *ability* to plan a line of action to the actual *achievement* of actions (from dreams to deeds) transports us away from the realm of cognition, in a strict sense, to the arena of practice, or effective action. Here we impinge on the sphere of will—certainly a crucial component in the ways in which we actually lead our lives, but one that I have also elected to skirt in this study of human intelligences.

ORIGINALITY

A second cognitive capacity that may elude our theory of intelligences is that of *originality*, or *novelty*—the skill of fashioning an unfamiliar and yet worthy product within a particular realm, be it an innovative story or dance, the solution of a personal conflict or a mathematical paradox. To my own way of thinking, originality or novelty does in fact occur principally, if not exclusively, within single domains: one rarely if ever encounters individuals who are original or novel across the intellectual board, though clearly some individuals have attained skills of a highly creative sort in more than one domain—the Leonardo phenomenon. Thus, the need to explain this capacity may reduce to the need to explain novelty within those particular domains where it is in fact found—and to explain why a few individuals succeed in more than one.

As in other facets of this work, I find it useful to take a developmental perspective on the issue of novelty. Early in life, most children give the appearance of engaging in original or novel behavior. I think that they do so because of two related factors. First of all, the young child is not keenly aware of boundaries between domains, and so more readily transgresses them, thereby arriving ofttimes at unusual and appealing juxtapositions and associations. Second of all, the young child does not have an affective stake in arriving at a single literal interpretation of a situation or a problem: he is not bothered by inconsistencies, departures from convention, nonliteralness. This insouciance, too, contributes to the apparently higher incidence of novel products, though it by no means ensures that these products will be cherished—or even properly interpreted—by others.

Early originality and novelty, however compelling they may be to the analyst or the parent, are distant from those original and novel creations that we can await—though not necessarily expect—from highly skilled practitioners in a field. It is worth noting that such originality and novelty, while often accepted as an unalloyed good in contemporary Western society, is in fact deemed undesirable in many cultures, in which adherence to an earlier consolidated tradition is the unquestioned goal. However, according to my own analysis, genuinely original or novel activities can come about only when an individual has achieved mastery in the field where he has been working. Only such an individual possesses the necessary skills and sufficient understanding of the structure of the field to be able to sense where a genuine innovation will lie and how best to achieve it.

But we do not actually know at which point in development such originality or novelty can come about, and whether it is, in fact, an option for every individual who has worked his way through an intellectual domain to its highest levels. If he has done so, it is up to the skilled practitioner himself whether he in fact produces original work or is simply satisfied with realizing a prior tradition. Perhaps, however, the seeds for originality date back far earlier and reflect basic temperament, personality, or cognitive style: on this analysis, individuals would be marked early on as potential creators of original works. These specially earmarked individuals would then become likely candidates for original productions even if they have not reached the top of their field; in contrast, others who lack these personal attributes will never be original, even if they attain superlative technical skills.

Modest empirical support for the latter position comes from an informal study that some colleagues and I conducted a few years ago. We interviewed several individuals who had become highly original musical composers. In each case, we found that as early as ten or eleven years of age, these future composers were not satisfied simply to perform the pieces of music presented to them but had already begun to experiment in various ways, searching for variations that were more appealing. In other words, as we saw in the case of Igor Stravinsky at an even younger age, certain gifted young musicians were already composing and decomposing. So far as I have been able to determine, this experimentation at an early age is not common among those individuals who become superlative performers but do not regularly compose. Individuals do not begin as Menuhins and end up as Mozarts. Further support for this point of view comes from numerous studies of the "creative" personality. These studies document that certain personality traits—such as ego strength and willingness to defy tradition—characterize the outstanding creative individuals within a particular domain; they also help to explain the *lack* of a relationship between scores on creativity measures and scores on more conventional tests of intellectual strengths, at least above a certain level of I.Q.

METAPHORICAL CAPACITY

Capacities that prove more challenging to account for in terms of M.I. theory include the abilities to make *metaphors*, to perceive *analogies*, and to cut across various intellectual domains in the process of forging such illuminating connections. In fact, this family of capacities seems at odds with the whole notion of separate intelligences, for the metaphoric intelligence (if we may so tentatively label this set of capacities) is defined by the very capacity to integrate diverse intelligences. It is this sort of realization which apparently encouraged Jerry Fodor to posit a central processor which could integrate the inputs from separate modules. Nor is a proponent of M.I. theory made more confident in his claims by the knowledge that Aristotle singled out the capacity to create metaphors as the very mark for genius: it would be an inadequate cognitive theory indeed that would allow genius to slip through its analytic fingers.

But M.I. theory does offer some ways of approaching the issue of metaphoric ability. To begin with, it may be the particular hallmark of logical-mathematical intelligence to perceive patterns wherever they may be: thus an individual with strong logical-mathematical abilities may be in a favorable position to discern metaphors, though not necessarily to judge their worth. Some modest support for this speculation comes from the fact that scores on the widely used Miller Analogies Test (MAT) correlate highly with other measures of logical power. It is also possible—in fact, highly likely—that the capacity to discern metaphors and analogies exists within particular domains. As I noted earlier, the capacity to contrive spatial images or metaphors has been of great usefulness to scientists who are trying to discover new relationships or to convey to a wider audience those relationships that they have uncovered. Moreover, it is quite possible that practitioners become skilled at discovering relationships within their chosen domains. Thus, within the language domain, the poet will discern many analogies and metaphors across semantic categories, even as the painter, the architect, or the engineer may discover numerous metaphors and analogies within the particular symbol systems favored in their respective domains. Thus, at least within particular domains, individuals with well-honed skills may well be the prime candidates to become effective metaphorizers.

But this line of explanation still circumvents that genius figure, the individual whose abilities extend across various domains, and who, indeed, is marked by the capacity to find connections between language and music, dance and social communion, the spatial and the personal realms. One could argue that these individuals have a highly developed metaphoric capacity in one domain (say logical-mathematical or spatial) which they are simply importing to other domains. But I myself do not find this explanation fully convincing. While it seems to me that any domain *might* serve as the principal vehicle (in a technical sense) for the forging of metaphors, it is unlikely to constitute the entire explanation for a highly skilled metaphoric ability.

Fortunately, there is evidence on the general development of metaphoric capacities, much of it courtesy of our own laboratory at Harvard Project Zero. We can detect at least three forms of analogic or metaphoric capacity in all normal children. To begin with perhaps the most remarkable form, young infants seem to be born with the capacity to note similarities across sensory domains—such as parallels in intensity or in rhythms—which are detectable in the auditory and visual realms. Thus, the six-month-old child can associate an auditory rhythm appropriately with a set of dots or a silent film that exhibits the same rhythm. There is a primitive but nonetheless accurate capacity in the young infant to effect domain-connections—a capacity that seems to fall outside the development of specific intelligences as I have described them in earlier chapters.

In the preschool years, after the child has become a symbol user, we encounter a second metaphoric capacity. This is the aforementioned time when the child finds it easy—and perhaps appealing—to effect connections among disparate realms: to note similarities among different forms within or across sensory modalities and to capture these in words (or other symbols); to make unusual combinations of words, or colors, or dance movements, and to gain pleasure in doing so. Thus the three- or four-year-old can note and describe the resemblances between a glass of ginger ale and a foot that has fallen asleep; or between a passage played on the piano and a set of colors; or between a dance and the movement of an airplane. As just suggested in the discussion of novelty, this metaphorizing proclivity gives rise to an early form of originality, one that may not be entirely conscious on the child's part, but that (as my colleagues have shown) is by no means totally accidental either.

The early school years are a period where overt metaphorizing is less likely. At this time, the child is striving to understand the structure of each domain and to master domain-relevant skills, and so any excursion to the realm of metaphorizing or analogizing may be unsettling. But once these domains have solidified satisfactorily, and once the child has achieved the requisite skills within desired domains, the possibility for metaphoric connection once again comes to the fore. Here, however, one begins to encounter wide individual differences, with some individuals rarely engaging in adventurous (or even routine) connections across domains, and with others proving more likely to effect these connections, wherever they might be.

My own belief is that these various early forms of metaphorizing represent a universal phenomenon, one that lies somewhat apart from the development of specific intelligences, but that constitutes part of the natural developmental process. Infants are so constituted that they can make certain cross-modal connections, just as they are wired to be able to imitate certain behavior patterns of adults. Preschoolers are similarly designed to note similarities and differences as part of their effort to make sense of the world. These are simply facts of development, and any comprehensive account of human development must allow for them. But whether they are directly involved in later, higher levels of intelligence, and if they are, whether the various "child" forms are all involved, is far from certain: thus the analyst is perhaps excused if he does not posit a possibly short-lived metaphoric intelligence or a set of intelligences which can be glimpsed during the first years of life.

When it comes to mature forms of metaphorizing, however, a crucial question arises: Is there an adult form of metaphoric capacity, apart from the separate intelligences, which some individuals have developed to a high degree, so that they can bring it to bear upon particular intellectual domains? And, if there is, what are the developmental origins of this much-prized adult activity? At present, I do not find sufficient evidence to decree a separate form of intelligence. Except for the indisputable existence of a developed end-state, metaphoric intelligence fails to exhibit those signs that have proved central in the identification of other intelligences. My own "fall-back position" is that individuals who are skilled metaphorizers have developed this ability in one or more domains, as part of their general learning process, but now feel sufficiently secure with this skill that they can apply it in the domains in which they happen to be involved. At his best, the superb metaphorizer will discern connections virtually everywhere and can censor those that appear unproductive or uncommunicative. Still, there will be a preferred locus for his metaphorizing capacities—namely, those fields in which he is most deeply knowledgeable, and in which his metaphorizing ability has found its most fertile grounds. Thus, a skilled metaphorizer like the scientific essayist Lewis Thomas will be able to discern and exploit resemblances in the areas of music or dance; but his chief mode of operation will still be in logical-mathematical areas. Similarly, the redoubtable poet W. H. Auden, another insightful (and inveterate) metaphorizer, will comb the world through his poems, but his principal metaphoric point of departure will remain the linguistic realm. Metaphor may spread to many localities, in other words, but it retains a favored "home intelligence" all the same.

WISDOM

A yet more general form of intelligence, somewhat akin to but broader than metaphorizing, has been variously called *general synthesizing power* or, even, *wisdom*. This intelligence is what one comes to expect from an older individual who has had a wide range of critical experiences in his earlier life and can now apply them appropriately and judiciously, in the proper circumstances.

On the surface, no capacity would seem further removed from the deployment of a single intelligence, or even of a pair of intelligences. Wisdom or synthesis offers by its very nature the widest view: to the extent that it is parochial or domain-specific, it seems inappropriate to call it "wisdom." My own hunch is that these terms are applied to individuals who have some combination of the abilities I have just reviewed: considerable common sense and originality in one or more domains, coupled with a seasoned metaphorizing or analogizing capacity. The individual can draw upon these abilities, at least in given circumstances, in order to make sage comments and to propose well-motivated lines of action. If this hunch is correct, then any explanation that can account for common sense, originality, and metaphorizing capacity ought to suggest the constituents of ultimate wisdom. Unfortunately, it will take a very wise person indeed to come up with a convincing formulation!

The preceding discussion indicates that, at least for some "higher-level" operations, it should be possible to offer an explanation in terms of the theory of multiple intelligences. These operations sometimes reduce to capacities in but a single domain (for example, interpersonal common sense or originality in sculpture); sometimes can be seen as the combination of an individual personality trait and an impressive ability in a given intellectual domain (as in the case of an original novelist); sometimes are better viewed as an emergent capacity which begins in one domain but spreads outward (as in certain metaphorizing abilities); and sometimes are best seen as an amalgam of different intellectual strengths (as in the case of wisdom).

All of these moves are frankly reductive: they are understandable, and perhaps permissible if one wants to salvage M.I. theory, but are certainly not necessary and perhaps unwise. The fact that the theory of multiple intelligences cannot explain everything does not invalidate the whole theory. At some point in the future course of this theory, it may make sense to add more general abilities or capacities (as Fodor has done) and to use them to garnish the competences that arise from individual capacities.

THE SENSE OF SELF REVISITED

It is appropriate to insert a few supplementary remarks at this point about the cognitive capacity that has already placed the greatest strain on the theory of multiple intelligences. I refer here to the *sense of self*—that prime candidate for status as a "second-order ability" which presides over the separate intelligences. In the previous chapter, I viewed the development of self in terms of the personal intelligences. According to my analysis there, the roots of a sense of self lie in the individual's exploration of his own feelings and in his emerging ability to view his own feelings and experiences in terms of the interpretive schemes and symbol systems provided by the culture. Some cultures will tend to minimize a focus on the self; and accordingly, the individual encased in such a culture will not allocate much active agency to his own efforts and will place a correlative emphasis on the behavior and the needs of others. But in other cultures, such as our own, there is a far greater emphasis on the self as an active decision-making agent possessing considerable autonomy, including the capacity to make pivotal decisions about one's own future existence. Every culture must, of course, strike a balance between the interpersonal and the intrapersonal aspects of knowledge—it is in this modulation that an ultimate sense of self consists; but those societies that are biased toward the intrapersonal, and hence toward an assertive sense of self, pose the gravest threat to any view of the intelligences as a simple conversation among equal elements.

As already mentioned in the preceding chapters, one may adopt a number of different strategic approaches to this problem. The first is simply to declare the development of the sense of self as a separate domain of intelligence—one growing out of that core ability to perceive oneself that we encountered in discussing the personal intelligences, but one that becomes fully on a par with the other intelligences that have been treated here. On this analysis, the sense of self would either become a new (eighth) intelligence or would become the mature form of intrapersonal intelligence. The second, more radical move is to declare the intelligence of the self as a separate domain, one inherently privileged from the start, since it serves as a kind of central processor, or reflector, upon the other capacities. This is the kind of move made by many developmental psychologists who have studied the growth of self. A third move, one that I currently favor, is to view the individual's sense of self as an emergent capacity. It is a capacity that grows initially out of the intrapersonal *and* the interpersonal intelligences but that has the option, in certain social settings, of exploiting the other intelligences as a means to a novel end. That novel end is the devising of a *special kind of explanatory model* encompassing everything that the individual is and everything that the individual does.

Let me try to explain in somewhat greater detail what I have in mind. Because human beings have at their disposal a range of symbol systems—such as language, gesturing, mathematics, and the like—they are able to take the inchoate understanding that lies at the core of intrapersonal intelligence and make it public and accessible to themselves (and, for that matter, to interested others). These representational systems enable the individual ultimately to create what is essentially an invented figure of speech—a fictional entity of the mind—a model of what that person is like, what he has done, what his strengths and weaknesses are, how he feels about himself, and the like. The individual can then operate upon this model, even as he can operate upon other models presented in other symbol systems. The fact that this model refers to that entity in life which is most sacred to him confers upon the model a special flavor and feeling; but the intellectual operations the individual brings to bear upon that model are not by their very nature different from those one imposes upon the model of a solar system, a biological organism, or another social creature. It just *feels* different—and more important.

Rather than viewing a sense of self as a domain apart, or as a second-order domain which has some inherent ontological priority over the others, I prefer at this juncture to think of the sense of self as explicable in terms of the existing multiple intelligences. I see this sense of self as the result of the natural evolution of intrapersonal intelligence within an interpreting cultural context, as aided by the representational capacities that emerge in the other forms of intelligence. In the end, the individual can offer an account of himself—one couched in language (or, more rarely, in other symbol systems) that puts forth in logically acceptable fashion all those properties of himself, and all of his own experiences, that seem worthy of note. And he can continue to edit this description of himself as events transpire over the years, and as his own "self-concept" alters. The particular account that is offered may or may not be valid, but that is not of the essence here. Crucial, rather, is that, through a combination of one's own intellectual competences, and through the interpretive schemes furnished by the rest of one's own culture, it is possible to put forth a description of oneself that appears to summarize, and regulate, the remainder of one's existence. Working together, the intelligences may give birth to an entity that seems larger than them all.

Disconfirming the Theory

Before bringing to a close this critical discussion of M.I. theory, it seems opportune to indicate the conditions under which the theory could be disproved. After all, if M.I. theory can explain (or explain away) all potentially disconfirming evidence, it is not a valid theory in the scientific sense of that term.

One might distinguish between two kinds of alterations of the theory. In the happier event, the general line of the theory will continue to be accepted, but minor or major revisions will be made regarding specific claims. For example, it may turn out that certain of the candidate intelligences violate major criteria and so are dropped from consideration; or, alternatively, ones that have been ignored or rejected might themselves earn a position among the select few. In another more substantial revision, it might turn out that the theory of multiple intelligences can account for a significant portion of human intellectual activity, but that it is also advisable to add some other components not presently included. Such would be added if the desirability of some horizontal component—such as perception or memory—was convincingly demonstrated, or if some other capacity—such as metaphor, wisdom, or a sense of self—could be shown to exist apart from the apparatus of multiple intelligence theory.

I can readily live with such revision. But it is also possible that the theory will be found deficient in some more fundamental way. If it turns out that the most significant human intellectual activities cannot be explained in terms of M.I. theory or can be better explained in terms of some competing theory, then the theory will deservedly be rejected. If it turns out that the kinds of evidence heavily weighted here—for example, neuropsychological and cross-cultural findings—are fundamentally flawed, then the whole line of inquiry forged here will have to be re-evaluated. It is also possible that further studies of the nervous system—or of other cultures—will suggest a vastly different picture of human intellective processes; and thus, there would also have to be a radical revamping of the theory. Finally, it might turn out that the whole Western inclination to pick out intelligence—or intelligences—as a "natural kind" may not be the best (or even a proper) way to slice up the human psyche or human behavior. And, in such a case, the present theory, like all those it purports to replace, will go the way of phlogiston. Being so discarded would give me little pleasure—but I would be far less disappointed than if I had put forth a theory whose very nature made it immune to refutation.

Conclusion

Even if my original list of intelligences can be salvaged by moves such as the ones just proposed, it is evident that the intelligences cannot be viewed merely as a group of raw computational capacities. The world is enwrapped in meanings, and intelligences can be implemented only to the extent that they partake of these meanings, that they enable the individual to develop into a functioning, symbol-using member of his community. As the earlier quotation from Robert Nozick reminds us, there may be "dumb" capacities at the center of intelligence; but it is equally true that these capacities must be made "smarter" if one is successfully to interact with the surrounding society.

It is the burden of the next chapter to begin the task of building from raw intellectual capacities to intelligences that can function in a complex and meaning-laden world. These meanings come to figure early on in the story, for the initial percepts and actions of the infant—and all which follow—are suffused with significance: from the very first, pleasures and pains are associated with them, and interpretations

297

are imposed upon them. Even more important, what characterizes human intelligences, as against those of other species, is their potential for being involved in all manner of symbolic activity—the perception of symbols, the creation of symbols, the involvement with meaningful symbolic systems of all sorts. This is another, and perhaps the most crucial, part of the story of human development in a world of meaning. Finally, with increasing age and experience, each individual comes to learn not only the particular consequences attached to individual acts and symbols, but the most general interpretive schemes of the culture—the way in which the worlds of persons and objects, physical forces and man-made artifacts are interpreted in the particular culture in which he happens to live. This immersion in the culture's *Weltanschauung* constitutes a final decisive aspect of the life of the human, defining the arena in which his several mature intelligences will be deployed in combination.

Talk of specific analyzers, of computers, of production systems, or even of modules no longer suffices once one encroaches upon this level of analysis. We must begin to think in terms of more encompassing categories—the individual's experiences, his frames of reference, his means of sense making, his overall world view. All of these would not be possible without specific intellectual computational capacities, but they would never come into being without human symbolic activity. Thus, the development of human symbol systems and symbolizing capacities becomes the next, essential part of the story to be related if we are to construct a bridge from intelligences to educational practice.

12

The Socialization
of Human
Intelligences
through Symbols

The Central Role of Symbols

Findings from biology and from anthropology stand at opposite extremes in any theory of human cognition. From study of the structures and functions of the nervous system, we should ultimately be able to specify certain limits on all human cognitive activities. From study of all known human cultures, we should eventually gain the fullest possible notion of the range of abilities, including thought processes, that have evolved over human history. By culling insights from these domains, we should receive a composite picture of the nature, the range, and the limitations of human intellectual prowess.

But from the perspective of interdisciplinary synthesis, biology and anthropology are too remote from one another. In other words, our two principal perspectives in this book do not partake of the same language. Biology furnishes a picture of human genetic potential as well as an account of the structure of cells, the synaptic connections, and the relatively molar regions of the brain. Anthropology ferrets out the different roles that exist in various societies, the various functions

299

that individuals perform, the circumstances under which these functions are carried out, the goals that individuals set, and the problems that they pose and attempt to solve. So far as I can see, there is no ready way to build a bridge directly between these two bodies of information: their vocabularies, their frames of reference are too disparate. It is as if one were asked to build a connecting link between the structure of a harpsichord and the sound of Bach's music: these entities are incommensurate.

Enter symbols, symbolic products, and symbolic systems. The domain of symbols, as it has been constituted by scholars, is ideally suited to help span the gap between the aforementioned entities—the nervous system with its structures and functions and the culture with its roles and activities. In dealing with symbols like words or pictures, with symbolic systems like mathematics or language, with symbolic products like scientific theories or literary narratives, we have commerce with entities and levels of analysis, that can "address" both biology and anthropology. Specifically, the nervous system is so constituted that, provided with certain kinds of experience, the organism is able to learn to apprehend and deal with such symbolic entities as words, sentences, and stories. For whereas the nervous system knows nothing of culture, its various regions are constituted to know a great deal about language. On the other hand, a culture—viewed here as the collectivity of inhabitants—is indeed able to examine the words, stories, theories, and the like that issue forth from its members. Thus anthropomorphized, the culture can evaluate these products, determine whether they are adequate, observe or advise changes, opt for tradition or for revolution. Those individuals most directly charged with the maintenance of cultural knowledge and tradition may know nothing of brain cells (or even of the role of the brain in cognition), but they are well equipped to know, and to evaluate, the dances, dramas, and designs fashioned by members. The realm of the symbol does indeed provide an indispensable level of analysis, an essential *tertium quid*, between the constraints of biology and the range of culture (or, if one prefers, between the range of biology and the constraints of culture).

It is through *symbols* and *symbol systems* that our present framework, rooted in the psychology of intelligences, can be effectively linked with the concerns of culture, including the rearing of children and their ultimate placement in niches of responsibility and competence. Symbols pave the royal route from raw intelligences to finished cultures. It is therefore necessary to comment on how one might envision this realm.

The Socialization of Human Intelligences through Symbols

I take a catholic view of symbols. Following my mentor Nelson Goodman and other authorities, I conceive of a symbol as any entity (material or abstract) that can denote or refer to any other entity. On this definition, words, pictures, diagrams, numbers, and a host of other entities are readily considered symbols. So, indeed, is any element—a line no less than a rock—so long as it is used (and interpreted) as representing some kind of information.

In addition to denoting or representing, symbols convey meanings in another equally important but less often appreciated way. A symbol can convey some mood, feeling, or tone—once again, just so long as the relevant community chooses to interpret a particular symbol in a particular way. Thus, a painting, whether abstract or representational, can convey moods of sadness, triumph, anger, or "blueness" (even if the painting itself is red!). By including this important expressive function within the armament of a symbol, we are able to talk about the full range of artistic symbols, from symphonies to square dances, from sculpture to squiggles, all of which have potential for expressing such connotative meanings.

Symbols can function alone as meaningful entities; but very commonly, they enter as components or elements in a more highly elaborated system. Thus, words figure in spoken or written language; numbers and other abstract symbols, in mathematical languages; gestures and other movement patterns, within dance systems; and the like. And a considerable range of meanings can be effectively conveyed when entire symbolic systems are used; mastering the deployment and the interpretation (the "reading" and the "writing") of such symbol systems constitutes a major task for every growing child.

Finally, symbols and symbol systems gain their greatest utility as they enter into the fashioning of full-fledged symbolic products: stories and sonnets, plays and poetry, mathematical proofs and problem solutions, rituals, and reviews—all manner of symbolic entities that individuals create in order to convey a set of meanings, and that other individuals imbued in the culture are able to understand, interpret, appreciate, criticize, or transform. These symbolic products are the ultimate *raison d'être* for symbol systems—the reasons they have come to evolve, and the reasons that human individuals go to the trouble of mastering diverse symbol systems.

Is there any limit on symbol systems, or can any conceivable set of elements be organized into systems, thereby yielding interpretable symbolic products? This is a difficult question. It seems almost self-defeating to posit *a priori* a fixed number of symbol systems, which

301

cannot be altered: this stricture constitutes a challenge that is almost too inviting, and doubtless a clever individual (or an enterprising culture) can invent an effective new symbol system. On the other hand, one risks opening a Pandora's box in arguing the opposite—in claiming that there can be an indefinite number of symbol systems. One would then have to explain why cultures the world over have tended to devise and favor the same kinds of symbol system, and why it is headline news in the anthropological community when effective new symbol systems are uncovered.

If one has indeed specified the nature of human intelligences—the raw materials for cognition—on the one hand, and the range of human cultural roles and functions, on the other, one ought to be able to generate a list of all possible symbol systems and, if you like, all the domains in which human beings can become intellectually engaged. It would be a long list, because the number of cultural roles is large indeed and may continually be expanded with the invention of new technologies. But, at least in principle, it should be possible to come up with an exhaustive list of symbolic systems. Such a list—or even a sketch of such a list—would be suggestive to educators, for it would indicate something of the possible systems of meanings which individuals growing up in a culture might be expected to master.

Of course, the introduction and mastering of symbolic systems is not just a matter of theoretical speculation. It is a major burden of childhood and might even be regarded as the principal mission of modern educational systems. It is therefore important to consider what is known about the way in which human beings become accomplished in the symbolic realm. Accordingly, I shall summarize the story of symbolic development, as I have come to view it, based in part on the findings of other workers, in part on the results of a decade of research by Dennie Wolf and other collaborators at Harvard Project Zero. Such a survey will serve a double function. On the theoretical plane, it will point the way toward an integration of a biologically based view of intelligence, on the one hand, with an anthropological inventory of various cultural roles, on the other. Then, turning to more practical concerns, a discussion of the normal course of symbolic development should introduce some of the challenges that face educators. These steps should place us in a better position to consider various pedagogical suggestions put forth in the concluding chapters of this work.

The Socialization of Human Intelligences through Symbols

The Emergence of Symbolic Competence

INTRODUCTION

According to my analysis, it is useful to think of the development of competence with symbol systems as entailing four distinct phases. During infancy, the child acquires certain basic understandings, on which later symbol use will piggy-back, and comes to evince capacities for certain mundane symbolic activities. During early childhood, a period of incredibly rapid advance spanning the ages from two to five, the child acquires basic competence in a range of symbol systems: this is also the time when there are at work two parallel aspects of symbolic development, which my colleagues and I have termed, respectively, the "waves" and the "streams" of development. During school age, having achieved some basic competence in symbolization, the child goes on to acquire higher levels of skill in certain culturally valued domains or "channels" of symbolization. This is also the time when he masters various notational or "second-order" symbol systems, those that prove extremely useful in carrying out complex cultural tasks. Finally, during adolescence and adulthood, the individual can become a fully competent user of symbols, one who is able to transmit symbolic knowledge to younger individuals, and who has at least the potential for fashioning original symbolic products.

Infancy. Aided by various examples drawn from my own work, I can now take a closer look at these steps of symbol development and begin to consider how they relate to the major themes of this essay. Starting with infancy, we know that the newborn child has available a relatively circumscribed set of skills and abilities through which he comes to know the world: "schemas" like sucking and looking. At first, these are brought to bear upon every available object; but very soon the child learns to direct certain activities to certain objects (sucking nipples and shaking rattles), while avoiding those activities in cases where they are less productive. Here we see the first examples of "meaning" becoming attached to behavior. The child pursues those activities that, for him, have come to be connected with pleasurable experiences, as well as those activities that lead to outcomes that he desires. In this, he is regularly aided by the interpretations adults confer upon his behavior and by the situations toward which he is guided (or away from which he is warned) by adults.

The child achieves certain basic forms of understanding during the first year of life. He comes to appreciate that individuals can carry

303

out certain roles with associated behavior (like shopping or feeding); that events have consequences (if you throw the bottle, it will fall on the ground); that there exist categories of objects, like dolls or flowers, which should not be confused with one another; and the like. These understandings are important for negotiating one's way around the world of persons and objects. In addition, they constitute an initial introduction to many facets of experience which will ultimately be expressed via diverse symbolic means.

A history of the first year of life can also be written in terms of the initial operations of specific intelligences. As we have already seen, the child is able to carry out numerous operations specific to each intellectual domain: he can recognize differences in pitches and tonal sequences, commonalities among tokens of the same phoneme type, the numerosity of small sets of objects; he comes to appreciate the structure of the space around him, the use of his body to gain desired objects, the characteristic behavior patterns of other individuals, and his own set of customary reactions and feelings. Indeed, considerable progress occurs within each of these separate intellectual domains during the first year of life.

Yet just as important are the ways in which these intelligences come to interact with one another. Smooth reaching requires the intercalation of spatial abilities with bodily activities: searching for hidden objects requires the linking of logical-mathematical, spatial, and bodily capacities; a feeling of anxiety when the mother leaves or a stranger comes upon the scene involves the connection of intrapersonal and interpersonal forms of intelligence.

Finally, we see a combination of intelligences at work in the first forms of proto-symbolic behavior detected toward the end of the first year of life: the ability to appreciate the meanings of single words and the ability to "read" pictorial depictions of objects in the real world. The child of one is able to respond appropriately to words like *mother*, *cookie*, or *doggie*, because he can both make the proper linguistic discriminations and link these envelopes of sound to objects perceived in the world and to actions or feelings characteristically associated with those objects. By the same token, the child is able to appreciate the linkage between a depicted form and an object in the real world, an object that again features a whole range of perceptual, motor, and affective associations. By virtue of these capacities, the child is able to enter for the first time into the world of public meanings—and he will build upon this baptism into the symbolic realm in the many additional symbol-using tasks that lie ahead.

The Child from Two to Five. During the following several years of life, epoch-making events occur in the child's symbolic development. The ages of two to five mark the time when *basic symbolization* develops, when the child becomes able to appreciate and to create instances of language (sentences and stories), two-dimensional symbolization (pictures), three-dimensional symbolization (clay and blocks), gestural symbolization (dance), music (songs), drama (pretend play), and certain kinds of mathematical and logical understanding, including an appreciation of basic numerical operations and simple causal explanations. By the close of the period, the time when children in our society enter school, they possess an initial or "first-draft" knowledge of symbolization; they may then go on in the years that follow to achieve fuller symbolic mastery.

An intuition for the several steps involved in the acquisition of such "first-draft" knowledge of symbolization can be gained from the following example of the child at play with blocks. Given a block, the one-year-old will simply place it in his mouth, knock it against a surface, or throw it down—nothing symbolic is going on here. Symbolic activity of a mundane variety begins in the perceptual realm, as the child can relate the block to a picture of a block or can hand over a block when requested to do so ("Give Mommy the block"). An important next step in block use occurs around the age of two, when the child is able to pick up two blocks, to announce one block as the "mommy" and the other as the "baby," and then to have the two blocks "take a walk." At age three, the child can take a number of blocks, place the smaller ones atop the bigger ones, and declare, "This is a snowman," or "This is a pyramid." At age four, the child is able to use the blocks in a numerically precise way—for example, building a staircase in which each column has one more (or one less) block than the abutting column. Finally at age five or six, the child can, for the first time, exploit the various squiggles on the side of the blocks, in order to compose simple words like *C A T* or confirm simple number facts like $2 + 4 = 6$.

STREAMS OF SYMBOLIZATION

Our analysis of such events which occur predictably during early childhood has turned up a number of factors at work: these are, respectively, the *streams*, *waves*, and *channels* of symbolization. In their manner of operation lies the key to symbolic development during the preschool years.

First of all, there occurs a progression that is unique to each particular symbolic system. In language, for example, there is a lengthy evolution of syntactic capacities, from the ability to concatenate a pair of words (at the age of eighteen months) to the ability to speak in complex sentences, to pose "Why" questions, and to utter passive constructions (by the age of four or five). This progression occurs exclusively within language and has few, if any, direct ramifications in other symbol systems—hence, it can be thought of as a separate *stream* in the child's evolving family of competences. In music, much of the activity involves working out the basic relations to pitch that obtain within a scale. In blocks, the basic streamlike challenge entails an understanding of the dimensions of extent, contour, and continuity which enter into and regulate the construction of buildings and other architectonic structures. In number, the core activities involve an understanding of the operations of plus 1 and minus 1, and the growing capacity to coordinate these operations with the knowledge of basic numerical sets. And so on, for each remaining symbol system.

It seems legitimate to think of this streamlike development as the articulation of a particular intelligence once that intellectual capacity has become susceptible to involvement in (or appropriation by) appropriate symbol systems of the culture. Thus, the core aspects of musical intelligence (pitch and rhythm) are marshaled by the symbolic aspects of music, such as *expression* (this is a happy piece) and *reference* (this alludes to an earlier section of the song). In the case of language, the core syntactic and phonological aspects come to express certain kinds of meaning (for example, a string of words describes an agent carrying out an action that has consequences) and to create certain kinds of effect (for example, a certain plot conveys a scary aura). In drawing, the working out of spatial relations in two and three dimensions enters into the depiction of objects and sets of objects in the world, including ones that are farther from, overlap, or are smaller than another object. Here, in each case, a once "raw" and unmediated intellectual competence is being marshaled by an available symbolic vehicle in order to allow the realization of the symbolic potential of that particular competence. An intelligence developing properly after the first year of life necessarily intermeshes increasingly with various symbolic functions and systems. Indeed, only in brain-injured or autistic individuals does the intelligence continue to unfold in "pure" or raw form, untouched by a symbolic envelope.

WAVES OF SYMBOLIZATION

But there is another, equally intriguing aspect to symbolic development, an aspect that runs concurrently with its streamlike or encapsulated aspect. I refer here to certain psychological processes that we call "waves" of symbolization: these sprawling processes typically begin within a particular symbolic realm but, by their very nature, spread rapidly and sometimes even inappropriately into other symbolic domains.

As an initial example, take the "wave" of *role*, or *event structuring*: the ability of the two-year-old child to indicate that an action has been carried out or a role occupied by an agent. The normal symbolic means for expressing such meanings is through words ("Mommy sleep," "Fido jump") or through "pretend" play (the child puts a doll to sleep, the child loops a toy stethoscope around her neck): language and "pretend" play are the "proper loci" of event-structuring knowledge. We find, however, that this psychological process does not remain simply within its proper symbolic realm. Rather, whatever the symbolic domain of a given task, the child of this age is likely to import event-structuring means. Hence, given a marker and asked to draw a truck, the child may instead grab the pen, rub it alongside the paper, and say, "Vroom Vroom." He has transformed the marker into a truck, and his actions serve to re-create the sound and feel of a vehicle in motion. Or, take a task in which the child is asked to select that block which resembles a toothbrush. Paying scant heed to the long cylindrical block, the child will simply grab the next available block, whatever its shape, and place it in his mouth, pretending that the block is a brush. Once again, the structure of the role and the event have taken over.

A second wave, which we call *analogical* or *topological mapping*, comes to the fore about a year later, at approximately the age of three. In analogical mapping, the child's use of the symbol captures, within the actual symbolic vehicle itself, some relations originally observed in the field of reference that he is symbolizing. And so, for the first time, in drawing, the child becomes able to extend two appendages from the base of a circular form and dub the resulting form "person." Or the child is able to place several blocks atop one another and declare the resulting form a "snowman." The symbols bear an analogic resemblance to their referents. In a perhaps related development in the realm of music, the child can capture such analogic relations as whether the "target" song goes up or down, becomes faster or slower, but cannot capture the exact pitch or the metrical relations. Given the sprawling nature of a wave of symbolization, the child also uses a relational form of symbolization even in circumstances where it is not appropriate. Asked to match the number of elements in an array, he will note whether there are many or a few, but will not fix the values with proper precision. Or, asked to retell a story with several characters, he will reduce the protagonists to two individuals—one representing good, the other representing evil, forces. The proclivity for capturing relative sizes, shapes, or valences proves an all-encompassing wave at this point.

A succeeding wave, occurring around the age of four, explores the other side of the coin. Riding this wave of *digital*, or *quantitative, mapping*, the child is now intent on getting the number of elements in an array precisely correct. No longer does the child settle for rough approximations of the number of toes on a foot, of characters in a story, of pitches in a song: the child now gets his quantities just right. However, even this apparently beneficent advance exacts its cost: rather than capturing the feelings and mood of a particular form of behavior (the sense of a person running in a dance or in a drawing), the child may be so intent on depicting the movement exactly correctly that crucial aspects of tone and nuance can be lost. After all, sometimes the qualities of a referent prove more important to capture than the quantities (particularly for aesthetic purposes).

There are important points associated with the appearance and the proliferation of these wavelike capacities. First of all, each of these waves goes on to have a further history, for event structuring, analogical mapping, and digital mapping each figure in later life. We might think of the novelist, the sculptor, and the mathematician as adult "masters" of the three wave capacities just described. But perhaps more germane to my purposes, the wide scope of the waves indicates that certain symbolic processes, whatever their origin, are not inviolably tied to a particular domain of symbolization. Instead, they become available as more general coin, to be exploited appropriately (or inappropriately) by a much wider range of symbol systems.

I touch here on a crucial aspect of human intellectual powers. Whereas most animals possess some computational capacities that are highly developed—consider song in birds or dances in bees—these competences are almost invariably encapsulated: that is, they remain rigidly restricted to a certain avenue of expression. In contrast, human intelligence is far more flexible. Given a new and valuable ability, humans have a much greater proclivity to deploy that ability widely, to try it out in remote symbolic domains, and to see whether "it flies." Indeed, we humans may not be able to resist experimenting with certain newly evolving capacities, even where they are not entirely appropriate. In the end, human beings become supple symbol users because of our ability to mobilize those operations that prove peculiar to one symbolic domain as well as certain versatile operations which lend themselves to deployment across a range of symbolic domains.

The relation of the waves of symbolization to autonomous intelligences poses a difficult problem. Whereas the streams map comfortably onto our initial intelligence, the waves by their very nature do not respect the boundaries that demarcate intellectual domains. My own view is that each wave of symbolization originates within one intelligence: thus, event-structuring is most closely tied to linguistic intelligence; analogue mapping, to spatial intelligence; digital mapping, to logical-mathematical intelligence. However, for reasons that are not yet clear, powerful forces operate to guide these symbolic waves to remote intellectual realms.

Having negotiated the three waves during the period when the individual streams of development continue to unfold in several symbolic domains, the child of five indeed has attained a first-draft knowledge of numerous symbolic products. He knows what a story is and how to spin a short but suitable one; he exhibits comparable knowledge about songs, plays, dances, designs, and numerous other symbolic products. Indeed, this age is often described as a flowering of symbolic activity, for the child enthusiastically and effortlessly can produce instances in each of these symbolic domains. Moreover, these examples often strike the observer (at least in our aesthetically permissive era) as novel, charming, creative, and original. The child is able to express himself freely without undue critical apprehension and has no commitment to producing just what others have fashioned. He is willing to transcend boundaries, to link domains, to effect unusual juxtapositions—in short, to exhibit some of the experimentation and flavorfulness that we associate with the mature artist. It is a heady time.

CHANNELS OF SYMBOLIZATION

Yet a new ensemble of symbolic processes is also beginning to come to the fore. These processes emerge spontaneously (at least in our society) when the child begins on his own, during a game, to make little "counting" marks on a piece of paper; or when asked to go to the store and purchase a dozen items, the child tries to invent a simple notation to aid him in his task. At around the age of five, six, or seven, children become capable of *notational symbolization*—the capacity to invent or use various notational systems which, in "second-order" fashion, themselves refer to basic symbol systems. There is written language that refers to spoken language; the written numerical system that refers to spoken (or otherwise symbolized) numbers; there are assorted maps, diagrams, codes, musical, or dance notational systems, each of which has been devised in order to capture salient points of a symbolic display. We might consider this new development the final and most decisive wave of symbolization.

Notational symbolization differs from earlier waves. First of all, the capacity to create notations is a second-order capacity: it features a symbol system that itself refers to other symbol systems. Notationality thereby opens up possibilities of a most happy, but unanticipated sort: now the child can continue to invent symbol systems of an ever higher and more complex order, which take a previously mastered notational system as their referent. Much of mathematics and science is built upon this recursive possibility, where a third-order system can refer to a second-order system, and so forth.

Perhaps most important, the hand of the culture can be seen with crystalline clarity at this point of symbolic development. Whereas the streams and the waves of earlier years have an endogenous quality and may well be observed in roughly comparable forms across the cultures of the world, notations clearly come largely from the surrounding culture. Hence, they constitute *channels* of symbolization—means of codifying information that have evolved within a given culture and are now furnished directly to the younger learner. While the inclination to invent notations might well be present even in individuals who live in societies with scant notational practices, it seems probably that only individuals who live in societies with many channels of notation will go on to use notations regularly in their own lives. Here may lie one of the principal differences between schooled and nonschooled societies, and hence, between the kinds of individuals each characteristically produces.

Once he becomes enwrapped in a world of notations, the child is bent upon mastering new systems and using them in a precise and prescribed way. The child is now engaged in earnest in obtaining the symbol skills of his culture; and, in a sense, the fun is over. The child attends especially to the symbolic channels favored by his culture, be they the dances in a ritual or the language in a historical textbook; and, correlatively, he comes to ignore those symbolic potentials that are neglected within his own culture. Whereas, until this time, much of the mastery of symbolization has taken place in an informal, almost invisible manner, the learning of these explicit notational systems typically occurs within a formal setting and, ofttimes, in an actual school. It is hardly an exaggeration to assert that *education*—as the term is used today—refers to the processes whereby children are introduced to, and come to master, the principal notational channels of their culture.

At least within our own society, there is an intriguing, if somewhat discouraging, cognitive corollary to the advent of notational symbolization. In his zeal to master certain symbolic systems, the child often becomes extremely literal-minded. He wants to use the symbol system just in the proper way and so will brook no deviations or experimentation. In fact, figurative language, unusual juxtapositions, and other departures from the conventional are out. This banishment makes the child's work seem prosaic and drab—in contrast to the freer if more idiosyncratic works of earlier years.

But this "literal stage" may well constitute an essential aspect of symbolic development; and it would be a radical pedagogue indeed who would attempt to circumvent or subvert it altogether. Perhaps one must master the symbolic system, as it is supposed to be mastered, before one can take fresh advantage of it. And, indeed, most adults seem content simply to gain some competence in the major symbol systems of their culture and to make sure that their youngsters achieve similar (or perhaps greater) competence. There is in most populations little interest in innovative uses of symbol systems, in departures from the *status quo*. It is given to only a few individuals in most cultures to reach the apogee of symbolic competence and then to move off in unanticipated directions, experimenting with symbol systems, fashioning unusual and innovative symbolic products, perhaps even attempting to devise a new symbol system.

OVERVIEW

Through this rapid survey of the highlights of symbolic development, as they have emerged in the research at Project Zero, I have attempted to suggest the way in which the raw intelligences come to be exploited and absorbed in the devising and the interpretation of symbolic products. Thus, in infancy there may be instances of the raw intelligences, but these are almost immediately enwrapped in meaningful activities, as a result of their affective consequences for the young child, and in light of the rich interpretations perpetually supplied by the surrounding culture. Then, during the preschool years, each intelligence is increasingly involved in the mastery and the deployment of diverse symbol systems. During this time, some aspects of the development of symbolic competences respect the boundaries of an intelligence, proceeding along relatively confined streams; while other aspects are likely to overrun the boundaries between intellectual domains in broad waves. Finally, during the period of notational symbolization, the culture itself intrudes, as various channels provided by the culture come to exert an ever greater effect on the child's symbolic practices and achievements. By this time, the dynamic within an individual intelligence must somehow have become intermeshed with the agenda of the culture, lest the child engage in activities that, from the culture's point of view, are unproductive, if not frankly autistic. Indeed, most individuals become so caught up in the mastering of the symbol systems—as defined by the culture—that sparks of original creativity remain in only a small minority of the population.

The study of the developmental course of human symbolization has barely begun, and essentially all research has been conducted from the perspective of behavioral science. Yet, with my interest in the biological bases of cognition, I shall risk a few speculative remarks. First of all, it seems apparent that participation in the symbolic process is part of the human condition. Humans are as "prepared" to engage in symbolic processes (from language to dreams) as squirrels are prepared to bury nuts: it would take extraordinary pressures to keep an organism (raised in a cultural setting) from becoming a symbolic creature. As a second point, the forms and kinds of symbolization in which humans participate may also be guided by biological processes. While clearly there exists a wide range of symbolic routes, and cultures can conjure up fascinating and unexpected symbolic complexes, it seems likely that the main avenues of symbolization, the main forms of symbol use, and our trio of streams, waves, and channels are also courtesy of our species membership.

A final point concerns the rhythms of symbolic development. In my view, there is a period of relatively great flexibility or plasticity during the first years of symbolic development: at this time, one has many options for the exploration of particular symbolic systems, the devising of unusual symbolic combinations, or the actual transgression of symbolic boundaries. This period may be likened to the phase of early plasticity found in a range of biological systems in a range of organisms. At the same time, there may also be sensitive or critical periods, when involvement with the "stuff" of particular symbolic systems is particularly crucial, and failure to become involved especially costly. Correlatively, (within and across cultures) particular triggering events or crystallizing experiences may guide individuals down particular symbolic paths. The growing reluctance to experiment with symbol systems in late childhood, may reflect a decline of flexibility and plasticity, paralleling the increased rigidity found elsewhere in the processes of biological development. Just why a select group of individuals can retain—or recapture—the flexibility of early childhood remains one of the most puzzling of all dilemmas in the biological domain.

While it has proved possible to indicate certain ways in which the individual intelligences continue to develop during the periods when symbolization comes to the fore, it is important to underscore once again that certain aspects of development do not fall easily into the "pure intelligence" mode of analysis. I refer, for example, to various amodal (or cross-modal) forms of representation, which may not respect the boundaries among intelligences. From the first months of infancy, it will be recalled, infants display some abilities to link information across diverse sensory modalities and even to recognize abstract qualities like continuity, intensity, height, and the like, which are encountered across diverse intellectual domains. Similar kinds of amodal sensitivity may well enable the child during the period of basic symbolization to effect mappings across diverse systems. And, during later childhood, such amodal sensitivities may spur the development of more general analogic or synthetic powers which can prove extremely important for creative output. Thus far, for reasons spelled out in the previous chapter, I have resisted the impulse to label these capacities as a separate "amodal" or "cross-modal" form of intelligence; but it is important that they not be omitted from any consideration of the trajectory of human symbolic development.

Even as we should allow the possibility that symbolic development may involve abilities that resemble neither streams nor waves, we must keep in mind the powers of the individual intelligences. As we saw in earlier chapters, linguistic intelligence will emerge even in individuals deprived of the normal auditory-oral channels of communication, just as spatial intelligence will emerge even in individuals blinded from birth. Such findings provide powerful evidence that intelligences are sufficiently canalized (in the biological sense) as to be manifest even in the absence of normal spurs to growth. To be sure, intelligences may well be funneled by cultures to extremely diverse ends, but ultimately it is unlikely that the most basic human potentials can be altogether distorted or stifled.

Issues in Symbolic Development

I have so far intimated a consensus within the community of developmental researchers on the issues of symbolic development. In a way, this portrait is permissible, because the number of researchers plumbing this area is very small, and the initial task of charting has itself consumed most of our energies. Moreover, it is fair to say that most of the researchers have been strongly influenced by Piaget and therefore find it natural to espouse a view of development as occurring in stages. Still, it is likely that any discussion among students of symbolic development would uncover significant disagreements and tensions as well. Consistent with my project of subjecting M.I. theory to discussion and criticism, it is appropriate to indicate where some of these tensions might lie.

First of all, while many authorities see learning as increasingly canalized and rigidified with age, so that the older individual has available fewer avenues for flexibility, some investigators have put forth an alternative point of view. In this latter view the young child is a prisoner of his abilities and gifts, which may exist in exquisite form but also lie in splendid isolation from one another, unable to be productively linked; while the mature individual is able to gain *conscious* access to his various modular abilities and to mobilize them for diverse ends. According to Ann Brown and Paul Rozin, two psychologists who have pondered this issue, once a new ability has been brought to consciousness, it can then be applied to all kinds of diverse programs and ends. Naturally, such a bubbling up to consciousness is less likely to occur in the two-year-old than in the twenty-year-old. Here, then, is a view that may account for the striking originality and flexibility found among at least some adults.

As far as I am concerned, these two positions are not necessarily in conflict. Perhaps the ability to master a particular program in a smooth and effortless way is easier in earlier life, but the ability to mobilize this ability and put it to fresh uses may be the prerogative of the developed individual. In any case, the issue of when abilities are flexible and/or accessible, as opposed to canalized and/or inaccessible, proves vital for anyone concerned with educational interventions in the symbolic domains.

A second controversial area concerns the existence of stages of development, and the extent to which such stages may be linked to certain ages. As articulated by Piaget, the strongest position here holds that there are indeed discrete stages of development, which are qualitatively different from one another and stipulate characteristic world views. Moreover, as part of this point of view, there is the frequent rider that the stages of development are age-linked; and that, if the child does not pass smoothly through a stage at the appropriate age, his subsequent development will be forever askew.

The past decade has not been friendly to the strong version of the stage hypothesis. It turns out that young children are capable of many operations once withheld from them; and that, under certain circumstances, adults must pass through stages of learning paralleling those realized by the young child. It is difficult, in the light of these findings, to adhere to a rigid view of the stage theory. Nonetheless, in my own view, there is still utility in recognizing different mental organizations associated with different levels of understanding (for example, in the picture of symbolic development I have rendered); and it is the foolhardy optimist who, confident that certain symbolic skills can be easily acquired by the adult, would withhold crucial symbolic experiences from children. To be sure, adults can attain mastery in many areas, sometimes even more quickly than children can, but mature individuals may well be using different kinds of abilities and strategies (including ones to which they have conscious access); there may well be certain facets of the material (such as accent or connotation in language) that the adult will never be able to negotiate as successfully as the naïve child.

Returning for a moment to the argument of earlier chapters, I find it most plausible that each domain of intelligence and, by extension, each symbolic domain harbors its own series of steps through which the individual can advance. There is no reason to think that these intelligences or symbol systems align with complete consistency alongside one another: that kind of general stage notion has almost surely been discredited. Nor is it reasonable to assume that the limits and the possibilities of adult learning are the same across diverse symbol systems. Rather, it seems more productive at this point to look for stagelike sequences, and for age-linked limitations, in each of the separate intelligences and to see whether any systematic patterns can be observed. It is equally important to examine putative stage sequences across different cultures to see, for example, whether the steps of development in drawing or dance are revealingly different, depending upon the cultural contexts in which they unfold. Only after such careful empirical work will it be opportune to return to more general issues such as the utility of stage concepts altogether and the relationships that may obtain between learning by children and learning by adults.

A final controversial issue pertains both to the range of abilities or potentials that one can find within a population and to the extent to which that range can be affected by environmental manipulations. This is a classical dilemma. Scholars of a hereditarian persuasion generally believe in fairly wide individual differences, which cannot be much affected by environmental manipulations; those of an empiricist or environmentalist persuasion tend to minimize differences among individuals and to feel that whatever differences may exist lend themselves readily to reduction (or intensification). Of course, it is possible to find hereditarians who believe in only small differences among individuals, as well as to find empiricists who are impressed by the large (initial or culturally formed) differences among individuals as well.

What is striking is that, with the passage of time and the accumulation of mountains of information, most disputants remain committed to their original position. Not even the demonstrations that a normal college student can increase his short-term memory tenfold, or that most differences in school performance can be virtually eliminated by tutoring, or that seemingly average Japanese children can become violin virtuosos, suffice to convince the committed hereditarian that individual differences can be fully dissolved by judicious intervention. Indeed, even I myself confess to being unpersuaded that there are not inborn differences, sometimes ones of great moment, and that at least some of them can never be erased.

What recent research has shown, virtually incontrovertibly, is that whatever differences may initially appear, early intervention and consistent training can play a decisive role in determining the individual's ultimate level of performance. If a particular behavior is considered important by a culture, if considerable resources are devoted to it, if the individual himself is motivated to achieve in that area, and if proper means of crystallizing and learning are made available, nearly every normal individual can attain impressive competence in an intellectual or a symbolic domain. Conversely, and perhaps more obviously, even the most innately talented individual will founder without some positive supporting environment. Discovery of an individual's inherent intellectual profile, which I believe may be possible, need not serve, then, as a means of pigeonholing the individual or of consigning him to an intellectual junkheap; rather, such discovery should provide a means for assuring that every individual has available to him as many options as possible as well as the potential to achieve competence in whatever fields he and his society deem important.

Interaction among Intellectual Competences

In alluding to the roles valued by a society, I approach the question of the ways in which intelligences are ultimately to be deployed. It is evident that, with few exceptions, societies are not interested in "pure" intellectual competences: there are few occupational roles that the *idiot savant* of linguistic, logical, or bodily intelligence can perform. Rather, in nearly all socially useful roles, one sees at work an amalgam of intellectual and symbolic competences, working toward the smooth accomplishment of valued goals.

In a sense, then, my description of individual intelligences, and even of the early stages of symbolic development, is a fiction, one chiefly useful for scientific purposes. Neither the several intelligences nor the various streams exist in pristine isolation; rather, such "ideal systems" are always encountered in a cultural setting, one that comes to exert decisive control of their developmental course. And so, in this present study, I have crossed a conceptual Rubicon: from this point on, I shall (with rare exceptions) be concerned with how human proclivities and skills unfold within a supportive cultural context.

Especially in a complex society, there is clearly no one-to-one correspondence between intellectual strengths and social roles. To begin with, the individual with impressive ability in one form of intelligence can use it to a number of ends. Thus, the individual in our society with well-developed spatial skills might end up as engineer or architect or, equally, as artist or sculptor. Likewise, an individual with well-developed interpersonal skills could end up as teacher or social worker, minister or magician. An intellectual strength opens up possibilities; a combination of intellectual strengths spawns a multiplicity of possibilities.

From the opposite perspective, it is equally evident that a valued cultural role can be filled by individuals who present distinctive intellectual profiles. Take, for example, the role of lawyer in our society. There is room in (and at the top of) the legal profession for the individual who has outstanding linguistic skills: one who can excel in the writing of briefs, the phrasing of convincing arguments, the recall of facts from hundreds of cases, and the like. There is room also for the individual with highly developed interpersonal skills: one who can speak eloquently in the courtroom, skillfully interview witnesses and prospective jurors, and display an engaging personality—the so-called society lawyer. Finally, there is room for the individual with highly developed logical skills: one who is able to analyze a situation, to isolate its underlying factors, to follow a torturous chain of reasoning to its ultimate conclusion.

Still in the area of legal reasoning, the forms themselves can be differentiated in various ways. Analysts of the legal profession, like

Paul Freund and Edward Levi, designate a variety of reasoning abilities that can be used by lawyers, including reasoning by analogy, pursuing lengthy syllogistic chains, engaging in dialectical thinking, finding the best precedent, overlooking marginal details, and testing hypotheses (in the manner of a scientist). Lawyers may begin from first principles, from earlier cases, or from the conclusion that a client wants one to reach. They may rely on reflection, authority, or intuition—the recognition of a solution through instantaneous, nonreflective means. Members of the legal profession also differ in whether they rely on straight logical deduction, in whether they value elegance in presentation, or in whether they are preoccupied with ethical issues or overwhelmed by personal ties to a client.

It is obvious even from this brief excerpt that the mere evocation of "logical-mathematical reasoning" is too simple to account for the kinds and the combinations of reasoning skills that are cultivated in lawyers. Doubtless, a similar differentiated analysis can be carried out for each of the roles within a complex society, ranging from performers to physicians, from scientists to salesmen. Moreover, once one begins to consider combinations of intelligences, one encounters an even larger set of ways in which an individual can be competent. Thus, it seems evident that a lawyer is well served if he has highly developed linguistic, logical, and interpersonal intelligences (though it is less obvious how musical or kinesthetic intelligence would bear on his practice). And the number of ways in which linguistic, logical, and interpersonal intelligences can be combined in effective legal practice is staggering even to contemplate.

As we toy with these sets of intelligences, we can readily see how various combinations might be exploited by different kinds of practitioner both in our culture and in others. Taking the lawyer as the paradigm of a combination of logical and linguistic intellectual abilities, we might contrast this mix of intelligences with several other couplets. The skilled politician may combine linguistic and social intelligence to a high degree but have relatively little need for logical ability; the grace involved in kinesthetic intelligence might prove an asset as well. As for public figures in other, less legalistically oriented societies, it is possible that social factors might again emerge as more important than logical ones. According to Stanley Tambiah, for example, advocates in African societies are less concerned with whether their statements can be disproved and more concerned with their persuasive powers. In the case of the theatrical performer, a premium may be placed on linguistic and bodily intelligence: on the other hand, I am not persuaded that interpersonal intelligence *per se* figures prominently in the skillful execution of dramatic roles, though it may be important for a director who must orchestrate large numbers of individuals.

Other combinations of intelligences lead in yet different directions. The individual with strongly developed logical-mathematical and spatial abilities has the gifts to become a physical scientist: the logical abilities may prove relatively more important for the theoretically oriented individual; the spatial abilities, for the experimental scientist. An individual equipped with these abilities along with a combination of linguistic and social skills would make an ideal administrator of a large scientific laboratory. Paradoxically, this latter combination of abilities might also be useful for the sorcerer in a traditional society, for he, too, needs skills in language, interpersonal relations, and logic, though perhaps in a different mix.

It is tempting to regard the particular intelligences as elements in a mentalistic chemistry set and to engage in the cocktail-party exercise of analyzing different social roles in terms of their preferred blend of intellectual flavors. I have myself succumbed to this temptation. But I hope I have not obscured the serious point: there is always a dialectic at work between the roles and the functions valued in a culture, on the one hand, and the individual intellectual skills possessed by its inhabitants on the other. The purpose of the professional marketplace or of the personnel director is to effect the most productive match between the demands of various roles and the profiles of specific individuals. One might even speculate that the smoothly functioning society has found a proper mechanism for effecting this correspondence (or has roles that nearly anyone can fill), while the dysfunctional society is packed with individuals whose intellectual profiles do not jibe with important roles. I would suspect that this kind of mismatch is most likely to occur during periods of rapid change. At such times, a new host of roles (for example, those involved in science and technology) need to be manned; but the traditional training of individuals has neglected (or actively rejected) those combinations of intellectual and symbolic skills essential to the effective execution of these newly emerging roles.

In this chapter, I have sought to broaden the analyses of earlier parts of the book, by showing how our raw intellectual competences constitute the basis on which human symbol-using capacities of the most diverse sort are constructed and then deployed for societal ends. In my view, it is through an understanding of how individuals obtain competence with various symbol systems and learn to fashion diverse

319

symbolic products, that we are most likely to gain a better understanding of the means by which one becomes (or fails to become) a productive member of one's community. To elaborate my position, I have put forth one theory of how symbolic development occurs and have touched as well upon a number of still controversial issues about the form of symbolic development.

Alternative Approaches to Human Intelligence

In the final chapters of this book, I turn to the educational implications of the theory. I am concerned with the ways in which the theory of multiple intelligences might be used to inform, and perhaps alter, policies implemented by people who are responsible for education, child care, and human development. But now, after having outlined the basic features of the theory, but before leaving the halls of scholarly inquiry for the trenches of educational policy, I shall revisit some major alternative approaches to intelligence and indicate how they appear to differ from my own approach. *In no sense is this brief survey meant to be a thorough discussion of how my theory relates to other extant theories:* that task would take another book. (Indeed, I have cited the names of individual scholars solely for illustrative purposes.) But some indication of the form that such a critical document might take would not be inopportune at the present time.

HEDGEHOGS AND FOXES AGAIN

I begin with those views most directly connected to the concept of intelligence as it is ordinarily employed in psychology. Classically, as I mentioned in chapter 2, there are two major views concerning the construct of intelligence: one set of "hedgehog" scholars sympathetic to the notion of a general intelligence ("g"), like Charles Spearman and Arthur Jensen; and an opposing set sympathetic to a pluralistic view of intelligence, such as those "foxes" who take a multifactorial approach to intellect like L. L. Thurstone and J. P. Guilford. It will be obvious that the conclusions of M.I. theory are much closer to those of the "foxes" and are not compatible with the beliefs of those who hold to a strong "g" view of intelligence.

My own analysis suggests that apparent support for "g" comes chiefly from the fact that most tests of intelligence are paper-and-pencil exercises which rely heavily on linguistic and logical-mathematical abilities. Hence, individuals strong in these two areas will perform well on tests of general intelligence, in contrast to individuals whose strengths lie elsewhere. Schools cherish these capacities for "mental manipulation," which is why "g" can predict success in school with some accuracy.

Where, then, does M.I. theory depart from the multifactorial point of view? First of all, the latter does not question the existence of general horizontal abilities, like perception and memory, which may cut across different content areas. Indeed, the multifactorial point of view exhibits a studied indifference to this issue, because some factors are indeed horizontal forms of memory or perception, while others reflect strict content areas, like spatial ability. Second, the multifactorial point of view does not make intellectual contact with biology but is strictly empirical, the result of correlations among test scores, and of nothing more. Third, and perhaps most crucial, the multifactorial approach does not allow one to sample the range of intellectual competences I have considered here. So long as one is content to use paper-and-pencil or brief interviewing techniques, lasting minutes rather than hours, there is simply no way to sample an individual's competence in such areas as bodily expression, musical ability, or the forms of personal intelligence. Thus while laudably more pluralistic than the "g" school, the multifactorial approach provides only that extremely partial glimpse of intelligence that reflects the Western scientific ethos.

PIAGET AND INFORMATION PROCESSING

The work of two subsequent schools, the Piagetian and the information-processing approaches, represents to my mind a step forward in scientific power but not necessarily any progress in the analysis of intellectual profiles. The Piagetian school is more closely attuned to the child's daily activities and skills, thereby providing a more holistic and veridical notion of his intellectual capacities. An interest in strategies, in tell-tale errors, in the relations among bodies of knowledge is to be applauded, and the clinical interviewing method perfected by Piaget is an innovation of great utility for the student of intellectual growth.

Yet the classical structuralist view of intellect is even narrower than that held by the intelligence-test makers and, in fact, is restricted almost completely to logical-mathematical thinking. Perhaps for that reason, it remains studiously blind to content: the clear assumption obtains that mental operations unfold in the same fashion across diverse materials. In the work of Piaget's follower Kurt Fischer, there is a welcome recognition that development may not occur at the same rate in diverse domains; that, in fact, in Piaget's terminology, *décalage* (loosely speaking, "variation") across domains is the rule rather than the exception. Still there remains the conviction that development occurs in the same sequenced fashion across all domains, and there is insufficient sensitivity to the possibility that the course of development in various content domains might be decisively different. It is poignant that Piaget, a biologist by training who believed that he was studying the biology of cognition, should have been so insensitive to diverse biological proclivities in the cognitive realm.

Information-processing psychology represents an advance over Piaget in the sense that more careful attention is paid to the actual processes by which individuals solve problems from moment to moment. The meticulous task analysis that is part and parcel of this approach has helped us to realize that many of Piaget's apparent stages and sequences are artifacts of particular task configurations, and that younger individuals possess many abilities that Piaget had mistakenly withheld from them.

But because information processing is more of an approach than a theory, it has been of little help in forging a coherent picture of human intellectual abilities. One can find in this approach some comfort for the notion that all problems are solved in essentially the same way, but virtually equal comfort for the notion of total task-specificity, where every task requires its own abilities, and there is no interesting transfer. By the same token, one finds support for the notion that the child processes information in just the way that adults do (but simply possesses less knowledge), but virtually equivalent support for the notion that the child has a less tenacious short-term memory, a less adequate encoding capacity, and other qualitative divergences from the information-processing machinery of the adult.

The very fact that information-processing psychology can yield such diverse conclusions may signify only the immaturity of the field. However, to my mind, it may reflect deeper lacks: the absence of a biological perspective on the nature of the tasks that are employed, as well as the lack of a theory of what constitutes the domain under scrutiny. Instead, one has the vague model of the child as a kind of computational device—a model that has certain advantages, but that, like all models, is only partial. And, as Allan Allport has suggested, depending upon the kind of computer one selects, and the analysis of the computer one embraces, one will secure a very different picture of what the information processor is like.

CHOMSKY'S STANCE

All the approaches reviewed until now center upon the individual, seeing him in Cartesian fashion, as almost entirely alone, engaged in sophisticated problem solving in an environment that plays little formative role in his skills, his attitudes, or his ultimate performance. This perspective is taken to an extreme in the work of Noam Chomsky (and, to some extent, in that of his colleague Jerry Fodor). Here the child is regarded as a collection of separate computational devices, each of which unfolds according to its own preordained (and preformed) laws, with little influence of any sort (except triggering) from the environment. Indeed, Chomsky rejects traditional notions of learning and development: in their stead, he nominates a model of intellectual unfolding which borrows heavily from embryology.

It should be obvious that I have some sympathy with Chomsky's point of view, feeling that it serves as a needed corrective to uncritically empiricistic accounts of knowledge acquisition spawned during earlier eras. And Chomsky's (and Fodor's) account of domains squares well with mine, though I fail to locate any attempt in his work to indicate how a domain might be defined and delimited in a systematic way. Where Chomsky's view seems unforgivably weak, however, is in its failure to countenance the ways in which an intelligence must unfold in an environment filled with meanings and interpretations: there is simply no recognition of how various symbolic capacities develop and interact, or of how the human biological substrate can be exploited to achieve many different ends, depending upon the particular values and functions of the society under consideration. By denying the role of culture—or, at any rate, by failing to confer upon it any importance—Chomsky fashions a theory that is completely skeletal. We are left with no way of understanding how a society accomplishes its work, of how (or even why!) education takes place, of why young children differ from one another, and of why they differ even more from adults in various societies. In other words, the superstructure is completely missing, even though the infrastructure may have been inferred with intuitive brilliance.

The Theory

FOCUS ON CULTURE

The superstructure dominates the attention of another group of analysts, those concerned with the effects of culture upon the development of the individual. Chief representatives of this tradition include Michael Cole, Sylvia Scribner, Jean Lave, and their psychologically oriented colleagues, as well as Clifford Geertz, the anthropologist interested in symbolic systems. These scholars direct almost all of their attention to the components of the surrounding culture, contending that it is through a careful analysis of the culture, with its different forms and forces, that the proper account of the acquisition of cognitive capacities is most likely to be found. Geertz quotes with approval Gilbert Ryle's caution that "the mind is not even a metaphorical 'place.' On the contrary, the chessboard, the platform, the scholar's desk, the judge's bench, the lorry driver's seat, the studio and the football field are among its places"; and he himself adds, "Men without culture would be monstrosities with some useful instincts, few identifiable feelings, and no intelligence." No doubt reacting to the perceived excessive mentalism of traditional philosophical approaches, when all mental abilities were conceded directly to the individual, and also to contemporary theorists like Chomsky, who at most pay lip service to culture, these anthropologically oriented commentators underscore the extent to which individuals gain their symbols, their ideas, their ways of thinking from those around them and, more generally, from the collected wisdom of the culture.

In many ways, this anthropological perspective introduces an important new element in the understanding of cognition. For instance, Cole and his colleagues have examined the performances of individuals drawn from several cultures on standard tests of intelligence and reasoning, and have concluded that most apparent differences in performances can be explained by the different previous experiences of the subjects. When these experiences are taken into account, and suitable alterations are made in testing procedures, most apparent differences evaporate; and, indeed, individuals from putatively less developed cultures may even perform at a superior level. Certainly, there is no need to introduce any notions of inherent ethnic differences.

The general argument put forth by these investigators runs as follows: While the products of reasoning, and the kinds of information to which individuals are sensitive, may differ significantly across cultures, the processes of thinking are the same everywhere: cultures mobilize these basic information-processing capacities—these core intelli-

324

gences—and fashion them to their own ends. As a further part of this reorientation of cognitive theories, scholars like Cole stress the extent to which every individual's mental powers are absorbed from the outside—first being constituted in the knowledge and actions of other persons, and only gradually becoming internalized into one's own representational capacities. We count and we write not because we have ourselves developed in certain ways but because we have seen other individuals make use of these notations. Nor is this process ever completed: no matter what the society, the individual always depends upon other intellectual contributions by other individuals in order to carry out his daily tasks and to ensure his own survival. How many individuals are truly self-sufficient, even in a cognitive sense? The answer underscores the extent to which even one's own mind is perennially dependent upon the many other minds around.

Naturally, this anthropologically oriented approach does not display much sympathy for endogenous developmental trajectories. Nor is there any need to posit a series of relatively autonomous mental computers: the individual will perform as required in the culture in which he happens to live. The belief in autonomous mental components would be criticized from at least two perspectives. First of all, the autonomous theory proceeds as if initial development were regulated by factors internal to the organism; whereas in actuality, the culture (and its interpretive mechanisms) are present from the first. Second, the autonomous theory tends to assume that the range of possible developmental outcomes is sharply canalized, if not actually fixed in advance. A more culturally oriented approach stresses the likelihood that certain as yet undiscovered cultures might perform operations that we cannot even envision, or that cultures evolving in the future will also mold our intellectual proclivities in unanticipated directions.

Conclusion

All of these insights seem to be well worth absorbing into a comprehensive account of human cognition. But what is missing from this analysis through anthropological lenses is a recognition of the ways in which, even treated in the most appropriate and equivalent ways, individuals within a culture can still differ significantly from one another—in intellectual strengths, in ability to learn, in ultimate use of their faculties, in originality and creativity. I see no way—short of a more psychological (and biological) approach—of dealing with this variable of difference in performance. Such an environmentally oriented approach also overlooks both the extent to which the individual may progress in a field, using only modest help from the surroundings, and how a few isolated individuals can go on to truly remarkable accomplishments. In a sense, the approach of these anthropologically oriented scholars is most suitable for explaining how the average individual in an average situation *functions,* and perhaps gives a misleading notion of how average all of us, in fact, are.

Somewhere between the Chomskian stress on individuals, with their separate unfolding mental faculties, the Piagetian view of the developing organism passing through a uniform sequence of stages, and the anthropological attention to the formative effects of the cultural environment, it ought to be possible to forge a productive middle ground: a position that takes seriously the nature of innate intellectual proclivities, the heterogeneous processes of development in the child, and the ways in which these are shaped and transformed by the particular practices and values of culture. It is this effort that I have undertaken in this book. It must be stressed, therefore, that I have relied heavily on the aforementioned authors, and on many other psychologists of development who have been interested in educational issues. In an earlier chapter, I have stated that my own view on the centrality of symbol systems, and on the need for an analysis in terms of cultural domains, grows out of collaborative efforts with Gavriel Salomon, David Olson, and most especially David Feldman. I should underscore again my indebtedness to these contemporary scholars of development and education. And I should add to this list the name of Jerome Bruner, who—more than any other developmental psychologist of our time— has been interested in education and has proved sensitive to the range of issues discussed in the latter part of this book: the child's biological heritage, his preferred avenues of development, and the formative effects of the culture, including the role of tools, symbol systems, media, and other prostheses in the devising and the transmission of knowledge. I owe a large debt to Jerome Bruner for attuning me (as he has so many others) to this nexus of issues.

I have now laid out the major tenets of multiple intelligence theory, indicated some of its major weaknesses as I see them, and related the current version of the theory to other competing perspectives on the intellect. The time has come to see whether this framework can help us to understand better the processes of education as they have taken place in the past, and as they might possibly be refashioned in the future. This task will first require some consideration of the various ways in which knowledge has, in fact, been transmitted throughout the course of human history; and it is to this fascinating, but little understood, issue that I shall next turn.

Part III

Implications and
Applications

13

The Education
of Intelligences

Introduction

It is time to beckon back to center stage the three figures whom we first encountered at the opening of this book. There is the Puluwat youth in the course of acquiring those vaunted navigational skills I have already reviewed in the discussion of spatial intelligence. There is the young Islamic scholar, capable of that facility at memorizing which I noted in treating linguistic intelligence. And there is the Parisian adolescent seated at a computer terminal preparing to compose a work of music—a young person who is combining, in a way scarcely imaginable some years ago, aspects of logical-mathematical and musical intelligence.

It was in an effort to understand better the skills involved in these disparate feats, to offer an account of the educational processes that develop such competences, and to consider how these competences can be assessed in an appropriate way, that I initially undertook this inquiry. I have, in preceding chapters, examined each of the candidate intelligences in some detail and have also undertaken a critique of the theory. Then, in chapter 12, I began the process of relating the "raw" and relatively autonomous intellectual competences to the concerns and practices of the larger society. I described the way in which the use of symbols develops in normal individuals. And I considered how human intelligences can be marshaled in the service of specific roles by the symbolic systems, codes, and interpretative frameworks of the wider culture.

Though arguably valid, this picture still has focused on the developing individual, *qua* individual. Consistent with the psychologists' biases, the culture has been viewed primarily as a backdrop, with its products and systems a means of fostering personal development. But one may examine the same encounters, the same sets of circumstances, from a vastly different perspective—that of the society at large. After all, from the point of view of the culture, numerous individuals are continually being born, each of whom needs to be socialized according to prevailing norms, values, and practices. It is the means used by the society—and in particular, the various modes of education and training —that will concern us as I consider here the education of intelligences.

The anthropologist Jules Henry reminds us of the central role played by education in all societies from the earliest days:

> Throughout his historical course, *Homo sapiens* has been a "status seeker"; and the way he has had to follow, by compulsion, has been education. Furthermore he has always had to rely on those superior to him in knowing and social status to enable him to raise his own status. . . . instructing the young in the tribal ways is as natural as breathing; [adults] have a vital interest in the children they teach, and they often seem to have even a broader interest in the tribal existence as a whole.

Surely in focusing upon the educational process, we are considering a domain of utmost importance in all cultures, as well as an optimal area in which to observe the intelligences at work. And yet, as we shift our perspective from the individual to the educational situation as a whole, we move into largely uncharted waters. The number of variables entailed in describing educational systems is so enormous that any hope of controlled experimentation, or of scientific modeling, must be suspended.

My mode of presentation, accordingly, becomes increasingly descriptive and allusive. Furthermore, in the final pages of this book, I become yet more speculative as I consider the options available to the educational practitioner, and attempt to lay forth the problems that he or she confronts, and even to offer some practical suggestions. It is only fair to warn the reader of this significant change in scope and in tone. I trust that the shift is justified by the urgency of the educational problems being faced the world over and by the need to consider these problems from a perspective broader than that of the solitary individual.

In this effort to elucidate particular forms of learning as they are found in the world today, I shall proceed as follows. First, I shall briefly survey the major components of any educational situation—components including the kinds of intelligences which are involved, the principal transmitting agents, the general context or situation within which such transmission of knowledge occurs. Taken together, these components constitute a framework that can be applied to any educational situation and that should point up similarities and differences among diverse educational situations.

Following the introduction of this framework, I will consider in turn the three educational situations embodied by our three prototypical learners—the youthful navigator, the Koranic student, and the young programmer. Of course, to isolate any trio of instances is radically to reduce the range of educational variation actually encountered in the world today. It is important to underscore, then, that these examples are used only for illustrative purposes. I will actually draw on information about numerous comparable educational settings as a means of arriving at generalizations about three prototypical forms of learning: (1) the acquisition of specialized skills in a nonliterate society (exemplified by the sailor); (2) attainment of literacy in a traditional religious school (exemplified by the Koranic student); and (3) the transmission of a scientific curriculum in a modern secular school (exemplified by the programmer).

A principal reason for developing an analytic framework is to explain why certain contemporary educational efforts have achieved success, while many others have met a less happy fate. I shall turn to this task in the concluding chapter of the book. To aid us in this effort, I have in the final pages of this chapter considered three components that typically occur together in modern secular education—attendance at a school, acquisition of various literacies, and deployment of the scientific method. It is, after all, the coincidence of these independent factors that gives the contemporary Western educational setting its peculiar flavor. And it is through an examination of these factors (and their consequences) that we may come to understand better the operation of educational processes quite different from our own, and the difficulties that arise when attempts are made to impose "our" forms upon other cultures.

A Framework for Analyzing Educational Processes

I begin by listing the various components that should be taken into account in the analysis of any educational encounter. Given the complexity of any situation in which one or more individuals are charged with the transmission of knowledge to another set of individuals, it is essential to consider a large set of components and thus, unfortunately, to be confined to a summary account of each. At the conclusion of this section on page 339, I have included a chart, which indicates the ways in which the framework might be applied to our three specimen learning situations. The detailed text of the chart is likely to become clear only after one has digested the individual sections on each of the educational encounters. Nonetheless, it may be of aid to readers to consult this chart, both during the introduction of the specific components in the paragraphs that follow, and in the course of reading the more detailed descriptions of each educational encounter in the following sections.

With this brief aside to the potentially perplexed, I shall turn first to a component of special import in this book—the particular *intelligences used in an educational encounter*. Even this component turns out to be multifaceted: For example, the abilities entailed in an intelligence can be used as a *means of acquiring information*. Thus, individuals may learn through the exploitation of linguistic codes, of kinesthetic or spatial demonstrations, or of interpersonal bonds. Even as various intelligences can be exploited as means of transmission, the actual *material to be mastered* may itself fall squarely within the domain of a specific intelligence. If someone learns to play an instrument, the knowledge to be acquired is musical. If someone learns how to calculate, the knowledge to be gained is logical-mathematical (even if the means is linguistic in nature). And so it turns out that our various intellectual competences can serve both as means and as message, as form and as content.

Related to, but separate from, the intelligences involved are the actual *ways of learning* exploited in one or another setting. Perhaps most basic is *direct* or *"unmediated" learning*: here the learner observes an adult activity *in vivo*, as when a Puluwat child watches an elder construct a canoe or prepare to sail. Closely related to direct observation but involving more overt participation by the learner, are various forms of *imitation*, where the child observes and then imitates (either immediately or subsequently) the actions performed by the model.

334

In these forms of *observational learning*, spatial, bodily, and interpersonal forms of knowledge are often at a premium. Linguistic knowledge may also be involved, but typically in an incidental manner—for example, to call attention to a feature of the performance. Sometimes, adages or general propositions are invoked as well: at this point "know-that" is joined to "know-how."

But instruction in a specific skill may also occur *outside the context* in which that skill is customarily practiced. Sometimes, a small model is constructed so that the learner can practice: for instance, the young Puluwat sailor learns the star configurations by setting up pebbles on the floor of a canoe house. Sometimes a ceremony or ritual is held, in which the learner is exposed to secrets or given specialized practice that can be utilized later on "in context." And as societies become more complex, and tasks more intricate and multifaceted, learning takes place increasingly in contexts remote from the actual site of practice— for example, in those special buildings called "schools." I shall examine such elaborated forms of learning as I turn to schools, ranging from informal bush schools, to traditional religious schools, to those contemporary secular schools with which most readers will have an intimate familiarity.

As we survey these different ways or settings of learning, we encounter three additional variables that must find their place within any equation of learning. To begin with, various *means* or *media* are used to transmit knowledge. While direct forms of learning are largely unmediated, involving at most a simple verbal description or a line diagram sketched "in the sand," more formal forms of learning rely heavily on discrete media of transmission. These may include articulated symbol systems, such as language or mathematics, as well as an ever-expanding family of media, including books, pamphlets, charts, maps, television, computers, and various combinations of these and other modes of transmission. Naturally, these media differ in the kinds of intelligence required for their proper use, as well as the kinds of information that they present most readily.

Next, there are the *particular sites* or *loci* where learning takes place. Much education, particularly in traditional societies, takes place *on site:* the learner is simply placed near (or gravitates toward) the model, who is at the time doing "his thing." On-site learning can occur at home, when that is the customary locus of the activity, be it learning how to prepare a meal or coming to "identify" with a parent who is always studying. As I have already noted, when societies become more complex, they are likely to set up *specialized institutions for learning.* Schools are the most prominent instances; but ateliers, shops, or laboratories where apprenticeships are available are also pertinent examples. And sometimes specialized settings, such as those used for initiation rites or ceremonies, facilitate the rapid and effective transmission of pivotal knowledge (and, as often, potent affect). Presumably, almost any kind of information could be transmitted at any site; but, as I have suggested, linguistic and logical-mathematical forms of knowing are most likely to be transmitted in settings devised expressly (and used primarily) for the transmission of knowledge.

A third variable in the equation of knowledge concerns the *particular agents* entrusted with this task. Classically, teachers are parents or grandparents, generally of the same sex as the learner; other relatives or members of one's caste or clan may also serve as the repository of special wisdom. Siblings and peers are often transmitters of knowledge as well: in fact, for some tasks, children learn more readily from their older siblings than from unrelated teachers. Not infrequently there is a *pairing* of individuals within a culture. Youngsters end up being trained by those adults who possess the skills that it is most important for them, the youngsters, to acquire: this kind of matching may occur because of blood relationships, proximity, or, less typically, a perceived fit on the part of the community between the model's skills and the youngster's aptitude. (Such matching is more likely to occur in societies with informal schooling.) Finally, in certain societies, there emerges a wholly separate class of teachers and leaders—initially religious, later secular in orientation—whose job it is to teach some, or perhaps even all, the youngsters in a community a given body of knowledge. Sometimes the teacher is expected to have an exemplary moral character; though in secular settings, technical expertise has become the key requirement. Possibly for the first time, a prior relationship between the child and the adult is no longer a necessary precursor for entering into an educational relationship: instead, one encounters a contractual situation where residence in a geographical area or membership in a religious body suffices as an entry card into an educational relationship.

A word, finally, about the *general context in which learning takes place*. Each of our prototypical instances of learning tends to occur in a particular cultural context. In a traditional nonliterate society, most learning is considered a requirement for survival. The same forms of knowledge are accordingly found among all, or most, inhabitants. Relatively little knowledge has been drawn up in explicit codes, and most required knowledge can be accrued simply by observing individuals at practice in their customary milieus. As these forms of knowledge are relatively straightforward, I shall not consider them further here. Instead, I shall turn to those forms of knowledge within a traditional society that do require a lengthy learning process, such as engages our young Puluwat sailor or a youth who is becoming a bard in a nonliterate Yugoslavian circle.

In societies where literacy is transmitted in a traditional religious setting, a somewhat different state of affairs obtains. Here a certain segment of the society, usually the young males, acquires a skill that will set its members apart from those who lack it. There is a gradual winnowing process, as a result of which some individuals end up with but a smidgeon of this specialized knowledge, while the most knowledgeable persons become the religious or the secular heads of the community. Outside the school setting, there may be further division of labor; often, however, the relatively simple technological and economic structure of the society permits most individuals to possess the same general set of skills and knowledge.

Representing an opposite extreme are modern technological societies that feature a wide range of roles and skills. As no individual can conceivably master all of them, there is considerable division of labor, with institutionalized formats for the transmission of knowledge and explicit standards for assessing success. Nearly all acquisition of skills takes place in specialized settings, ranging from technical schools to ateliers, from factories to corporations. While, in the traditional society, nearly everyone has some understanding of the knowledge possessed by others, the technological society features experts, whose particular store of knowledge proves as mysterious to the average citizen as does literacy to the nonliterate individual.

The kinds of intelligence that are highly valued differ markedly across these disparate contexts of learning. In the traditional nonliterate societies, there is a high valuing of interpersonal knowledge. Spatial and bodily forms of knowledge tend to be heavily exploited, while linguistic and musical forms of knowledge may also be at a premium in certain specialized circumstances. In a society that harbors traditional religious schools, linguistic knowledge comes to be esteemed. There is a continued cultivation of interpersonal knowledge, accompanied at the highest levels by the fostering of certain forms of logical-mathematical knowledge. Finally, in modern secular educational settings, logical-mathematical knowledge is at a premium, and certain forms of linguistic competence are also of value; in contrast, the role of interpersonal knowledge is generally reduced, even as intrapersonal forms of understanding may loom much larger.

I have briefly surveyed an analytic framework and a set of categories that can be applied to a range of educational settings and experiences. Naturally, *any application of this framework must be preliminary and tentative, pending both close observation of the particular society in question and the development of means for applying the categories in an unambiguous and reliable manner.* One can gain a feeling for how the framework might be applied to our three specimen settings, and to others of comparable scope, by studying the chart on page 339. Of course the chart samples just three possible cultural settings; a consideration of other educational settings would no doubt yield many other combinations of features and might as well bring to the force agents, loci, media of transmissions, or forms of intelligence that have not been considered here. Indeed, one virtue of such a framework is that, far from being Procrustean, it can help bring to our awareness aspects of the educational equation which might otherwise remain invisible.

SKILLS IN THE NONLITERATE SOCIETY

Until a few thousand years ago, nearly all human beings lived in societies where energies were consumed in providing for basic needs, primarily through hunting, gathering, farming, and the preparation of food. In such societies, most forms of knowledge were widely shared, as it was important for individuals in the society (or, at least, for all members of one sex) to be able to provide for themselves and others for whom they had responsibility. By and large, these forms of knowledge were acquired relatively early in life by the young, usually through simple observation and imitation of the adults in their families. There was little need for explicit codes, specialized training, or articulated levels of gradation or skill.

But even in nonliterate societies, one finds skills that are complex, highly elaborated, and restricted to individuals with considerable expertise—and it is these skills that are of particular significance for our inquiry. Sailing in the Puluwat Islands in the Caroline chain of Micronesia is an excellent example of such a skill. The status of "master navigator," achieved by only a handful (perhaps half a dozen) of males in the society, proves extremely difficult to attain. Indeed, many males do not even attempt to acquire any more than rudimentary knowledge of sailing; and of those who make the attempt, substantially fewer than half complete the course and become skilled navigators. By the same token, the building of canoes is also an elaborate skill, which requires considerable training and is achieved by only a small minority of the population.

The Framework for Analyzing Educational Processes Applied to Three Cultural Settings

Component of Education	Type of Learning		
	Specialized Skill in Nonliterate Society	*Literacy in Traditional Religious School*	*Scientific Curriculum in Modern Secular School*
Examples Mentioned in Chapter 13	Puluwat sailing; Yugoslavian oral verse	Koranic school; Hindu gurukula; Hebrew cheder; Medieval cathedral school	Elementary and secondary schools in Europe, North America, and Japan; Programming on microcomputer
Intelligences	Linguistic, musical (oral verse); Spatial (sailing); Bodily-kinesthetic; Interpersonal	Linguistic; Interpersonal; Logical-mathematical (among advanced students)	Logical-mathematical; Intrapersonal; Linguistic (less emphasized)
Media of Transmission	Mostly unmediated (direct observation); Some oral linguistic instruction	Oral verse or books	Great variety, including books, charts, computers, films, etc.
Locus of Learning	On site	Separate building or inside religious building	Separate building; Some learning can be done in a private home or study
Agents Who Transmit Knowledge	Skilled elders, typically relatives	Individuals trained in literacy and argument; high moral comportment expected; status high except at entry level positions	Individuals with training in education at lower level; individuals with specialized training at higher levels; moral caliber not germane
General Context of Learning	Most individuals share some basic skills, including sailing; a few may be experts	Most males start out in religious school; gradual winnowing process; successful students often enter clergy or community elect	Universal primary and secondary education; many individuals have specialized postsecondary education; possibility of life-long individual-initiated education

From the study undertaken by Thomas Gladwin, and reported in chapter 8, we have obtained considerable understanding of the processes involved in becoming a Puluwat sailor. Gladwin delineates two distinct courses of learning that are necessary for eventual success in navigation. One portion of learning is oral and takes place "off site": it involves the committing to memory of vast amounts of factual information, such as the identities and locations of all of the islands, and the identities and courses of all the stars, which the navigator could conceivably need to know. Gladwin points out that there is no need to keep this lore secret since

no one could possibly learn it except through the most painstaking and lengthy instruction. . . . It is taught and memorized through endless reiteration and testing. The learning job is not complete until the student at his instructor's request can start with any island in the known ocean and rattle off the stars both going and returning between that island and all the others which might conceivably be reached directly from there.

This aspect of Puluwat navigation, which relies on linguistic intelligence, is necessary but scarcely sufficient for the aspiring sailor. The more important part of his training can be acquired only by considerable practice at sailing. He needs a first-hand acquaintance with the currents, with specific conditions that obtain in traveling between various groups of islands, with the system used for keeping track of distance traveled, with the kinds of information that the waves convey, and with the procedures for navigation in storms, for finding one's way in the dark, for forecasting the weather, for dealing with sea life, and for using the stars to guide one's course. Much of this process involves the building up of "mental models" so that the navigator can conceive of himself traversing his course with everything moving past except the stars poised overhead. For these core aspects of sailing, linguistic knowledge proves of little help; at a premium are keen sensory capacities and the deployment of spatial and bodily-kinesthetic knowledge.

Forming an instructive contrast to the Puluwat navigators are those individuals in rural Yugoslavia who become singers of oral verse. According to Millman Parry and Albert Lord, hardly any formal training is involved in becoming an epic singer—an individual who can sing, for example, a different song all night for each of the forty nights of the Islamic month of Ramadan. Rather, the future singer simply listens night after night to the performances, learning the plot of the story and, more important, the various linguistic and musical formulae out of which new performances are constructed. After years of such listening and absorbing, the individual begins to practice the formulae himself, learning how to expand or ornament songs he hears, or perhaps even to create new songs. According to Lord, "it is a process of imitation and of assimilation through listening and much practice on his own." Finally, the singer has the opportunity to perform the song in front of a sympathetic but critical audience. Here at last he has the chance to see whether the feat that he has mastered, by observation and solitary practice, can exert the desired effects upon members of his community.

Both the Puluwat sailor and the Yugoslavian singer attain a high level of skill, one that sets them apart from others in their society. In both cases, a capacious linguistic memory, subjected to extensive rehearsal, is an important possession of the would-be expert. But whereas the sailor depends on his spatial and bodily abilities, the singer is reliant on his musical abilities and also on the interpersonal skill of communicating with an audience. Nearly all of the learning by the Yugoslavian poet takes place "on site," without formal instruction: he is, in a strong sense, self-taught. In contrast, explicit teaching procedures are used for Puluwat sailors, and at least some of these take place "off site"—for example in a canoe house, where pebbles signify stars. In the case of learning to build canoes, the offspring almost always works with his father; but in the case of navigation and oral verse, kinship ties themselves do not suffice. Many members of a family will lack the abilities (or the inclination) to become skilled practitioners, and it is possible for an otherwise talented individual to succeed even if his own kin are not engaged in the aforementioned skilled activities. Nonetheless, as in most other activities in a traditional society, one is far more likely to engage in an activity, and to attain high levels of expertise, if that activity has belonged to one's family's customary pursuits for many generations.

The acquisition of such expertise by a small caste within a traditional society is, as I have said, something of an anomaly, since most activities in the society are within the ken of all normal adults. (Indeed, all adults in the Puluwat islands have some rudimentary navigating capacity, even as all adults in the Yugoslavian society have some knowledge of oral verse.) As we move toward consideration of a schooled society, we encounter an environment in which specialized knowledge becomes more common. Our understanding of such societies may be increased if we consider briefly three institutions that one may find within a traditional society, each of which stands apart from

341

the normal course of observational learning and thereby anticipates the more formal processes associated with a schooled society.

THREE TRANSITIONAL FORMS OF EDUCATION

Initiation Rites. We begin with a more formally organized occasion of learning—the initiation rite. Much written about, these are ceremonial occasions which can last for hours or for years. Typically, youths of a culture are subjected to challenging experiences and asked to master particular behaviors or information as a step—often the decisive one— in effecting the transition from childhood to adulthood. Sometimes these rites are brutal: a youth may be subjected to harsh physical pain, as among the Thonga of Africa, or left alone in the wilds for long periods of time, as in the case of some American Indian tribes. Sometimes, as among the Tikopia of Polynesia, the rites are more benign, as the ceremonies are performed by relatives, and there is much affection, celebration, exchange of gifts and food.

One might well ask what is learned through these more or less traumatic rites of transition, whether they should, in fact, be considered occasions of learning. Answers in terms of sheer volume of information are probably beside the point. In general, the initiation rite is better viewed as marking a change of status than as an opportunity for mastering skills and lore; though in certain cases (for example, during the three-month circumcision rite in Senegambia), much learning does take place. But coming to understand that one is now a member of the adult society, and that there are specific expectations and privileges connected with that role, is in itself a crucial form of knowledge in traditional societies: one's beliefs about oneself constitute a powerful factor and reflect an assessment of whether one is able (or unable) to perform in the prescribed manner. Here is a task central to the development of intrapersonal intelligence and of a sense of self. Moreover, the initiation rite also marks a time of intensive affective learning— learning about one's feelings and one's relationship to others in one's group. The tension, thrill, and fear surrounding these experiences probably serve as a model for those affects associated with other important experiences in life which the youth must learn to handle—for instance, hunting, marriage, childbirth, and death: the individual's relationship to his community is confirmed as he undergoes these rites (even as it is undercut if, for some reason, the initiate does not perform adequately). One might regard the initiation rite as a kind of crystallizing experience in the personal realm—a critical moment when the

child-turned-adult must come to grips with the range of feelings that
he has as a person in his own right and as a member of the larger
society.

Bush Schools. While such affective and personal forms of learning
can perhaps be telescoped into days and months, other skills in a traditional society take a longer time to master. This situation has given rise
to two other institutions—neither of them schools in a fully institutionalized sense, but both lasting for longer periods of time and sharing some of the characteristics of a formal educational institution. The
first of these is the so-called bush school—a separate locus where an
individual child can learn how to perform arts, crafts, and other skills
important for the life of the community. In traditional West African
bush schools, boys and girls are enrolled for several years and are
trained as part of a secret society. The grandmaster is an individual of
high status. The youngsters are divided into groups according to ages
and aptitudes and receive instruction in the assorted lore of native life.
Included also are tests to determine individual aptitudes. There are
mock battles and skirmishes to test one's war-making abilities. As part
of involvement in the bush school, there is an initiation rite where the
youth attains a new name; those who do not show sufficient endurance
may simply be allowed to die. In some of these schools, there is a
particular stress on the historical background of the population as a
means of stimulating group consciousness, political sophistication, and
greater courage.

Apprenticeship Systems. One additional means of training those
skills that are not readily acquired by sheer imitation, or through involvement in an initiation rite, is the apprenticeship system. In the
most familiar form, as exemplified in the guilds of the late medieval
period, a youngster leaves home during the pre-adolescent or the adolescent period and goes to dwell for several years in the home of a
master of a particular craft. There he first becomes a member of the
household, running errands, watching the master at work, forming
bonds with the other apprentices and those who have already become
journeymen. When the apprentice is judged ready, he is slowly initiated into the skills of the craft, through the posing of more difficult
tasks, through constant evaluations by the master, through sharing of
the secrets of effective craftsmanship. If the lessons are well learned,
and the interpersonal tie has been properly maintained, the apprentice
has the opportunity to make his way to the higher levels of performance within the particular specialty. Admission to the society of masters itself depends upon the completion of a task or a piece that is

suitable for the particular guild. This "masterpiece" is in effect the final examination. Ultimately, the journeyman will be allowed to join the ranks of the masters, to be privy to all of their secrets, and to take on apprentices in his own atelier.

The apprenticeship system seems to have evolved in an effective form in diverse regions of the world, perhaps even independently, including many places bereft of literacy or schools. For example, the Anang of Nigeria have an apprenticeship system for the mastery of carving. While youngsters often learn from their fathers, a young man can learn to carve by paying a large stipend to, and serving a year's apprenticeship with, a master carver. There are even carving villages, where numerous individuals specialize in teaching and practicing this craft. In ancient India, technical and other craft skills became organized into guilds—a practice that may, in fact, have given rise to the Jati or caste system. In Egypt, the arabesque wood workers have long had a lengthy and intricate apprenticeship system whereby the secrets of that complex trade are slowly meted out to the most promising young individuals. And, indeed, though not usually labeled as such, the procedures whereby the adolescent Puluwat gains skills in sailing can be considered a kind of apprenticeship system. Less able students are dropped during the rigors of oral memorization or of early "trial runs" at sea, while the most successful students are eventually granted admission to the small society of master navigators.

The progression I have noted here is worth underlining. Forms of learning that are direct and unmediated suffice for relatively uncomplicated activities but may prove inadequate when a process is lengthier and features elements that are not readily observed or comprehended by the untutored eye. Once skills within a domain have reached a certain level of complexity, sheer observation or even informed interaction with the instructor will rarely suffice to yield a product of quality. Accordingly, it becomes advisable for the society to develop formal mechanisms for ensuring that youths with promise are trained to high levels of proficiency. Both the bush schools and the craft guilds are mechanisms for increasing the probability that at least the more talented males in a society will achieve the necessary level of competence. Some division of labor within the society is essential for this procedure to work.

In these forms of knowledge transmission, the technical skills—be they bodily, musical, or spatial—are rarely divorced from the interpersonal facets of life within a culture. The bush schools culminate in initiation rites, and the guilds themselves may be viewed as a kind of elaborate initiation rite, complete with secrets that are withheld, sometimes unnecessarily, simply to prolong the period of indenture. Individuals who do not possess the requisite interpersonal skills are unlikely to negotiate this series of hurdles successfully; indeed, interpersonal sensitivity may prove as important as personal courage or manual dexterity. And, ofttimes, the very opportunity to participate in the process depends upon pre-existing interpersonal ties within or between families.

The emergence of bush schools and craft guilds also marks a transition from the direct methods favored by many traditional societies to the mode of formal schooling which has arisen in the last thousand years in many parts of the world. Formal schools arise from a network of reasons, the chief one of which may be the need for an efficient and effective way of teaching reading and writing to certain of the young in a society. With the rise of schools, we behold a transition from tacit knowledge to explicit forms of knowledge, from ceremonial rituals to technical requirements, from oral preservation of knowledge to written forms of communication, from a religious orientation to a secularized stance and, eventually, to the rise of a scientific approach to knowledge. All of these are tremendously complex trends, none identical with any other; and none of them is as yet sufficiently well understood. Still, if we are to probe the educational challenges that today confront much of the world's population, it is important to try to understand the nature of schooling in its various guises and the ways in which schooling makes use of (and develops) the different intellectual potentials of individuals.

Varieties of School

KORANIC EDUCATION

Islam spans one fifth of the entire world population, covering half of the globe; and from North Africa to Indonesia, young Islamic males undergo similar forms of education. At some point between the ages of four to eight, the young child enters a Koranic school. The word *Koran* means "recitation," and the principal goal of these schools is (as it has been for centuries) the memorization of the entire Koran. Initial entry to school is an important and joyous time, marked by prayers and cele-

345

bration; but soon attention turns to the serious business at hand. At first the young child listens to the Koran being read and learns a few verses. He is introduced to the Arabic alphabet as he learns the names of the letters, what they look like, and how they are written.

From then on, learning proceeds along two parallel tracks. Part of the curriculum involves regular recitation of the Koran. The child must learn to recite the Koran using the proper rhythm and intonation, which he acquires by imitating his master slavishly. The emphasis falls on the correct sound rather than on understanding the meaning, and many individuals will commit to memory the whole Koran—a process that can take six to eight years—without comprehending the words they are speaking. Total recall of the Koran is considered a singular virtue in its own right, irrespective of whether its words are understood.

The remainder of the curriculum involves learning to read and write Arabic, a process achieved chiefly through the mastery of the Koran. First, the student learns how to trace or write the letters. Then he learns to copy whole lines from the Koran. Later steps involve learning to write from dictation and coming to understand the meaning of the words in what is, to many of the children, a foreign tongue. While most students do not go beyond these elementary literacy skills, the most diligent and successful students are eventually allowed to read other texts, to enter into discussion about the meaning of texts, to engage in the processes of argument, analysis, and interpretation.

Of course, the details of Koranic education differ in various schools, in various parts of the islamic world. The extent to which other subject matter—such as arithmetic, astronomy, poetry, or logic—is offered, and the extent to which learning of other languages, or reading of secular texts, is permitted differs widely across nations and social environments. But at the core of Islamic education everywhere, even today, is the linguistic mastery of a sacred text, a mastery that always entails oral recitation and typically involves as well the gaining of literacy in the Arabic language.

TRADITIONAL PATTERNS IN TRADITIONAL SCHOOLS

The regimen of the Koranic school, with its emphasis on rote memorization of a text in a language unfamiliar to the student, may strike contemporary readers as remote and even bizarre. It is therefore important to underscore that similar procedures and processes have characterized a range of schools that existed during the last thousand years, including many in medieval Christian Europe and other pockets of the literate world, such as the Hebrew cheder and yeshiva, the Islamic Koranic schools and madrasas, the Japanese terakoyas, the Hindu gurukulas. Following the work of Michael Fischer and of my colleagues Robert LeVine and Susan Pollak, I will indicate a number of features that characterize these traditional schools. Obviously there are instructive differences in these prototypes; but for the most part, it is remarkable how far similar features arose in disparate corners of the earth, which were hardly in constant contact with one another.

As I have already noted, these traditional schools are almost invariably religious: operated by religious individuals for religious ends. (Of course, in a society that supports traditional schools, there are few realms not permeated by religion.) The teachers are not only religious personages but are also expected to be individuals of high moral character who are afforded considerable liberty to punish wayward students (when necessary) and who are expected to serve as paragons of virtue in the community. An immoral teacher is seen almost as a contradiction in terms.

The principal curriculum in the schools, particularly for the first years of education, is simple: the student must learn how to read and write in the language of the sacred texts. As this is almost always a language other than the vernacular, the students will be involved for several years in learning a foreign language. Also, little effort is exerted to make this language familiar and "friendly" to the user; the task is to learn the language through rote drill and memorization. Typically one starts with letters of the alphabet whose strokes are copied and memorized. Words and phrases are then copied as well, and soon the student is learning to produce and to memorize the sight and the sound of lengthier passages. It is pretty much left up to the individual to work out (on his own) the elements of grammar and of the sound structure of the language. (Clearly, linguistic intelligence is at a premium here: the child so gifted—like our mythical Iranian youth—is most likely to succeed at this "decoding.") The sequence generally moves from mastering of the alphabet, to decoding of the language, to the understanding of the texts. At the highest levels, individuals are able to move on to texts other than sacred ones and, eventually, to the public interpretation of and disputation over the meaning of certain texts. But this goal takes many years to reach, and most students never get beyond the memorization of the more familiar sacred texts.

For the most part, students in these traditional schools are young males. In some communities, early education is obligatory; whereas in

347

others, it is limited (or quickly reduced) to an élite group. The first day of school is marked as a special occasion, and the child is given to understand that the opportunity to learn to read the sacred scripture is wonderful and properly marked by celebration. But pleasures become infrequent thereafter as daily drill and memorization take over. Individuals with skills in these tasks of literacy are rapidly separated from those who show little talent. A keen linguistic memory is probably the most important feature for advancement, and thus gifts or techniques for remembering well are at a premium. While memorization is often not the overt goal of the regimen, it seems to be a necessary step; after all, much of later interpretation and disputation presupposes rapid and faithful recollection of the text, which contains the relevant answers to the principal dilemmas of life, and whose existence has been the *raison d'être* for the school in the first place. There may be periodic celebrations as major milestones are passed. Those individuals who, like our Iranian youth, succeed at their studies, and are otherwise approved of by their community, are allowed to proceed to the highest level of studies—the yeshivas, the medieval universities, or the madrasa in the sacred Islamic cities. These individuals have the option of devoting their lives to scholarship; and even if they will never become as affluent as some of their peers, they are honored by their community.

While linguistic and logical abilities have obviously come to the fore in this mode of training, the interpersonal aspects of traditional education over the centuries should not be minimized. Except for those relegated to teaching the very youngest children, teachers have typically commanded great respect. In the past, much of the educational process came to center on a single magnetic figure—a guru, a mullah, a rabbi, a Confucian scholar who took promising students under his wing and helped them to scale the heights of knowledge. Moreover, a primary purpose of the schools was to maintain social cohesion in the community, which supported the schools and took great pride in the success of the best students. While talent was often recognized and often rewarded, it did not occur in an atmosphere free of personal favorites, contacts, and bonds. The secularization and impersonalization of education had still to come (and may never arrive completely).

It must be underscored that these schools did not arise in a vacuum. During the medieval period, there was considerable contact among the religious groups that lived in areas surrounding the Middle East, and even frank borrowing of certain features amongst these traditional schools. Doctrines of competing religions often served as the focus for debate among those who had entered into the ranks of "higher education." I must note as well the existence of definite differences among the systems, differences that I have ignored for the purposes of exposition, but that must be taken into account in any consideration of the traditional school. Religious schools themselves built upon earlier traditions: the training of scribes and copyists in ancient Egypt and Mesopotamia; the scholastic institutions in China and India some three thousand years ago; the Classical academies of ancient Athens, where the Iliad and the Odyssey formed the center of learning, but where music, physical development, arithmetic, geometry, astronomy, philosophy, and political leadership were all featured. Indeed, with the breakdown of the Classical world, this varied curriculum fell by the wayside: much ancient knowledge was lost, and the form of schooling which arose in the early Middle Ages was notably narrower.

There was, indeed, a general feeling in the Middle Ages, in Europe, that the amount of information to be learned was finite. Richard McKeon comments that "if you wanted to know what the culture of the twelfth century was, you could list, let's say, three thousand quotations that every intellectual would know . . . you can tabulate it." The method of teaching, even at the higher levels of learning, was largely memorization, through set question-and-answer formats, formalized definitions, or even whole lectures. Indeed, only a privileged few were allowed to participate in relatively free debate. Even at a university, students could not afford books and so had to memorize many lectures. This remained the case until the Renaissance, as can be seen by this description of an Italian Renaissance university before the widespread use of printing:

the students had no notes, grammars, lexicons or dictionaries of antiquities and mythology to help them. It was therefore necessary for the lecturer to dictate quotations, to repeat parallel passages at full length, to explain geographical and historical allusions, to analyze the structure of sentences in detail. . . . Scores of students, old and young, with nothing but pen and paper before them, sat patiently recording what the lecturer said. At the end of his discourses . . . each of them carried away a compendium volume containing a transcript of the author's text, together with a miscellaneous mass of notes, critical, explanatory, ethical, aesthetical, historical, and biographical. In other words a book had been dictated and as many scores of copies as there were attentive pupils had been made.

As Michael Fischer points out, in his instructive discussion of such traditional schools, this description could have applied to schools in Iran as late as the nineteenth century.

The factors that gave rise to the various traditional schools were diverse and cannot be considered apart from specific historical, cultural, and religious conditions. Nonetheless, the surprising similarity in form in many parts of the world and over a long time suggests that we are dealing with a variety of education that was remarkably adaptive and exploited the ways of knowing of which many individuals are capable. Building upon the role of memorization, which plays so important a role in a nonliterate society, these schools continued to cultivate the art of memory, while embroidering verbal recall skills with the ability to read (and eventually to write) texts that were not already known to the student. Recognizing the importance of a central figure as a transmitter of knowledge, these schools featured a respected and often charismatic "master" to whom students would feel a bond, and whose assessment of their progress would determine whether they could pass to the next level of achievement. While the institutions of learning were housed separately from the ongoing economic life of the community, they were scarcely estranged from the community. Rooted in religious practice, often located in temple or mosque, they were seen by all as absolutely central to the life of the community and therefore could be considered, in a sense, "on site" or "contextual." Except for books, there were few media of transmission: except for the most successful students, whose participation in disputations invoked logical skills, the featured intelligences were those linguistic and interpersonal forms that have always held sway in a traditional society. Where they differed from traditional nonliterate modes of education was in their relative indifference to spatial and bodily intelligences. Thus, while the traditional religious schools cannot be assimilated to the direct on-site learning of a Yugoslavian bard or a Puluwat sailor, their ties to the less formal institutions of learning are still apparent.

Writing a few hundred years after the heyday of the medieval traditional school, the French author Rabelais ridiculed the constraining elements in this form of education. He wrote of the great doctor of theology, Master Tubal Holofernes, who succeeded

in making his pupil stupider and stupider by forcing him to spend five years on the alphabet until he could recite it backwards, then keeping him for thirteen years, six months, and two weeks on the worst of the medieval textbooks, until he knew them backwards, too, and following that with sixteen years on the crude Late Roman compilers whose work had been all that was available for the early barbarians.

Francis Bacon, writing at the beginning of the seventeenth century, declared that "the method of discovery and proof according to which the most general principles are first established, and then intermediate axioms are tried and proved by them, is the parent of error and the curse of all science." Yet, these critiques are one-sided: medieval scholastic schooling was in many ways appropriate to the structure and the goals of the society of its time and allowed the transmission of the most important skills and knowledge in an effective way.

The decline of the traditional schools and the rise of the modern secular school occurred first in the West, particularly in England and Germany. Of crucial importance was the development of modern science and its gradual acceptance throughout Europe and North America. The many other epochal religious, political, economic, and social changes that occurred in the period from 1400 to 1800 are so well known and have so often been cited that it is unnecessary to rehearse them again here. But in their wake there arose a citizenry much more in need of formal education, much more willing to sacrifice so that its children could gain that education, much more oriented toward the sciences and toward technology, much less oriented toward the learning of sacred texts and the reading of classical literature. As each of the great industrial revolutions occurred—the revolution of textiles and heavy machinery in the eighteenth century, the revolution of chemicals, electrical engineering, and steel in the nineteenth century, the revolution of computers and information technology in the twentieth century—further changes have been wrought in the educational system. By now the modern school in Europe, the United States, the Soviet Union, Israel or Egypt, India or Japan bears little resemblance to the prototype that I have just sketched.

THE MODERN SECULAR SCHOOL

Prototypical Features. What features came to distinguish the secular schools—those modes of transmitting knowledge which will be most familiar to, if not taken for granted by, readers of this book? First of all, secular schools no longer centered upon religious texts and, in fact, began to treat all accumulated knowledge as equally within their province. Second, they were no longer manned exclusively, or even primarily, by members of the clergy; instead, there arose a set of civil servants, teachers in the employ of the state, who became the agents of instruction, and who were chosen on the basis of intellectual credentials rather than of moral fiber. Education began early in life: Erasmus recommended that it commence at three, and some modern authorities would favor an even earlier age. The family sought to contribute to education

351

in whatever ways it could: the use of the vernacular, of simple and direct forms of expression, of games, puzzles, and books written just for children became acceptable and eventually widespread. Females were permitted to study and, eventually, to teach. Finally, the overall goals of education changed. Education was designed to foster productive labor and proper citizenship within one's own country: it could also stimulate personal development and provide skills that individuals could use however they wished.

Of course, individual goals differed from one secular society to another, and the extent to which any were fully realized is debatable. Moreover, the line between traditional and secular schools must not be overdrawn: not all traditional schools were, strictly speaking, religious; and many otherwise secular schools have maintained some religious ties or moorings. But it is undeniable that most schools in the industrialized world have come to assume this secular garb.

With a shift in type of schooling have come decided alterations in the mix of intelligences. Determining for certain just which intelligences were featured, in which way, is a task for future research, and any such determination must take into account the fact that shifts affect relative emphases rather than the absolute presence or absence of a particular intelligence. Nonetheless, if one bears these caveats in mind, it is instructive to consider some of the changes that appear to have taken place over the centuries.

To begin with, the relative importance of interpersonal intelligence has been reduced in the contemporary educational scene: one's sensitivity to other individuals as individuals, one's capacity to form a close tie to a single mentor, one's ability to get along with others, to read their signals and respond appropriately assumes less importance now than it did in centuries past. In contrast, intrapersonal skills are continually—even increasingly—germane, as the individual must monitor his own reactions and plan his future course of study and, indeed, the rest of his life. Certain purely linguistic skills are less important: with the ready availability of books, it is important to be able to read quickly and to take good notes, but skills of sheer memorization and uncritical "parroting" have little importance (and may even be regarded with suspicion). Rather, a combination of linguistic and logical skills has been brought to the fore, as individuals are expected to abstract, synthesize, and criticize the texts they read, and to devise new arguments and positions to replace the contemporary wisdom. And with the rise of computers and other contemporary technologies, even the word itself takes on less importance: the individual can now perform much of his work purely through the manipulation of logical and numerical symbols. Traditional schools replaced the "direct methods" of spatial and bodily intelligences, with a stress on linguistic facility, while retaining much of the interpersonal element; the modern school places increasing premium on logical-mathematical ability and on certain aspects of linguistic intelligence, along with a newly found premium on intrapersonal intelligence. The remaining intellectual capacities are, for the most part, consigned to after-school or recreational activities, if they are taken notice of at all. It is no wonder that individuals living in societies that had only traditional schooling exhibit severe strain when they are expected to make a rapid transition to a computer-centered educational system.

An Adolescent Programmer. Let us pause for a moment to consider our hypothetical Parisian student, who is programming a musical composition on her home microcomputer. This activity presupposes the evolution of a highly industrialized and technological society, as well as a degree of affluence which allows an individual to purchase equipment that was the stuff of science fiction a generation or two ago. After all, no one can build a computer society—or a computer—from scratch.

Yet, what is striking is the extent to which our student can proceed on her own, having remarkably little interaction with other members of her culture. Equipped with the rudiments of programming, which can be acquired from a manual or a brief course, she is free to go to her terminal at will, to purchase whatever software she desires, and to produce works that meet her own desires and specifications. She is equally at liberty to revise, reject, or transform the compositions, to share them with others or keep them for herself. As much depends on her own planning, on her knowledge of what she wants and how best to achieve it, intrapersonal knowledge assumes a central role in the activities she selects and in the ways in which she evaluates them. (Similarly, she has greater leverage about important life decisions— role, mate, place of residence—than do her peers from a traditional religious culture.) In working with a computer, she is necessarily embracing logical-mathematical abilities to a far greater extent than do most individuals in most other societies. Life in a computerized society also involves a combination of logical-mathematical intelligence with other intellectual forms—most typically linguistic; but, as our Parisian student exemplifies, logical–mathematical intelligence can also be yoked to musical thinking. One may continue to exercise other intellectual capacities, such as spatial, kinesthetic, or interpersonal forms; but this pursuit remains a personal option rather than a societal imperative.

The adolescent at work with her personal computer stands at the opposite end of an educational continuum from a youth in a traditional society who is learning to hunt, plant, or make a simple tool, and is remote as well from the student at a cheder or a madrasa who is mastering a religious text. Still, it is important not to exaggerate the distinctions in the profiles of intelligence favored across different school settings. Certainly interpersonal relationships retain importance in some modern educational contexts: for example, much of graduate education, in the sciences no less than in the arts, is based upon the forging of a close link between the master professor and his promising students. While intellectual strengths of a nonpersonal sort may underlie the initiation of the link, its preservation over a long period of time constitutes an important ingredient in the younger colleagues' eventual success within a field. It is also worth noting that nearly every society with modern secular schools has in some way tried to preserve aspects of traditional schooling. A society may have after-school religious education or weekend "Sunday schools." There are frequently special schools for Hebrew or Islamic studies which individuals attend in addition to their secular schools. In Japan, teachers often cultivate certain traditional values in their regular classrooms, while their students attend after-school "jukus" designed in secular fashion to prepare them for the rigorous college entrance examinations they must eventually pass. In India, the "patashalas" exist to provide secular treatment of many disciplines, while the "gurukulas" are a throwback to an earlier era. And, even within the modern West, one can also discern an attempt to maintain the classical orientation of the earlier traditional schools alongside the more scientific orientation of the modern secular schools. Thus we have high schools of the arts and of Latin as opposed to technical high schools, and *Humanistische* as opposed to *Technische Gymnasia*. And we can also contrast "terminal" elementary schools, devised to ensure that individuals will have some rudiments of literacy before they take jobs as laborers or farmers, with élite private schools, where aspects of classical education continue to be stressed even as a certain proportion of individuals is introduced to the lore and the methods of the sciences. Finally, the numerous optional or extracurricular activities available in developed countries ensure that the full range of intelligences can be cultivated, given time, desire, and a certain measure of affluence.

Critiques of Schooling. Since modern secularized schools have been a reality for many years throughout much of the West, our society has had the opportunity to reflect upon this institution, to identify its weak points as well as its strengths. We have been able to consider what may have been lost by an adoption of schooling in general and by an uncritical acceptance, during the past century, of modern secularized schooling, with its focus on certain uses of mind and its relative lack of integration with the long-term spiritual and moral life of the community. This soul-searching has given rise, in recent decades, to blistering attacks on schooling by the gamut of educationally oriented scholars. There are Ivan Illich, who has called on us to "de-school society"; Paolo Freire, who objects to the use of schools as élite tools for manipulating oppressed people; Ronald Dore, who condemns the credentialing function of schooling, where the focus lies on obtaining a diploma, when there are few jobs available for the certified; Ulric Neisser, who decries the narrow academic skills which reign in the classroom; Christopher Jencks (along with various other American commentators), who claims that schools as a whole do not even attain their avowed goals of helping individuals scale the ladder of success (social class background and luck prove more important); and nostalgic commentators like Michael Maccoby and Nancy Modiano who declare:

If the peasant child is not dulled by village life, he will experience the uniqueness of events, objects, and people. But as the city child grows older, he may end by exchanging a spontaneous less alienated relationship with the world for a more sophisticated outlook which concentrates on using, exchanging, or cataloguing. What industrialized urban man gains in an increased ability to formulate, to reason, and to code the ever more numerous bits of complex information he requires, he may lose in a decreased sensitivity to people and to events.

These critics need not necessarily carry the day. A recent influential study by Michael Rutter and his colleagues in London indicates that schools can make a positive difference in the lives of children. If a school has sufficient resources, a competent principal, an emphasis on teaching by teachers who are punctual and responsible, and a clear and justly administered system of rewards and demerits, then children will tend to learn more, to like school better, and to avoid delinquent behavior. Similar reports come from the challenging environment of New York City. Principals and principles matter! And for populations who are disadvantaged, a program of early enrichment which begins to develop intellectual skills in the first years of life, can have measurable long-term effects on student attitudes and achievement.

It is not my purpose here, however, to take issue (or sides) with the defenders or the critics of schools. Rather, my analytic framework may help to identify those features of modern schools which are part of

355

their explicit program, as well as some of the consequences that may be unintended side-effects of such schooling. Among those observers partial to spatial, bodily, or musical forms of knowing, as well as those who favor a focus on the interpersonal aspects of living, an inclination to indict contemporary schooling is understandable. The modern secular school has simply—though it need not have—neglected these aspects of intellectual competence. In contrast, those commentators who favor the cultivation of logical-mathematical and intrapersonal skills and the utilization of meritocratic rather than subjective measures of quality find much to admire in the modern school. Still, it is worth noting that among the factors that contribute to the effectiveness of schools are the personal qualities of the principal and the teachers. Despite promises of a microcomputer alongside (or, in place of) every desk, these individuals cannot be replaced, at least not yet.

While the actual effects and effectiveness of modern schools can (and will continue to) be debated, the overall impact of a schooled society (as against one without formal education) is rarely a matter of dispute. It seems evident to nearly all observers that attendance at school for more than a few years produces an individual—and, eventually a collectivity—who differs in important (if not always easy to articulate) ways from members of a society that lacks formal schooling. There are, of course, differences between the traditional and the modern secular schools: in terms of our overall framework, a society featuring the traditional school may be thought of as marking an intermediate point between a society without any formal schooling and a society dominated by modern secular schools.

Three Features of Modern Education

Whatever its preferred mode of transmitting knowledge, nearly every society in the contemporary world has had to confront the accomplishments of the modern "industrialized," or "developed," world. And few societies, whatever their doubts about the European, the American, or the Japanese examples, have been able to turn their backs on the educational systems of these societies and to remain content with their traditional forms of knowledge transmission.

In order to make informed decisions about which paths to follow and which to abjure, educational planners have sought to understand better the effects and implications of the principal features of education in the developed world—such features as enrollment in a secular school, acquisition of literacy, and mastery of the scientific method. Each of these areas is enormous, and none is as yet well understood. Moreover, they tend to be correlated with one another: most contemporary schools in the developed world feature several literacies as well as scientific thought, and so it is scarcely a straightforward matter to disentangle the effects of each and to determine the ways in which they typically interact. Nonetheless, given the importance of these factors in any contemporary educational equation, it is germane to consider what is known about each form, whenever possible in isolation, and to see whether its features can be illuminated by the framework that I have introduced earlier in this chapter.

SCHOOLING

With these caveats in mind, we may consider the features that are generally believed to accompany this trio of factors. Probably the effects of schooling have been most often probed. Authorities generally agree that, outside of schooled settings, children acquire skills through observation and participation in the contexts in which these skills are customarily invoked. In contrast, in the standard classroom, teachers talk, often presenting material in abstract symbolic form and relying on inanimate media such as books and diagrams in order to convey information. Schooling generally treats subject matter that one cannot readily see or touch, even as those sensory modes of taking in information seem singularly inappropriate for most school tasks (except for the visual act of reading). Children skilled in the ways of school are accustomed to the presentation of problems and tasks, often out of context, and learn to tackle these assignments just because they are there. Children learn to look for clues, to devise steps and strategies, and to search doggedly for answers that are not known. Some of the skills learned in school prove to be general: once one can read, one can read a book on any topic; once one can write, one can write on many topics; skills of calculation, diagram reading, and the like are similarly versatile. Indeed, dealing with notational systems altogether may be a chief survival skill inculcated in school.

Surveying a wide range of studies, Michael Cole and Roy D'Andrade indicate some of the consequences that one can regularly expect following years of schooling. Individuals who have been to school regularly outperform those who have not, on tasks where one must focus

357

on language itself, where specialized information-processing strategies (like chunking) are required, or where one must spontaneously use certain taxonomic classification systems (putting together objects that belong to the same superordinate class). Conversely, one typically finds little or no difference between schooled and unschooled populations on tasks where materials are familiar, where the kinds of relationship sought after are functional, or where the desired modes of classification have been modeled in a familiar and non-threatening situation. Such findings underscore the effectiveness of school in calling attention to language and in teaching students to classify in certain ways and to use certain informational approaches. The missing skills may well be trainable even in unschooled children, but it is important to stress that they do not arise spontaneously in the course of tackling tasks typically posed by experimental investigators.

In terms of our framework, then, schooling involves a novel site of learning (outside of the usual context where skills are deployed for productive labor), with specialized agents of transmission and numerous media of transmission that are not generally featured in a non-schooled environment. This combination, in turn, cultivates mental skills that are difficult to acquire when transmission of knowledge occurs only in on-site, unmediated contexts. A more sophisticated and self-conscious use of language may well be a byproduct of most schooling, even as a new set of literacies and a commitment to logical thinking are frequent concomitants. The forms of personal knowledge will differ depending upon the kind of school; while, in general, spatial, bodily-kinesthetic, and musical forms of knowing will have only an incidental or an optional status. Differences in schools will depend chiefly on whether they tend toward the traditional religious model—where linguistic and interpersonal forms are at the fore—or toward the modern secular pole—where logical-mathematical and intrapersonal forms of intelligence prove most germane to the goals of the system. It should be noted that in some societies, such as Japan, strong efforts are made to foster interpersonal knowledge within the formal school setting. Furthermore, in some strict traditional schools, such as the Koranic ones which focus only upon reading and writing, some of the cognitive revolutions associated with secular schooling may not occur.

LITERACY

Turning next to the effects of literacy, we find discussions of a somewhat separate, though certainly related set of skills. Like schooling, literacy encourages fresh and, in many ways, more reflective attention to language. In a nonliterate society, language tends to be invisible: all that is noticed are the effects of what has been said. In contrast, in a literate society, the individual becomes aware that there are elements like words, that they are combined in certain acceptable ways (grammar), and that these linguistic elements can themselves be referred to (meta-language). Individuals learn that it is possible to be precise and unambiguous in articulating what one means, to have a completely accurate record of what has been said, and to distinguish between what may have been meant ("Pass the salt") and what has actually been said ("Would you mind passing the salt?"). Literate persons become able to relate readily with one another in other than a direct face-to-face manner: they can even come to know someone whom they have never met and, if correspondence is possible, establish a relationship with that individual. Interpersonal relations can take on a new, hitherto almost inconceivable flavor.

It may well be that, at least in certain contexts, the ability to read and write encourages a more abstract form of thinking, for one can now define terms with precision, refer back to facts and definitions that were presented some time before, and weigh the logical and persuasive elements of an argument. The capacity to employ various symbolized notations enables one to supplement one's memory, organize one's future activities, and communicate at one time with an indefinite number of individuals (the set of all potential readers).

Mastery of different literacies—for example, reading musical scores, mathematical proofs, or intricate diagrams—exposes one to once-inaccessible bodies of knowledge and allows one to contribute new knowledge within these traditions. And literacy may also have profound social consequences: the individual who can write may not only place himself in a powerful situation vis-à-vis his illiterate contemporaries but may also establish a reputation as a certain kind of person. For instance, if he maintains faithful records of public transactions and uses them judiciously, he can serve as a kind of "honest broker" or judge of the behavior of other individuals. No wonder that chiefs of nonliterate societies are often observed to feign literacy as soon as they become aware of its existence!

So much for the alleged consequences of literacy. Even as Michael Cole and his colleagues have helped us to understand the effects (and the limits) of years spent in school, they have recently added materially to our understanding of the implications of literacy. Taking advantage of a unique experiment in culture, Cole, Sylvia Scribner, and their colleagues spent several years studying a group of Vai individuals in Liberia. This population is special because some inhabitants are literate only in English, some are literate only in Arabic (acquired in the study of the Koran), and about 20 percent of the adult Vai males have learned a special script restricted to their geographical region: a syllabary devised in the nineteenth century primarily for writing letters and keeping personal records. Though used for these valued purposes, the Vai script does not entail any contact with new knowledge or record scientific, philosophical, or literary information.

The Cole team uncovered the surprising fact that attaining even a high degree of literacy in one of these systems does not in itself produce widespread cognitive consequences. In fact, it is the attending of school, rather than the acquisition of literacy *per se*, that produces most of the aforementioned differences in problem solving, classification and analytic skills, and even that sensitivity to language which might seem part and parcel of an immersion in literacy. What mastery of each script does accomplish, however, is the enhancing of certain skills integral to the practice of that particular literacy. Thus, Vai literates prove better than other individuals at integrating syllables into meaningful linguistic units; Arabic literates have a selective ability to remember a string of words (as they must do in learning the Koran) but are otherwise not remarkable. On this analysis, literacy should be seen not as a panacea for various cognitive deficiencies but, rather, as a set of specific cognitive skills that may have some generality but do not by any means change a worldview. It is literacy in the context of schooling which alters a larger family of linguistic and cognitive operations.

We see, then, that a particular languagelike skill need not have the revolutionary effects that typically surround it in a schooled situation. Consistent with the theory of this book, a particular use of linguistic intelligence does not necessarily implicate other intellectual strands. True, a general concern with literacies and notations is likely to produce an individual who is both aware of the possibilities of recoding information and facile in acquiring additional literacies (for example, new programming languages for the computer). Moreover, occurring as it typically does in a schooled setting, the acquisition of literacies enables the individual to master much additional information in a context-free setting. In a sense, reading opens up the world. But the Scribner-Cole study reminds us that we must be careful before assuming that any new form of education necessarily entails broad consequences. And indeed, as one considers the vast differences between a bush school and a traditional religious school, or between a traditional religious school and a modern secular school, it seems clear that the kind of school makes as big an intellectual difference as the fact of schooling *per se*.

SCIENCE

The chief pretender in our times to an altering of worldviews is our third factor—science, that body of procedures and findings which arose in the Renaissance and its aftermath and has led to many of the most important innovations of our time. The adoption of scientific and technological measures has made possible unprecedented affluence (as well as numerous unanticipated physical and social upheavals): no corner has escaped its effects or its appeal.

In the scientific method, at least two aspects work hand in hand. On the one side, there is an interest in collecting facts, a desire to be objectively empirical and to find out as much as one can about a subject matter, along with a willingness (or even eagerness) to change one's mind in the light of new facts. Complementing this descriptive aspect of science is the building of an explanatory superstructure—a theoretical framework which explains the nature of, and the relations among, objects and forces, how they come about, what can make them change, and under what conditions such changes are likely to take place. The theoretical structure depends upon reasoning: deductive reasoning, where implications are drawn from general assumptions; and inductive reasoning, where general principles are arrived at from the examination of individual cases. These elements existed to some extent in Classical times (certainly in Aristotle's vicinity) and also in other corners of the world for many years, but it is the particular genius of European culture after the Middle Ages to have brought them together into a "scientific synthesis" whose results have already been dramatic and whose ultimate effects are incalculable.

Much discussion of the differences between the modern and the "traditional," "pre-literate," or "primitive" mind centers around the role of scientific thinking. Authorities like Claude Lévi-Strauss have argued that the traditional mind is not fundamentally different from the modern mind: the same operations are used but applied to different materials. In fact, primitive science is best viewed simply as a science of the concrete, whose operations can be seen at work as individuals classify objects or weave mythic explanations. Other observers in sympathy with pre-modern ways of thinking have criticized Western science for spawning an ethnocentrism about our current way of making sense of the world, which they see as simply one of numerous equivalent worldviews.

On the other side, authorities like Robin Horton have argued, to my mind rather convincingly, that while both scientific and nonscientific or pre-scientific ways of thinking are efforts to explain the world, there remains a fundamental difference between them. Specifically, in its effort to explain the world, the scientific mind includes a credo that involves the positing of hypotheses, the stipulation of the conditions under which a hypothesis can be rejected, and the willingness to abandon the hypothesis and to entertain a new one should the original one be disconfirmed. Hence, the system is inherently open to change. The pre-modern or nonscientific mind has available all the same thought processes as has the scientific mind, but the system within which the former works is essentially closed: all premises have already been stated in advance, all inferences must follow from them, and the explanatory system is not altered in the light of the new information that has been procured. Rather, in the manner described in my discussion of traditional religious education, one's rhetorical powers are simply mobilized to provide ever more artful justifications of the conclusions, the worldviews, that were already known in advance and for all time.

Even if one accepts (as many do not) this difference between scientific and nonscientific thinking, it is important not to exaggerate its pervasiveness or decisiveness. When it comes to cosmic matters, individuals in nonscientific societies may well reason in a closed manner; yet it seems much less likely that they adopt this mode of reasoning in every-day matters. Unless they use an essentially experimental method in daily life—for example, rejecting foods that make one sick—they cannot survive. By the same token, even if Western scientists do indeed employ a method of reasoning which has allowed them to build the ever-changing structures of science, it is scarcely the case that they stand, in the rest of their lives, immune from aspects of closed thinking. In addition to whatever superstitious, mystical, or religious beliefs many of us hold onto unswervingly, an overall belief in science can be viewed as a kind of a myth, one that scientists are as loath to relinquish as our nonscientific brethren are reluctant to abandon their own mythic-poetic systems.

Though scientific thinking may well yield a different worldview, one fundamentally alien to and even incommensurate with nonscientific worldviews, it need not entail a new form of intelligence. Rather, I think that the scientist is characterized by a willingness to use linguistic and logical-mathematical modes of thought in areas where they have customarily not been used before (for example, the devising of new notational systems or the positing of testable theories) and to combine them with careful observation in ways that have not generally been employed. Put differently, the components of the scientific method have existed for thousands of years, in any number of societies, ranging from ancient China to Classical Greece to medieval Islamic society. It has been the special genius of modern science to combine these sensory, logical, and linguistic approaches in a new way and to dissociate them from the personal and religious forms of knowing in which they have been hitherto embedded.

Just as it is possible to have literacy without the effects of schooling, it is possible to have schooling without the effects of science. Indeed, both the informal schools of the nonliterate society and the traditional schools of the literate society have existed for many years without any involvement in the scientific world. It is even possible to feature logical-mathematical thinking within the traditional school setting: in such instances, sophisticated linguistic and logical-mathematical abilities are harnessed in order to justify certain predetermined conclusions. What distinguishes contemporary science, whether or not it is practiced in a schooled setting, is a particular use of logical-mathematical thinking in order systematically to investigate new possibilities, to develop fresh explanatory frameworks, to test those frameworks, and then to revise or scuttle them in the light of the results. Interpersonal ties may well be important in the mastery of the scientific method—particularly for one who wants to collaborate with other workers; but in practice, much scientific work involves an immersion in one's own thought processes, and achievement of one's own ensemble of goals, ranging from the development of a particular computer program to an entirely novel scientific explanation. These activities exploit the intrapersonal rather than the interpersonal forms of understanding. In sum, while scientific thinking does not in itself entail any new form of intelligence, it represents a combination of intelligences that has hitherto not been utilized in this particular way. This form of thinking is possible only in settings with certain goals and values—witness the moving plight of Galileo in his struggle with the Church or of contemporary scientists in totalitarian societies. Like schooling and literacy, science is a social invention to which human intelligences can be marshaled only if the society is willing to accept the consequences.

The Three Youths Revisited

I have in this chapter examined, in schematic fashion, a large number of trends. I have observed that, as one effects a transition from "direct" forms of knowledge to informal forms of schooling, from informal to traditional schooling, and from traditional to modern schools, there has been a steady minimization of bodily, spatial and interpersonal forms of knowledge—first in favor of linguistic forms, and then, increasingly, in favor of logical-mathematical and intrapersonal forms of thinking.

This shift of emphasis can be seen clearly as one considers the skills utilized by the three hypothetical students. The Puluwat sailor relies primarily on his bodily and spatial capacities: linguistic abilities assume importance at one point in the learning process, while logical-mathematical capacities are scarcely at a premium. Both the Puluwat youth and the Iranian adolescent are embedded in an interpersonal situation: each youth's relationship to the elders who will instruct him assumes great importance for the success of the educational encounter. But where the Puluwat youth learns primarily in the "natural" context of sailing, the Iranian youth is mastering a far less transparent body of knowledge in a setting remote from significant daily activities. He is therefore thrown more squarely upon his linguistic capacities, which must include not only skills in rote verbal memory but ultimately the ability to "crack the code" of the Arabic language.

An equally sizable gulf separates the Iranian youth from the Parisian composer at her computer terminal. While the skills necessary for the mastery of music and computing may well have been acquired in an interpersonal setting, this adolescent works chiefly alone: she must engage in a great deal of solitary planning about what she proposes to do and how she expects to carry it out. Thus, a much greater emphasis is placed upon the cultivation of intrapersonal intelligence and an autonomous sense of self. Far more than her youthful counterparts in other parts of the world, she also must rely on logical-mathematical skills: successful writing of a program depends upon cultivated abilities in the numerical and inferential spheres. Of course, as a composer, she is also dealing with musical elements—indeed, these will be central to her work. Were she involved in videographics or in spatial reasoning, she would be relying on still other forms of intelligence. By virtue of her engagement with computers, this youth must inevitably deal with linguistic codes as well: but since various handbooks are available, she has no need to rely on the extensive memorization prized by the Iranian and Puluwat youths. Once she has learned to read, this skill can serve as an aid to the acquisition of required forms of logical and mathematical knowledge.

Of course, outside their particular learning settings, these individuals retain the options of using a much wider set of intelligences, and there is no reason to think that they do not do so. Life consists of more than the deployment of particular combinations of intelligence for specific educational purposes. I must also point out that these intelligences are not mutually exclusive of one another. Cultivation of one intelligence does not imply that others cannot be acquired: some individuals (and some cultures) may develop several intelligences to a keen extent, while others may highlight only one or two. One should not think of intelligences as involved in a zero sum situation: nor should one treat the theory of multiple intelligences as a hydraulic model, where an increase in one intelligence necessarily entails a decrease in another. Still, on a statistical basis, it seems reasonable to speculate that different individuals—and different cultures—place their bets differently in their deployment of intelligences.

It is possible to interpret the transition from the sailor to the Koranic scholar to the computer programmer as the course of progress; and, indeed, from the perspective of Western experience, the ability of an individual to create works of art upon a computer can be seen as a crowning achievement. But it is equally possible to see this sequence of episodes as a systematic devaluation of certain forms of intelligence, such as interpersonal, spatial, or bodily intelligence, and as a destruction of certain important linguistic capacities. No less an authority than Socrates declared (with respect to the advent of writing):

For this invention of yours will produce forgetfulness in the minds of those who learn it, by causing them to neglect their memory inasmuch as, from the confidence in writing they will recollect by the external aid of foreign symbols and not by the internal use of their own faculty.

The invention of various technological aids may, paradoxically, leave an individual less well prepared to rely on his own abilities. And the sequence witnessed in the Western world is certainly not the only conceivable one and, quite possibly, not the optimal one.

The evolution from a pre-scientific to a scientific way of thinking, from observational learning to schooling, and from nonliteracy to literacy may have worked with some smoothness in the West and in certain other regions of the world. The story of the West is, however, not a

365

universal saga, and it is a grave mistake to assume that it should be. In my view, many of the most problematic aspects of modernization have resulted from an uncritical attempt to apply the model and the history of the West to alien traditions, with different histories, different traditions of education, and different favored blends of intelligence. Just how to balance these various factors to produce effective educational systems is a most vexing question, which I can hardly pretend to be able to answer. However, in the concluding chapter, I want to offer some speculations about how my theoretical framework might prove germane to such an effort.

14

The Application
of Intelligences

Intelligences in the Air

In April of 1980, I visited the Suzuki Talent Education Center in Matsumoto, Japan. There I met with individuals who administered the program and attended a concert by youngsters enrolled in the various
classes at the center. The performances were virtually incredible. Children as young as seven or eight were playing movements from violin
concerti drawn from the concert repertoire; a pre-adolescent played a
virtuoso piece of the Romantic era; children hardly old enough to hold
a violin performed in startling unison a number of pieces that any
Western schoolchild would be proud to have mastered. The youngsters
performed with style, gusto, and accuracy, clearly enjoying themselves
and clearly giving satisfaction to the audience—largely mothers of the
performers—who were leaning eagerly forward, lest they miss a single
bowing. Indeed, the only individual who seemed discomfited was a
talented cellist of perhaps eleven, whose performance was being vigor-
ously—though not unkindly—criticized by a visiting master cellist
from Europe.

Clearly, if I had simply heard one of the Suzuki preschoolers play
an instrument while he remained hidden behind a curtain, I would
have thought the performance to be by a much older child. Indeed, I
would probably have concluded that the child was a prodigy (or a

367

fraud) if I had been told that he was only three or four years of age. And, in using the term *prodigy*, I would probably have been attributing to the luck of heredity what is actually a talent nurtured through a shrewd educational intervention. On the other hand, I think it would be equally mistaken to infer that genetic factors have been invariably absent in other examples of early musical precocity. Had I the opportunity to listen to the youthful Mozart, or to an autistic child who is able to sing hundreds of melodies, I would in all likelihood have been witnessing the fruition of a strong hereditary inclination.

I have taken some pains in this book to avoid pitting genetic against cultural factors. Social scientists need a framework that, while taking into account genetic predisposition and neurobiological factors, recognizes the formative role played by the environment. Even if the individuals enrolled in the Suzuki class are to some extent a selected group, the scions of musically gifted families, they clearly reached such heights of performance at at youthful age because of the ingenuity of the program and the dedication displayed by their parents. More on that later. In this chapter, I shall be concerned with the ways in which the theory of multiple intelligences may help us to understand better the reasons for the effectiveness—or the ineffectiveness—of various programs designed to help individuals realize their potential. And, in conclusion, drawing on the framework introduced in chapter 13, I will set forth some principles that may help planners and policy makers think through more effectively the goals and the means of various contemplated interventions.

As compared with one hundred or even with thirty years ago, talk about the development of intelligence, the realization of human potential, and the role of education is very much in the international air. These topics are being explored not only by the usual lobbying groups but also by such unexpected (and unexpectedly formidable) institutions as banks for economic development and national governments. Rightly or wrongly, the powers-that-be in the worlds of international development and national sovereignty have become convinced that the ingredients for human progress, success, and happiness are closely linked to better educational opportunities for their client citizenry and, particularly, for young individuals. This provides, to my mind, a rare opportunity for the psychological and the pedagogical sciences to show that they have some usefulness. If this opportunity is not exploited, it is unlikely to present itself again for some time.

Judiciously, but clearly audibly, an organization like the World Bank questions a policy of exclusive funding for agriculture and tech-

368

nological enterprises and, instead, calls for investment in human development and education. Robert S. McNamara, then president of the Bank, declared in a 1980 speech, "Development is clearly not economic progress measured in terms of gross national product. It is something much more basic: it is essentially human development, that is the individual's realization of his or her inherent potential." He went on to note that human development—which he defined as better education, health, nutrition, and family planning at the local level—promotes economic growth as effectively as does capital investment in physical plans. In *Learning to Be*, the prestigious UNESCO report of 1972, Edgar Faure, former prime minister of France, and his colleagues made the provocative statement that "the human brain has a very large unused potential which some authorities—more or less arbitrarily—have assessed at 90 percent." The job of education—to realize this unused potential.

Consistent with these sentiments, the international "think-tank" the Club of Rome commissioned a report on how education and learning might assume their proper roles in the world of today and tomorrow. As the president of the Club, Aurelio Peccei, declared:

any solutions to the human gap as well as any guarantees for the human future can be sought nowhere else but within ourselves.What is needed is for all of us to *learn* [Peccei's italics] how to stir up our dormant potential and use it from now on purposefully and intelligently.

The authors of the resulting volume, *No Limits to Learning*, concurred that "for all practical purposes there appear to be virtually no limits to learning." As their chosen vehicle for bridging the various gaps and solving the vexing problems that plague contemporary societies, they recommended *innovative learning*: a second-order learning in which individuals plan in concert for the kind of world which is likely to evolve in the future, and take joint actions to exploit opportunities and avoid disasters. As they describe it:

Innovative learning is problem formulation and clustering. Its main attributes are integration, synthesis, and the broadening of horizons. It operates in open ... situations or open systems. Its meaning derives from dissonance among contexts. It leads to critical questioning of conventional assumptions behind traditional thoughts and actions, focusing on necessary changes. Its values are not constant, but rather shifting. Innovative learning advances our thinking by reconstructing wholes, not by fragmenting reality.

The tone of this passage reflects accurately the flavor of the study as a whole. Laudable in its aspirations, and hortatory in its exposition, the Club of Rome report invokes a capacity that would clearly be of greatest utility to develop both in individuals and in collectivities. The problem with the report, however, is that it contains little in the way of concrete suggestions about how anticipatory learning might be inculcated, equally little about possible biological and cultural constraints upon adopting such an enlightened, unselfish, and forward-looking orientation toward particular problems. The report remains mired at the level of slogans.

Far less circumspect is the astonishing platform on which stands Luis Alberto Machado, a Venezuelan politician, the first and (so far as can be ascertained) the only minister in the world for the Development of Human Intelligence. Surveying the world's philosophical thinkers and the range of human sciences, Minister Machado has reached the conclusion that every human being has the potential to become intelligent. Consider some of his statements:

we all have the same potentialities which throughout life are incarnated in different ways according to each person's existence

man is offered unlimited possibilities, that are materialized through learning and teaching

Einstein learned intelligence in the same way that a person learns to play the piano "by ear"

government should be, then, the teaching of intelligence

the development of man's intelligence allows him to rationally direct the biological evolution of his own species and to eradicate chance and need from the entire process of that evolution

the free intelligence of every man is also the image and likeness of God's intelligence

Based on this optimistic analysis of the capacity of human beings to become geniuses (in Machado's phrase), he and his colleagues have embarked on an ambitious program to raise the intelligence of the Venezuelan populace:

We [Venezuelans] are going to completely transform our educational system. We are going to teach how to develop intelligence every day, from kindergarten to college, and we are going to teach parents, especially mothers, how to teach their children from the moment of their birth, and even before, how to develop all of their capabilities. In this manner we will be offering our people and all the peoples of the world a real new future.

With the collaboration of scientists from all over the world (but chiefly from the West), the Machado Project features fourteen separate programs, initially developed elsewhere, which are now being injected into Venezuelan contexts, ranging from the nursery and the elementary school to the work setting and the military.

The grandiosity of the Machado Project is there for all to see and is perhaps too inviting a target for cynical observers of the world scene. It would be easy to take potshots at this overly ambitious and perhaps somewhat ill-conceived undertaking and to show why it is unlikely to succeed in its avowed terms. After all, we really know little about what intelligence is (or what intelligences are), about how such capacities can be better developed, and about how to implant into an alien setting a set of skills which evolved under one set of historical and cultural circumstances. The same kind of critique could be initiated with equal facility with reference to other contemporary grandiose programs, such as those launched by the Institutes for the Achievement of Human Potential in Philadelphia. This eccentric organization claims to be able to teach the whole range of "school skills" to toddlers, even to those who have suffered brain damage, and it blithely contends in its workbook of "cardinal facts" that "our genetic potential is that of Leonardo, Shakespeare, Mozart, Michelangelo, Edison, and Einstein." Unfortunately, however, this organization has not, to my knowledge, allowed objective evaluators to assess the success of its interventions.

But such hatchet jobs are more likely to give momentary pleasure to the wielder of the ax than genuine profit to practitioners earnestly trying to better the skills and the knowledge base of growing human populations. The obligation of the pragmatically oriented social scientist is to offer a better set of tools and to suggest how, when adopted, these would be more likely to culminate in positive results, less likely to engender another set of dashed expectations. In what follows, I undertake some modest efforts in this direction.

Using M.I. Theory to Elucidate Examples

INTRODUCTION

Attempts to think about human intelligence should begin with a confrontation of what the human species is like, and with a consideration of the spheres in which its members are inclined to perform effectively, given adequate resources and timely interventions. From these perspectives, invocations of "no limits to learning" are of little utility: not only is it false to think that a human being can do anything; but where everything is possible, there are no guidelines about what ought to be attempted and what not. My seven "core" forms of intelligence are an effort to lay out seven intellectual regions in which most human beings have the potential for solid advancement, and to suggest some of the milestones that will be passed as these intellectual competences are realized, by gifted individuals and by individuals who, though entirely normal, apparently possess no special gifts in a given realm.

We have seen, however, that except perhaps in the case of certain exceptional individuals, these intellectual competences never develop in a vacuum. Rather, they become mobilized by symbolizing activities in ongoing cultures where they have practical meaning and tangible consequences. Thus, the inborn capacity to process certain (linguistic) sounds in certain ways becomes exploited for human communication through speaking and, in many contexts, through writing. Ultimately, these nurtured abilities become central in certain social roles, ranging from the lawyer or the poet in contemporary Western civilization to an oral storyteller, shaman, or political leader in a traditional society.

A lengthy educational process is necessary before the raw intellectual potential—be it linguistic, musical, or logical-mathematical—can be realized in the form of a mature cultural role. Part of this process simply involves certain "natural" processes of development, whereby a capacity passes through a predictable set of stages as it matures and is differentiated. I have noted some of the developmental milestones that occur in the area of language, and could provide similar portraits of "streamlike" development in other intellectual realms. But when it comes to the transmission of specific skills and knowledge, one beholds a more complex, less "natural" process at work. I made an initial effort, in the previous chapter, to analyze this process of transmission by noting the kind of knowledge that is to be transmitted, the agents of transmission, the modes or media by which the knowledge is to be transmitted, and the locus of transmission. To my mind, an analogous analysis ought to be conducted whenever a policy maker recommends that some educational course be followed.

Through such an analysis, it becomes evident that human intellectual competences can be mobilized in a variety of ways. As I have already noted, human linguistic competence can become the method whereby some other nonlinguistic skill is acquired: language is often exploited as an aid in teaching an individual some bodily process (like a dance) or some mathematical process (like a proof). Language itself can constitute a subject matter, as, for instance, when an individual is learning his own language, or another tongue, or is mastering a subject matter that is in itself highly linguistic in content—like history or political science. Finally, developmental factors surrounding linguistic competence are also relevant: if, for example, individuals exhibit the highest aptitude for learning language during the first ten years of life, and a diminished ability to do so after the second decade; and if, furthermore, young children are especially able to master materials through rote learning of associations—then, these facts, too, must enter any equation describing the transmission of knowledge.

This brief aside indicates, I hope, that the adoption of a perspective like M.I. theory may permit a more differentiated and precise analysis of how various educational goals might be viewed and pursued. It should be pointed out, once again, that even if one's cognitive mechanisms are in order, educational progress will not necessarily result. Most contemporary psychological analyses assume an individual eager to learn; but, in fact, such factors as proper motivation, an affective state conducive to learning, a set of values that favors a particular kind of learning, and a supporting cultural context are indispensable (though often elusive) factors in the educational process. Indeed, one of the Venezuelan-supported research projects has concluded that proper motivation to learn may well be the single biggest difference between a successful and an unsuccessful educational program (and learner). Be that as it may, analysis of educational experiments must attend to such factors as motivation, personality, and value: the fact that my own analysis focuses heavily on "purely cognitive components" must be considered a limitation of the present formulation.

THE SUZUKI TALENT EDUCATION METHOD

Returning to the opening example, it should be possible (and certainly desirable) to explain something of the success of the Suzuki music program through our framework of human intelligences. Before doing so, it is helpful to provide some more information about this unusual and unusually effective experiment. For these details, I draw upon my observations at Matsumoto and on my own experiences as a Suzuki parent, as well as on the valuable study of the Suzuki program undertaken by Lois Taniuchi at Harvard.

The Talent Education Program, devised just before the Second

World War by a sensitive Japanese violinist Shinichi Suzuki, is a carefully structured technique of music education which begins virtually at birth and has as a principal goal the training of accomplished musical performance in young children. Crucial to success in the program is the child's mother, who, particularly at the beginning, is the locus of the program and remains throughout a vital catalyst for child involvement and progress.

In a typical version of the program, as perfected in Japan and recently adopted in other countries, the child is exposed daily during the first year of life to recordings of great performances. Toward the end of the first year of life, the child begins to hear, on a fairly regular basis, the twenty short songs that will constitute his curriculum once he begins to study an instrument.

Six months before beginning his own lessons, at perhaps the age of two, the child starts to attend group lessons. These lessons, which last perhaps an hour and a half, bring together children of different ages and levels of performance, covering a total age span of perhaps two or three years. The children attend with their mothers who participate with the children and the teacher in a group of games and exercises. The lessons themselves are divided between general exercises in which all children participate and from which all children are expected to benefit, and short performances by each of the students of the pieces on which they have been working. The future student listens attentively and participates to the extent that he can. At these lessons, he has an opportunity to observe what he will be doing in his own lessons once they have begun. The emphasis always falls on one's own progress from one week to the next, never on competition with the other youngsters.

Meanwhile, back at home, the child's own interest in playing is being deliberately aroused. The mother has received a small violin, of the same size that the child himself will one day play, and begins to perform by herself each day. (If she does not know how to play the violin, she takes lessons of the same sort that her child will soon be taking.) The child watches with mounting excitement, and finally one day the mother allows the child to touch the instrument himself. This is a thrilling moment. Shortly thereafter, when mother and teacher decide that the child's interest has reached a fever pitch, the child is invited to join the group he has been observing, and is given an individual lesson on his own instrument. Another milestone has been passed. The mother and child then go home and work very hard on the lesson in order to surprise the teacher with the youngster's progress during the week interval. Over the next months, mother-and-child lessons and practice continue together: gradually the mother's involvement as an active student and fiddler stops, and the attention focuses completely on the child.

Over the next years, the child follows faithfully a curriculum that has been worked out with painstaking care by Suzuki and his colleagues. The agents, loci, and media of transmission are all specified in the program. Each step in the curriculum is carefully structured so that it advances the child but does not cause him frustration or undue difficulty. Correct performance is constantly modeled through recordings and through the mother's and the teacher's own examples. The child does not proceed to a new lesson or piece until he has thoroughly mastered the previous one, and he returns repeatedly to old pieces to make sure that the models and the lessons have been retained. Much is made of repetition and practice, and the child strives to duplicate exactly the sounds heard on the recording. This makes for impressive group performances, though it does not generate interesting variations in performance. (Perhaps these facts explain why the cello student I witnessed could not readily deal with the vigorous criticism offered by the non-Suzuki master.) An avowed goal of the program is to produce appealing sounds, and children are often asked explicitly to make a piece sound beautiful. In Suzuki's classes for advanced students, one of the most difficult challenges is total mastery of a single note. In Zen fashion, students are asked to practice a note up to one thousand times a week until they come to understand how it feels to play a tone perfectly.

Over the next few years, the child continues this daily regimen of practice, together with weekly individual and group lessons. Naturally children will progress at different rates, but even the less remarkable pupils will perform at a level that astonishes Western observers. One of thirty students beginning at age two or three will be able to play a Vivaldi concerto at age six and a Mozart one by nine or ten, and even the average student will have reached this competence but a few years later. In sharp contrast to the Western context, children do not have to be cajoled or wheedled into practicing; in fact, it is the child who comes to request the practicing time. (If the child does not want to practice, the mother is considered to be at fault; and she is counseled on how to restore motivation and initiative to the child.)

It is worth emphasizing that the goal of producing outstanding performances, which may seem all-encompassing to outside observers, is in fact not Suzuki's avowed aim. He is interested, rather, in forming

375

an individual with a strong, positive, and attractive character and regards exquisite musical performance as simply as means to that end—a means that could be achieved by any intensive artistic experience. For this reason, it is not particularly relevant that many of the Suzuki students stop playing their instruments when they become adolescents. However, it is worth noting that approximately 5 percent of Suzuki children do go on to become professional musicians, and that the percentage of Suzuki students is rising in major Western conservatories, such as the Juilliard School of Music.

A CRITIQUE OF THE SUZUKI APPROACH

How can we make sense of this amazing experiment, in terms of the framework of intellectual competences? Certainly pivotal from this perspective is the fact that Suzuki has focused on one of the intelligences—that of music—and has helped individuals of a presumably wide range of native talents advance rapidly within that domain. Indeed, it is hardly an exaggeration to say that, thanks to Suzuki's ingenious program, the kind of domain proficiency that David Feldman has discerned in child prodigies has been made available to a much wider population. The success of the program is integrally tied, in my judgment, to an intuitive understanding of the natural milestones of musical development in a young child and of the manner in which—through pieces that pose successively just the right amount of difficulty—these milestones might be most effectively and most smoothly negotiated.

Yet the effectiveness of this program depends on more than a shrewd sense of how musical abilities may unfold. To my mind, Suzuki has performed a superbly keen analysis of a whole range of factors—from the agents of transmission to the kinds of intelligence—which are relevant to the attainment of skilled performances. As a start, he has realized the special importance and heightened sensitivity of the early years of life: not only does formal instruction begin at the age of three or so, but the groundwork has been carefully laid in the opening years of life through ample exposure to the materials that will eventually be learned. Musical pieces are as much "in the air" as the child's native language.

To the extent that there may be a critical period for the acquisition of musical competence, and to the extent that the brain of the young child is especially plastic for this kind of learning, Suzuki has certainly taken advantage of important neurobiological factors. Second, and perhaps more important, Suzuki has brilliantly exploited the mother-child relationship, making it central to the initial acquisition of motivation and competence in violin playing. Through his sensitivity to interpersonal knowledge—the mother's knowledge of her child and the child's knowledge of his mother—and his appreciation of the strong affective bonds which define this mother-child relationship, Suzuki has succeeded in fostering a tremendous commitment on the part of both individuals to the child's mastery of the violin. The instrument becomes a privileged means of maintaining intimacy between child and parent. Nor should the role of other children be minimized: the fact that so much of Suzuki instruction and performance takes place in a "learning context" rich in other children exploits a youngster's tendency to imitate the behavior of peers in his vicinity. If one had to reduce the complex Suzuki method to a formula, one might speak of strong interpersonal knowledge being used as a means to negotiate a complex musical pathway, in the context of a great deal of cultural support for such an undertaking. It is no accident that a program clearly built upon the mother's total involvement with her child, and taking advantage of the support of other individuals as well, was devised in Japan.

All regimens have their costs, and some equivocal aspects of the Suzuki method should also be noted. The method is very much oriented toward learning by ear—probably a highly beneficent decision, considering the age of the children who are enrolled. Much time would be wasted in trying to get preschoolers to read notation, and the insistence in many quarters on beginning with the score often makes many otherwise musically inclined children hostile to their music lessons. On the other hand, since the learning of notation is devalued in the Suzuki method, children often fail to master sight reading. Shifting to a notation-based strategy after the ages of six or seven would seem to be a desirable ploy, if the habits acquired by ear-and-hand have not become too completely entrenched by this time. The very plasticity that initially allowed rapid learning may already have given way to a rigid and difficult-to-alter style of performance.

A more serious charge against the Suzuki method pertains to the limited character of the musical skills and knowledge which it develops. For one thing, the music played is exclusively Western music from the Baroque through the Romantic periods—a circumscribed sample of Western music and an even smaller proportion of the world's repertoire. Yet, again, because the children are so deeply immersed in (or "imprinted upon") this common idiom during the most formative and "critical" years of their musical training, the Suzuki program may engender an unnecessarily parochial taste.

Much of the method focuses on a slavish and uncritical imitation of a certain interpretation of the music—for example, a Fritz Kreisler recording of a classical sonata. Children are likely to come away with the notion that there is but one correct way to interpret a piece of music, rather than there being a range of equally plausible interpretations. Even more problematically, children receive the impression that the important thing in music is to replicate a sound as it has been heard and not to attempt to change it in any way. No wonder that few, if any, Suzuki-trained children display any inclination toward composing. The whole notion of doing it another way, of *de*composing a piece into one's own preferred variations, is bypassed in such a highly mimetic form of learning. In this case, a single mode of transmission may exact severe costs.

Finally, there are definite personal costs to this undertaking. From the point of view of the child, he is devoting many hours each week to a single kind of pursuit and to the development of a single intelligence—at the cost of stimulating and developing other intellectual streams. More dramatically, this regimen makes great demands upon the mother: she is expected to devote herself unstintingly to the development in her child of a certain capacity. If she succeeds, plaudits are likely to come to the child; if she fails, she will probably be blamed. (A mother once complained to Suzuki that teaching her child took up too much of her time. He immediately responded, "Then why did you bear him?") Finally, whether or not the child ultimately succeeds in musical mastery, he will eventually leave the home; meanwhile, the mother's own personal skills and qualities may not have been significantly enhanced, a result that (at least to Western eyes) is lamentable.

These deficits are perhaps minor in comparison with the pleasures of skilled playing that the Suzuki method has given to many individuals (including mothers!). Nonetheless, it is worth considering which alterations could minimize these deficiencies while still preserving the key points of the method. According to my analysis, there is no reason for the children not to acquire a wider repertoire, and little reason for them not to attain high levels of competence in the notational realm. The media available to the child could certainly be broadened. More problematic is the tension between ideal production of someone else's model and the production of one's own pieces of music in one's own way. The transition from skilled performance to original composition is difficult to make in any case, and my own guess is that the Suzuki method makes it nearly impossible. As for the interpersonal costs, they also seem intrinsic to the program. In societies where mothers do not invest themselves so completely, the Suzuki program is not nearly so successful and, in fact, comes to resemble "standard" musical training.

The Suzuki focus upon music is probably apt, since an individual can advance quite far in that intellectual domain without needing much general knowledge about the world. However, as I have indicated, the choice of the musical domain is not particularly decisive as far as Suzuki himself is concerned: other arts from flower arrangement to painting could yield many of the same traits of character, particularly if pursued with the same rigor, vigor, and faith. There is a preschool and kindergarten in Matsumoto where a much wider set of curricular materials is used, apparently with marked success; and in Japan today, the potential of preschool children to master a range of tasks—including reading, mathematics, and writing—is estimated to be quite high (even in comparison with child-centered middle-class America). The founder of SONY, Masuru Ibuka, has even written a best-seller, *Kindergarten Is Too Late!*, which articulates the profound belief among Japanese in the primacy of the first quinquennium of life.

THE JAPANESE CASE: PRO AND CON

Success has a thousand fathers, and the phenomenal success of Japan in the era after the Second World War naturally has produced numerous candidates for the "prime cause." There seems to be little question that the Japanese are skilled at studying examples in other lands and then absorbing the best from other individuals and groups. The Japanese also have a strong dedication to discipline, education, and technological expertise; and each of these ends has been pursued to a high point during the last thirty years. Indeed, this success has invaded practically every domain: Japanese youths today are significantly taller and have significantly higher I.Q.'s than their counterparts of thirty years ago—the strongest proof (if proof be needed) that early educational and nutritional experiences can make an enormous difference. Yet sheer imitation is not enough, for the impulse to imitate the West has been found in many developing countries that have not in any way matched the Japanese success story. From all indications, the ability to learn from other cultures has also been matched by a capacity to maintain what is suitable and distinctive in the Japanese cultural tradition.

According to my own analysis, and to that of colleagues on the Project on Human Potential, the Japanese have succeeded in striking an effective balance between the maintenance of group feeling and solidarity, on the one hand, and individual attainment of proficiency and skill, on the other. Both forms of personal intelligence seem to be exploited here. This balance can be seen at a variety of levels of achievement. For example, in primary school classes, individuals are expected to learn arithmetic. In most parts of the world, elementary arithmetic is taught principally through rote learning, with little attention to the underlying concepts, which often perplex not only the youngsters but also the teachers. In Japan, however, according to recent reports by Jack and Elizabeth Easley, challenging problems are posed to entire classes, whose members then have the opportunity to work together over several days in an effort to solve these problems. The children are encouraged to talk to, and to help, one another and are allowed to make mistakes; at times, older children visit the classrooms and aid the younger ones. Thus, what is potentially a tension-building and frustrating situation is alleviated through the involvement of children in a common effort to understand; there is plenty of support for the general collaborative effort, accompanied by a feeling that it is all right not to come up with an answer right away, so long as one keeps plugging away at the problems. Paradoxically, in our much more overtly competitive society, this risk of *not* knowing the answer at the end of the class seems too great; neither teacher nor student can readily handle the tension, and so a potentially valuable learning opportunity is scuttled.

Even in Japan's large business corporations, one encounters the same delicate balance. Much of the competitive urge, of course, is deflected to competition with other societies, where Japan has enjoyed great success, and toward anticipating future trends in the market, where again, Japan has displayed far more foresight than have its principal competitors. Moreover, within the Japanese company itself, it is proper for different individuals to make different contributions to problem formulation and problem solution. An individual identifies strongly with his firm, with which he expects to have life-long relations, and has relatively little sense of being in direct competition with fellow employees. Similarly, no premium is placed on a single individual's—particularly a single young individual—possessing all the requisite competences himself. If anything, such a precocious polymath could be deemed inappropriate and somewhat anachronistic. Thus, we might even say that the Japanese corporation has realized, in an intuitive way, that there is a profile of human intelligences, and that individuals with different profiles can make their own distinctive contributions to the success of the firm.

As with the Suzuki Talent Education Program, there are costs to the Japanese corporate system; and as the successes become better known, these costs have also become more evident. The opportunity to work in the corporation rests upon success in the academic system; and this success, in turn, depends heavily on the peculiarities and particularities of the Japanese child-rearing and educational systems. An early key to a child's eventual success is believed to lie in the relationship of the young child (particularly the boy) to his mother. While the strong bond can help to yield early achievements, it can also exert negative effects as children feel ensnared in a bargain with their mother to achieve: if they fail to do so, there may be severe frustration, tension, and even overt aggression against the mother. The public school system attempts to maintain a friendly and cooperative spirit among students, but this communal conviviality overlooks the reality that there are far fewer places in the university than there are youths intent on occupying them. Hence, the propagation of the alternative school, or *juku*, where youths are trained to do well on their college-entry examinations. From all reports, the atmosphere in the jukus is much more frankly competitive; and, again, one encounters severe psychological costs (and sometimes suicides) among those youths who do not perform satisfactorily on the examinations. Finally, the skill of the Japanese at absorbing appropriate models from other settings is now seen to have its limits, as the models from elsewhere grow less relevant, and as the Japanese are thrown more on their own innovative powers. Many Japanese commentators have decried the dearth of original scientists from this interpersonally oriented culture and have noted, with even greater sadness, that the Japanese scientists (and artists) whose originality turns out to be the most prized are those who have moved to the West.

Other Educational Experiments

I have dwelled at some length on Japan because in today's world the Japanese example is particularly striking and because I feel that the analytic framework developed here ought to be applied in the first instance to educational experiments that have been successful. It is crucial to note, however, that Japanese success with a program like Talent Education does not simply reflect expert design. Were that the case, then the Suzuki program would prove equally successful everywhere (and in every field of learning)—as is decidedly not the case. No, the key to the success of the Suzuki program in Japan lies in the comfortable fit between the abilities and inclinations of the target population (young children) and the particular values, opportunities, and institutions of the society in which they happen to be growing up. Such programs can be successfully exported only if similar support systems exist in the new "host" country; or, alternatively, if suitable alterations are made so that the educational program meshes with the dominant values, procedures, and intellectual orientation of the host land.

Here, indeed, may lie some clues to the success of other educational interventions as well. In the case of teaching the fundamentals of literacy, for example, two notable successes of recent years have both taken shrewed advantage of the situations as they exist in particular host countries. One such case is Paolo Freire's efforts to teach reading to illiterate adult Brazilian peasants. Freire has developed a method in which individuals are introduced to key words which have strong personal value and feature a phonetic and morphological structure relevant to the learning of future words. This much is skillful linguistic pedagogy. But the Freire program is embedded within a much larger program of political action, which has profound meaning for students and helps to spur them on to heroic efforts. Here the context of learning makes a critical difference. A totally different but also highly successful approach to reading instruction can be found in the television programs "Sesame Street" and the "Electric Company" which have taught the fundamentals of reading to a generation of American schoolchildren. Once again, these procedures build upon tried-and-true methods of training reading. But through a commercial-style format, as well as a tempo suited to the medium of television, these programs succeed in holding the audience's attention. In both the Brazilian and the American cases, attempts have been made to transplant the reading programs to very different populations. My own guess is that these efforts will be successful to the extent that the particular conditions that obtained in the countries of origin can also be encountered—or constructed—in novel cultural settings. In my terms, an analysis in terms of the intellectual skills to be cultivated and of those already valued in the host society should precede any contemplated intervention.

Alas, the incidence of educational experiments that have not succeeded is high in the contemporary world. One need only think of the attempts in Iran to Westernize the educational system during the last thirty years, or of the various flirtations in the People's Republic of

China with a technologically oriented education. In each case, attempts were made to impose a more Western-style curriculum—one organized around scientific thinking—upon a society that had previously favored traditional modes of schooling of the sort considered in the previous chapter. Tremendous stress resulted when schools that had been largely concerned with teaching one form of literacy were asked to convey "open thinking," the weighing of conflicting theories, and the primacy of logical-mathematical reasoning. The relative de-emphasis of social ties, the dramatic shift in the uses to which language was put, and the insistence on the application of logical-mathematical thinking to diverse realms of existence proved too jarring in these entrenched cultural contexts.

Not surprisingly, in both the Iranian and the Chinese cases, a dramatic counterreaction resulted. A reflexive opposition to everything Western, modern, and technological characterized the Cultural Revolution in China, as well the Islamic Revival in Iran. Clearly, in the absence of continuity with the past, an educational innovation is unlikely to hold.

Pointers for Policy Makers

GENERAL CONSIDERATIONS

Such a review of pedagogical experiments—successful or not—calls upon a close analysis of educational processes as they have traditionally existed in a culture, as well as on a careful consideration of how these processes might be mobilized to meet novel needs in a changing world. I am frankly somewhat uncomfortable, as a neophyte in matters of policy, in recommending a particular course of action in situations that are exceedingly complex and ever fluid. Nonetheless, it seems opportune at this concluding point to mention some of the considerations that policy makers might bear in mind as they attempt to decide about the education—and in a sense the future lives—of those individuals over whom they have responsibility.

It is always judicious to begin with a review of the goals of a particular intervention or of a whole educational program. The more specifically these goals can be articulated, the more shorn of rhetoric or generalities, the better. Thus, "educating individuals to achieve their potential" or "to be an informed citizenry" is not helpful; but "achieving sufficient literacy to read a newspaper or discuss a current political problem" is instructively precise. For the latter type of specific goal, one can analyze the constituent intellectual skills and devise ways of assessing success (or degrees of success or failure); for the former grandiose goal, there is no implied evaluation metric. Statement of explicit goals also brings to the fore potential conflicts or contradictions: for example, a goal of attaining a certain level of literacy, skill in scientific thinking, or facility in discussing political issues might well conflict with a goal of maintaining traditional religious values, political attitudes, or a homogeneous outlook throughout the population. Though such conflicts are unfortunate, it is better that they be confronted explicitly rather than ignored, denied, or swept under a rhetorical rug.

Following the review of goals, a next step entails a sober assessment of the means currently available for achieving these goals. Some of this analysis ought to focus on the traditional methods that are available: observation learning, informal interaction, apprenticeship systems, prevalent media, varieties of school, the curriculums (explicit or implicit) that currently exist. But it is also advisable to cast the net more widely and to consider the agents and the loci of transmission, as well as the ways in which values, roles, and procedures have in fact been transmitted across generations.

For every goal currently being pursued, there is presumably a set of intelligences which could readily be mobilized for its realization, as well as a set of intelligences whose mobilization would pose a greater challenge. Moreover, with different cultures, there appear to be characteristic blends of intelligences which have been favored over the years. Determining the exact blend is no easy matter, but it is possible to delineate those configurations that have been relatively prominent in diverse cultural settings. Thus, one would expect that, in a traditional agrarian society, interpersonal, bodily-kinesthetic, and linguistic forms of intelligence would be highlighted in informal educational settings which are largely "on site" and feature considerable observation and imitation. In a society in the early stages of industrialization, one would anticipate traditional forms of schooling that focus on rote linguistic learning but where logical-mathematical forms of intelligence are beginning to be used. In highly industrialized societies, and in post-industrial society, one would predict a prizing of linguistic, logical-mathematical, and intrapersonal forms of intelligence: quite probably, modern secular schools would be yielding to individual computerized instruction. The shift from any of these forms to the "next" one would clearly involve costs; an attempt to shift directly from agrarian to post-industrial modes of transmission (as in the aforementioned Iranian case) could be expected to yield especially severe strains.

384

In societies with limited resources, it may seem necessary to move directly from an inventory of goals and means to a decision about the optimal way to proceed with the population as a whole. However, it is a principal assumption of this study that individuals are not all alike in their cognitive potentials and their intellectual styles and that education can be more properly carried out if it is tailored to the abilities and the needs of the particular individuals involved. Indeed, the cost of attempting to treat all individuals the same, or of trying to convey knowledge to individuals in ways uncongenial to their preferred modes of learning, may be great: if at all possible, it is advisable to devise methods for assessing the intellectual profiles of individuals.

There does not yet exist a technology explicitly designed to test an individual's intellectual profile. I am not sure it would be wise to attempt to set up such an explicit testing program, particularly given the ways in which such testing programs tend to become standardized and commercialized. But it is clear from my analyses that certain ways of assessing individual profiles are better than others. I would now like to indicate how one might—given sufficient resources (and benevolent intentions!)—assess an individual's profile of intelligences.

ASSESSING INTELLECTUAL PROFILES

A first point is that intelligences should not be assessed in the same ways at different ages. The methods used with an infant or a preschooler ought to be tailored to the particular ways of knowing that typify these individuals and may be different from those employed with older individuals. My own belief is that one could assess an individual's intellectual potentials quite early in life, perhaps even in infancy. At that time, intellectual strengths and weaknesses would emerge most readily if individuals were given the opportunity to learn to recognize certain patterns and were tested on their capacities to remember these from one day to the next. Thus, an individual with strong abilities in the spatial realm should learn to recognize target patterns quite quickly when exposed to them, to appreciate their identity even when their arrangement in space has been altered, and to notice slight deviations from them when they are presented on subsequent trials or subsequent days. Similarly, one could assess pattern-recognition abilities in other intellectual domains (like language or number) as well as the ability to learn motor patterns and to revise and transform them in adaptive ways. My own hunch about strong intellectual abilities is that an individual so blessed does not merely have an easy time learning new patterns; he in fact learns them so readily that *it is virtually impossible for him to forget them*. The simple melodies continue to play on in his mind, the sentences linger there, the spatial or gestural configurations are readily brought to the fore, although they may not have been tapped for a while.

Even if such intellectual profiles could be drawn up in the first year or two of life, I have little doubt that profiles at that early date can be readily shifted. In fact, that is what early neural and functional plasticity is all about. A principal reason for early assessment is to allow an individual to proceed as rapidly as seems warranted in those intellectual channels where he is talented, even as it affords an opportunity to bolster those intellectual endowments that seem relatively modest.

At a somewhat later age (all the way up through the preschool years!) it should prove possible to secure a contextually rich and reliable assessment of an individual's intellectual profile. The preferred route for assessment at this age is to involve children in activities which they themselves are likely to find motivating: they can then advance with little direct tutelage through the steps involved in mastering a particular problem or task. Puzzles, games, and other challenges couched in the symbol system of a single intelligence (or of a pair of intelligences) are particularly promising means for assessing the relevant intelligence.

Involvement with such inherently engrossing materials provides an ideal opportunity to observe intelligences at work and to monitor their advances over a finite period of time. If one could watch a child as he learns to build various constructions out of blocks, one would receive insight into his skills in the areas of spatial and kinesthetic intelligence: similarly, the child's capacities to relate a set of stories would reveal facets of his linguistic promise, even as his capacity to operate a simple machine would illuminate kinesthetic and logical-mathematical skills. Such involvements in rich and provocative environments are also most likely to elicit "markers"—those signs of early giftedness that are readily noticed by adults expert in a particular intellectual domain. The future musician may be marked by perfect pitch; the child gifted in personal matters, by his intuitions about the motives of others; the budding scientist, by his ability to pose provocative questions and then follow them up with appropriate ones.

Note how this approach to assessment differs from that employed in traditional intelligence testing. In the conventional test, the child is confronted by an adult who fires at him a rapid series of questions. The

386

child is expected to give a single answer (or, when somewhat older, to write down his answer or to select it from a set of choices). A premium is placed on linguistic facility, on certain logical-mathematical abilities, and on a kind of social skill at negotiating the situation with an elder in one's presence. These factors can all intrude when one is trying to assess another kind of intelligence—say, musical, bodily-kinesthetic, or spatial. By removing the experimenter and his paraphernalia from the assessing situation—or, at least, by placing them firmly in the background—and by substituting the actual elements and symbols of the particular realm under consideration, it should prove possible to obtain a more veridical picture of the child's current intellectual abilities—and of his intellectual potential.

Proceeding from some ideas originally put forth by the Soviet psychologist Vygotsky, it should be possible to devise tests suitable for individuals who have had little or no prior experience with the particular material or symbolic elements in question, and to see how rapidly they can progress in a given area in a limited period of time. Such a mission places a particularly strong burden on the tester to locate problems that are intrinsically engaging and serve as "crystallizing experiences" for young and naïve but possibly talented individuals. In the present study of intelligences, I have noted some of the experiences that proved catalytic for particular individuals in particular domains: watching folk pageants, for the future dancer; looking at recurrent alternating visual patterns, for the young mathematician; learning long and intricate rhymes, for the future poet.

Naturally the specific experiences favored for the assessment of intellectual potential will differ, given the age, the sophistication, and the cultural background of the individual. Thus, when monitoring the spatial realm, one might hide an object from the one-year-old, pose a jigsaw puzzle to the six-year-old, or provide the pre-adolescent with a Rubik's cube. Analogously, in the musical realm, one might vary a lullaby for the two-year-old, provide the eight-year-old with a computer on which he can compose simple melodies, or analyze a fugue with an adolescent. In any case, the general idea of finding intriguing puzzles and allowing children to "take off" with them seems to offer a far more valid way of assessing profiles of individuals than the current favorites world-wide: standard measures designed to be given within a half-hour with the aid of paper and pencil.

My own guess is that it should be possible to gain a reasonably accurate picture of an individual's intellectual profile—be he three or thirteen—in the course of a month or so, while that individual is in-

volved in regular classroom activities. The total time spent might be
five to ten hours of observing—a long time given current standards of
intelligence testing, but a very short time in terms of the life of that
student. Such a profile should indicate which lines are already
launched in an individual, which lines show a decided potential for
development, which are more modestly endowed or entail some genuine obstacles (such as tone-deafness, meager visual imagery, or
clumsiness).

EDUCATING INTELLIGENCES

Now comes the decisive but delicate step in the educational planning process. Given the curricular ends that one has in mind for an
individual, and the individual's own intellectual profiles, a decision
must be made about which educational regimen to follow. First of all,
there must be a general strategic decision: does one play from strength,
does one bolster weakness, or does one attempt to work along both
tracks at the same time? Naturally this decision must be made in terms
of the resources available, as well as of the overall goals of both the
society and the individuals most directly involved.

Assuming room for developing more than a single faculty along a
single track, decisions of a far more focused sort must be made as well.
In the case of each individual, those charged with educational planning must decide which means can best be mobilized to help that individual attain a desired competence, skill, or role. In the case of the
highly talented individual, it may be necessary (and sufficient) to enable him to work directly with an acknowledged master, in a kind of
apprenticeship relation; it should also be possible to provide him with
materials that he can explore (and with which he can advance) on his
own. In the case of the individual with meager abilities, or even frank
pathologies, it will probably be necessary to devise special prostheses:
machinery, mechanisms, or other means whereby the information or
skills can be presented to him in such a way as to exploit the intellectual capacities he has, while circumventing (to as large an extent as
possible) his intellectual frailties. In the case of the individual who
does not fall at either extreme of the bell-shaped curve, there will
presumably be a larger set of procedures and curricula from which one
can draw, always acknowledging the limits of resources and the competing demands on the student's and the teacher's time.

Surprisingly little work has been done by educational psychologists in charting the general principles that may govern progress

through an intellectual domain. (This lack may be due in part to a lack of concern with particular domains—as opposed to general learning; in part, to extensive concern with just how a *specific* task is mastered.) Of various efforts in this direction, I find most suggestive the work by the Soviet school of psychology—such followers of Lev Vygotsky as V. V. Davydov, D. Elkonin, and A. K. Markova. These researchers believe that at each age children exhibit a different set of interests: thus, during infancy, the dominant activity involves emotional contact; at age two, the child is absorbed in manipulation of objects; at ages three to seven, role play and other kinds of symbolic activity come to the fore; during the ages of seven to eleven, the feature activity is formal study in school; and in adolescence, the youth pursues a combination of intimate personal relations and career-oriented exploration. Any educational program should keep these biases in mind; though, of course, the specific profile of interests may differ significantly across cultures.

Working within these broad parameters, the educator searches for *genetic primary examples*. These are problems or lessons that can be handled by the novice but, at the same time, harbor within them the most relevant abstractions within that domain. Mastery of a genetic primary example serves as an indication that an individual can successfully negotiate the succeeding steps within the field. For the educator, the challenge consists in planning the steps—the hurdles that the child must overcome so that he can progress satisfactorily through the domain, until he reaches the next phase and the next genetic primary example. If the kind of analysis put forth by Soviet psychologists could be merged with the approach being developed here, it might be possible to chart an optimal path of educational progress in each of the intellectual domains with which I have been concerned. Such an analysis would reveal the path or the set of paths to be negotiated by normal children as well as by those with special gifts or particular difficulties.

Given a wide range of cultural goals, and an even greater variety of intellectual profiles, the challenge of obtaining a match between student and method may seem overwhelming. In fact, however, students have managed to learn even when lessons are in no way tailored for them, presumably because most curricula are redundant, and because the students themselves possess an array of intellectual strengths and strategies on which they can draw. A "matching system" should help ensure that a student can rapidly and smoothly master what needs to be mastered, and thus be freed to proceed further along both optional and optimal paths of development.

Of course, the idea of matching individuals with particular subject matters and/or styles of teaching is familiar and has implicitly guided much instruction since Classical times. It is therefore disappointing to note that attempts to document significant improvements as a result of matching students with appropriate teaching techniques have not met with much success.

Educational scholars nonetheless cling to the vision of the optimal match between student and material. In my own view, this tenacity is legitimate: after all, the science of educational psychology is still young; and in the wake of superior conceptualizations and finer measures, the practice of matching the individual learner's profile to the materials and modes of instruction may still be validated. Moreover, if one adopts M.I. theory, the options for such matches increase: as I have already noted, it is possible that the intelligences can function both as subject matters in themselves and as the preferred means for inculcating diverse subject matter.

Carrying out relevant research is a task for the future. The most I can do here is to sketch some expectations. In the case of learning to program a computer, for example, it seems plausible that a number of intellectual competences may prove relevant. Logical-mathematical intelligence seems central, because programming depends upon the deployment of strict procedures to solve a problem or attain a goal in a finite number of steps. Writing the program requires that the steps be clear, precise, and organized in a strictly logical order. Linguistic intelligence is also relevant, at least so long as manuals and computer languages make use of ordinary language. The metaphor of the program as a story (complete with subplots) may also help certain budding programmers with a linguistic bent. The intuitions that individuals have about particular domains may well help them in learning to program. Thus, an individual with a strong musical bent might best be introduced to programming by attempting to program a simple musical piece (or to master the use of a program that composes). An individual with strong spatial abilities might be initiated through some form of computer graphics—and he might also be aided in the task of programming through the use of a flow chart or some other spatial diagram. Personal intelligences can play important roles. The extensive planning of steps and goals carried out by the individual as he engages in programming relies on intrapersonal forms of thinking, even as the cooperation needed for carrying out a complex task or for learning new computational skills may rely on an individual's ability to work with a team. Kinesthetic intelligence may play a role in working with the computer itself, facilitate skill at the terminal, and be exploited in those cases where the subject matter of a program involves use of the body (programming a dance or a sequence of football plays).

Parallel lines of reasoning can be invoked in analyzing the task of learning to read. Particularly in the case of individuals who have initial difficulty in learning to read text, it may make sense to begin with an introduction to some other symbolic systems—for example, those used for musical notation, map making, or mathematics. Moreover, individuals with pronounced reading disabilities sometimes must resort to unusual measures of learning—for example, mastering the letters through tactile-kinesthetic exploration. The particular subject matter may also play an important role in improving reading comprehension: an individual who knows something about a field, or is interested in increasing his knowledge base, may find reading easier and will also be more highly motivated to read. Whether the actual process of reading involves, in significant measure, intelligences other than linguistic ones is problematic. However, in view of the various reading systems already invented by human beings (such as pictographic systems) and the kinds likely to be devised in the future (logical-mathematical systems for use with computers), it seems clear that one's facility in reading will depend on more than one's linguistic capacities.

Even as computers offer a useful way to think about the marshaling of intelligences to master educational goals, the potential utility of computers in the process of matching individuals to modes of instruction is substantial. While effecting a match between a student's intellectual profile and the instructional goals can be a highly demanding task for even the most gifted instructor, the relevant kinds of information could be readily handled by a computer that can, in a fraction of a second, suggest alternative pedagogical programs or routes. More important, the computer can be a vital facilitator in the actual process of instruction, helping individuals to negotiate sequences at their preferred pace by using a variety of educational techniques. I should point out, however, that the computer cannot assume certain roles of an interpersonal sort and seems less relevant for certain intellectual domains (say, kinesthetic) than for others (logical-mathematical). There is the risk that the electronic computer—a product of Western thinking and technology—may prove most useful for perpetuating just those forms of intelligence that led to its devising in the first place. It is also possible, however, that extensions of the computer—including robots—might eventually be developed which would facilitate learning and mastery in the full gamut of intellectual domains.

While it is desirable to consider the fine points of the learning process, it is important for the planner or policy maker not to lose sight of his overall educational agenda. Ultimately, the educational plans that are pursued need to be orchestrated across various interest groups of the society so that they can, taken together, help the society to achieve its larger goals. Individual profiles must be considered in the light of goals pursued by the wider society; and sometimes, in fact, individuals with gifts in certain directions must nonetheless be guided along other, less favored paths, simply because the needs of the culture are particularly urgent in that realm at that time. The synthetic ability entailed in this form of decision making involves its own blend of intelligences—if not a special form of intelligence. It is important that a society find some way of training, and then using, those abilities that permit a vision of a large and complex whole.

A Concluding Note

These scattered notes are as far as I feel prepared to go in trying to draw some educational and policy implications from the framework introduced in this book. The framework has been taken principally from findings in the biological and cognitive sciences, and it first needs to be amply discussed and tested in those circles before it provides a handbook, a red book, or a white paper for any practitioner. Even good ideas have been ruined by premature attempts at implementation, and we are not yet certain of the goodness of the idea of multiple intelligences.

After the euphoria of the 1960s and early 1970s, when educational planners felt that they could readily ameliorate the world's ills, we have come to the painful realization that the problems dwarf our understanding, our knowledge, and our ability to act prudently. We have become much more aware of the roles of history, politics, and culture in circumscribing or thwarting our ambitious plans and in guiding them down paths that could not have been anticipated. We are even more keenly aware that particular historical events and technological developments can mold the future in a way that would have been difficult to envision even a decade ago. For every successful planner and implementer, for every "Sesame Street" or Suzuki method, there are dozens, perhaps thousands of failed plans—so many, in fact, that it is difficult to know whether the few successes are happy accidents or the fruits of rare genius.

Nonetheless, problems and potentialities will not go away, and people—teachers of preschoolers no less than ministers of education—will continue to hold the major responsibility for developing other individuals. This trust they will exercise wisely or poorly, productively or counterproductively. That they should do so with some awareness of what they are doing, with some knowledge of the alternative methods and outcomes, would seem to be preferable to operating completely from intuition or wholly from ideology. In this book, I have urged that educators pay close heed to the biological and psychological proclivities of human beings and to the particular historical and cultural context of the locales where they live—a task, of course, easier said than done. Nonetheless, knowledge is accruing and will—I hope—continue to accrue about what human beings are like, when considered in relative isolation and as members of a functioning cultural entity. And since some individuals will continue to assume responsibility for planning the lives of others, it seems preferable that their efforts be framed by our growing knowledge of human minds.

Notes

[The numbers in brackets following a short title refer to the page number of its original, complete citation in that chapter.]

Chapter 1. The Idea of Multiple Intelligences

Page

5   On the Suzuki method of violin training, see S. Suzuki, *Nurtured by Love* (New York: Exposition Press, 1969); B. Holland, "Among Pros, More Go Suzuki," *The New York Times*, 11 July 1982, E9; L. Taniuchi, "The Creation of Prodigies through Special Early Education: Three Case Studies," unpublished paper, Harvard Project on Human Potential, Cambridge, Mass., 1980.

     On the LOGO method of introducing mathematical thinking, see S. Papert, *Mindstorms* (New York: Basic Books, 1980).

     On programs for the realization of human potential, see World Bank, *World Development Report* (New York: Oxford University Press, 1980); H. Singer, "Put the People First: Review of World Development Report, 1980," *The Economist*, 23 August 1980; J. W. Botkin, M. Elmandjra, and M. Malitza, *No Limits to Learning: Bridging the Human Gap: A Report to the Club of Rome* (Oxford and New York: Pergamon Press, 1979); and W. J. Skrzyniarz, "A Review of Projects to Develop Intelligence in Venezuela: Developmental, Philosophical, Policy, and Cultural Perspectives on Intellectual Potential," unpublished paper, Harvard Project on Human Potential, Cambridge, Mass., November 1981.

6   The authorities on the role of intelligence throughout Western history are quoted in J. H. Randall, *The Making of the Modern Mind: A Survey of the Intellectual Background of the Present Age* (New York: Columbia University Press, 1926, 1940).

     St. Augustine is quoted on p. 94 of Randall's *Making of the Modern Mind*, cited in previous note.

     Francis Bacon is quoted on p. 204 of the same book.

     Dante is quoted on p. 105 of the same book.

7   Archilochus' distinction between "hedgehogs" and "foxes" is reviewed in I. Berlin, *The Hedgehog and the Fox: An Essay on Tolstoy's View of History* (London: Weidenfeld & Nicolson, 1953; New York: Simon & Schuster, 1966).

     For a general discussion of faculty psychology, see J. A. Fodor, *The Modularity of Mind* (Cambridge, Mass.: M.I.T. Press, 1983).

Page
7   On Franz Joseph Gall, see E. G. Boring, *A History of Expermental Psychology* (New York: Appleton-Century-Crofts, 1950).

For an elaboration of Guilford's views, see J. P. Guilford, "Creativity," *American Psychologist* 5 (1950):444–54; and J. P. Guilford and R. Hoepfner, *The Analysis of Intelligence* (New York: McGraw-Hill, 1971).

On a general factor of intelligence, see. C. Spearman, *The Abilities of Man: Their Nature and Measurement* (New York: Macmillan, 1927); and C. Spearman, " 'General Intelligence' Objectively Determined and Measured," *American Journal of Psychology* 15 (1904): 201–93.

For a discussion of the debate in child development between those who favor general structures of mind and those who favor a set of specific mental skills, see H. Gardner, *Developmental Psychology*, 2nd ed. (Boston: Little, Brown, 1982).

On the view that there is a family of primary mental abilities, see L. L. Thurstone, "Primary Mental Abilities," *Psychometric Monographs*, 1938, no. 1; and L. L. Thurstone, *Multiple-Factor Analysis: A Development and Expansion of "The Vectors of the Mind"* (Chicago: University of Chicago Press, 1947).

Chapter 2. Intelligence: Earlier Views

12   For a discussion of the theories of Franz Joseph Gall, see. E. G. Boring, *A History of Experimental Psychology* (New York: Appleton-Centry-Crofts, 1950).

On phrenology, see H. Gardner's *The Shattered Mind: The Person after Brain Damage* (New York: Alfred A. Knopf, 1975), pp. 20–21.

13   See M. J. P. Flourens's critique in *Examen de phrénologie* (Paris: Hachette, 1842).

On Pierre-Paul Broca's work on aphasia, see Gardner, *Shattered Mind* [12], p. 21; P. Broca, "Remarques sur le siège de la faculté de langage articulé," *Bulletin de la Société d'anthropologie* 6 (Paris, 1861); and E. G. Boring, *A History of Experimental Psychology* (New York: Appleton-Century-Crofts, 1950), pp. 28–29.

For a discussion of linguistic impairment resulting from lesions in the left hemisphere, see Gardner, *Shattered Mind* [12], chap. 2.

15   On Francis Galton's methodology, see F. Galton, *Inquiries into Human Faculty and Its Development* (London: J. M. Dent, 1907; New York: E. P. Dutton, 1907); and Boring, *History of Experimental Psychology* [12], pp. 482–88.

Binet and Simon's pioneering efforts are described on pp. 573–75 of Boring's history, cited in the previous note.

16   Controversies over the I.Q. test are discussed in A. Jensen, *Bias in Mental Testing* (New York: Free Press, 1980); and N. Block and G. Dworkin, eds., *The IQ Controversy* (New York: Pantheon, 1976).

Eysenck's statement is quoted in M. P. Friedman, J. P. Das, and N. O'Connor, *Intelligence and Learning* (New York and London: Plenum Press, 1979), p. 84.

Thomas Kuhn's theory is found in *The Structure of Scientific Revolutions* (Chicago: University of Chicago Press, 1970).

On C. Spearman, see his *The Abilities of Man: Their Nature and Measurement* (New York: Macmillan, 1927); and " 'General Intelligence' Objectively Determined and Measured," *American Journal of Psychology* 15, (1904):201–93.

On L. L. Thurstone, see his "Primary Mental Abilities," *Psychometric Monographs*, 1938, no. 1; and *Multiple-Factor Analysis: A Development and Expansion of "The Vectors of the Mind"* (Chicago: University of Chicago Press, 1947).

The views of scholars who posit several independent factors of intelligence are discussed in G. H. Thomson, *The Factoral Analysis of Human Ability* (London: University of London Press, 1951).

17   The mathematical problems in interpreting test scores are reviewed in S. J. Gould, *The Mismeasure of Man* (New York: W. W. Norton, 1981).

Page

On Piaget's career and theories, see H. Gardner, *The Quest for Mind: Piaget, Lévi-Strauss, and the Structuralist Movement* (Chicago and London: University of Chicago Press, 1981); J. P. Flavell, *The Developmental Psychology of Jean Piaget* (Princeton: Van Nostrand, 1963); and H. Gruber and J. Vonèche, eds., *The Essential Piaget* (New York: Basic Books, 1977).

18   The example of an individual who loses the frontal lobes, and still functions at close to genius level on I.Q. tests, is described in D. O. Hebb, *The Organization of Behavior* (New York: John Wiley, 1949).

On the concept of a zone of proximal development, see L. Vygotsky, *Mind in Society*, M. Cole ed. (Cambridge, Mass.: Harvard University Press, 1978); and A. L. Brown and R. A. Ferrara, "Diagnosing Zones of Proximal Development: An Alternative to Standardized Testing?," paper presented at the conference on Culture, Communication, and Cognition: Psychosocial Studies, Chicago, October 1980.

20   I. Kant's basic categories of time, space, number, and causality are introduced in *The Critique of Pure Reason*, Norman Kemp Smith, trans. (New York: Modern Library, 1958; originally published in 1781).

21   K. Fischer argues that *décalage* has become the rule in studies of cognitive development, in "A Theory of Cognitive Development: The Control of Hierarchies of Skill," *Psychological Review* 87 (1980):477–531.

21   The often precocious responses obtained when Piaget's tasks are conveyed nonlinguistically are discussed in H. Gardner, *Developmental Psychology*, 2nd ed. (Boston: Little, Brown, 1982), chap. 10. See also P. Bryant, *Perception and Understanding in Young Children* (New York: Basic Books, 1974).

22   On cognitive psychology and information-processing psychology, see R. Lachman, J. Lachman and E. C. Butterfield, *Cognitive Psychology and Information Processing: An Introduction* (Hillsdale, N.J.: Lawrence Erlbaum 1979); and G. R. Claxton, ed., *Cognitive Psychology: New Directions* (London: Routledge & Kegan Paul, 1980).

23   R. Sternberg attempts to identify the operations involved in solving standard intelligence test items, in "The Nature of Mental Abilities," *American Psychologist* 34 (1979): 214–30.

24   On the "magic number" of seven chunks, see G. A. Miller, "The Magical Number Seven, Plus or Minus Two: Some Limits on Our Capacity for Processing Information," *Psychological Research* 63 (1956):81–97.

25   The following works are by philosophers who have taken a special interest in human symbolic capacities: E. Cassirer, *The Philosophy of Symbolic forms*, vols. 1–3 (New Haven and London: Yale University Press, 1953–1957); S. Langer, *Philosophy in a New Key: A Study in the Symbolism of Reason, Rite, and Art* (Cambridge, Mass.: Harvard University Press, 1942); and A. N. Whitehead, *Modes of Thought* (New York: Capricorn Books, Macmillan, 1938).

26   D. Feldman addresses the problem of reconciling a pluralistic approach to intelligence with Piaget's developmental scheme, in his *Beyond Universals in Cognitive Development* (Norwood, N.J.: Ablex Publishers, 1980).

28   G. Salomon discusses the media of transmission of symbols in his *Interaction of Media, Cognition, and Learning* (San Francisco: Jossey-Bass, 1979).

D. Olson's work on the prostheses that may enable individuals to acquire information from alternative media is discussed in his *Cognitive Development* (New York: Academic Press, 1970).

D. Olson discusses the role of the symbol systems in literacy in "From Utterance to Text: The Bias of Language in Speech and Writing," *Harvard Educational Review* 47 (1977): 257–82.

On work at the Harvard Project Zero on the fine structure of development within symbol systems, see D. P. Wolf and H. Gardner, *Early Symbolizations*, in preparation.

Research at the Boston Veterans Administration Medical Center on the breakdown of symbolic capacities is described in W. Wapner and H. Gardner, "Profiles of Symbol Reading Skills in Organic Patients," *Brain and Language* 12 (1981):303–12.

29   For N. Goodman's work on symbols, see his *Languages of Art: An Approach to a Theory of Symbols* (Indianapolis: Hackett Publishing, 1976).

On lesions that may cause a disturbance in the ability to read one type of symbols but leave unharmed the ability to read a different type, see H. Gardner, *Art, Mind, and Brain: A Cognitive Approach to Creativity* (New York: Basic Books, 1982), part IV.

Chapter 3. Biological Foundations of Intelligence

Page

33   On the "cracking of the genetic code," see J. D. Watson, *The Double Helix: A Personal Account of the Discovery of the Structure of DNA* (New York: Signet Books, New American Library, 1968).

34   Combinations of genes that are correlated with each other are described by L. Brooks in her paper, "Genetics and Human Populations," a technical report for the Harvard Project on Human Potential, June 1980.

      On the controversy over the heritability of intelligence, see S. Scarr-Salapatek, "Genetics and the Development of Intelligence," in F. Horowitz, ed., *Review of Child Development Research*, vol. IV (Chicago: University of Chicago Press, 1975); S. Gould, *The Mismeasure of Man* (New York: W. W. Norton, 1981); and N. Block and G. Dworkin, eds., *The IQ Controversy* (New York: Pantheon, 1976).

35   On the Suzuki Violin Talent Education Program, see S. Suzuki, *Nurtured by Love* (New York: Exposition Press, 1969); B. Holland, "Among Pros, More go Suzuki," *The New York Times*, 11 July 1982, E9; L. Taniuchi, "The Creation of Prodigies through Special Early Education: Three Case Studies," unpublished paper, Harvard Project on Human Potential, Cambridge, Mass., 1980.

      On "genetic drift" in the South Sea islands, see C. Gajdusek, "The Composition of Musics for Man: On Decoding from Primitive Cultures the Scores for Human Behavior," *Pediatrics* 34 (1964):1, 84–91.

37   The pioneering work of D. Hubel and T. Wiesel is concisely summarized in H. B. Barlow, "David Hubel and Torsten Wiesel: Their Contributions toward Understanding the Visual Cortex," *Trends in Neuroscience*, May 1982, pp. 145–152.

      On the singing capacities of birds, see F. Nottebohm, "Brain Pathways for Vocal Learning in Birds: A Review of the First 10 Years," *Progress in Psychobiological and Physiological Psychology* 9 (1980):85–124; M. Konishi in R. A. Hinde, ed., *Bird Vocalization* (Cambridge: Cambridge University Press, 1969); and P. Marler and S. Peters, "Selective Vocal Learning in a Sparrow," *Science* 198 (1977):519–21.

      On canalization, see C. H. Waddington, *The Evolution of an Evolutionist* (Ithaca: Cornell University Press, 1975). See also J. Piaget, *Behavior and Evolution* (New York: Pantheon, 1978).

      C. H. Waddington is quoted in E. S. Gollin, *Developmental Plasticity: Behavioral and Biological Aspects of Variations in Development* (New York: Academic Press, 1981), pp. 46–47.

38   On the nervous system's adaptation to environmental influences, see Gollin, *Developmental Plasticity* [37], p. 236.

      M. Dennis describes the capacity of the human infant to learn to speak even if one cerebral hemisphere is lost; see M. Dennis, "Language Acquisition in a Single Hemisphere: Semantic Organization," in D. Caplan, ed., *Biological Studies of Mental Processes* (Cambridge, Mass.: M.I.T. Press, 1980).

      On residual plasticity and on the limits of plasticity in cases of early injury or deprivation, see the following summaries of D. Hubel and T. Wiesel's work: J. Lettvin, "'Filling out the Forms': An Appreciation of Hubel and Wiesel," *Science* 214 (1981):518–20; and Barlow, "Hubel and Wiesel: Their Contributions" [37].

39   On the emerging consensus that each species is specially "prepared" to acquire certain kinds of information, see J. Garcia and M. S. Levine, "Learning Paradigms and the Structure of the Organism," in M. R. Rosenzweig and E. L. Bennett, eds., *Neural Mechanisms of Learning and Memory* (Cambridge, Mass.: M.I.T. Press, 1976); M. E. P. Seligman, "On the Generality of the Laws of Learning," *Psychological Review* 77 (1970):406–18; and P. Rozin, "The Evolution of Intelligence: An Access to the Cognitive Unconscious," *Progress in Psychology and Physiological Psychology* 6 (1976):245–80.

      The work on the songs of female sparrows is reported in M. Baker, "Early Experience Determines Song Dialect Responsiveness of Female Sparrows," *Science* 214 (1981):819–20.

40   W. M. Cowan's studies are reviewed in his article, "The Development of the Brain," *Scientific American* 241 (1979):112–33.

      Patricia Goldman's findings on nervous system adaptation were drawn from P. S. Goldman and T. W. Galkin, "Prenatal Removal of Frontal Association Cortex in the Fetal

Page

Rhesus Monkey: Anatomical and Functional Consequences in Postnatal Life," *Brain Research* 152 (1978):451–85.

40   Concerning "critical periods" in development, see Gollin, ed., *Developmental Plasticity* [37].

On the high degree of modifiability in regions like the corpus callosum, see G. M. Innocenti, "The Development of Interhemispheric Connections," *Trends in Neuroscience* 1981, pp. 142–44.

41   On the acquisition of speech following removal of an entire hemisphere early in life, see Dennis, "Language Acquisition" [38].

On the cat's visual system, see D. H. Hubel and T. N. Wiesel, "Brain Mechanisms of Vision," *Scientific American* 241 (3 [1979]):150–62; and Barlow, "Hubel and Wiesel: Their Contributions" [37].

On the long-term effects of injury to the brain and nervous system, see P. S. Goldman-Rakic, A. Isseroff, M. L. Schwartz, and N. M. Bugbee, "Neurobiology of Cognitive Development in Non-Human Primates," unpublished paper, Yale University, 1981.

42   The study by M. Rosenzweig and his colleagues on rats in enriched and impoverished environments: M. R. Rosenzweig, K. Mollgaard, M. C. Diamond, and E. L. Bennett, "Negative as Well as Positive Synaptic Changes May Store Memory," *Psychological Review* 79, (1 [1972]):93–96. See also E. L. Bennett, "Cerebral Effects of Differential Experiences and Training," in Rosenzweig and Bennett, *Neural Mechanisms* [39].

William Greenough's findings on animals raised in complex environments are reported in his "Experience-Induced Changes in Brain Fine Structure: Their Behavioral Implications," in M. E. Hahn, C. Jensen, and B. C. Dudek, eds., *Development and Evolution of Brain Size: Behavioral Implications* (New York: Academic Press, 1979).

43   F. Nottebohm correlates the size of two nuclei in the canary's brain with the appearance of singing, in "Ontogeny of Bird Song," *Science* 167 (1970):950–56.

The observations by O. and A. Vogt were reported by Arnold Scheibel in a paper given at the Academy of Aphasia, London, Ontario, October 1981. See also R. A. Yeo, et al., "Volumetric Parameters of the Normal Human Brain: Intellectual Correlates," unpublished paper, University of Texas at Austin, 1982.

On the production of an excess of neuronal fibers, see J. P. Changeux and A. Danchin, "Selective Stabilization of Developing Synapses as a Mechanism for the Specification of Neuronal Networks," *Nature* 264 (1976):705–12.

44   On the period of "selective cell death," see W. M. Cowan, "The Development of the Brain," *Scientific American* 241 (1979):112–33. Also see M. Pines, "Baby, You're Incredible," *Psychology Today*, February 1982, pp. 48–53.

The tremendous growth of cell connections after lesions was described by Gary Lynch in a paper presented at the International Neuropsychology Society, Pittsburgh, Pa., February 1982.

The reduction in the rate of death of retinal ganglion cells when one eye is removed at birth, is documented in D. R. Sengelaub and B. L. Finlay, "Early Removal of One Eye Reduces Normally Occurring Cell Death in the Remaining Eye," *Science* 213 (1981):573–74.

On U-shaped phenomena, see S. Strauss, ed., *U-Shaped Behavioral Growth* (New York: Academic Press, 1982).

Peter Huttenlocher discusses changes in the density of synapses with age, in "Synaptic Density in Human Frontal Cortex: Developmental Changes and the Effects of Aging," *Brain Research* 163 (1979):195–205.

45   On neural changes in later life, see M. C. Diamond, "Aging and Cell Loss: Calling for an Honest Count," *Psychology Today*, September 1978; S. McConnell, "Summary of Research on the Effects of Aging on the Brain," unpublished technical report, the Harvard Project on Human Potential, Cambridge, Mass., 1981; R. D. Terry, "Physical Changes of the Aging Brain," in J. A. Behnke, C. E. Finch, and G. B. Moment, eds., *The Biology of Aging* (New York: Plenum Press, 1979); M. E. Scheibel and A. B. Scheibel, "Structural Changes in the Aging Brain," in H. Brody, D. Harman, and J. M. Ordy, eds., *Aging*, vol. 1 (New York: Raven Press, 1975); J. M. Ordy, B. Kaack, and K. R. Brizzee, "Life-Span Neurochemical Changes in the Human and Nonhuman Primate Brain," in H. Brody, D. Harman, and J. M. Ordy, eds., *Aging*, vol.1 (New York: Raven Press, 1975).

Page

On bird song, see Marler and Peters, "Selective Vocal Learning in a Sparrow," [37]. Also see Nottebohm, "Brain Pathways," [37], and "Ontogeny of Bird Song" [43].

46   E. R. Kandel described his work on the simplest forms of learning in aplysia, in "Steps toward a Molecular Grammar for Learning: Explorations into the Nature of Memory," paper presented at the Bicentennial Symposium of the Harvard Medical School, 11 October 1982, p. 9.

47   Kandel's summary is from p. 35 of the paper cited in the previous note.

48   On the link between poor nutrition and unstable emotions in children, see J. Cravioto and E. R. Delicardie, "Environmental and Nutritional Deprivation in Children with Learning Disabilities," in W. Cruickshank and D. Hallahan, eds., *Perceptual and Learning Disabilities in Children*, vol. II (Syracuse: Syracuse University Press, 1975).

49   Vernon Mountcastle's view of the organization of the cerebral cortex may be found in his "An Organizing Principle for Cerebral Function: The Unit Module and the Distributed System," in G. M. Edelman and V. B. Mountcastle, eds., *The Mindful Brain* (Cambridge, Mass.: M.I.T. Press, 1978).

David Hubel and Torsten Wiesel's statement is from their article, "Brain Mechanisms of Vision, *Scientific American* 241 (3 [1979]):161. On frontal lobe organization, see W. Nauta, The Problem of the Frontal Lobe: A Reinterpretation," *Journal of Psychiatric Research* 8 (1971):167–87; P. S. Goldman-Rakic, A. Isseroff, M. L. Schwartz, and N. M. Bugbee, "Neurobiology of Cognitive Development in Non-Human Primates," unpublished paper, Yale University, 1981.

On the responses of cortical cells in the visual system to color, direction of movement, and depth, see Hubel, and Wiesel, "Brain Mechanisms" [49], p. 162.

On the relaying of information from one cortical area to the next, see Lettvin, " 'Filling out the Forms' " [38].

50   For details on the speculations by P. Goldman and M. Constantine-Paton, see F. H. C. Crick, "Thinking about the Brain," *Scientific American* 241 (3 [1979]):228.

Crick's remark is from p. 228 of the article cited in the preceding note.

51   Sources on brain laterality include B. Milner, "Hemispheric Specializations: Scope and Limits," in F. O. Schmitt and F. G. Worden, eds., *The Neurosciences: Third Study Program* (Cambridge, Mass.: M.I.T. Press, 1974), pp. 75–89; and M. Kinsbourne, "Hemisphere Specialization and the Growth of Human Understanding," *American Psychologist* 37 (4 [1982]): 411–20.

On linguistic disorders resulting from lesions in different areas of the brain, see H. Gardner, *The Shattered Mind: The Person after Brain Damage* (New York: Alfred A. Knopf, 1975).

D. Hubel's statement is from his article, "Vision and the Brain," *Bulletin of the American Academy of Arts and Sciences* 31 (7 [1978]):7, 17–28.

52   On language zones in the deaf, see H. J. Neville and U. Bellugi, "Patterns of Cerebral Specialization in Congenitally Deaf Adults: A Preliminary Report," in P. Siple, ed., *Understanding Language through Sign Language Research* (New York: Academic Press, 1978).

The gestural language developed by deaf children is discussed in S. Goldin-Meadow, "Language Development without a Language Model," paper presented at the Biennial Meeting of the Society for Research in Child Development, Boston, April 1981; to appear in K. Nelson, ed., *Children's Language*, vol. V (New York: Gardner Press).

The case of Genie, a severely abused child who acquired language through the use of her right hemisphere, is described by S. Curtiss in *Genie: A Linguistic Study of a Modern-Day Wild Child* (New York: Academic Press, 1977).

53   The view of the brain as an "equipotential organ" is put forth by Karl S. Lashley in his paper, "In Search of the Engram," in *Symposia of the Society for Experimental Biology* 4 (1950):454–82.

For flaws in Lashley's conception of equipotentiality, see R. B. Loucks, "Methods of Isolating Stimulation Effects with Implanted Barriers," in D. E. Sheer, ed., *Electrical Stimulation of the Brain* (Austin: University of Texas Press, 1981).

54   The findings that specific lesions lead to impairments in the performance of rats running mazes are reported in J. Garcia and M. S. Levine, "Learning Paradigms and the Structure of the Organism," in Rosenzweig and Bennett, *Neural Mechanisms* [39].

On the importance of the posterior parietal regions for tasks measuring "raw" intelligence, see E. Zaidel, D. W. Zaidel, and R. W. Sperry, "Left and Right Intelligence: Case

Studies of Raven's Progressive Matrices Following Brain Bisection and Hemidecortica-tion," *Cortex* 17 (1981):167–86.

The effects of right and left hemisphere impairments on different aspects of drawing are described in chapter 8 of Gardner, *Shattered Mind* [51]; see also references cited therein.

55   The view that human cognition consists of many cognitive devices may be found in J. A. Fodor, *The Modularity of Mind* (Cambridge, Mass.: M.I.T. Press, 1983).

See also M. Gazzaniga and J. Ledoux, *The Integrated Mind* (New York: Plenum Press, 1978); and P. Rozin, "The Evolution of Intelligence and Access to the Cognitive Uncon-scious," *Progress in Psychobiology and Physiological Psychology* 6 (1976):245–80.

For Allport's view on special purpose cognitive devices, see D. A. Allport, "Patterns and Actions: Cognitive Mechanisms Are Content Specific," in G. L. Claxton, ed., *Cognitive Psychology: New Directions* (London: Routledge & Kegan Paul, 1980).

P. Rozin discusses the special capacity of becoming aware of the operation of one's own information-processing system, in his "The Evolution of Intelligence and Access to the Cognitive Unconscious," cited in the previous note.

57   For evidence that the growth by alternative routes, which plasticity permits, is not always advantageous, see B. T. Woods, "Observations on the Neurological Basis for Initial Language," and N. Geschwind, "Some Comments on the Neurology of Language," in Caplan, *Biological Studies* [38].

Chapter 4. What Is an Intelligence?

61   On the development of the ability to recognize faces, see S. Carey, R. Diamond, and B. Woods, "Development of Face Recognition—A Maturational Component?" *Developmental Psychology* 16 (1980):257–69.

Larry Gross's five modes of communication are discussed in his "Modes of Communi-cation and the Acquisition of Symbolic Capacities, in D. Olson, ed., *Media and Symbols* (Chicago: University of Chicago Press, 1974).

On Paul Hirst's seven forms of knowledge, see his *Knowledge and the Curriculum* (Lon-don: Routledge & Kegan Paul, 1974).

62   On Selfridge's "demon model" of intelligence, see O. G. Selfridge, "Pandemonium: A Paradigm for Learning," in *Symposium on the Mechanization of Thought Processes*, vol. I (London: H. M. Stationery Office, 1959).

63   For a discussion of *idiots savants*, see chapters 5 and 6 in H. Gardner, *The Shattered Mind: The Person after Brain Damage* (New York: Alfred A. Knopf, 1975).

68   Discussion of the decisional aspects of deploying an intelligence can be found in my colleague Israel Scheffler's forthcoming book, tentatively titled "Of Human Potential."

The "know-how" versus "know-that" distinction is treated in G. Ryle, *The Concept of Mind* (London: Hutchinson, 1949).

Chapter 5. Linguistic Intelligence

73   The Gilbert Islander's statement is from R. Finnegan, "Literacy versus Non-Literacy: The Great Divide?" in R. Horton and R. Finnegan, eds., *Modes of Thought: Essays on Thinking in Western and Non-Western Societies* (London: Faber & Faber, 1973).

Lillian Hellman's description of writing is from her autobiography, *An Unfinished Woman* (New York: Bantam, 1970).

Page

Keith Douglas's correspondence with T. S. Eliot is described in A. Coleman's article, "T. S. Eliot and Keith Douglas," *London Times Literary Supplement*, 7 February 1970, p. 731.

74   T. S. Eliot's search for the right words is detailed in C. Ricks, "Intense transparencies," review of *The Composition of "Four Quartets,"* by Helen Gardner, *London Times Literary Supplement*, 15 September 1978, pp. 1006–8.

Robert Graves's search for the right word is described in his *On Poetry: Selected Talks and Essays* (Garden City, N.Y.: Doubleday, 1969), pp. 417–19.

Stephen Spender's search for the right words is described in B. Ghiselin, ed., *The Creative Process* (New York: Mentor, New American Library, 1952), p. 112.

76   T. S. Eliot's observation on the logic of the poet is from his preface to St. John Perse's *Anabasis* (New York: Harcourt, Brace, Jovanovich, 1970).

W. H. Auden's remark is from C. D. Abbott, ed., *Poets at Work* (New York: Harcourt, Brace, 1948), p. 171.

H. Read's statement on the visual nature of poetic words is from his *The Philosophy of Modern Art* (London: Faber & Faber, 1964), p. 147.

77   Helen Vendler discusses Robert Lowell's poetry classes in her "Listening to Lowell," *New York Times Book Review*, 3 February 1980.

N. Frye's statement is from the "Polemical Introduction" to his book, *The Well-Tempered Critic* (Bloomington: Indiana University Press, 1963), p. 5.

The importance of sensitivity to the subtle shades of difference in words is discussed in J. L. Austin, *Philosophical Papers*, 3rd ed., J. O. Urmson and G. J. Warnock, eds. (Oxford and New York: Oxford University Press, 1979), p. 274.

78   Major points of N. Chomsky's theory are laid out in his *Language and Mind* (New York: Harcourt, Brace, Jovanovich, 1968).

79   On the functions of language, see R. Jakobson, "Closing Statement: Linguistics and Poetics," in T. A. Sebeok, ed., *Style in Language* (Cambridge, Mass.: M.I.T. Press, 1960).

On the development of linguistic ability in children, see H. Gardner, *Developmental Psychology*, 2nd ed. (Boston: Little, Brown, 1982), chapter 4; and P. Dale, *Language Development: Structure and Function* (Hillsdale, Ill.: Dryden, 1972).

80   Evidence for the claim that certain initial assumptions about the operation of language are built into the nervous system may be found in K. Wexler and P. Culicover, *Formal Principles of Language Acquisition* (Cambridge, Mass.: M.I.T. Press, 1980). See also D. Osherson, "Thoughts on Learning Functions," unpublished paper, University of Pennsylvania, 1978; and N. Chomsky, *Rules and Representations* (New York: Columbia University Press, 1980).

81   J. P. Sartre's statement, "By writing I was existing," is from his autobiography, *The Words: The Autobiography of Jean-Paul Sartre* (New York: George Braziller, 1964), p. 153. His statement "My pen raced . . ." (describing his activities at the age of nine) is on p. 181.

82   Auden's discussion of the pitfalls that threaten to ensnare the young writer, and his analogy of a young lad courting, are from his *Forewords and Afterwords* (New York: Vintage, 1973), p. 13.

Stephen Spender's discussion of his sheer memory for experiences is quoted in Ghiselin, *Creative Process* [74], pp. 120–21.

Auden discusses the undeveloped poet, and the worth of writing a dozen rhopalic hexameters, in his *Forewords and Afterwords.* [82], pp. 224–25.

83   Thornton Wilder's comment is quoted in M. Cowley, ed., *Writers at Work: The Paris Review Interviews* (New York: Viking Press, 1959), p. 117.

Walter Jackson Bate's comment on Keats is from W. J. Bate, *John Keats*. (New York: Oxford University Press, 1966), p. 438.

Igor Stravinsky describes Auden's ability to write verse on command, in I. Stravinsky, *Stravinsky in Conversation with Robert Craft* (Harmondsworth, England: Pelican Books, 1962), p. 280.

Karl Shapiro's statement on genius in poetry is quoted in Abbott, *Poets at Work* [76], p. 94.

84   On Einstein's life and work, see B. Hoffman, *Einstein* (Frogmore, St. Albans, Herts, Great Britain: Paladin, 1975).

Language-disturbed children's simplification of sentences was discussed by H. Sinclair-de-Zwart in a lecture at Harvard University in May 1976. Also see H. Sinclair-de-Zwart, "Language Acquisition and Cognitive Development, in T. E. Moore, ed., *Cognitive*

Page

Development and the Acquisition of Language (New York: Academic Press, 1973); and A. Sinclair, et al., *The Child's Conception of Language,* (Springer Series in Language and Communication: vol. II [New York: Springer-Verlag, 1979]).

85   On hyperlexic children, see C. C. Mehegan, and F. E. Dreifuss, "Exceptional Reading Ability in Brain-Damaged Children," *Neurology 22,* (1972):1105–11; and D. E. Elliot and R. M. Needleman, "The Syndrome of Hyperlexia,," *Brain and Language* 3 (1976):339–49.

On brain laterality and language, see J. M. Ranklin, D. M. Aram, and S. J. Horowitz, "Language Ability in Right and Left Hemiplegic Children," *Brain and Language* 14 (1981):292–306. Also see M. Dennis, "Language Acquisition in a Single Hemisphere: Semantic Organization," in D. Caplan, ed., *Biological Studies of Mental Processes* (Cambridge, Mass.: M.I.T. Press, 1980).

86   Genie's case is documented in S. Curtiss, *Genie: A Linguistic Study of a Modern-Day Wild Child* (New York: Academic Press, 1977). On the capacity of deaf children with hearing parents to develop a gestural language system, see S. Goldin-Meadow, "Language Development without a Language Model," paper presented at the biennial meeting of the Society for Research in Child Development, Boston, April 1981; to appear in K. Nelson, ed., *Children's Language,* vol. V. (New York: Gardner Press).

87   Evidence that language is more strongly focalized in the left hemisphere in males is cited in M. H. Wittig and A. C. Petersen, eds. *Sex-Related Differences in Cognitive Functioning* (New York: Academic Press, 1979); A. Kertesz, "Recovery and Treatment," in K. M. Heilman and E. Valenstein, eds., *Clinical Neuropsychology* (New York: Oxford University Press, 1979); and J. Levy, "Cerebral Asymmetry and the Psychology of Man," in Wittig and Peterson, *Sex-related Differences,* previously cited in this note.

For evidence from studies of the brain that written language "piggybacks" on oral language, see H. Gardner, *The Shattered Mind: The Person after Brain Damage* (New York: Alfred A. Knopf, 1975), chap. 3.

88   On the decoding of *kana* versus *kanji* symbols, see S. Sasnuma, "Kana and Kanji Processing in Japanese Aphasics," *Brain and Language* 2 (1975):369–82.

On the ability of certain grossly aphasic individuals to perform well on other cognitive tasks, see H. Gardner, "Artistry Following Damage to the Human Brain," in A. Ellis, ed., *Normality and Pathology in Cognitive Functions* (London: Academic Press, 1982).

On idioglossia, anomic aphasia, and the different writing styles produced by different lesions, see Gardner, *Shattered Mind* [87], chaps. 2 and 3.

90   On the evolution of the brain, see M. LeMay, "Morphological Cerebral Asymmetries of Modern Man, Fossil Man, and Nonhuman Primate," in S. R. Harnad, H. D. Steklis, and J. Lancaster, *Origins and Evolution of Language and Speech* (New York: New York Academy of Sciences, 1976), vol. 280.

91   For N. Chomsky's views on the evolution of language, see his *Reflections on Language* (New York: Pantheon, 1975). I learned of C. Lévi-Strauss's view that language evolved in a single moment in time from a personal communication, June 1981.

On the evolution of language in man and apes, see G. W. Hewes, "The Current Status of the Gestural Theory of Language Origin," in Harnad, Steklis, and Lancaster, *Origins and Evolution* [90], vol. 280.

On the evolution of language in chimpanzees, see T. A. Sebeok and J. Umiker-Sebeok, eds., *Speaking of Apes: A Critical Anthology of Two-Way Communication with Man* (New York: Plenum Press, 1980).

The evolution of the human capacity for speech is also discussed in P. Lieberman, "On the Evolution of Language: A Unified View," *Cognition* 2 (1974):59–95.

On contemporary singers of verse, see A. B. Lord, *The Singer of Tales* (New York: Atheneum, 1965).

92   On the mnemonic demands of chess, see W. Chase and H. Simon, "The Mind's Eye in Chess," in W. G. Chase, ed., *Visual Information Processing* (New York: Academic Press, 1973).

On E. F. Dube's finding that illiterate Africans remember stories better than do schooled Africans or schooled New Yorkers, see "A Cross-Cultural Study of the Relationship between 'Intelligence' Level and Story Recall," unpublished Ph. D. dissertation, Cornell University, 1977. Dube's findings are also cited in W. W. Lambert's *Introduction to Perspectives,* vol. 1 of the *Handbook of Cross-Cultural Psychology,* H. C. Triandis and W. W. Lambert, eds. (Boston: Allyn & Bacon, 1980), p. 29.

Page

G. Bateson, *Naven* (Stanford, Calif.: Stanford University Press, 1958), p. 222. The importance of memory in classical and medieval times is described in F. Yates, *The Art of Memory* (London: Routledge & Kegan Paul, 1966).

Ericcson and Chase's findings on the memory of digits can be found in K. A. Ericcson, W. G. Chase, and S. Faloon, "Acquisition of a Memory Skill," *Science* 208 (1980):1181–82.

93   Susanne Langer's introspection on verbal memory is from the article, "A Lady Seeking Answers," *New York Times Book Review* 26 May 1968.

A. R. Luria describes his study of a mnemonist in *The Mind of the Mnemonist* (New York: Basic Books, 1968).

Verbal dueling among the Chamula of Chiapas, Mexico, is discussed by G. Gossen in his paper, "To Speak with a Heated Heart: Chamula Canons of Style and Good Performance," in R. Bauman and J. Sherzer, eds., *Explorations in the Ethnography of Speaking* (Cambridge: Cambridge University Press, 1974).

94   The Mayan language, Tzeltal, is described in B. Stross, "Speaking of Speaking: Tenejapa Tzeltal Metalinguistics," in the same book by Bauman and Sherzer.

Deep Kpelle is described in M. Cole, J. Gay, J. A. Glick, and D. W. Sharp, *The Cultural Context of Learning and Thinking* (New York: Basic Books, 1971).

J. Comaroff discusses the Tshidi of Botswana in his "Talking Politics: Oratory and Authority in a Tswana Chiefdom," in M. Bloch, ed., *Political Language and Oratory in Traditional Society* (London: Academic Press, 1975).

E. Havelock discusses Greek oral culture in his *Preface to Plato.* (Cambridge, Mass.: Harvard University Press, 1963), p. 126.

97   Henry James's statement is taken from his *The Art of the Novel*, R. Blackmur, ed. (New York: Charles Scribner's, 1950; originally published, 1934), p. 122.

"Of language calling attention to itself": R. Jakobson is quoted in I. A. Richards, "Jakobson on the Subliminal Structures of a Sonnet," *The London Times Literary Supplement*, 28 May 1980.

Chapter 6. Musical Intelligence

99   Hoene Wronsky's definition of music is quoted in D. H. Cope, *New Directions in Music* (Dubuque, Iowa: Wm. C. Brown, 1978), p. 87.

101   R. Sessions's discussion of composing music is taken from *Questions about Music* (New York: W. W. Norton, 1970), p. 89.

Sessions's definition of "logical musical thinking" may be found on p. 110 of his *Questions about Music*, cited in the preceding note.

102   On the task of the composer, also see A. Copland, *What to Listen for in Music* (New York: McGraw-Hill, 1939). Aaron Copland's statement on composing as a natural act is from p. 20.

Arnold Schoenberg's remark is quoted in C. Rosen, "The Possibilities of Disquiet," a review of B. Tagebuch's book *Arnold Schoenberg*, J. Rufer, ed., *The London Times Literary Supplement*, 7 November 1975, p. 1336.

Harold Shapero's views are quoted in B. Ghiselin, *The Creative Process* (New York: New American Library, 1952), pp. 49–50.

103   Sessions discusses the process of composition in his *Questions about Music* [101], pp. 29–30.

Igor Stravinsky's remark occurs in his *Conversations with Robert Craft* (London: Pelican Books, 1971), p. 29.

Arnold Schoenberg quotes Schopenhauer's view in Rosen, "The Possibilities of Disquiet," [102], p. 1335.

C. Levi-Strauss's phrase "whose minds secrete music" is from his *The Raw and the Cooked: An Introduction to a Science of Mythology* (New York: Harper & Row, 1969), p. 18.

Page

    A. Copland discusses the intelligent listener in his *What to Listen for in Music* [102], p. 17.

104   E. T. Cone's view of "active listening" is taken from his *Musical Form and Musical Performance* (New York: W. W. Norton, 1968), p. 21.

    Cone's remarks on adequate musical performance are on p. 31 of the previously cited book.

    Stravinsky discusses his intended audience in his *Conversations with Robert Craft* [103], p. 32.

    The different musical emphases in different cultures are described by E. May in *Musics of Many Cultures* (Berkeley: University of California Press, 1980).

105   Sessions's remark is from his *Questions about Music* [101], p. 42.

    Arnold Schoenberg's definition of music is taken from his *Letters*, E. Stein, ed. (New York: St. Martin's Press, 1965), p. 186.

    S. Langer discusses the emotional implications of music in her *Philosophy in a New Key: A Study in the Symbolism of Reason, Rite, and Art* (Cambridge, Mass.: Harvard University Press, 1942).

106   Sessions's statement is from his *Questions about Music* [101], p. 14.

    Stravinsky's remark and his later recantation may be found in R. Craft and I. Stravinsky, *Expositions and Developments* (London: Faber & Faber, 1962), pp. 101–2.

    Paul Vitz's studies are described in P. Vitz and T. Todd, "Preference for Tones as a Function of Frequency (Hz) and Intensity (db)," *Psychological Review* 78 (3[1971]):207–28.

107   The "middle-ground" approach to research on music is taken in C. Krumhansl, "The Psychological Representation of Musical Pitch in a Tonal Context," *Cognitive Psychology* 11 (1979):346–74.

    A review of findings on the psychology of music can be found in E. Winner, *Invented Worlds* (Cambridge, Mass.: Harvard University Press, 1982).

108   Mechthild and Hanus Papoušek's studies are described in M. Papoušek, "Musical Elements in Mother-Infant Dialogues," paper presented at the International Conference on Infant Studies, Austin, Texas, March 1982.

109   On the development in children of musical competence, see L. Davidson, P. McKernon, and H. Gardner, "The Acquisition of Song: A Developmental Approach," in *Documentary Report of the Ann Arbor Symposium* (Reston, Va.: Music Educators National Conference, 1981).

110   J. C. Messenger describes music and dance among the Anang of Nigeria in "Reflections on Esthetic Talent," *Basic College Quarterly* 4 (20–24 [1958]):pp. 20–21.

    A. Merriam describes musical training among the Venda at Northern Transvaal in A. Merriam, *The Anthropology of Music* (Evanston, Ill.: Northwestern University Press, 1964), p. 148; the Griots in Senegambia are discussed on p. 158. Also see E. May, *Musics of Many Cultures* (Berkeley: University of California Press, 1980).

    On J. Bamberger's work, see E. Winner, *Invented Worlds* [107]; and J. Bamberger, "Growing up Prodigies: The Mid-Life Crisis," *New Directions for Child Development* 17 (1982):61–78.

112   On the Suzuki Talent Education Program, see S. Suzuki, *Nurtured by Love* (New York: Exposition Press, 1969); B. Holland, "Among Pros, More go Suzuki," *The New York Times*, 11 July 1982, E9; and L. Taniuchi, "The Creation of Prodigies through Special Early Education: Three Case Studies," unpublished paper, Harvard Project on Human Potential, Cambridge, Mass., 1980.

113   On L. Vygotsky's notion of a zone of proximal development, see his *Mind in Society*, M. Cole, ed. (Cambridge, Mass.: Harvard University Press, 1978).

    On A. Rubinstein's early years, see his *My Young Years* (New York: Alfred A. Knopf, 1973). Rubinstein reflects on the lack of musical gifts in his family on p. 4

    Rubinstein's description of his musical play in the drawing room is also from p. 4 of this book.

    On Rubinstein's meeting with Joachim, see p. 7 of the same book.

114   R. Serkin is quoted in M. Meyer, "He Turned the Store Upside Down," *The New York Times*, 7 December 1969, D1.

    Stravinsky's reflection is found in Stravinsky and Craft, *Expositions and Developments* [106], p. 21.

115   On music in other cultures, see Merriam, *Anthropology of Music* [110]; and B. Nettl,

Page

Music in Primitive Culture (Cambridge, Mass.: Harvard University Press, 1956).

John Lennon is quoted in B. Miles, "The Lennon View," *The Boston Globe*, 11 December 1980, p. 1.

On the evolution of music, see J. Pfeiffer, *The Creative Explosion: An Inquiry into the Origins of Art and Religion* (New York: Harper & Row, 1982).

116   On bird song, see F. Nottebohm, "Brain Pathways for Vocal Learning in Birds: A Review of the First 10 Years," *Progress in Psychobiological and Physiological Psychology*, 9 (1980):85–124; M. Konishi in R. A. Hinde, ed., *Bird Vocalization* (Cambridge: Cambridge University Press, 1969); and P. Marler and S. Peters, "Selective Vocal Learning in a Sparrow," *Science*, 198 (1977):519–21.

117   The statement "bird songs are promise of music . . ." is from I. Stravinsky, *The Poetics of Music in the Form of Six Lessons* (New York: Vintage, 1956), p. 24.

On D. Deutsch's finding of 40 percent error in recall of tones, see her "The Organization of Short-Term Memory for a Single Acoustic Attribute," in D. Deutsch and J. A. Deutsch, eds., *Short-term memory* (New York: Academic Press, 1975), p. 112; see pp. 108–12 for evidence that verbal material does not interfere with melodic material.

118   The effects of brain damage on musical abilities are described in M. I. Botez, T. Botez, and M. Aube, "Amusia: Clinical and Computerized Scanning (CT) Correlations," *Neurology* 30 (April 1980):359.

For review of the findings on Ravel, Shebalin, and other composers, as well as for a survey of the neuropsychology of music, see H. Gardner, "Artistry Following Damage to the Human Brain," in A. Ellis, ed., *Normality and Pathology in Cognitive Functions* (London: Academic Press, 1982).

119   H. Gordon's findings are described in his article, "Degree of Ear Asymmetries for Perception of Dichotic Chords and for Illusory Chord Localization in Musicians of Different Levels of Competence," *Journal of Experimental Psychology: Human Perception and Performance* 6 (1980):516–27.

120   On *idiots savants* with unusual musical skills (Harriet), see B. M. Minogue, "A Case of Secondary Mental Deficiency with Musical Talent," *Journal of Applied Psychology* 7 (1923): 349–57; W. A. Owens and W. Grim, "A Note Regarding Exceptional Musical Ability in a Low-Grade Imbecile," *Journal of Educational Psychology* 32 (1942): 636–37; and D. S. Viscott, "A Musical Idiot Savant," *Psychiatry* 33 (1970): 494–515.

121   Peter F. Ostwald's statement about a young composer is from his paper, "Musical Behavior in Early Childhood," *Developmental Medicine and Child Neurology* 15 (3 June 1973):368.

Stravinsky's reminiscences on the fife-and-drum marine band are from Stravinsky and Craft, *Expositions and Developments* [106], pp. 21, 28.

Stravinsky's recollection of the singing of the countrywomen is from p. 36 of the same book.

122   On the properties of music valued in Japan, see W. Malm, "Some of Japan's Musics and Musical Principles," in May, *Musics of Many Cultures* [110], p. 52.

G. Bateson, *Naven*, 2nd ed. (Stanford, Calif.: Stanford University Press, 1958).

123   Lévi-Strauss discusses music in *The Raw and The Cooked* [103], p. 18.

Stravinsky states that music must be seen to be properly assimilated, in *Poetics of Music* [117].

Harris discusses the importance of spatial abilities for composers, in L. J. Harris, "Sex Differences in Spatial Ability," in M. Kinsbourne, ed., *Asymmetrical Functions of the Brain* (Cambridge: Cambridge University Press, 1978).

On A. Lintgen's astonishing ability to recognize musical pieces from the grooves on the phonograph record, see B. Holland, "A Man Who Sees What Others Hear," *The New York Times*, 19 November 1981; also, "Read Any Good Records Lately?" *Time*, 4 January 1982.

124   The case of the composer who sustained right hemisphere damage, yet remained able to teach and write books about music, is described in H. Gardner, "Artistry following Damage to the Human Brain," in A. Ellis, ed., *Language Functions and Brain Organization* (London: Academic Press, 1982). The musician who lost his aesthetic feeling is described in K. Popper and J. Eccles, *The Self and Its Brain* (New York: Springer International, (1977), p. 338.

125   On the search for parallels between music and language, see F. Lerdahl and R. Jacken-

Page

doff, "Toward a Formal Theory of Tonal Music," *Journal of Music Theory*, Spring 1977, pp. 111–71; and J. Sundberg and B. Lindblom, "Generative Theories in Language and Music Descriptions," *Cognition* 4 (1976):99–122.

On the connections between music and math, see E. Rothstein, "Math and Music: The Deeper Links," *The New York Times*, 29 August 1982.

126 Stravinsky's statement on the relationship of music to mathematics is from his *Conversations with Robert Craft* [103], p. 34.

Stravinsky's statement "I know . . . that these discoveries . . ." is from Stravinsky and Craft, *Expositions and Developments* [106], p. 99.

127 Stravinsky's contention that music and mathematics are not alike comes from his *Poetics of Music* [117], p. 99.

G. H. Hardy's statement is quoted in Anthony Storr's article "The Meaning of Music," *The London Literary Supplement*, 28 November 1970.

Chapter 7. Logical-Mathematical Intelligence

128 Whitehead's statement is from A. N. Whitehead, *Science and the Modern World* (New York: New American Library, 1948), p. 26.

Piaget relates the anecdote about the childhood of a future mathematician in his *Genetic Epistemology* (New York: W. W. Norton, 1971).

Piaget's work on the development of logical-mathematical thought may be found in his *The Child's Conception of Number* (New York: W. W. Norton, 1965); J. Piaget and B. Inhelder, *The Psychology of the Child* (New York: Basic Books, 1969). Also see H. Gardner, *The Quest for Mind: Piaget, Lévi-Strauss, and the Structuralist Movement* (Chicago and London: University of Chicago Press, 1981); J. P. Flavell, *The Developmental Psychology of Jean Piaget* (Princeton: Van Nostrand, 1963); and H. Gruber and J. Vonèche, eds., *The Essential Piaget* (New York: Basic Books, 1977).

On the child's numerical development, see R. Gelman and R. Gallistel, *The Child's Understanding of Number* (Cambridge, Mass.: Harvard University Press, 1978).

134 For a critical treatment of Piaget's theory, see C. Brainerd, *Piaget's Theory of Intelligence* (Englewood Cliffs, N.J.: Prentice-Hall, 1978).

135 B. Rotman's view is from his book *Jean Piaget: The Psychologist of the Real* (Ithaca, N.Y.: Cornell University Press, 1977), p. 77.

Euler is quoted in G. Polya, *How to Solve It* (New York: Anchor Books, 1957), p. 3.

Quine's distinction between logic and mathematics may be found in his *Methods of Logic* (New York: Holt, Rinehart, & Winston, 1950), p. xvii. See also the article, "You Cannot Be a Twentieth-Century Man without Maths," *The Economist*, 27 October 1979, p. 107.

Whitehead and Russell's views are discussed in J. G. Kemeny, *A Philosopher Looks at Science* (New York: D. Van Nostrand, 1959).

Russell is quoted on p. 20 of Kemeny, *A Philosopher Looks at Science*, cited in preceding note.

Whitehead's statement is from his *Science and the Modern World*. [128], p. 27.

136 On the scientist and the world of practice, see W. V. Quine, "The Scope and Language of Science," in *The Ways of Paradox and Other Essays* (Cambridge, Mass., and London: Harvard University Press, 1966).

A. M. Gleason's figure of speech is from his essay, "The Evolution of Differential Topology," in COSRIMS, eds., *The Mathematical Sciences: A Collection of Essays* (Cambridge, Mass.: M.I.T. Press, 1969), p. 1.

The complex sentence is quoted by M. Polanyi in his *Personal Knowledge: Towards a Post-Critical Philosophy* (Chicago: University of Chicago Press, 1958), p. 118.

The two quotations of Henri Poincaré are from B. Ghiselin, ed., *The Creative Process* (Berkeley: University of California Press, 1952), p. 35.

Page
138   A. Adler's statement is from his article "Mathematics and Creativity," *The New Yorker*, 19 February 1972, pp. 39–40.

        Adler's statement regarding the qualities of mathematicians is from p. 44 of the article cited in the previous note. Adler's statement "A great new edifice . . . ," is from p. 45 of the same article.

139   G. H. Hardy's statement, "It is undeniable . . ." is from his *A Mathematician's Apology* (Cambridge: Cambridge University Press, 1967), p. 70.

        Hardy's statement "A mathematician . . ." is from the same source, p. 86.

        On Andrew Gleason, see COSRIMS, *Mathematical Sciences* [136], p. 177.

        S. Ulam's statement is from his *Adventures of a Mathematician* (New York: Charles Scribner's, 1976), p. 180.

        H. Poincaré is quoted in J. Hadamard, *An Essay on the Psychology of Invention in the Mathematical Field* (Princeton, N.J.: Princeton University Press, 1945), p. 106.

140   On errors of omission and of commission, see A. N. Whitehead, *Science and the Modern World* [128], p. 29.

        Adler describes the levels of abstraction in mathematics in his article "Mathematics and Creativity" [138], pp. 43–44.

141   Ulam's suggestion is from his *Adventures* [139], p. 120.

        On the ability to find an analogy between analogies, see Ulam, *Adventures* [139], p. 26.

142   Ulam discusses von Neumann on p. 76 of the same source.

        Bronowski's exchange with von Neumann is from J. Bronowski, *The Ascent of Man* (Boston: Little, Brown, 1973), p. 433.

        Julian Bigelow on von Neumann, in S. J. Heims, *John von Neumann and Norbert Wiener: From Mathematics to the Technologies of Life and Death* (Cambridge, Mass., and London: M.I.T. Press, 1980), p. 127.

143   The statement "Beyond anyone else . . ." is from p. 129 of the same book.

        Ulam's statements are from his *Adventures* [139], p. 292.

        Arthur Rubinstein's comment that mathematics is impossible for him is from his autobiography, *My Young Years* (New York: Alfred A. Knopf, 1973).

144   General pointers for mathematical problem solving may be found in A. Newell and H. Simon, *Human Problem-Solving* (Englewood Cliffs, N.J.: Prentice-Hall, 1972); and in G. Polya, *How to Solve It* [135].

145   Newton's role as one of the inventors of the calculus is described in the *Economist* article "You Cannot Be a Twentieth-Century Man without Maths," [135], p. 108.

146   J. Piaget describes the parallel between the evolution of science and the development of logical-mathematical thought in his *Logique et Connaissance Scientifique* (Paris: Encyclopédie de la Pléiade, 1967).

        H. Butterfield's comment is from his *The Origins of Modern Science* (New York: Free Press, 1965), p. 117.

147   Newton's view of himself as an explorer is quoted in Bronowski, *Ascent of Man* [142], p. 237.

        Bronowski's statement is from p. 223 of the previous title.

        A. Einstein's statement on "Truth in physical matters . . . ," is from Jeremy Bernstein's profile of Albert Einstein, *The New Yorker*, 5 March 1979, p. 28.

        Einstein's discussion of his career decision is from B. Hoffman, *Einstein* (Frogmore, St. Albans, Herts, Great Britain: Paladin, 1975), p. 8.

148   Ulam's statement is from his *Adventures* [139], p. 447.

        W. Heisenberg discusses Niels Bohr in his *Physics and Beyond* (New York: Harper & Row, 1962), p. 37.

        Heisenberg relates his conversation with Einstein on p. 68 of the previously cited book.

150   G. Holton's views are from his "On the Role of Themata in Scientific Thought," *Science* 188 (April 1975):328–38.

        Einstein is quoted in Kemeny, *A Philosopher Looks at Science* [135], p. 62.

        Holton's statement, "The awareness of themata . . ." is from "On the Role of Themata" [150], p. 331.

151   Frank Manuel's discussion of Newton is from F. Manuel, "Isaac Newton as Theologian," *The London Times Literary Supplement*, 29 June 1973, p. 744.

        Einstein's recollections of his early years are quoted in Hoffman, *Einstein* [147], p. 9.

Page

Ulam's recollections of his childhood are from his *Adventures* [139], p. 10.

152   On patterners and dramatists, see D. Wolf and H. Gardner, "Style and Sequence in Symbolic Play," in N. Smith and M. Franklin, eds., *Symbolic Functioning in Childhood* (Hillsdale, N.J.: Erlbaum Press, 1979).

On Pascal's youth, see C. M. Cox, "The Early Mental Traits of Three Hundred Geniuses," in L. M. Terman, ed., *Genetic Studies of Genius*, vol. 2 (Stanford, Calif.: Stanford University Press, 1926), p. 691.

B. Russell's reminiscence is quoted in R. Dinnage, "Risks and Calculations," review of Ronald W. Clark's "The Life of Bertrand Russell," *The London Times Literary Supplement*, 31 October 1975, p. 1282.

Ulam's account of the course of development of a passion for mathematics is from his *Adventures* [139], p. 19.

153   The anecdote about Saul Kripke is from T. Branch, "New Frontiers in American Philosophy," *The New York Times Sunday Magazine*, 14 August 1977.

Descartes's statement is quoted in G. Polya, *How to Solve It* [135], p.93.

154   G. H. Hardy's statement is from his *A Mathematician's Apology* (Cambridge: Cambridge University Press, 1967), p. 63.

I. I. Rabi's observation is quoted in Jeremy Bernstein's profile of I. I. Rabi, *The New Yorker*, 20 October 1975, p. 47.

Adler's statement that mathematical productivity drops with age is from his article "Mathematics and Creativity," [138], p. 40.

The view that humanistic scholarship gets better with age is discussed in M. W. Miller, "Unusual Promotion Granted in English," *Harvard Crimson*, 29 September 1982, p. 1.

155   On the calculating abilities of the mathematician Gauss and the astronomer Truman Safford, see K. R. Lewis and H. Plotkin, "Truman Henry Safford, the Remarkable 'Lightning Calculator,'" *Harvard Magazine*, September–October 1982, pp. 54–56.

On Obadiah and George, mathematical *idiots savants*, see W. A. Horwitz, et al., "Identical Twin-'idiot savants'—Calendar Calculators," *American Journal of Psychiatry*, 121 (1965):1075–79; and A. Phillips, "Talented Imbeciles," *Psychological Clinic* 18, 1930:246–65.

The *idiot savant* L. is described in M. Scheerer, E. Rothmann, and K. Goldstein, "A Case of 'Idiot Savant': An Experimental Study of Personality Organization," *Psychology Monographs* 269 (1945):1–61. Also see B. M. Minogue, "A Case of Secondary Mental Deficiency with Musical Talent," *Journal of Applied Psychology*, 7 (1923):349–57; W. A. Owens and W. Grim, "A Note Regarding Exceptional Musical Ability in a Low-Grade Imbecile," *Journal of Educational Psychology* 32 (1942):636–37; D. S. Viscott, "A Musical Idiot Savant," *Psychiatry* 33 (1970):494–515; A. C. Hill, "Idiot Savants: A Categorization of Abilities," *Mental Retardation* 12 (1974):12–13; E. Hoffman and R. Reeves, "An idiot savant with unusual mechanical ability," *American Journal of Psychiatry* 136 (1979):713–14; and R. M. Restak, "Islands of Genius," *Science* 82, May 1982, p. 63.

156   On the Gerstmann syndrome, see H. Gardner, *The Shattered Mind: The Person after Brain Damage* (New York: Vintage, 1974), chap. 6.

John Holt's question is raised in *How Children Fail* (New York: Delta Books, Dell Publishing, 1964), p. 92.

157   On the precursors to numerical ability in animals, see O. Kohler, in the Society for Experimental Biology publication *Physiological Mechanisms in Animal Behavior*, 1950.

On the dance language of bees, see K. von Frisch, *Dance Language and Orientation of Bees*, L. E. Chadwick, trans. (Cambridge, Mass.: Harvard University Press, 1967).

On the capacity of primates to make probability estimates, see D. Premack, *Intelligence in Ape and Man* (Hillsdale, N.J.: Erlbaum, 1976).

The importance of the right hemisphere for understanding numerical relations and quantities is discussed in N. Dahmen, W. Hartje, A. Büssing, and W. Sturm, "Disorders of Calculation in Aphasic Patients—Spatial and Verbal Components," *Neuropsychologia* 20 (2 [1982]):145–53; A. Basso, A. Berti, E. Capitani, and E. Fenu, "Aphasia, Acalculia, and Intelligence," paper presented at the International Neuropsychology Society, June 1981, Bergen, Norway; and E. K. Warrington, "The Fractionation of Arithmetic Skills: A Single Case Study." *Quarterly Journal of Experimental Psychology* 34A (1982):31–51.

158   On the importance of the left parietal lobes and of certain contiguous areas for logic and math, see J. Grafman, D. Passafiume, P. Faglioni, and F. Boller, "Calculation Disturbances in Adults with Focal Hemisphere Damage," *Cortex* 18 (1982):37–50.

Notes to Pages 158–165

Page

A. R. Luria discusses the effects of lesions in the area of the angular gyrus in his *Higher Cortical Functions in Man* (New York: Basic Books, 1966).

159   A. Gervais's studies document the involvement of both hemispheres during the solution of mathematical problems; the results are briefly described in "Complex Math for a Complex Brain," *Science News* 121, (23 January, 1982):58. Also see R. H. Kraft, O. R. Mitchell, M. L. Langvis, and G. H. Wheatley, "Hemispheric Asymmetries during Six-to-Eight-Year-Olds' Performance of Piagetian Conservation and Reading Tasks," *Neuropsychologia* 18 (1980):637–43.

160   Experimental tasks that "primitives" perform better than the investigators are described in B. N. Colby, "Folk Science Studies," *El Palacio*, Winter 1963, pp. 5–14.

161   On the design and appropriate use of elaborate hierarchically organized systems, see M. Cole, J. Gay, J. A. Glick, and D. W. Sharp, *The Cultural Context of Learning and Thinking* (New York: Basic Books, 1971).

On bargaining and trading skills, see M. Quinn, "Do Mfantse Fish Sellers Estimate Probabilities in Their Heads?" *American Ethnologist* 5 (2 [1978]):206–26. Also see H. Gladwin and C. Gladwin, "Estimating Market Conditions and Profit Expectations of Fish Sellers at Cape Coast, Ghana," in G. Dalton, ed., *Studies in Economic Anthropology*, Anthropological Studies, no. 7, P. J. Bohannon, ed. (Washington, D.C.: American Anthropological Association, 1971).

The statement on the skills of hunters in the African Bush is from Nicholas Blurton-Jones and Melvin Konner, "!Kung Knowledge of Animal Behavior," in R. B. Lee and I. DeVore, eds., *Kalahari Hunter-Gatherers* (Cambridge, Mass.: Harvard University Press, 1976), p. 35.

On the estimation abilities of Kpelle adults in Liberia, see J. Gay and M. Cole, *The New Mathematics and an Old Culture* (New York: Holt, Rinehart & Winston, 1967), pp. 43–44.

162   On the arithmetical game *kala*, see C. Zaslavsky, *Africa Counts: Number and Pattern in African Culture* (Boston: Prindle, Weber, & Schmidt, 1973), p. 130.

Cole's description of the strategies of winning players is from M. Cole, et al., *Cultural Context* [161] pp. 182–84.

The intertwining of mathematical thinking and religious pursuits is described in J. Goody, ed., *Introduction to Literacy in Traditional Societies* (Cambridge: Cambridge University Press, 1968); see p. 18 on the use of magic squares to ward off disease. Also see Zaslavsky, *Africa Counts* [162] p. 138.

The statement, "Mathematicians were denounced . . . " is from H. W. Smith, *Man and His Gods* (New York: Grosset & Dunlap, 1952), p. 261 (cited in Zaslavsky *Africa Counts* [162], p. 274).

On the mathematical systems of the medieval Indians, see K. Menninger, *Number Words and Number Symbols: A Cultural History of Numbers*, P. Broneer, trans. (Cambridge, Mass.: M.I.T. Press, 1969), p. 12.

The statement that even today elaborate systems of numbers are used by Islamic scholars to convey messages was made by L. Sanneh in a personal communication, September 1982.

163   On the controversy over the rational nature of primitive thought, see R. A. Shweder, "Rationality 'Goes without Saying,'" *Culture, Medicine and Psychiatry* 5 (4 December 1981):348–58. Also see D. Sperber, *Rethinking Symbolism*, Cambridge Studies in Social Anthropology, J. Goody, general ed. (Cambridge: Cambridge University Press, 1975).

Edwin Hutchins's study in the Trobriand Islands is described in his *Culture and Inference: A Trobriand Case Study* (Cambridge, Mass.: Harvard University Press, 1980), pp. 117–18.

164   On the urge to challenge established wisdom in "schooled" versus "primitive" societies, see G. N. Seagrim and R. J. Lendon, *Furnishing the Mind: Aboriginal and White: A Report on the Hemannsburg Project*, Behavioral Development: A Series of Monographs (New York: Academic Press, 1981), p. 297.

165   B. Rotman's statement on the various attitudes toward mathematics at different points in history is found in his *Jean Piaget* [135], p. 73.

Thomas Kuhn's theory is set forth in his *The Structure of Scientific Revolutions* (Chicago: University of Chicago Press, 1970).

Paul Feyerabend questions the distinction between science and non-science in his book *Against Method* (Atlantic Highlands, N.J.; Humanities Press, 1975).

410

Page
166   G. H. Hardy's account of the Indian mathematician Ramanujan is from J. R. Newman, *The World of Mathematics*, vol. 1 (New York: Simon & Schuster, 1956), pp. 366–67.

W. V. Quine's statement is from his *Methods of Logic* (New York: Holt, Rinehart, & Winston, 1950), p. *xiv*.

168   D. Hofstadter, *Gödel, Escher, Bach: An Eternal Golden Braid* (New York: Basic Books, 1979).

Chapter 8. Spatial Intelligence

170   Capablanca is quoted in B. Schechter, "Electronic Masters of Chess," *Discover*, December 1982, p. 110.

For examples of spatial problems, see R. H. McKim, *Experiences in Visual Thinking* (Belmont, Calif.: Brooks Cole, 1972); and E. J. Eliot and N. Salkind, *Children's Spatial Development* (Springfield, Ill.: Charles C Thomas, 1975).

On spatial ability, also see M. I. Smith, *Spatial Ability* (London: University of London Press, 1964).

172   The description of Einstein's theory of relativity is from p. 118 of Eliot and Salkind's *Children's Spatial Development* in the previous note.

174   Roger Shepard's study is described in R. N. Shepard and G. W. Cermak, "Perceptual Cognitive Explorations of a Toroidal Set of Free Form Stimuli," *Cognitive Psychology* 4 (1973):351–57. See also R. N. Shepard and J. Metzler, "Mental Rotation of Three-Dimensional Objects," *Science* 171 (1971):701–3, from which figure 3 is drawn.

175   On L. L. Thurstone, see his "Primary Mental Abilities," *Psychometric Monographs*, 1938, no. 1; and *Multiple-Factor Analysis: A Development and Expansion of "The Vectors of the Mind."* (Chicago: University of Chicago Press, 1947). Also see M. I. Smith, *Spatial Ability* [170], p. 85.

On El-Koussy's distinction between two- and three-dimensional spatial aptitude, see A. A. H. El-Koussy, *The Directions of Research in the Domain of Spatial Aptitudes*, Edition of the Centre National de la Recherche Scientifique, Paris, 1955.

For a more detailed discussion of spatial abilities and mental imagery, see U. Neisser and N. Kerr, "Spatial and Mnemonic Properties of Visual Images," *Cognitive Psychology* 5 (1973): 138–50; and Z. Pylyshyn, "What the Mind's Eye Tells the Mind's Brain: A Critique of Mental Imagery," *Psychological Bulletin* 80 (1973):1–24.

176   Lewis Thomas's analogies are from *The Lives of a Cell* (New York: Bantam Books, 1975). On images of wide scope, see H. Gruber, *Darwin on Man* (Chicago: University of Chicago Press, 1981).

177   On mental models and the role of imagery in mundane problem solving, see P. N. Johnson-Laird, *Mental Models* (Cambridge, Mass.: Harvard University Press, 1983).

R. Arnheim's statement is from his *Visual Thinking* (Berkeley: University of California Press, 1969), p. *v.*

178   Lee R. Brooks describes his studies on imagery in his article "Spatial and Verbal Components of the Act of Recall," *Canadian Journal of Psychology* 22 (1968):349–50.

Piaget's work on spatial abilities may be found in J. Piaget and B. Inhelder, *The Child's Conception of Space* (London: Routledge & Kegan Paul, 1956). Also see H. Gardner, *The Quest for Mind: Piaget, Lévi-Strauss, and the Structuralist Movement* (Chicago and London: University of Chicago Press, 1981); J. P. Flavell, *The Developmental Psychology of Jean Piaget* (Princeton: Van Nostrand, 1963); and H. Gruber and J. Vonèche, eds., *The Essential Piaget* (New York: Basic Books, 1977). For a review of other work, see H. Gardner, *Developmental Psychology* (Boston: Little, Brown, 1972), chap. 10.

181   Effects of damage to the right posterior regions are described in J. Wasserstein, R. Zappulla, J. Rosen, and L. Gerstman, "Evidence for Differentiation of Right Hemisphere Visual-Perceptual Functions," unpublished paper, New School for Social Research, New York, 1982.

Page

On the effects of lesions to the right parietal regions on visual attention, spatial orientation, imagery production, and memory, see H. Gardner, *The Shattered Mind: The Person after Brain Damage* (New York: Alfred A. Knopf, 1975), chap. 8.

The work of Nelson Butters and his colleagues on visual-spatial difficulties is described in N. Butters, M. Barton, and B. A. Brady, "Role of the Right Parietal Lobe in the Mediation of Cross-Modal Associations and Reversible Operations in Space," *Cortex* 6 (2 [1970]): 174–90.

182   For B. Milner and D. Kimura's work, see D. Kimura's article, "The Asymmetry of the Human Brain," *Scientific American* 228 (3 [1973]): 70–80.

On the difficulty that right-hemisphere-injured patients have in making drawings, see E. K. Warrington and A. M. Taylor, "Two Categorical Stages of Object Recognition," *Perception*, 7 (1978):695–705. Also see Gardner, *Shattered Mind*, [181], chap. 8.

Moira Williams's anecdote is quoted in L. J. Harris, "Sex Differences in Spatial Ability," in M. Kinsbourne, ed., *Asymmetrical Function of the Brain* (Cambridge: Cambridge University Press, 1978), p. 124.

On imagery in right-hemisphere-damaged patients, see E. Bisiach, E. Capitani, C. Luzzatti, and D. Perani, "Brain and Conscious Representation of Outside Reality," *Neuropsychologia* 19 (4 [1981]):543–51.

183   On Hubel and Wiesel, see D. H. Hubel and T. N. Wiesel, "Brain Mechanisms of Vision," *Scientific American* 241 (3 [1979]):150–62; and H. B. Barlow, "David Hubel and Torsten Wiesel: Their Contributions towards Understanding the Primary Visual Cortex," pages 145–52.

For studies of the inferior temporal regions of the primate brain, see C. G. Gross, C. E. Rocha-Miranda, and D. Bender, "Visual Properties of Neurons in Inferotemporal Cortex of the Macaque," *Journal of Neurophysiology* 35 (1972):96–111; and M. Mishkin, "Visual Mechanisms Beyond the Striate Cortex," in R. W. Russell, ed., *Frontiers in Physiological Psychology* (New York: Academic Press, 1967). Other aspects of spatial functioning are discussed in J. E. LeDoux, C. S. Smylie, R. Ruff, and M. S. Gazzaniga, "Left Hemisphere Visual Processes in a Case of Right Hemisphere Symptomatology: Implications for Theories of Cerebral Lateralization," *Archives of Neurology* 37 (1980):157–59; and M. Gazzaniga and J. LeDoux, *The Integrated Mind* (New York: Plenum, 1978).

The importance of the frontal lobes for remembering spatial location was described by Michael Goldberg in a paper presented at the International Neuropsychology Symposium, June 1982, Ravello, Italy.

184   The spatial memory of the Eskimos is discussed in J. S. Kleinfeld, "Visual Memory in Village Eskimo and Urban Caucasian Children," *Arctic* 24 (2 [1971]):132–38.

On sex differences in spatial skills, see R. L. Holloway, "Sexual Dimorphism in the Human Corpus Callosum," *Science* 216 (1982):1431–32; and S. G. Vandenberg and A. R. Kuse, "Spatial Ability: A Critical Review of the Sex-linked Major Gene Hypothesis," in M. A. Wittig and A. C. Peterson, eds., *Sex-related Differences in Cognitive Functioning* (New York: Academic Press, 1979).

For Wolfgang Köhler's work with the great apes on Tenerife, see his *The Mentality of Apes*, 2nd ed. (London: Routledge & Kegan Paul, 1973; first published in English in London, in 1925).

185   On the spatial abilities of the blind, see J. M. Kennedy, *A Psychology of Picture Perception: Images and Information* (San Francisco: Jossey-Bass, 1974).

See S. Millar, "Visual Experience or Translation Rules? Drawing the Human Figure by Blind and Sighted Children," *Perception* 4 (1975):363–71; S. Millar, "Effects of Input Conditions on Intramodal and Crossmodal Visual and Kinesthetic Matches by Children," *Journal of Experimental Child Psychology* 19 (1975):63–78.

186   G. S. Marmor, "Mental Rotation by the Blind: Does Mental Rotation Depend on Visual Imagery?" *Journal of Experimental Psychology: Human Perception and Performance* 2 (4 [1976]): 515–21; the statement quoted is from p. 520.

B. Landau, "Early Map Use by the Congenitally Blind Child," paper presented at the American Psychological Association, Los Angeles, August 1982; and B. Landau, H. Gleitman, and E. Spelke, Spatial Knowledge and Geometric Representation in a Child Blind from Birth," *Science* 213 (1981):1275–78.

On the effects of Turner's syndrome on visual perception, see L. J. Harris, "Sex Differences in Spatial Ability: Possible Environmental, Genetic, and Neurological Factors," in Kinsbourne, *Asymmetrical Function of the Brain* [182].

Page
187   On the special difficulties of brain-damaged children in visual-spatial tasks, see R. G. Rudel and H.-L. Teuber, "Spatial Orientation in Normal Children and in Children with Early Brain Injury," *Neuropsychologia* 9 (1971):401–7; and R. G. Rudel and H.-L. Teuber, "Pattern Recognition within and across Sensory Modalities in Normal and Brain-injured Children, *Neuropsychologia* 9 (1971):389–99.

On S. Kosslyn's work, see his *Image and Mind* (Cambridge, Mass: Harvard University Press, 1980).

Francis Galton's observation of poor visual imagery in scientists is discussed in his *Inquiries into Human Faculty and Its Development* (London: Dent, 1907).

E. B. Titchener is quoted in Arnheim, *Visual Thinking* [177], p. 107.

Aldous Huxley's statement is from his *The Doors of Perception* (New York: Harper & Row, 1970), p. 46.

The description of Nikola Tesla's abilities is found in McKim, *Experiences in Visual Thinking* [170], p. 8.

188   Rodin is quoted in H. Read, *The Art of Sculpture* (New York: Pantheon Books, 1961), p. 73.

Henry Moore is discussed on p. *ix* of Read's *Art of Sculpture*, cited in previous note.

The Japanese Yamashita and Yamamura are discussed in D. Doust, "Still life," *The London Sunday Times*, 1977.

On Nadia, see L. Selfe, *Nadia: A Case of Extraordinary Drawing Ability in an Autistic Child* (London and New York: Academic Press, 1977).

190   The statement about Einstein is from "The Talk of the Town" section of *The New Yorker* 5 March 1979, p. 28.

Einstein is quoted in McKim, *Experiences in Visual Thinking* [170], p. 9.

191   Kekulé is quoted on p. 9 in McKim, *Experiences in Visual Thinking* [170].

E. S. Ferguson describes the thinking processes of scientists and engineers in his article, "The Mind's Eye: Nonverbal Thought in Technology," *Science* 197 (4306 [1977]):827–36.

192   M. I. Smith examines the relative importance of spatial ability in the different sciences in his *Spatial Ability* [170], pp. 236–37.

The statement about "thinking in three dimensions" is from G. H. Colt, "The Polyhedral Arthur Loeb," *Harvard Magazine*, March–April 1982, p. 31.

A. Binet's study of mnemonic virtuosity in blindfolded chess may be found in A. Binet, "Mnemonic Virtuosity: A Study of Chess Players," *Genetic Psychology Monographs* 74 (1966):127–62.

193   Dr. Tarrasch's statement, "Some part of every . . . " is quoted in Binet, "Mnemonic Virtuosity" [192], p. 135.

Mr. Goetz's statement "I grasp it . . . " is quoted on p. 147 of the same book.

Binet's comments, "it is the multitude . . . " and "The move itself . . . " are from p. 147 of the same book.

194   The paragraph beginning "To envision a position . . . " is from Dr. Tarrasch, quoted on p. 152 of the same book.

Mr. Tarrasch's statement "The player absorbed . . . " is quoted on p. 159 of the same book.

Binet's conclusion is on p. 160 of the same book.

Napoleon's view of a battle plan is described in McKim, *Experiences in Visual Thinking* [170], p. 105.

195   Adrian de Groot and his colleagues describe chess masters in A. D. de Groot *Thought and Choice in Chess* (The Hague: Mouton, 1965).

W. Chase and H. Simon study the chess master in "The Mind's Eye in Chess," in W. G. Chase, ed. *Visual Information Processing* (New York: Academic Press, 1973).

196   Vincent Van Gogh's statements are from *Dear Theo: The Autobiography of Vincent Van Gogh*, I. Stone and J. Stone, eds. (New York: Grove Press, 1960), pp. 176 and 55, respectively.

Le Corbusier is quoted in R. L. Herbert, *Modern Artists on Art* (Englewood Cliffs, N.J.: Prentice-Hall, 1964), p. 64.

The Dürer woodcut of 1527 is often reprinted; for example in McKim, *Experiences in Visual Thinking* [170], p. 72.

197   G. Vasari discusses Leonardo in his *Lives of the Artists* (New York: Noonday Press, 1957), p. 148; Vasari describes Michelangelo on p. 322.

W. Hogarth is quoted in H. Gardner, *The Arts and Human Development: A Psychological*

Page

Study of the Artistic Process (New York: John Wiley, 1973), p. 260.

Leonardo da Vinci's advice to his painting students is related in G. Bachelard, The Poetics of Space (New York: Orion Press, 1964), p. 144.

Picasso's claim is found in Arnheim, Visual Thinking [177], p. 56.

198   Arnheim's statement is from Arnheim, Visual Thinking [177], p. 273.

Ben Shahn's description is from his The Shape of Content (New York: Vintage, 1960), pp. 58, 88.

Sir Herbert Read's description is from his The Philosophy of Modern Art (New York: Meridian Books, 1955), p. 11

Picasso is quoted in Read, Philosophy of Modern Art, p. 30.

Constable is quoted in Read, Philosophy of Modern Art, p. 17.

Cézanne is quoted in Read, Philosophy of Modern Art, p. 17.

Clive Bell's statement is from C. Bell, Old Friends: Personal Recollections (London: Chatto & Windus, 1956), p. 95.

199   Picasso is quoted in A. Malraux, "As Picasso Said, 'Why Assume That to Look Is to See?' A Talk between Malraux and the Master," The New York Times Magazine, 2 November 1975.

K. Clark discusses pure aesthetic sensation in his Another Part of the Wood: A Self-Portrait (New York: Ballantine, 1976), p. 45.

K. Clark's comment "It never occurred . . ." is from p. 46 of his Another Part of the Wood, cited in the previous note.

200   Clark's statement "the finest training . . ." is from p. 107 of the same book.

Clark describes the task of the connoisseur on p. 153 of the same book.

On the Gikwe Bushmen of the Kalahari, see Yi-Fu Tuan, Topophilia (Englewood Cliffs, N.J.: Prentice-Hall, 1974), p. 78.

201   On the Kikuyu in Kenya, see C. Zaslavsky, Africa Counts: Number and Pattern in African Culture (Boston: Prindle, Weber, & Smith, 1973), p. 225.

On the Shongo people of the Congo, see Zaslavsky, Africa Counts, cited in previous note, pp. 111–12.

On the visual acuity of Eskimos, see Kleinfeld, "Visual Memory" [184].

See also P. R. Dasen, "Piagetian Research in Central Australia," in G. E. Kearney, P. R. de Lacy, and G. R. Davidson, eds., The Psychology of Aboriginal Australians (Sydney: John Wiley, 1973), p. 5.

202   On Puluwat navigation, see T. Gladwin, East is a Big Bird: Navigation and Logic on Puluwat Atoll (Cambridge, Mass.: Harvard University Press, 1970).

Gladwin's statement, "No one set . . ." is from p. 146 of his East Is a Big Bird, cited in the previous note.

203   Gladwin's statement "The learning job . . ." is from pp. 131 and 155 of the same book.

On the use of reference islands, see p. 186 of the same book.

On the ability to point out distant islands, see p. 182 of the same book.

Gladwin's statement, "We in the Western world . . ." is from p. 219.

204   Henry Moore is quoted in G. Glueck, "Henry Moore," The New York Times, 11 July 1978, section III, p. 5.

Chapter 9. Bodily-Kinesthetic Intelligence

206   M. Simmel describes Marcel Marceau in her article, "Anatomy of a Mime Performance," The Justice (Brandeis University) Tuesday, 6 May 1975. Also see M. Simmel, "Mime and Reason: Notes on the Creation of the Perceptual Object," The Journal of Aesthetics of Art Criticism 31 (2 [1972]):193–200.

207   The emphasis on harmony between mind and body in ancient Greece is described in M. N. H'Doubler, Dance: A Creative Art Experience (Madison: University of Wisconsin Press, 1940), p. 9.

Page

Norman Mailer is quoted in B. Lowe, *The Beauty of Sport: A Cross-Disciplinary Inquiry* (Englewood Cliffs, N.J.: Prentice-Hall, 1977), p. 255.

208   On the recent stress on the link between body use and cognition, see N. Bernstein, *The Coordination and Regulation of Movements* (London: Pergamon Press, 1967).

Frederic Bartlett's analogy is presented in his *Thinking* (New York: Basic Books, 1958), p. 14.

209   On the grasping skills of prosimians and higher primates, see C. Trevarthen, "Manipulative Strategies of Baboons and the Origins of Cerebral Asymmetry," in M. Kinsbourne, ed., *Asymmetrical Function of the Brain* (New York: Cambridge University Press, 1978).

On the hand movements of expert pianists, see L. H. Shaffer, "Performances of Chopin, Bach and Bartok: Studies in Motor Programming," *Cognitive Psychology* 13 (1981):370–71.

Suzanne Farrell is quoted in W. Goldner, "The Inimitable Balanchine," *The New York Times Magazine*, 30 May 1976, p. 35.

210   Roger Sperry is quoted in E. Ewarts, "Brain Mechanisms in Movement," *Scientific American* 229 (1 [July 1973]): 103.

For an account of the way the body executes motor actions, see M. Clynes, *Sentics: The Touch of Emotions* (New York: Anchor Press/Doubleday, 1978).

A detailed explanation of hand-eye interaction was given by E. Bizzi in a paper presented at the International Neuropsychology Symposium, Ravello, Italy, June 1982.

211   On feedback from voluntary movements, see N. Bernstein, *The Coordination and Regulation of Movements* (London: Pergamon Press, 1967).

On the view that the individual's perception of the world is affected by the status of his motor activities, see H. L. Teuber, "Perception," in J. Field, ed., *Handbook of Physiology; Neurophysiology*, vol. 3 (Washington, D.C.: American Physiological Society, 1960), pp. 1595–668.

Manfred Clynes's statement is from his *Sentics* [210], p. 21.

Noam Chomsky quotes G. B. Kolata's statement, "Many motor programs . . ." in N. Chomsky, *Rules and Representations* (New York: Columbia University Press, 1980), p. 40. Also see G. B. Kolata, "Primate Neurobiology: Neurosurgery with Fetuses," *Science* 199 (March 1978):960–61.

212   On the capacity for brain dominance, see "Neural Parallels and Continuities," part XII, in S. R. Harnad, H. D. Steklis, and J. Lancaster, eds., *Prigins and Evolution of Language and Speech* (New York: New York Academy of Sciences, 1976).

On the selective motor impairments produced by left hemisphere injuries, see E. A. Roy, "Action and Performance," in A. W. Ellis, *Normality and Pathology in Cognitive Functions* (London and New York: Academic Press, 1982), p. 281.

Limb-kinetic, ideomotor, and ideational apraxia are described by H. Hécaen and M. L. Albert in their *Human Neuropsychology* (New York: John Wiley, 1978).

213   L. Squire described the retention of motor patterns in patients without verbal memory, in a paper presented at the Conference on Cognition, Education, and the Brain, Warrenton, Va., March 1982.

214   On the cases of Earl and Mr. A., see A. C. Hill, "Idiots Savants: A Categorization of Abilities," *Mental Retardation* 12 (1974):12–13; and E. Hoffman and R. Reeves, "An Idiot Savant with Unusual Mechanical Ability," *American Journal of Psychiatry* 136 (1979):713–14.

Bernard Rimland's story of the autistic youth Joe is quoted in R. M. Restak, "Islands of Genius," *Science 82*, May 1982, p. 63. Also see B. M. Minogue, "A Case of Secondary Mental Deficiency with Musical Talent," *Journal of Applied Psychology* 7 (1923):349–57; W. A. Owens and W. Grim, "A Note regarding Exceptional Musical Ability in a Low-grade Imbecile," *Journal of Educational Psychology* 32 (1942):636–37; D. W. Viscott, "A Musical Idiot Savant," *Psychiatry* 33 (1970):494–515; W. A. Horwitz, et al., "Identical Twin—'Idiot Savants'—Calendar Calculators," *American Journal of Psychiatry* 121 (1965):1075–79; A. Phillips, "Talented Imbeciles," *Psychological Clinic* 18 (1930):246–65; and M. Scheerer, E. Rothmann, and K. Goldstein, "A Case of 'Idiot Savant': An Experimental Study of Personality Organization," *Psychology Monographs* 269 (1945):1–61.

Bettelheim discusses "Joey, the Mechanical Boy" in B. Bettelheim, *The Empty Fortress: Infantile Autism and the Birth of the Self* (New York: Free Press, 1967), pp. 233–39; the quotation comes from p. 235.

Page
215   On the lack of tool use in animals below the primate order, and on tool use in lower primates, see D. Preziosi, *Architecture, Language and Meaning* (Bloomington: Indiana University Press, 1979), p. 20.

On the history of tool use in higher primates, see W. C. McGrew, "Socialization and Object Manipulation of Wild Chimpanzees," in S. Chevalier-Skolnikoff and F. E. Poirier, eds., *Primate Bio-social Development: Biological, Social and Ecological Determinants* (New York: Garland Publishing, 1977), p. 269.

Geza Teleki's description of chimpanzee termite fishing is found in his "Chimpanzee Subsistence Technology: Materials and Skills," *Journal of Human Evolution* 3 (1974):575–94; his statement about selection proficiency is from p. 587.

216   On termite fishing in the Gombe chimpanzee population in Tanzania, see W. C. McGrew, C. E. G. Tutin, and P. J. Baldwin, "Chimpanzees, Tools, and Termites: Cross-Cultural Comparisons of Senegal, Tanzania, and Rio Muni," *Man (N.S.)* 14 (1979):185–214.

217   On the speculation that three sets of factors determine whether primates will learn to use a tool, see B. Beck, *Animal Tool Behavior* (New York: Garland STPM Press, 1980); and W. A. Mason, "Social Experience and Primate Cognitive Development," in G. M. Burghardt and M. Bekoff, eds., *The Development of Behavior: Comparative and Evolutionary Aspects* (New York: Garland STPM Press, 1978).

On the evolution of tool use, see A. Marshack, "The Ecology and Brain of Two-Handed Bipedalism," paper presented at the Harry Frank Guggenheim Conference on Animal Cognition, 2–4 June 1982, Columbia University; Preziosi, *Architecture, Language and Meaning* [215]; and S. L. Washburn, "The Evolution of Man," *Scientific American*, September 1978.

219   On symbolization by Paleolithic man, see J. Pfeiffer, *The Creative Explosion* (New York: Harper & Row, 1982).

On the relationship between the development of hominids and the development of children, see S. Parker and K. R. Gibson, "A Developmental Model for the Evolution of Language and Intelligence in Early Hominids," *The Behavioral and Brain Sciences*, 1979, Cambridge University Press.

220   On the role of greater overall brain size and newly emerging brain regions in the evolution of humans, see H. T. Epstein, "Some Biological Bases of Cognitive Development," *Bulletin of the Orton Society* 30 (1980):46–62.

221   On the relationship of knowledge to the development of skills, see J. S. Bruner, "The Growth and Structure of Skill," paper presented at the Ciba Conference, London, November 1968; and K. Fischer, "A Theory of Cognitive Development: The Control of Hierarchies of Skill, "*Psychological Review* 87 (1980):477–531.

222   Edith Kaplan's anecdote about apraxia was a personal communication, February 1975.

On the evolution of dance, see A. Royce, "*The Anthropology of Dance* (Bloomington, Ind.: Indiana University Press, 1977).

Judith Hanna's definition of dance is found in her *To Dance Is Human* (Austin: University of Texas Press, 1979), p. 19.

223   Anthony Shay's views on the many purposes of dance are describe on p. 79 of Royce's *Anthropology of Dance*, cited in the previous note.

The statement on the Nuba Tira tribe is from Hanna, *To Dance Is Human* [222], p. 183.

Margaret Mead describes dance among the Samoans in her *Coming of Age in Samoa* (New York: William Morrow, 1928).

Dance among the Hopi Indians is described in Royce, *Anthropology of Dance* [222] p. 140.

224   Paul Taylor describes the task of the dancer in S. J. Cohen, ed., *The Modern Dance* (Middleton, Conn.: Wesleyan University Press, 1965), p. 91.

The many possible combinations of movement are described in M. N. H'Doubler, *Dance* [207].

Balanchine's remark is from p. 97 of Cohen, *Modern Dance* [224].

Isadora Duncan's statement is quoted in Tamara Comstock, ed., *New Directions in Dance Research: Anthropology and Dance (the American Indian)* (New York: Committee on Research on Dance, 1974), p. 256.

Martha Graham's remark is from her *The Notebooks of Martha Graham* (New York: Harcourt Brace Jovanovich, 1973).

Page

José Limón is quoted in Cohen, *Modern Dance* [224], p. 23.

225   Nijinsky's promise as a young ballet student is described in J. Russell, "Pas de Deux," a review of Irina Nijinska and J. Rawlinson, eds. and trans., *Bronislava Nijinska: Early Memoirs, New York Review of Books*, 3 December 1981.

Amy Greenfield described her early ballet lessons at the Harvard Graduate School of Education, panel on Choreography in the 1980's, 14 April 1982.

Alwin Nikolai is quoted in Cohen, *Modern Dance* [224], p. 67.

Donald McKayle is quoted on p. 57 of Cohen, *Modern Dance* [224].

226   Baryshnikov's comment is from M. Baryshnikov and M. Swope, *Baryshnikov at Work* (New York: Alfred A. Knopf, 1976), p. 10.

Ron Jenkins describes his training to be a Balinese clown in his article, "Becoming a Clown in Bali," *The Drama Review* 23 (2[1979]):49–56.

227   Richard Boleslavsky stresses the absolute concentration necessary for acting in *Acting: The First Six Lessons* (New York: Theatre Arts, 1970)

His discussion of the actor's special memory for feelings is from p. 36 of the same book.

His statements on the "gift of observation" are on pp. 93 and 101, respectively, of the same book.

Constantin Stanislavski underscores the crucial role of emotion in acting in his *An Actor Prepares* (New York: Theatre Arts, 1948), p. 266.

His statement, "Some musicians . . ." is from p. 158 of the same book.

228   J. Martin discusses the sixth sense of kinesthesis in his *Introduction to the Dance* (New York: Dance Horizons, 1965).

Martin's statement on the dancer's function is from pp. 53–54 of the same book. His statement "The building becomes . . ." is from p. 48 of the same book.

Ruth Benedict's statement is from her *The Chrysanthemum and the Sword* (New York: Meridian Books, 1946), p. 269.

On the mimicking hand movements of spectators at Balinese cockfights, see G. Bateson and M. Mead, *Balinese Character: A Photographic Analysis:* Special publications of the New York Academy of Sciences, vol. 11 (New York: New York Academy of Sciences, 1942), p. 18.

229   For an account of the impetus for the childhood antics of several comedians, see Steve Allen, *The Funny Men* (New York: Simon & Schuster, 1956).

230   B. Lowe's description of "stuff" is from his *The Beauty of Sport: A Cross-Disciplinary Inquiry* (Englewood Cliffs, N.J.: Prentice-Hall, 1977), p. 308.

The qualifications necessary for pitching baseball are described in D. Owen, "The Outer Limits of Excellence," *Inside Sports* 3 (November 1981): 62–69.

Jack Nicklaus is quoted in Lowe's *Beauty of Sport* [230] p. 177. Also see J. Nicklaus, *Golf My Way* (New York: Simon & Schuster, 1974).

231   Wayne Gretzky's skill is described in P. Gzowski, "The Great Gretzky," *Inside Sports* 3 (November 1981): 90–96; the passage quoted is from p. 94.

On the similarities in the training of the athlete and the artistic performer, see B. Bloom, ed., *Taxonomy of Educational Objectives* (New York: David McKay, 1956).

232   John Arnold describes how he goes about making new printing devices in M. Hunt, *The Universe Within: A New Science Explores the Human Mind* (New York: Simon & Schuster, 1982), p. 309.

233   Tracy Kidder discusses computer "whiz-kids" in, *The Soul of a New Machine* (New York: Avon, 1981) pp. 216 and 93, respectively.

The statement about the Greeks' respect for the human body from E. Hawkins, "Pure Poetry," in Cohen, *Modern Dance* [224], pp. 40–41.

On dance among the Ibo of Nigeria, see Hanna, *To Dance Is Human* [222], p. 34.

234   John Messenger's statement appears in his "Reflections on Esthetic Talent," *Basic College Quarterly* 4 (20–24 [1958]): 23.

On the seafaring skills of Manus children, see M. Mead, *Growing Up in New Guinea* (New York: William Morrow, 1975).

The descriptions of attention to bodily skill in Bali are from Bateson and Mead, *Balinese Character* [228] pp. 15 and 17.

Chapter 10. Personal Intelligences

Page
237   S. Freud, *Origins and Development of Psychoanalysis* (New York: Regnery-Gateway, 1960). The exchange between James and Freud is quoted in H. Stuart Hughes, *Consciousness and Society* (New York: Alfred A. Knopf, 1963), p. 113.

238   James's statement to a confidant, "I hope that Freud . . . ," is quoted in H. A. Murray, *Endeavors in Psychology: Selections from the Personology of Henry A. Murray* (New York: Harper & Row, 1981), p. 340.

       James's famous phrase "A man has as many social selves . . ." may be found in his *Psychology*, abridged ed. (New York: Fawcett, 1963), p. 169.

       A discusson of the social origins of knowledge may be found in J. M. Baldwin, *Mental Development in the Child and the Race* (New York: Macmillan, 1897). See also G. H. Mead, *Mind, Self, and Society*, (Chicago: University of Chicago Press, 1934).

241   For David Wechsler's skeptical views on social intelligence, see *The Measurement of Adult Intelligence*, 3rd ed. (Baltimore: Williams & Wilkins, 1944), pp. 88–89.

244   Harry Harlow's work on motherless monkeys may be found in H. Harlow, "Love in Infant Monkeys," *Scientific American* 200 (June 1959):68–74; H. Harlow, *Learning to Love* (New York: Ballantine Books, 1971); H. Harlow and M. K. Harlow, "Social Deprivation in Monkeys," *Scientific American* 207 (1962):136–44; and H. Harlow and M. K. Harlow, "Effects of Various Mother-Infant Relationships on Rhesus Monkey Behaviors," in B. M. Foss, ed., *Determinants of Infant Behavior*, vol. 4 (New York: Barnes & Noble, 1969).

       On the bond between infant and caretaker, and on the effects of infant institutionalization, see J. Bowlby's *Attachment* (New York: Basic Books, 1969), and *Separation: Anxiety and Anger* (New York: Basic Books, 1973), vols. I and II, respectively, of his *Attachment and Loss*.

       For evidence of a universal set of facial expressions, see I. Eibl-Eibesfeldt, *Ethology: The Biology of Behavior* (New York: Holt, Rinehart, & Winston, 1970); C. E. Izard, *The Face of Emotion* (New York: Appleton-Century-Crofts, 1971); and C. Darwin, *The Expression of the Emotions in Man and Animals* (Chicago and London: University of Chicago Press, 1965).

       On the inference that there are bodily and brain states associated with facial expressions of emotion, see M. Clynes, *Sentics: The Touch of Emotions* (New York: Anchor Press/Doubleday, 1978).

245   On the task of discriminating the moods of familiar others, see J. M. Baldwin, *Mental Development in the Child and the Race* (New York: Macmillan, 1897).

       On infants' ability to imitate facial expressions, see A. N. Meltzoff and M. K. Moore, "Imitation of Facial and Manual Gestures by Human Neonates," *Science* 198 (1977): 75–78.

       On the empathic abilities of young children, see M. L. Simner, "Newborn's Response to the Cry of Another Infant," *Developmental Psychology* 5 (1971):136–50; and H. Borke, "Interpersonal Perception of Young Children: Egocentrism or Empathy?" *Developmental Psychology*, 5 (1971):263–69.

       On the distinctive brain wave patterns yielded when an infant distinguishes between different affective expressions, see R. Davidson, "Asymmetrical Brain Activity Discriminates between Positive versus Negative Affective Stimuli in Ten-Month-Old Human Infants," *Science* 218 (1982):235–37.

       Gordon Gallup's studies are described in "Chimpanzees: Self-Recognition," *Science* 167 (1970):86–87.

246   On the child's distress when he violates standards, see J. Kagan, *The Second Year* (Cambridge, Mass., and London: Harvard University Press, 1981); and M. Lewis and L. Rosenblum, eds., *The Origins of Fear* (New York: John Wiley, 1975).

247   On sexual identity as a form of self-discrimination, see L. Kohlberg, "A Cognitive-Developmental Analysis of Children's Sex-Role Concepts and Attitudes, in E. Maccoby, ed., *The Development of Sex Differences* (Stanford: Stanford University Press, 1966).

       For an introduction to the Freudian account of the young child's development, see S. Freud, *New Introductory Lectures on Psychoanalysis* (New York: W. W. Norton, 1965).

       For Erik Erikson's account of the struggle between feelings of autonomy and of shame, see E. H. Erikson, *Childhood and Society* (New York: W. W. Norton, 1963).

       On the egocentrism of the young child, see J. Piaget and B. Inhelder, *The Psychology of the Child* (New York: Basic Books, 1969).

Page

On the "symbolic-interactionist" school of George Herbert Mead and Charles Cooley, see G. H. Mead, *Mind, Self and Society* (Chicago: University of Chicago Press, 1934); and C. H. Cooley, *Social Organization* (New York: Charles Scribner, 1909).

On the "mediationist" accounts, see L. Vygotsky, *Mind and Society* (Cambridge, Mass.: Harvard University Press, 1978); and A. R. Luria, *The Making of Mind* (Cambridge, Mass.: Harvard University Press, 1981).

For details on personal development, see H. Gardner, *Developmental Psychology* (Boston: Little, Brown, 1982), chaps. 5, 8, and 12.

251   Erik Erikson discusses identity in his books *Childhood and Society* [247]; and *Identity, Youth and Crisis* (New York: W. W. Norton, 1968).

252   Erik Erikson discusses the later phases of the maturing self in his "Identity and the Life Cycle," *Psychological Issues* 1 (1959).

For an example of the perspective of one school of social psychologists on determinants of behavior, see E. Goffman, *The Presentation of Self in Everyday Life* (New York: Doubleday, 1959); and E. Goffman, *Relations in Public* (New York: Basic Books, 1971).

253   T. S. Eliot is quoted in R. W. Hepburn, "The Arts and the Education of Feeling and Emotion," in R. F. Deardon, P. Hirst, and R. S. Peters, eds., *Education and the Development of Reason*, part III: Education and Reason (London: Routledge & Kegan, Paul, 1975).

254   On the importance of the individual's understanding of his own feelings, see R. S. Peters, "The Education of the Emotions," in M. B. Arnold, ed., *Feelings and Emotion* (New York: Academic Press, 1970). Hepburn, "The Arts and the Education of Feeling and Emotion" [253]; and E. T. Gendlin, J. Beebe, J. Cassens, M. Klein, and M. Oberlander, "Focusing Ability in Psychotherapy, Personality, and Creativity," *Research in Psychotherapy* 3 (1968):217–41.

255   On primitive forms of consciousness in higher animals, see D. Griffin, *The Question of Animal Awareness*, rev. ed. (Los Altos, Calif.: W. Kaufmann, 1981).

On the socialization of young chimpanzees, see W. C. McGrew, "Socialization and Object Manipulation of Wild Chimpanzees," in S. Chevalier-Skolnikoff and E. E. Poirier, eds., *Primate Bio-Social Development: Biological, Social, and Ecological Determinants* (New York: Garland, 1977).

256   On the adaptiveness of the nuclear family, see L. L. Cavalli-Sforza, "The Transition to Agriculture and Some of Its Consequences," essay prepared for the 7th International Smithsonian Symposium, Washington, D.C., November 1981; and C. O. Lovejoy, "The Origin of Man," *Science* 211(4480 [23 January 1981]):341–350; S. Moscovici, *Society against Nature* (Sussex, Eng.: Harvester Press, 1976).

257   Harry Jerison's comments on the difference between perception of others and the perception of self is found in his *Evolution of the Brain and Intelligence* (New York: Academic Press, 1973), p. 429.

N. K. Humphrey's views are developed in his "The Social Function of Intellect" in P. P. G. Bateson and R. A. Hinde, eds., *Growing Points in Ethology* (Cambridge, England: Cambridge University Press, 1976); the quote is on p. 312.

258   On the workings of the "attack system" in cats, see J. P. Flynn, S. B. Edwards, and R. J. Handler, "Changes in Sensory and Motor Systems during Centrally Elicited Attack," *Behavioral Science* 16(1971):1–19; and F. Bloom, *The Cellular Basis of Behavior*, a Salk Institute Research Report (San Diego, Calif.: Salk Institute , n.d.).

Studies inducing depression in rats were by W. Sullivan, "Depletion of Hormone Linked to Depression," *The New York Times*, 25 August 1982, p. A15. On evoking fear in chimpanzees, see D. O. Hebb, *The Organization of Behavior* (New York: John Wiley, 1949).

259   On Harry Harlow's motherless monkeys, see his "Love in Infant Monkeys" and *Learning to Love*, and Harlow and Harlow, "Social Deprivation" and "Various Mother-Infant Relationships" [244].

For Ronald Myers's studies of the primate nervous system, see his "Neurology of Social Communication in Primates," *The 2nd International Congress on Primates* (Atlanta, Ga.) 3(1968):1–9; E. A. Frazen and R. E. Myers, "Age Effects on Social Behavior Deficits Following Prefrontal Lesions in Monkeys," *Brain Research* 54(1973):277–86; and R. E. Myers, C. Swett, and M. Miller, "Loss of Group-Affinity Following Prefrontal Lesions in Free-ranging Macaques, *Brain Research* 64(1973):257–69.

260   Ross Buck discussed distinct systems for volitional and spontaneous expressions of emotions in his "A Theory of Spontaneous and Symbolic Expression: Implications for

Page
Facial Lateralization," paper presented at the meeting of the International Neuropsychological Society, Pittsburgh, Pa., 4 February 1982.

On the importance of the frontal lobes in various forms of personal knowledge, see H. Gardner, *The Shattered Mind*, (New York: Knopf, 1975), chap. 10.

261   On the effects of injury to the orbital area of frontal lobes, see D. Blumer and D. F. Benson, "Personality Changes with Frontal and Temporal Lobe Lesions," in D. F. Benson and D. Blumer, eds., *Psychiatric Aspects of Neurological Disease* (New York: Grune & Stratton, 1975).

A. R. Luria describes Zasetsky in his *The Man with a Shattered World: The History of a Brain Wound*, Lynn Solotaroff, trans. (New York: Basic Books, 1972)

The statement from Zasetsky's notebook is quoted on p. 421 of Luria's book cited in the previous note.

262   Walle Nauta's view of the frontal lobes as a meeting place for information is put forth in his, "The Problem of the Frontal Lobe: A Reinterpretation," *Journal of Psychiatric Research* 8(1971):167–87.

263   On autism, see B. Rimland, *Infantile Autism* (New York: Appleton-Century-Crofts, 1964).

264   On the effects of damage to the right hemisphere (cases where personality is altered, but verbal skills remain essentially intact), see Gardner, *Shattered Mind* [260], chap. 9, and references cited therein.

265   On the contrast between patients with Alzheimer's disease and those with Pick's disease, see Gardner, *Shattered Mind* [260], chap. 7 and references cited therein. On temporal lobe epilepsy, see Gardner, *Shattered Mind* [260], chap. 10.

266   David Bear's work on epilepsy was described in his "Hemispheric Specialization and the Neurology of Emotion," unpublished paper, Harvard Medical School, 1981.

On "split-brain patients," see M. Gazzaniga, *The Bisected Brain* (New York: Appleton-Century-Crofts, 1970); and N. Geschwind, "Disconnexion Syndromes in Animals and Man," *Brain* 88(1965):273–348, 585–644. My critique of the characterizations of the two hemispheres appears in *Art, Mind, and Brain* (New York: Basic Books, 1982), part IV.

268   Clifford Geertz sketches different cultural conceptions of the self in his "On the Nature of Anthropological Understanding," *American Scientist* 63(January/February 1975):1, 47–53.

Geertz's statement on the Javanese appears on p. 49 of the article cited in the previous note.

269   Geertz's statement on the Balinese appears on p. 50 of the same article.

271   Harry Lasker's metaphor of "particle" and "field" societies is a personal communication, the Harvard Project on Human Potential, March 1980.

The statement on the French literary tradition is from S. Sontag, "Writing Itself: On Roland Barthes," *The New Yorker*, 26 April 1982, p. 139.

272   Sartre's remark: "Hell is other people," is from J. P. Sartre, *No Exit* (New York: Alfred A. Knopf, 1947.

On the contrast between the Dinka of southern Sudan and western "particle society," see G. Liennhart, *Divinity and Experience: The Religion of the Dinka* (Oxford: Clarendon Press, 1961).

On Yoga psychology, see A. Rawlinson, "Yoga Psychology," in P. Heelas and A. J. Locke, eds., *Indigenous Psychologies: The Anthropology of the Self* (New York: Academic Press, 1981); and M. Eliade, *Yoga* (London: Routledge & Kegan Paul, 1958).

On the Maori of New Zealand, see J. Smith, "Self and Experience in Maori Culture," in P. Heelas and A. J. Locke, eds., *Indigenous Psychologies: The Anthropology of the Self* (New York: Academic Press, 1981).

On traditional China, see I. A. Richards, *Mencius on the Mind: Experiments in Multiple Definition* (London: Routledge & Kegan Paul, 1932).

On the Ojibwa of the Lake Superior area, see A. I. Hallowell, *Culture and Experience* (Philadelphia: University of Pennsylvania Press, 1971).

273   On "minimum message communication" among the Japanese, and on *jikkan*, see T. S. Lebra, *Japanese Patterns of Behavior* (Honolulu: University Press of Hawaii, 1976).

The statement on the Ixils in Guatemala is from B. N. Colby and L. M. Colby, *The Daykeeper: The Life and Discourse of an Ixil Diviner* (Cambridge, Mass. Harvard University Press, 1981), p. 156.

Page

On "negative capability," see W. J. Bate, *John Keats* (New York: Oxford University Press, 1963).

274   On the emergence of a sense of personal identity, see T. Luckmann, "Personal Identity as an Evolutionary and Historical Problem," in M. Von Cranach and K. Koppo, et al., eds., *Human Ethology* (Cambridge: Cambridge University Press, 1980.)

Chapter 11. A Critique of the Theory of Multiple Intelligences

279   Robert Nozick's statement is from his *Philosophical Explanations* (Cambridge, Mass. Belknap Press of Harvard University Press, 1981), p. 633.

280   For a nontechnical introduction to cognitive psychology and cognitive science, see M. Hunt, *The Universe Within* (New York: Simon & Schuster, 1982). For a more technical treatment, see A. Newell and H. A. Simon, *Human Problem Solving* (Englewood Cliffs, N.J.: Prentice-Hall, 1972).

281   On Allport's view of the human mind, see D. A. Allport, "Patterns and Actions: Cognitive Mechanisms Are Content Specific," in G. L. Claxton, ed., *Cognitive Psychology: New Directions* (London: Routledge & Kegan Paul, 1980).

        Allport's statement "Overwhelming evidence . . ." is from p. 5 of the book cited in the previous note.

282   Jerry Fodor's defense of the modularity of mind may be found in his *The Modularity of Mind* (Cambridge, Mass.: M.I.T. Press, 1983).

283   Z. Pylyshyn distinguishes between impenetrable and penetrable processes in his article "Computation and Cognition: Issues in the Foundations of Cognitive Science," *The Behavioral and Brain Sciences*, 3(1980):111–69.

        On the parallel model of the operations of the nervous system, see G. E. Hinton and J. A. Anderson, ed., *Parallel Models of Associative Memory* (Hillsdale, N.J.: Lawrence Erlbaum, 1981).

        The speculations of Gazzaniga and his colleagues are found in J. LeDoux, D. H. Wilson, and M. S. Gazzaniga, "Beyond Commisurotomy: Clues to Consciousness," in M. Gazzaniga, ed., *Handbook of Neuropsychology* (New York: Plenum, 1977).

285   Israel Scheffler proposes a new framework for viewing the concept of potential in his forthcoming book, tentatively entitled "Of Human Potential."

288   On creativity, see "Studies of the Creative Personality," C. Taylor and F. Barron, eds., *Scientific Creativity* (New York: John Wiley, 1963).

290   On the Miller Analogies Test, see N. E. Wallen and M. A. Campbell, "Vocabulary and Nonverbal Reasoning Components of Verbal Analogy Tests," *Journal of Educational Research* 61(1967):87–89. Also see reviews of the MAT in O. K. Buros, ed., *Intelligence Tests and Reviews* (Highland Park, N.J.: Gryphon Press, 1975).

291   On Harvard Project Zero's investigation of the development of metaphoric capacities, see E. Winner, M. McCarthy, and H. Gardner, "The Ontogenesis of Metaphor," in R. Honeck and R. Hoffman, eds., *Cognition and Figurative Language* (Hillsdale, N.J. Lawrence Erlbaum, 1980); and H. Gardner, E. Winner, R. Bechhofer, and D. Wolf, "The Development of Figurative Language," in K. Nelson, ed., *Children's Language* (New York: Gardner Press, 1978).

293   Lewis Thomas's gifts can be enjoyed in any of his collections of essays. See, for example, *The Lives of a Cell* (New York: Viking, 1974).

Chapter 12. The Socialization of Human Intelligences through Symbols

Page
301   The views of Nelson Goodman on symbols and symbol systems may be found in his *Languages of Art: An Approach to a Theory of Symbols* (Indianapolis: Hackett Publishing, 1976).

302   On Harvard Project Zero's research of symbolic development, see H. Gardner and D. P. Wolf, "Waves and Streams of Symbolization," in D. R. Rogers and J. A. Sloboda, eds., *The Acquisition of Symbolic Skills* (London: Plenum Press, 1983).

312   On the notion of crystallizing experiences, see L. S. Vygotsky, *Mind in Society: The Development of Psychological Processes* (Cambridge, Mass.; Harvard University Press, 1978).

314   On isolated versus linked skills, see P. Rozin, The Evolution of Intelligence and Access to the Cognitive Unconscious, *Progress in Psychobiology and Psychology* 6(1976):245–80; A. Brown and J. C. Campione, "Inducing Flexible Thinking: The Problem of Access," in M. Friedman, J. P. Das, and N. O'Connor, eds., *Intelligence and Learning* (New York: Plenum Press, 1980); and A. L. Brown, "Learning and Development: The Problems of Compatibility, Access and Induction," *Human Development* 25(2 [1982]):89–115.

315   B. Bloom holds that most differences in performance can be virtually eliminated by tutoring: see B. Bloom, ed., *Taxonomy of Educational Objectives* (New York: David McKay, 1956).

316   On the ability of the college student to increase his short-term memory tenfold, see K. A. Ericcson, W. G. Chase, and S. Faloon, "Acquisition of a Memory Skill," *Science* 208(1980):1181–82.

317   For an analysis of the skills involved in the legal profession, see P. A. Freund, "The Law and the Schools," in A. Berthhoff, ed., *The Making of Meaning* (New York: Boynton/Cook, 1981); and E. H. Levi, *Introduction to Legal Reasoning* (Chicago: University of Chicago Press, 1949).

318   On advocates in African societies, see S. Tambiah, "Form and Meaning of Magical Acts: A Point of View," in R. Horton and R. Finnegan, eds., *Modes of Thought* (London: Faber & Faber, 1973), p. 219; E. Hutchins, *Culture and Inference: A Trobriand Case Study* (Cambridge, Mass.: Harvard University Press, 1980).

320   On the "g" or general view of intelligence, see D. K. Detterman, "Does "g" Exist?" *Intelligence* 6(1982):99–108.

322   On the finding that *décalage* across domains is the rule rather than the exception, see K. Fischer, "A Theory of Cognitive Development: The Control of Hierarchies of Skill," *Psychological Review* 87(1980):477–531.

        On information-processing psychology, see A. Newell and H. A. Simon, *Human Problem Solving* (Englewood Cliffs, N. J.: Prentice-Hall, 1972).

323   Alan Allport suggests that the picture of the human mind gained from the approach of information-processing psychology varies depending on the type of analysis used and on the type of computer considered. See D. A. Allport, "Patterns and Actions: Cognitive Mechanisms Are Content Specific, in G. L. Claxton, ed., *Cognitive Psychology: New Directions* (London: Routledge & Kegan Paul, 1980).

        On N. Chomsky, see his *Reflections on Language* (New York: Pantheon, 1975). On J. A. Fodor, see his *The Modularity of Mind* (Cambridge, Mass.: M.I.T. Press, 1983).

324   The following are works concerned with the effects of culture on the development of the individual: J. Lave, "Tailored Learning: Education and Cognitive Skills among Tribal Craftsmen in West Africa," unpublished paper, University of California at Irvine, 1981; M. Cole, J. Gay, J. A. Glick, and D. W. Sharp, *The Cultural Context of Learning and Thinking* (New York: Basic Books, 1971); and S. Scribner and M. Cole, *The Psychology of Literacy* (Cambridge, Mass.: Harvard University Press, 1981).

        Clifford Geertz quotes Gilbert Ryle in C. Geertz, *The Interpretation of Cultures* (New York: Basic Books, 1972), p. 54.

        Geertz's own statement is quoted in L. A. Machado, *The Right To Be Intelligent* (New York: Pergamon Press, 1980), p. 62.

        M. Cole examines the performance of individuals from different cultures on tests of intelligence and reasoning in "Mind as a Cultural Achievement: Implications for IQ

Page

Testing," Annual Report 1979–1980, Research and Clinical Center for Child Development, Faculty of Education, Hokkaido University, Sapporo, Japan.

326   The following works are by contemporary scholars of development and education: J. S. Bruner, *Toward a Theory of Instruction* (Cambridge, Mass.: the Belknap Press of Harvard University Press, 1966); J. S. Bruner, *The Process of Education* (New York: Vintage, 1960); J. S. Bruner, J. J. Goodnow, and G. A. Austin, *A Study of Thinking* (New York: Science Editions, Inc., 1965); J. S. Bruner, A. Jolly, and K. Sylva, *Play: Its Role in Development and Evolution* (New York: Penguin, 1976); D. H. Feldman, *Beyond Universals in Cognitive Development* (Norwood, N.J.: Ablex Publishing, 1980); D. E. Olson, ed., *Media and Symbols: The Forms of Expression, Communication, and Education* (Chicago: University of Chicago Press, 1974); and G. Salomon, *Interaction of Media, Cognition and Learning* (San Francisco: Jossey-Bass, 1979).

Chapter 13. The Education of Intelligences

332   Jules Henry discusses the central role of education in his "A Cross-Cultural Outline of Education," *Current Anthropology* 1(4 [1960]):267–305; the quotation is on p. 287.

336   On the "agents" of education in different cultures, see p. 297 of the title in the previous note.

338   On becoming a Puluwat navigator, see T. Gladwin, *East Is a Big Bird: Navigation and Logic on Puluwat Atoll* (Cambridge, Mass.: Harvard University Press, 1970).

340   Gladwin's statement "no one could possibly . . . " is from p. 131 of the book cited in the previous note.

Gladwin's discusson of the building of "mental models" is from p. 182 of the same book.

On the training involved in becoming an epic singer, see A. B. Lord, *The Singer of Tales* (New York: Atheneum, 1965).

341   Lord's statement concerning imitation is from p. 24 of his book cited in the previous note.

342   On the rites of the Thonga of Africa, see J. W. M. Whiting, C. Kluckhohn, and A. Anthony, "The Function of Male Initiation Ceremonies at Puberty," in E. E. Maccoby, T. M. Newcomb, and E. L. Harley, eds., *Readings in Social Psychology*, 3rd ed. (New York: Henry Holt, 1958), p. 308.

On the rituals of American Indian tribes and on the Tikopia of Polynesia, see M. N. Fried and M. H. Fried, *Transitions: Four Rituals in Eight Cultures* (New York: W. W. Norton, 1980).

Lamin Sanneh describes the three-month circumcision rite in Senegambia, in a personal communication.

343   On schooling in the West Afrcian bush, see M. H. Watkins, "The West African 'Bush' School," *American Journal of Sociology* 48(1943):666–77; and A. F. Caine, "A Study and Comparison of the West African 'Bush' School and the Southern Sotha Circumcision School, Master of Arts thesis, Northwestern University, Evanston, Ill., June 1959.

On the apprenticeship system, see J. Bowen, *A History of Western Education*, vol. I (London: Methuen, 1972), p. 33.

344   On apprenticeship in ancient Egypt, see p. 42 of Bowen's history, cited in the previous note.

On the history of Indian education, see K. V. Chandras, *Four Thousand Years of Indian Education* (Palo Alto, Calif.: R & E Research Associates, 1977).

On apprenticeship among the Anang of Nigeria; see J. Messenger, "Reflections on Esthetic Talent," *Basic College Quarterly*, Fall 1958.

On the apprenticeship system of the arabesque wood worker in Egypt, see A. Nadim, "Testing Cybernetics in Khan-El-Khalili: A Study of Arabesque Carpenters," unpublished doctoral dissertation, University of Indiana, 1975.

Notes to Pages 345–358

Page

345   On Koranic education, see D. A. Wagner, "Learning to Read by 'Rote' in the Quranic Schools of Yemen and Senegal," paper presented in the Education, Literacy and Ethnicity: Traditional and Contemporary Interfaces symposium, of the American Psychological Assocation, Washington, D.C., December 1980; S. Scribner and M. Cole, *The Psychology of Literacy* (Cambridge, Mass.: Harvard University Press, 1981; and S. Pollak, "Traditional Islamic Education," unpublished paper, Harvard Project on Human Potential, March 1982.

347   On the characteristics of traditional education, see M. J. Fischer, *Iran: From Religious Dispute to Revolution* (Cambridge, Mass.: Harvard University Press, 1980); R. A. LeVine, Western Schools in non-Western Societies: Psychosocial Impact and Cultural Responses," *Teachers College Record* 79 (4, [1978]):749–55; S. Pollak, "Of Monks and Men: Sacred and Secular Education in the Middle Ages," unpublished paper, Harvard Project on Human Potential, December 1982; S. Pollak, "Traditional Jewish Learning: Philosophy and Practice," unpublished paper. Harvard Project on Human Potential, December 1981; and S. Pollak, "Traditional Indian Education," unpublished paper, Harvard Project on Human Potential, April 1982.

348   On the frequent contact between religious groups in the Middle East in medieval times, see Fischer, *Iran* [347].

349   Richard McKeon is quoted in Fischer, *Iran* [347], p. 51.

      J. Symonds's description of a Renaissance university is cited in Fischer, *Iran* [347], pp. 40–41. Fischer's statement is from p. 40 of the same book.

      See also articles in D. A. Wagner and H. W. Stevenson, eds., *Cultural Perspectives on Child Development* (San Francisco: W. H. Freeman, 1982).

350   John Randall quotes Master Tubal Holofernes in J. Randall, *The Making of the Modern Mind* (New York: Columbia University Press, 1926, 1940, 1976), p. 215.

      Francis Bacon is also quoted on p. 215 of the book cited in the previous note.

351   Erasmus's views on education are described in J. Bowen, *A History of Western Education*, vol. II (London: Methuen, 1975), p. 340.

354   On the importance of forging close interpersonal relationships in the sciences, see M. Polanyi, *Personal Knowledge* (Chicago: University of Chicago Press, 1958).

      On the rise of the modern secular school, see M. Oakeshott, "Education: The Engagement and Its Frustration," in R. F. Deardon, P. Hirst, and R. S. Peters, eds., *Education and the Development of Reason, Part I: Critique of Current Educational Aims* (New York: Routledge & Kegan Paul, 1975). Also see, W. F. Connell, *A History of Education in the Twentieth Century World* (New York: Teachers College Press, 1980).

355   Criticisms of schooling in recent years have been made by I. Illich in his *Reschooling Society* (New York: Harper & Row, 1971); P. Freire, *Pedagogy of the Oppressed* (New York: Seabury, 1971). R. Dore, *The Diploma Disease: Education, Qualification, and Development* (Berkeley: University of California Press, 1976); U. Neisser, "General, Academic, and Artificial Intelligence," in L. B. Resnick, ed., *The Nature of Intelligence* (Hillsdale, N.J.: Erlbaum, 1976); C. Jencks, *Inequality* (New York: Basic Books, 1972); and M. Maccoby and N. Modiano, "On Culture and Equivalence," in J. S. Bruner, R. S. Oliver, and P. M. Greenfield, eds., *Studies in Cognitive Growth* (New York: John Wiley, 1966).

      Maccoby and Modiano's statement is from p. 269 of their article cited in the previous note.

      For studies reporting positive aspects of well-run modern schools, see M. Rutter, *Fifteen Thousand Hours* (Cambridge, Mass.: Harvard University Press, 1979); and I. Lazer and R. Darlington, "Lasting Effects of Early Education," *Monographs of the Society for Research in Child Development*, (1982) 175 (whole).

357   For a survey of the consequences that can be expected from years of schooling, see M. Cole and R. D'Andrade, "The Influence of Schooling on Concept Formation: Some Preliminary Conclusions," *The Quarterly Newsletter of the Laboratory of Comparative Human Cognition* 4 (2 [1982]):19–26.

358   On the skills developed through traditional schooling, see D. A. Wagner, "Rediscovering 'Rote': Some Cognitive and Pedagogical Preliminaries," S. Irvine and J. W. Berry, eds., *Human Assessment and Cultural Factors* (New York: Plenum, in press); and D. A. Wagner, "Quranic Pedagogy in Modern Morocco," in L. L. Adler, ed., *Cross-Cultural Research at Issue* (New York: Academic Press, 1982).

Page
On the cognitive changes resisted by strict traditional schools, see Scribner and Cole, *The Psychology of Literacy* [345]; and Wagner, "Learning to Read by 'Rote' " [345].

On the social consequences of literacy in traditional societies, see J. Goody, M. Cole, and S. Scribner, "Writing and Formal Operations: A Case Study among the Vai," *Africa* 47 (3 [1977]):289-304.

359   Lévi-Strauss observes that chiefs of nonliterate societies are often observed to feign literacy, in his *Tristes Tropiques* (New York: Atheneum, 1964).

360   The results of the study by Jack Goody, Michael Cole, Sylvia Scribner, and their colleagues on the Vai of Liberia are reported in their "Writing and Formal Operations" [358].

361   Lévi-Strauss's views on the differences between the "traditional" and the "modern" mind may be found in his *The Savage Mind* (Chicago: University of Chicago Press, 1966).

362   Robin Horton argues that there is a fundamental difference between scientific and nonscientific ways of thinking in R. Horton and R. Finnegan, eds., *Modes of Thought: Essays on Thinking in Western and non-Western Societies* (London: Faber & Faber, 1973).

On the similarities between scientific and nonscientific thinking, see R. Schweder, "Likeness and Likelihood in Everyday Thought: Magical Thinking in Judgments and Personality," *Current Anthropology* 18 (1977):637-58; and D. Sperber, *Le Savoir des anthropologues: Trois essais* (Paris: Hermann, 1982).

On the mythic beliefs of scientists, see J. Jaynes, *The Origin of Consciousness in the Breakdown of the Bicameral Mind* (New York: Houghton, Mifflin, 1976).

365   Socrates' statement is quoted in P. H. Coombs, *The World Educational Crisis: A Systems Analysis* (New York: Oxford University Press, 1968), p. 113.

Chapter 14. The Application of Intelligences

367   On the Suzuki Talent Education Center, see S. Suzuki, *Nurtured by Love* (New York: Exposition Press, 1969); B. Holland, "Among Pros, More go Suzuki," *The New York Times*, 11 July 1982, E9; L. Taniuchi, "The Creation of Prodigies through Special Early Education: Three Case Studies," unpublished paper, Harvard Project on Human Potential, Cambridge, Mass., 1980.

368   On the World Bank's call for investment in human development and education, see World Bank, *World Development Report, 1980* (New York: Oxford University Press, 1980); and H. Singer, "Put the People First: Review of World Development Report, 1980," *The Economist*, 23 August 1980, p. 77.

369   R. S. McNamara's statement is quoted in "Attack on Poverty: Will We Do Still Less? *The Boston Globe*, 3 October 1980.

Edgar Faure's statement is from his *Learning to Be: The World of Education Today and Tomorrow*, UNESCO report (New York: Unipub [a Xerox publishing company], 1973), p. 106.

For the Club of Rome's report, see J. W. Botkin, M. Elmandjra, and M. Malitza, *No Limits to Learning: Bridging the Human Gap: A Report to the Club of Rome* (Oxford and New York: Pergamon Press, 1979); Aurelio Peccei's statement is on p. xiii.

The statement "for all practical pruposes . . . " is from p. 9 of the book cited in the previous note.

The statement "Innovative learning is . . . " is from p. 43 of the same book.

370   Luis Alberto Machado's statements are from his *The Right to Be Intelligent* (New York: Pergamon Press, 1980: pp. 2, 9, 24, 30, 52, 59, respectively).

Machado's statement "We are going to completely transform . . . " is from his article "The Development of Intelligence: A Political Outlook, *Human Intelligence* 4 (September 1980):4. Also see E. de Bono and H. Taiquin, "It Makes You Think," *The Guardian*, 16 November 1979, p. 21; J. Walsh, "A Plenipotentiary for Human Intelligence," *Science* 214 (1981):640-41; and W. J. Skrzyniarz, "A Review of Projects to Develop Intelligence in

Page

Venezuela: Developmental, Philosophical, Policy, and Cultural Perspectives on Intellectual Potential," unpublished paper, Harvard Project on Human Potential, Cambridge, Mass., November 1981.

371   The statements of the Institutes for the Achievement of Human Potential are quoted in "Bringing Up Superbaby," *Newsweek*, 28 March 1983, p. 63. Also see K. Schmidt, "Bringing Up Baby Bright," *American Way*, May 1982, pp. 37–43.

376   David Feldman's discussion of domain proficiency and child prodigies may be found in his *Beyond Universals in Cognitive Development* (Norwood, N.J.: Ablex Publishing, 1980).

379   The advice of Masuru Ibuka, the founder of SONY, is reported in his best-selling book, *Kindergarten Is Too Late!* (New York: Simon & Schuster, 1980).

On Japan's success after the Second World War, see E. Vogel, *Japan as Number One: Lessons for America* (Cambridge, Mass.: Harvard University Press, 1979).

On Japan's success after the Second World War, also see R. A. Levine, "Western Schools in non-Western Societies: Psychosocial Impact and Cultural Responses," *Teachers College Record*, 79 (4 [1978]):749–55.

On early education in Japan and on the high I.Q. scores of Japanese youths compared with American youths, see M. Alper, "All Our Children *Can* Learn," *University of Chicago Magazine*, Summer 1982; D. P. Schiller and H. J. Walberg, "Japan: The Learning Society," *Educational Leadership*, March 1982; "I.Q. in Japan and America," *The New York Times*, 25 May 1982; D. Seligman, "Japanese Brains: Castroism for Kids," *Fortune*, 31 May 1982; and K. Kobayashi, "The Knowledge-Obsessed Japanese," *The Wheel Extended*, January-March, 1982, p. 1.

On the success of the Japanese in achieving a balance between various proficiencies and group feeling, see L. Taniuchi and M. I. White, "Teaching and Learning in Japan: Premodern and Modern Educational Environments," unpublished paper, Harvard Project on Human Potential, October 1982.

380   For Jack and Elizabeth Easley's reports on mathematics instruction in Japan, see J. Easley and E. Easley, *Math Can Be Natural: Kitamaeno Priorities Introduced to American Teachers* (Urbana, Ill.: University of Illinois Committee on Culture and Cognition, 1982). Also see F. M. Hechinger, "Math Lessons from Japan," *The New York Times*, 22 June 1982.

382   P. Freire describes his successful efforts to teach reading to illiterate Brazilian peasants in his *Pedagogy of the Oppressed* (New York: Continuum Publishing, 1980).

On the approach to teaching used in Sesame Street, see G. S. Lesser, *Children and Television: Lessons from Sesame Street* (New York: Random House, 1974).

383   On the attempt in China, during the Cultural Revolution, to expunge all Western educational influence, see T. Fingar and L. A. Reed, *An Introduction to Education in the People's Republic of China and U.S.–China Educational Exchange* (Washington, D.C.: U.S.–China Education Clearinghouse, 1982); S. L. Shirk, *Competitive Comrades: Career Incentives and Student Strategies in China* (Berkeley and Los Angeles: University of California Press, 1982); and J. Unger, *Education under Mao: Class and Competition in Canton Schools, 1960–1980* (New York: Columbia University Press, 1982).

On the failed attempt to westernize education in Iran, see M. J. Fischer, *Iran: From Religious Dispute to Revolution* (Cambridge, Mass.: Harvard University Press, 1980).

386   On "markers" or signs of early giftedness, see B. Bloom, "The Role of Gifts and Markers in the Development of Talent." *Exceptional Children* 48 (6 [1982]):510–22.

387   L. S. Vygotsky develops the notion of the "zone of proximal development" in his *Mind in Society: The Development of Higher Psychological Processes* (Cambridge, Mass.: Harvard University Press, 1978). Also see L. S. Vygotsky, "Play and the Role of Mental Development in the Child," *Soviet Psychology*, 5(1967):6–18.

On crystallizing experiences, dominant activities, and critical periods, see V. V. Davydov, "Major Problems in Developmental and Educational Psychology at the Present Stage of Developmental Education," *Soviet Psychology*, 15 (Summer 1977):4; V. V. Davydov and V. P. Zinchenko, "The Principle of Development in Psychology," *Soviet Psychology* 20 (1 [1981]): 22–46; D. B. El'konin, "Toward the Problem of Stages in the Mental Development of the Child," *Soviet Psychology* 10 (Spring 1972):3; and Feldman [376].

389   On genetic primary examples, see A. K. Markova, *The Teaching and Mastery of Language* (New York: M. E. Sharp, 1979), pp. 63–65.

On the attempts to document improvements resulting from matching students with

426

Page
     appropriate teaching techniques, see L. J. Cronbach and R. E. Snow, *Aptitudes and Instructional Methods* (New York: Irvington Publishers, 1977).

390   The role of cooperation in computer programming is illustrated in T. Kidder's *The Soul of a New Machine* (New York: Avon, 1982).

391   On the use of tactile-kinesthetic exploration in overcoming learning disabilities, see J. Isgur, "Letter-Sound Associations Established in Reading-Disabled People by an Object-Imaging-Projection Method," unpublished paper, Pensacola Florida Learning Disabilities Clinic, 1973.

NAME INDEX

Name Index

Name Index

SUBJECT INDEX

acting, 207, 226–29; and mimetic skill, 226–29
Alzheimer's disease, 265
amusia, 46, 118
aphasia, 46; anomic, 90; and bodily-kinesthetic intelligence, 210; Broca's, 51, 87, 90; and linguistic intelligence, 14, 52, 88–90; and logical-mathematical intelligence, 157; and musical intelligence, 118; and personal intelligence, 240, 264; Wernicke's, 51, 90, 118
aplysia, 46
apraxia, 212–13, 221
athletics, 230–31
autism, 63, 312; and bodily-kinesthetic intelligence, 213–15; and linguistic intelligence, 84–85; and musical intelligence, 113, 120–21, 368; and personal intelligence, 263; and spatial intelligence, 188–90; and symbolic development, 306

Bali: Balinese clowns, 226–28; and bodily-kinesthetic intelligence, 226–29; and personal intelligence, 268–70
behaviorism, 237
biology: cognitive psychology, 23–24; and intelligence, 10, 12–16, 23, 31–58, 299–300, 302, 326; see also listings under the separate intelligences
bird song, 45–46, 116–117; and amusia, 46; and cerebral hemispheres, 46, 116; development of, 45, 116; and human song, 117

blindness: drawing ability, 185–86; and figure rotation ability, 186; and spatial intelligence, 185–86
bodily kinesthetic intelligence, 205–36; and acting, 207, 226–29; and aphasia, 210; and apraxia, 212–13, 221; and athletics, 230–31; and autism, 213–15; and Balinese culture, 226–29; and biology, 212–13; and brain damage, 212–13; and brain structure, 212–13; and cerebral dominance, 213; and cerebral hemispheres, 212–13; and core operations, 206–22, 226–29, 231–32; cultural differences in, 207, 222–23, 226, 228; and dance, 207, 222–26, 233–34; development of, 219–21; evolution of, 215–20; and Greek Culture, 207, 233; and humor, 229; and *idiots savants*, 213; and invention, 207, 231–32; and linguistic intelligence, 213, 219; and mimetic ability, 206, 226–29; and motor skills, 206, 209, 211–12; and musical intelligence, 123; and neural feedback, 211; and nonhuman primates, 209, 212, 215–16; and object manipulation, 206, 231–32; and personal intelligence, 235–36; and Piagetian stages, 219; and Puluwat navigation, 341, 364; and symbolization, 219, 221; and tool use, 215–220
Boston Veterans Administration Medical Center, x
brain damage, 50–51; and bodily-kinesthetic intelligence, 212–13; and canalization, 42; as criteria for multiple intelligences, 9, 63; and flexibility, 38, 40, 41,

433

Subject Index

initiation rites: education, 342–43; and linguistic intelligence, 93; and personal intelligence, 342–43

Institutes for the Achievement of Human Potential, 371

intelligence: and biology, 10, 12–16, 23, 31–58, 299–300, 302, 326, *see also* the separate intelligences; Chomskian view of, 323–25; classical view of, 5; computer as model for, 23, 24, 278, 323; and culture, 10, 27, 299–300, 331–392, *see also* education, and the separate intelligences; environmental-learning view of, 8; executive function of, 281; "fox's" view of, 7, 16, 32, 320–21; "g" factor of, 7, 17, 320; and genetics, 15, 16, 34, 326; "hedgehog's" view of, 7, 16, 32, 53, 165, 320–21; and horizontal processes, 15, 21, 23, 39, 47, 54; information-processing view of, 22–24, 32, 321–23; intelligence quotient view of, 7, 24; modular view of, 280–85; nature/nurture controversy over, 5, 315–16, 368; Piagetian theory of, 7, 17–22, 26–28, 321–23; uniformist view of, 280; *see also the separate intelligences*; multiple intelligences

intelligence quotient, 3, 7, 17, 18; and genetics, 15, 16; theory of intelligence, 7, 24

intelligence tests, 7, 9, 15, 20, 22, 321; logical-mathematical bias of, 24; and spatial intelligence, 175–77; verbal bias of, 17–18, 24

interpersonal intelligence, 70, 237–76; definition of, 239; *see also* personal intelligence

intrapersonal intelligence, 237–76, 286, 288; definition of, 239; *see also* personal intelligence

Japanese education, 357, 379–81; and mother/child bond, 381

Juilliard School of Music, 376

Kalahari Bushmen: and logical-mathematical intelligence, 161; and spatial intelligence, 200–201

Koranic education, 4, 345–47, 357, 364–65;

and linguistic intelligence, 346; and memorization, 345–46; and multiple intelligences, 364

language, *see* linguistic intelligence

legal profession: and linguistic intelligence, 317–18; and logical-mathematical intelligence, 317–18; and personal intelligence, 317–18

linguistic intelligence, 70–98, 331; and aphasia, 14, 52, 88–90; and autism, 84–85; and biology, 41, 51–52, 54, 80, 84–90; and bodily-kinesthetic intelligence, 213, 219; and brain damage, 41, 51–52, 57, 84–90; and brain structure, 41, 51–52, 54, 57, 84–90; and canalization, 41, 52, 86; and cerebral hemispheres, 51–52, 54, 84–86, 89–90; and core operations, 81, 84–91, 278, 306; critical period in, 86; cultural difference in, 91–95; and deafness, 52, 79, 86, 98; development of, 41, 51–52, 79–81, 84–86, 98, 326; and education, 336, 345–48, 352, 357–59; and environment, 80; evolution of, 87, 90, 91, 97; and figurative language, 80; and flexibility, 41, 52, 85; genetic factors in, 80; and hyperlexia, 85; and idioglossia, 90; and *idiots savants*, 85; individual differences in, 81; and initiation rites, 93; and legal profession, 317–18; and literacy, 92, 346, 357–61, 363, 382; and literary talent, 73–77, 81–84, 94–98; and musical intelligence, 98, 115, 117, 125; in nonhuman primates, 91; in nonliterate society, 92–95, 345–46; and phonology, 77, 80, 84; and poetry, 73–77, 82–83, 94, 97, 98; and pragmatics, 78–79; "preparedness" for, 39; and Puluwat navigation, 341, 364; and retardation, 84; and rhetoric, 78; and semantics, 41, 76, 80, 85, 87, 89; and spatial intelligence, 177; and symbolization, 304–13, 372; and syntax, 79–80, 84–85; and verbal memory, 78, 92, 345–46

literacy: and education, 357–61, 363, 382, 391; and Koranic education, 346; and multiple intelligences, 357–59; and schools, 363; and verbal memory, 92

literary talent, 73–77, 81–84, 94–98

localization, 146; of brain structure, 7, 13–14, 53–54, 282; of spatial intelligence, 177

436

prodigies, 9, 30, 35, 63, 368, 376, 386; and domains theory, 27–28; in logical-mathematical intelligence, 153–54, 159; in musical intelligence, 99, 100, 112; and Piagetian theory, 27–28; in spatial intelligence, 188–90
pruning of nerve cells, 44
psychoanalysis, 237–39
psychology, 14–16, 59, 65, 237–39; see also cognitive psychology; development; neuropsychology
Puluwat navigation, 4, 331; and bodily-kinesthetic intelligence, 341, 364; and education, 334, 336, 338–41, 344, 350, 364–65; and linguistic intelligence, 341, 364; and linguistic intelligence, 341, 364; and logical-mathematical intelligence, 364; and personal intelligence, 341, 364; and spatial intelligence, 201–3, 331, 341, 364

retardation, 15, 35, 63; and linguistic intelligence, 84; and musical intelligence, 121; and personal intelligence, 263; and spatial intelligence, 188
rhetoric, 78
rhythm, 104–5; and deafness, 105

schools, 333, 335–36, 343–61, 363; bush, 343, 360–61; and literacy, 363; modern secular, 351–57, 360–61; and science, 363; traditional religious, 345–51, 356, 360–61
science, 135, 145–49; and aging, 154; and calculating ability, 155; and education, 361–63; history of, 145–46, 165–67; and intuition, 148; and mathematics, 145–49; and mysticism, 150–51; in nonliterate societies, 361–62; and originality, 176–77; and physical reality, 147–51; and spatial intelligence, 176–77, 190–92
sculpture, 96, 97, 100, 188, 195
self, see sense of self
semantics, 41, 76, 80; and brain damage, 85, 87, 89
sense of self, 237–76, 294–97; see also personal intelligence
sensori-motor stage, 19; of logical-mathematical intelligence, 129; of spatial intel-

ligence, 178
"Sesame Street," 382, 392
short-term memory, 14, 24, 145, 281
sickle cell anemia, 34
spatial intelligence, 70, 170–204; and aging, 204; and appreciation of visual arts, 198–200; and autism, 188–90; and biology, 51, 54, 181–84, 187; and blindness, 185–86; and brain damage, 181–83, 187; and brain structure, 51, 54, 181–84, 187; and cerebral hemispheres, 51, 54, 181–84; and cerebral palsy, 187; and chess, 192–95; and compositional sense, 176, 198; and concrete-operational stage, 179; and copying skills, 174; and core operations, 170, 174–76, 186, 306; cultural differences in, 200–204; development of, 178–80; and drawing, 182, 186, 188–90, 306; and eidetic imagery, 189; evolution of, 184–85; and Eskimos, 184, 201, 202, 203; and figure rotation ability, 174, 186; and idiots savants, 188, 193; and intelligence testing, 175, 177; and the Kalahari bushmen, 200–01; and the Kikiyu, 201; and linguistic intelligence, 177; localization view of, 177; and logical-mathematical intelligence, 168, 176–77, 204; and metaphorical ability, 176–77; and musical intelligence, 123; in nonhuman primates, 184; and painting, 188, 195–200; and patterning skills, 195; and Piagetian stages, 178–80; and prodigies, 188–90; and Puluwat navigation, 202–3, 341–64; and retardation, 188; and the sciences, 176–77, 191–92; and sculpture, 188, 195; sex differences in, 184; and the Shongo, 201; and Turner's syndrome, 186; and visual imagery, 173, 175–77, 187–95; and visual memory, 180–81, 192–95, 197, 201
streams of symbolization, 303, 306
structuralism, see Piagetian theory
Suzuki method, 5, 35, 99, 112, 367, 373–81, 392; and composing, 378; critique of, 376–79; and imitation, 377–78; and mother/child bond, 374–77; and personal intelligence, 377; and sight reading, 377
symbolic development, 26, 303–16, 331; and autism, 306; and brain damage, 306; and canalization, 314; and Chomskian theory, 323, 326; and flexibility, 314; and Piagetian stages, 314–15; and Piagetian theory, 314–15, 326